TOWARD EXPLAINING
HUMAN CULTURE:
A Critical Review of the Findings of
Worldwide Cross-Cultural Research

David Levinson and Martin J. Malone

With an Appendix: *Language Universals*
by
Cecil H. Brown and
Stanley R. Witkowski

HRAF Press
1980

International Standard Book Number:
  Cloth 0-87536-339-3
  Paper 0-87536-340-7
Library of Congress Number: 80-83324

ACKNOWLEDGMENTS

Many people have helped with this book. They all have our thanks and gratitude. We are particularly indebted to Raoul Naroll for his intellectual and administrative support. It was his idea to write a book-length review of the findings of holocultural research, and this review has benefited greatly from his careful critique. We thank Robert O. Lagace also for his administrative support and comments on the entire manuscript. An early draft of the holocultural portion of this volume, in the form of Levinson's Ph.D. thesis, was read and criticized by Professors Phillips Stevens, William Stein and David Hays; various sections of this volume have benefited from the careful reviews of Professors Edwin Erickson, Ronald Rohner, Charles Snyder and Stanley Witkowski. The comments and suggestions of all of them have made this book a more thorough, careful, and measured review of cross-cultural research.

We want to thank also the Human Relations Area Files staff members who helped with this book. First, we thank all of those who contributed to *A Guide to Social Theory: Worldwide Cross-Cultural Tests*. If we had not had the information in the *Guide* so readily available, the writing of this review would have been all but impossible. We thank Timothy J. O'Leary for continually supplying us with references to key works and often the works themselves. We thank Judith Camera and Victoria Crocco for typing the manuscript and Deborah Levinson for guiding the manuscript through various stages of typing and revision. And we thank Frada Naroll and Enid Margolis for their careful editing of the entire manuscript.

Finally, we thank our families—Deborah, Ethan and Diane—Jane, Brady and Megan—for their continual support, encouragement, and help.

D.L.
M.J.M.

Acknowledgment is gratefully made to the following publishers and authors for permission to reprint:

ACADEMIC PRESS, INC. and JOHN W. M. WHITING for:
Figure 3-1 from "A Model for Psychocultural Research," by John W. M. Whiting. From *Culture and Infancy*, P. Herbert Leiderman, Steven R. Tulkin, and Anne Rosenfield, eds. p. 30, 1977.

AMERICAN ANTHROPOLOGICAL ASSOCIATION and MELVIN EMBER for:
Tables 2 and 3 from "The Conditions Favoring Matrilocal versus Patrilocal Residence," by Melvin Ember and Carol R. Ember, *American Anthropologist* 73 (1971), 574.

AMERICAN ANTHROPOLOGICAL ASSOCIATION and JOHN L. FISCHER for:
Table 1 from "Art Styles as Cultural Cognitive Maps," by John L. Fischer, *American Anthropologist* 63 (1961), 83.

AMERICAN ANTHROPOLOGICAL ASSOCIATION and KEITH OTTERBEIN for:
Tables 2 and 3 from "An Eye for an Eye, a Tooth for a Tooth: A Cross-Cultural Study of Feuding," by Keith F. Otterbein and Charlotte Swanson Otterbein, *American Anthropologist* 67 (1965), 1473, 1474.

AMERICAN ANTHROPOLOGICAL ASSOCIATION and JOHN M. ROBERTS for:
Table 2 from "Games in Culture," by John M. Roberts, Malcolm J. Arth and Robert R. Bush, *American Anthropologist* 61 (1959), 600.

AMERICAN ASSOCIATION FOR THE ADVANCEMENT OF SCIENCE and ALAN LOMAX for:
Table 8 from *Folk Song Style and Culture*, Alan Lomax, ed. Pub. No. 88, 1968, © 1968, American Association of the Advancement of Science. Used by permission of the author.

ANTHROPOLOGICAL SOCIETY OF WASHINGTON and GERTRUDE E. DOLE for:
Table 4 from "Developmental Sequences of Kinship Patterns," by Gertrude E. Dole. From *Kinship Studies in the Morgan Centennial Year*, Priscilla Reining, ed. p. 155, 1972.

BARBARA AYRES for:
Tables 1 and 2 from "Pregnancy Magic: A Study of Food Taboos and Sex Avoidances," by Barbara Ayres. From *Cross-Cultural Approaches*, Clelland S. Ford, ed. pp. 116, 118, 1967.

WILLIAM T. DIVALE for:
Figure II.1 from "The Causes of Matrilocal Residence: A Cross-Ethnohistorical Survey." Ph.D. Dissertation, State University of New York at Buffalo. p. 25.

ETHNOLOGY and HERBERT BARRY, III for:
Table 3 from "Agents and Techniques for Child Training: Cross-Cultural Codes 6," by Herbert Barry III, Lili Josephson, Edith Lauer and Catherine Marshall, *Ethnology* 16 (1977), 218.

worth, *Journal of Marriage and the Family* 31 (1969), 326. © 1969, National Council on Family Relations. Reprinted by permission.

NATIONAL MUSEUMS OF CANADA for:
Tables 2 and 3 from "Correlations of Exploitative and Settlement Patterns," by George Peter Murdock, *National Museums of Canada Bulletin* 230 (1969), 144-145.

PLENUM PUBLISHING CORPORATION for:
Figure 4 from "Causal Inferences Concerning Inheritance and Property," by Jack Goody, Barrie Irving and Nicky Tahany, *Human Relations* 24 (1970), 306.

PRENTICE-HALL, INC. and STANLEY H. UDY, JR. for:
Table 2.2 from *Work in Traditional and Modern Society*, by Stanley H. Udy, Jr. p. 35. © 1970, Prentice-Hall, Inc., Englewood Cliffs, New Jersey.

SAGE PUBLICATIONS for:
Table 1 from "A Cross-Cultural Study of Aggression," by Martin G. Allen, *Journal of Cross-Cultural Psychology* 3 (1972), 264.

SCHENKMAN PUBLISHING CO., INC. and ERIKA BOURGUIGNON for:
Figure 1 from "Dreams and Altered States of Consciousness in Anthropological Research," by Erika Bourguignon. From *Psychological Anthropology*, new edition, Francis L. K. Hsu, ed. p. 424, 1972.

UNIVERSITY OF CHICAGO PRESS for:
"Scale and Social Relations," by Gerald D. Berreman, *Current Anthropology* 19 (1978), 226. © 1978, Wenner-Gren Foundation for Anthropological Research.

UNIVERSITY OF CHICAGO PRESS for:
Table 2 from "Correlates of the Long Postpartum Taboo: A Cross-Cultural Study," by Jean-François Saucier, *Current Anthropology* 13 (1972), 243. © 1972, Wenner-Gren Foundation for Anthropological Research.

UNIVERSITY OF SOUTH CAROLINA PRESS for:
Quotations from *Primitive War*, by Harry H. Turney-High. pp. 23, 30, 1949. Quoted by permission of University of South Carolina Press.

WENNER-GREN FOUNDATION FOR ANTHROPOLOGICAL RESEARCH and BEATRICE B. WHITING for:
Tables 1 and 2 from *Paiute Sorcery*, by Beatrice Blyth Whiting. pp. 85, 87, 1950. Reprinted from *Paiute Sorcery*, by Beatrice Blyth Whiting, Viking Fund Publications in Anthropology, No. 15. © 1950, Wenner-Gren Foundation for Anthropological Research.

CONTENTS

TABLES

FIGURES

SECTION I. Introduction

Chapter 1
Overview

This book is an attempt to review systematically and objectively all theories of human culture and behavior that have been tested or developed through holocultural research. We summarize and assess the theoretical findings of some 305 holocultural studies. By holocultural study we mean a study designed to test or develop a theory through statistical analysis of data on a sample of ten or more small-scale societies from three or more geographical regions of the world. This includes such studies as Murdock's *Social Structure* (1949), Swanson's *The Birth of the Gods* (1960), and Rohner's *They Love Me, They Love Me Not* (1975). Our review is based on the findings of some 1500 proposition tests reported in the 305 different holocultural studies conducted between 1889 and 1979.

This book is about theories of human culture. By theory we mean a statement of lawful regularity about two or more variables which predicts that the appearance or a change in the value of one variable will lead to or cause a change in the value of some other variable. We use the term human culture, in its broadest sense, not only to include the rules, practices, actions, and characteristics of entire cultures or societies, but also the thoughts, feelings, actions and characteristics of individual human beings. In fact, most of the research we look at here seeks to explain human behavior at the cultural or societal level. So, we look at theories about post-marital residence practices, kinship terminology, and religion as well as theories about crime, suicide, and child rearing practices, among others. Holocultural studies, based as they are on worldwide samples of small-scale societies, test theories about human behavior in a universal or worldwide sense. The findings of holocultural studies can often be generalized to a universe of all known small-scale societies, and sometimes to a universe of all societies. By a small-scale society we mean what others call primitive, nonliterate, preliterate, kin-based, or non-industrialized societies.

3

This book has two key features. First, it provides a comprehensive review of the theoretical findings of holocultural research, a review that updates and greatly expands the earlier reviews by Naroll (1970b; 1973a), Driver (1973) and Levinson (1977a). Second, it assesses the *trustworthiness* of these theories by evaluating the quality of the holocultural research used to test them. Thus, we distinguish among and discuss three categories of theory: (1) theories that have been carefully tested and supported; (2) theories that have been carefully tested and discredited; and (3) theories that have not been carefully tested. And, we sometimes mention a fourth category of theory—those that have been proposed but not yet tested holoculturally.

A tested theory is one that has been confronted with cross-cultural data in such a way that, if the theory is entirely incorrect, it will very likely be discredited. Holocultural research allows such testing. Trustworthy theories are those theories that have been tested carefully and supported, and a careful theory test is one that controls for certain key methodological problems that may confound the results of the study. To assess the quality of each holocultural theory test, we have relied primarily on the data presented in *A Guide to Social Theory: Worldwide Cross-Cultural Tests* (Levinson 1977b). The *Guide* provides profiles of 1350 theoretical propositions tested holoculturally. Each page of the *Guide* is a profile of one proposition and the holocultural research used to test it. Included in each profile are twenty-four items of information about the research design and method. These information items have allowed us to evaluate quickly the quality of each holocultural theory test. The specific methodological information we have used is summarized in Appendix A.

In assessing the trustworthiness of each theory we considered the following aspects of its testing: (1) sampling—we looked for a probability sample of thirty or more societies; (2) measure validity—if the measure of the theoretical variable was not manifestly valid, we looked for a formal test of validity; (3) regional variation—we looked for a test of regional variation if the sample was large enough (n=50 or more) to permit one; (4) Galton's Problem—we looked for a test to determine if the statistical relationship between the variables was influenced by a spuriously inflated sample size due to interdependence of the sample units; (5) group significance—we looked at the results of the group significance tests reported in *A Guide to Social Theory*; (6) systematic data errors—we looked for a test of the effect of systematic data errors resulting from ethno-grapher error on the results of the study; (7) replication—we looked for a re-test of the theory either by means of a second, independent holocultural study or another design such as a sample survey, case study, or experiment; (8) statistical test—we looked for a statistical test that showed whether or not the relationship was stronger than would be expected by chance alone at the .05 level. We considered, too, other methodological factors such as coder training and naivete, but based the evaluation on the eight items listed above. In Chapter 2 we discuss the significance of each of these for holocultural research.

Most holocultural studies have not been especially rigorous, although they are becoming more so (Schaefer and Levinson 1977). Nonetheless, many theories have been tested carefully enough so that we can reach some conclusions about the causes of various categories of human culture. Holocultural research has supported a number of trustworthy theories; it has also questioned or discredited a variety of other theories, including some that are widely believed to be true. Thus, holocultural research has served us well as a tool for testing, verifying and discrediting social theory.

All of the holocultural research reviewed here is from English language sources. We have omitted those few studies not published in English (Steinmetz 1930; van der Bij 1929; Tjim 1933). We looked at almost all holocultural studies published through 1977, and many published since then. Our choice of topics was determined solely by the topics covered in holocultural studies. Only if the topic is mentioned in at least one holocultural study do we mention it. Since most holocultural research has been conducted by anthropologists, many of the topics covered are those that traditionally interest anthropologists—kinship, cultural evolution, religion, taboos. But, because sociologists and psychologists have also tested some of their ideas holoculturally, we include sections on socialization, social problems, and other topics that interest a wider range of social scientists.

We want to emphasize again that *this is a book about theories of human culture that have been tested holoculturally*. We have deliberately excluded descriptive or conceptual studies—the kind of studies often associated with anthropological research. We have given little attention to theories not tested holoculturally. We do mention some of these theories, but only to suggest that they be tested holoculturally, not to argue for or against their trustworthiness. In regard to description and conceptualization, we try to avoid those debates that already occupy so much space in the anthropological literature. *Our definitions of the topics and variables discussed are based on the definitions used by the holocultural researchers whose work we review.*

This book is divided into seven general sections. In this section we discuss the uses, methods, advantages, and criticisms of holocultural research. In the second, third and fourth sections we review holocultural tests of theories about cultural evolution, kinship, and expressive culture. The fifth and sixth sections deal with holocultural research bearing on socialization and social problems. The seventh section presents our conclusions. Appendix B, by Cecil Brown and Stanley Witkowski, reviews research on language universals.

We believe that the ultimate goal of the social and behavioral sciences is the development and verification of universal laws of human culture and behavior. Holocultural studies let us test universal theories. This book consists of what we know about the causes of human culture and behavior in a universal cross-cultural sense as of 1978. We hope that others will expand and build on the knowledge summarized here.

Chapter 2
Holocultural Research

Worldwide comparative studies provide an especially effective method for social scientists interested in testing universal theories of human culture and behavior. Other theory-testing approaches such as case studies or experiments based on worldwide samples are often too costly and time-consuming to be effective. Worldwide comparative studies come in three forms. First, holocultural or cross-cultural studies whose samples consist largely of small-scale or peasant societies. Second, holonational or cross-national studies whose samples consist of modern nations. Third, holohistorical studies whose samples consist of specific historical time periods of given societies. Over nine hundred worldwide comparative studies are in print. About sixty percent of them are holonational studies, forty percent holocultural, and only three studies are holohistorical.

We review here the findings of 305 holocultural and holohistorical studies. Social scientists have been carrying out holocultural research for ninety years, but fully one-half of all published holocultural studies have appeared since 1960. Holocultural research has progressed through three stages of methodological sophistication (Naroll 1970b). The first phase, which includes all studies published before 1934 and Wright (1942), is characterized by an almost total lack of concern with methodology. The second phase, which began in 1934, is characterized by the use of statistical analysis, representative sampling of the world's areas, and unit definition. Murdock's (1949) *Social Structure* is the classic example of a second generation holocultural study. Most holocultural studies are still second generation studies. In 1970 Naroll suggested that we were moving into a third phase, characterized by the control of all or most of the leading methodological problems plaguing holocultural research. Third generation studies like Schlegel's (1972) *Male Dominance and Female Autonomy* measure and control for regional variation, data

7

inaccuracies, Galton's Problem, group insignificance, and other problems ignored by first and second generation studies.

This chapter is a brief introduction to holocultural research—its uses, advantages, disadvantages, and methods.

Uses of Holocultural Research

Holocultural or cross-cultural survey research is used by social scientists for three major reasons. First, it describes and categorizes human behavior; Ford and Beach's (1951) *Patterns of Sexual Behavior* is the best known study of this type. Such a study does not test theories, although hypotheses may be suggested that are tested in subsequent research. Second, and most commonly, it provides theory tests—sometimes they are "quick and dirty" theory tests. If confirmed, these theories will be further tested in more rigorous holocultural studies or through other approaches. Third, it develops new theories, primarily through the multivariate analysis of large batches of cross-cultural data. Here, we are mainly interested in holocultural studies as theory tests.

Comparativists do not agree about what is the most fruitful methodological approach to holocultural theory testing. Some advocate methodological rigor (Naroll, Michik and Naroll 1976; Rohner, Barry, Divale, Erickson, Naroll, Schaefer and Sipes 1978). Others prefer a more cost-effective, less rigorous approach (Murdock 1977). The cost-effective approach saves time and money by ignoring certain methodological procedures that may or may not bias the results. Thus, it is argued that major theories can be tested for little cost. The major disadvantage of this cost-effective approach is that the results cannot be considered trustworthy. The rigorous approach gives time and money to get trustworthy results. The possible confounding effects of methodological problems are measured and, if necessary, controlled. In the past, the major disadvantage of rigorous studies was their cost—in time and money. This is not true anymore. The general availability of cross-cultural samples, data, computer programs, and research guides designed specifically for holocultural research make rigorous research cost-effective, too. A third approach is the multi-method design followed at times by Roberts (Roberts and Forman 1971), by Whiting (Landauer and Whiting 1964), and by Rohner (1975). Here, theories are tested cross-culturally with holocultural studies and intraculturally with case studies and sample surveys. This approach is the most fruitful of all, but is also the most time-consuming and costly.

Advantages of Holocultural Research

Holocultural studies offer six major advantages for testing theories about human culture and behavior. First, and most important, holocultural studies sample a much wider range of variation in cultural activities than do studies based on a single society, a few societies, or even many nations. A reading of any introductory textbook demonstrates the breadth of worldwide variation in cultural behavior. Second, because of this variation, we can more confidently assume that irrelevant variables will vary randomly and will not influence the results of holocultural studies. Third, the range of variation allows researchers to consider cultural evolution, as measured by degree of cultural complexity, as a variable in their causal analysis. Cultural evolution influences much of human behavior, as we show in Chapter 4. Fourth, some variables—or aspects of some variables—can be explained only at the societal level. Language, religion, social structure, and cultural complexity are some crucial ones. Fifth, holocultural studies are objective. The theory tester (comparativist) and data collector (ethnographer) are different individuals. Thus, the data collector cannot consciously or unconsciously skew the data in favor of the theory being tested. Sixth, holocultural studies, even rigorous ones, are cost effective.

Disadvantages of Holocultural Research

Holocultural studies have four main disadvantages, although the six advantages clearly outweigh the four disadvantages. First, holocultural theory tests sacrifice variation within culture for variation across cultures. Variability within a single culture is often ignored for the sake of coding uniformity. Second, because it is archival and not collected with a particular theory in mind, data used in holocultural research tends to be less sensitive and precise than data used in case studies. Third, some topics are poorly described in the ethnographic literature and thus cannot be studied at all or studied easily. Often indirect, less precise measures must be used. The psychoanalytic aspects of personality theories discussed in Chapter 20 are examples of topics that are not especially amenable to holocultural testing. Fourth, because holocultural samples consist mostly of small-scale societies, the top end of the scale of cultural evolution is either under- or unrepresented.

General Criticisms of Holocultural Theory Testing

Holocultural theory testing has not been widely accepted within anthropology. This is so for a number of reasons: perhaps because anthropologists stress description over explanation; or because anthropologists place more value on field research; or because anthropologists are sometimes unfamiliar and uncomfortable with quantitative or statistical analysis. Holocultural studies have been widely criticized (Köbben 1952, 1967; Schapera 1953; Lewis 1956; Barnes 1971). They have also been widely defended (Whiting 1954, 1968b; Rohner 1977; Naroll, Michik and Naroll 1980). The situation is much different in sociology and psychology, where the findings of holocultural studies are more readily accepted.

Anthropological criticism raises four general questions about the validity and usefulness of holocultural theory testing.

1) Holocultural Studies Tear Traits from Their Cultural Context

By tearing traits from their cultural context, critics say, holocultural studies ignore or destroy cultural patterns or themes. This is perhaps the oldest criticism of holocultural studies. It is also one that, while once true, is no longer so. No one denies that nineteenth century comparativists like Frazer correlated traits from one culture with traits from other cultures. Trait A might come from one culture, trait B from a second culture, and trait C from a third culture. The traits were then correlated or aligned as if they all existed within the same culture. With the exception of Wright (1942), no holocultural study published in the past forty years has followed this practice. Instead, recent holocultural studies correlate cultural traits only with other traits existing in the same culture—and, in fact, more and more describe the same community within the cultural unit.

An axiom of cultural anthropology is that cultural elements or traits which form a cultural system are integrated with one another. These elements are formed into patterns by certain themes or beliefs that are present in all features of the cultural system (Spengler 1928;

Benedict 1946; Opler 1945; Kluckhohn 1941). The culture pattern or theme model of culture does not argue that the elements are related as cause to effect, only that the elements influenced as they are by a common theme or themes, are integrated. One criticism of holocultural research is that cultural patterns are ignored, that the focus is on only a few traits which are then correlated with one another. Although this line of reasoning can be dismissed on both logical and methodological grounds, the best evidence that it is unsound comes from those holocultural studies that test and consistently support the culture pattern model. Some key studies are those by Roberts, Arth and Bush (1959) on games, Sipes (1973) on aggression, Fischer (1961) on art style, Lomax (1968a) on song style, and the factor analysis research of Stewart and Jones (1972) and Russell (1972). Holocultural research does not ignore cultural patterns. It provides the major empirical evidence of the existence of cultural patterns.

2) *Holocultural Research Treats as Equivalents Cultural Traits that May Vary Widely in Meaning across the Cultural Universe*

Do comparativists measure oranges, apples, pears, and peaches and call them all oranges: Or, do comparativists measure limes, oranges, grapefruits, and tangerines and call them all citrus fruits? Critics complain that comparativists do the former. Holoculturalists argue that they do the latter. No one denies that a major problem of holocultural research is the development of universally applicable measures of cultural traits. What can be disputed, though, is the questionable assumption that certain traits may not be comparable because they vary widely in content, form, or meaning, that they are really different, not equivalent traits. This criticism is effectively answered by Goodenough (1970). Cultural specialists and comparativists study culture at different levels of abstraction. Culture experts study emics, concepts that define and explain characteristics of one culture. Comparativists study etics, concepts that define and explain characteristics of all cultures. The two approaches are compatible, not conflicting.

3) *Holocultural Studies Are Irrelevant*

Some skeptics argue that holocultural research, and perhaps cultural anthropology in general, is irrelevant to the needs and concerns of the modern world. After all, holocultural studies, based as they are on data from small-scale societies, test theories that apply only to those societies. And, small-scale societies are rapidly disappearing. Contemporary, modern societies are ignored. Is there any reason to believe that theories tested holoculturally tell us anything about the modern world? So goes this line of reasoning, expressed often by action-oriented critics. However, holocultural studies are relevant to contemporary concerns in two ways. First, they point to ways of life different from ours now. So long as our own way of life is less than perfect, we need to keep our minds open to alternatives. Second, the findings of holocultural research almost always agree with the findings of other studies using samples from modern, industrialized nations. For example, the tentative conclusions of the dozens of holocultural tests of Freudian theory reviewed in Chapter 20 agree completely with the conclusions reached by the hundreds of clinical and experimental tests reviewed by Fisher and Greenberg (1977). These clinical and experimental studies often used subjects from modern industrialized nations, and most often from the United States and Great Britain. Likewise, the conclusions of Sipes (1973) about aggression, Landauer and Whiting (1964) about stress, and Roberts, Arth and Bush (1959) about games all agree with subsequent case study research conducted in the United States. So, holocultural studies are relevant.

4) *Holocultural Studies Have Many Deviant Cases*

Deviant cases are societies which fail to conform to the universal pattern of association confirmed by the holocultural study. Holocultural studies are filled with deviant cases. Few holocultural studies find every case sampled behaving in the predicted fashion. This is as expected. Holocultural research, like all social science research, rests on a probability model. Holocultural studies predict that if A, then *probably* B. They do not predict that if A, then *always* B. The prediction is considered confirmed if the strength of the statistical association is greater than would be expected by chance alone. An acceptable chance risk level (level of statistical significance) is usually defined as five times in one hundred or less. Deviant cases appear for a variety of conceptual, methodological, and theoretical reasons (Köbben 1967). Analysis of deviant cases often leads to new hypotheses and more holocultural research.

Specific Methodological Problems

Like any research, a holocultural study must satisfy certain technical and methodological requirements if the findings are to be accepted as trustworthy. As we mentioned before, holocultural researchers do not agree on methodological standards. Some advocate the less rigorous, less costly approach, others the more costly, more rigorous approach. Both approaches are, of course, useful. But if the conclusions are to be accepted as trustworthy, the theory must be tested rigorously at least once. All or at least most of the specific methodological problems described below must be controlled for, and it is easier to do so now than it was even five years ago. *Worldwide Theory Testing* (Naroll, Michik and Naroll 1976) tells us how.

Along with other theory-testing approaches, holocultural studies require that (1) the sample be selected using probability techniques, (2) the measures of the theoretical variables be valid and reliable, (3) the scales be appropriate for the statistical tests, and (4) the data collectors be unaware of the hypothesis being tested. The trustworthiness of the findings is increased if the theory is retested with an independent sample.

Holocultural studies are also plagued by special methodological problems that necessitate the use of unique control procedures. Five problems are especially troublesome: (1) regional variation; (2) data inaccuracies; (3) Galton's Problem; (4) unit definition; and (5) group insignificance.

Regional variation is the problem of possible variation in the strength of the association among different geographical regions of the world. A number of associations thought to be worldwide actually vary greatly from one region of the world to another (Sawyer and LeVine 1966; Driver and Schuessler 1957; Bourguignon and Greenbaum 1973; Chaney and Ruiz-Revilla 1969; Erickson 1976). Regional variation can be measured by recomputing the associations for each region of the world.

Holocultural studies have been criticized for using *inaccurate ethnographic data* (Naroll 1962a; Webb, Campbell, Schwartz and Sechrest 1966; Haekel 1970; Naroll 1970a; Rohner, deWalt and Ness 1973; Rohner 1975). In a few studies, some findings have been shown to be the result of systematic data errors. Inaccurate data come from three sources—the people being studied may describe their culture inaccurately, the reporter may describe the culture inaccurately, or the comparativists may code the data inaccurately.

Holoculturalists have been most concerned with inaccuracies due to reporter error. The reporter is usually an ethnographer, but may also be a missionary, government official, or traveler. Recently there has been increased concern with coder errors (Kang 1976a; Sipes 1976; Whyte 1978b). The ethnographic record for some small-scale societies is incomplete, inaccurate, biased, distorted and contradictory. How does the comparativist produce "trustworthy conclusions from untrustworthy data"? It is a difficult but not impossible task. Newspaper reporters do it all the time. The possible confounding effects of systematic error can be identified and controlled with the control factor method of data quality control (Naroll 1962a, 1970a). The control factor method assumes that variation in the degree of accuracy in the ethnographic record is due to variations in the data collection process. A control factor is any aspect of the data collection process shown to be related to the accuracy of the data. Five control factors are known to be especially sensitive to data errors: (1) length of stay in the field—the longer the stay, the more accurate the data; (2) native language familiarity—the more familiarity with the native language, the more accurate the data; (3) time focus—the closer the field date to the period being described, the more accurate the data; (4) systematic checks on informants' statements—the more census taking, cross-checks, multiple interviews, the more accurate the data; (5) earlier publications cited—the more early reports about the same people cited by the fieldworker, the more accurate the data.

Galton's Problem has drawn more attention than any other methodological problem; it concerns the interdependence of cultural units in cross-cultural samples. The basic problem has been summarized by Naroll, Michik and Naroll (1974: 127) as follows:

> . . . if cultures are interdependent with respect to the characteristics being studied, the actual number of independent observations may be less than the number of cultures the investigator examined. The effect of interdependence on the significance tests of a study might be similar to that of systematic error. The spuriously high number of cases involved in the computation of statistical significance would tend to decrease the probability of chance occurrence indicated by those tests. This probability of chance [occurrence] decreases because the standard errors of measures of association are all inverse functions of the number of cases. In addition, the inclusion of interdependent cases can produce spuriously inflated (or deflated) coefficients of association . . . .

Galton's Problem has sometimes led researchers to accept as true a hypothesis that, in fact, was false (see, for example, the discussions in Erickson (1976) and Ross and Homer (1976). About a dozen solutions to Galton's Problem have been proposed. The strengths and weaknesses of these solutions are summarized by Strauss and Orans (1975) and Naroll (1976).

Holocultural studies have been criticized, too, for not *defining their sample units* precisely. This, of course, is a criticism of anthropology in general which has so far failed to produce a generally accepted definition of what constitutes a cultural unit. Naroll (1970a) lists ten criteria sometimes used to define a cultural unit. Ethnographer's unit, language unit, and political unit are the three most often used in holocultural research. Ethnographer's unit is the culture as defined by the ethnographer. Language unit is a group of people who speak a language distinct from that of its neighbors. A political unit is a territorial unit that welds a number of distinct local communities into a war-making entity.

Group insignificance concerns chance; when a large number of correlation coefficients are computed, a certain percentage can be expected to be statistically significant by chance alone. For example, if we compute a matrix of seventy correlation coefficients, we would expect that only about three would be significant by chance alone. Many holocultural studies, particularly those of book length, report dozens or even hundreds of correlations. The researcher needs to determine whether the number of significant correlations found is greater than the number that would be expected by chance alone.

We have now very briefly reviewed the major methodological problems confronting holocultural research. Only a few studies control for all these problems. Most studies ignore most of them. But, fortunately, the more rigorous studies often retest theories that were tested in the earlier, less rigorous ones.

Conducting a Holocultural Study

The number and variety of holocultural research tools available make it easy today to conduct a rigorous holocultural study. It is, of course, even easier to conduct a cost-effective one. Those who are unfamiliar with holocultural research would do well to skim through some model holocultural studies. We recommend the following: Divale (1974a) for its general rigor and use of ethnohistorical data;

Rohner (1975) for its general rigor and multi-method approach; Kang (1976a) for its general rigor and careful operationalization of a difficult and complex theory; Rosenblatt, Walsh and Jackson (1976) for its application of holocultural method to contemporary needs; and Pryor (1977) for its sophisticated theoretical and statistical analysis. These five studies provide an introduction to the complexities, advantages, limits, and methods of holocultural research.

General Methodology

Naroll, Michik and Naroll (1976) and Otterbein (1969) provide the basic instructions for conducting a holocultural study. Naroll, Michik and Naroll (1976) allow the investigator the luxury of choosing to conduct a preliminary, tentative, or rigorous level study. Schedules that have been used to rate the rigor of holocultural studies can be found in Sipes (1972), and Levinson (1977b).

Sampling

A cross-cultural sample of small-scale societies can be obtained in two ways. The researcher can select it. There is now enough ethnographic literature—especially in the Human Relations Area Files (HRAF)—to select a random sample of up to one hundred societies fairly easily. Or the researcher can choose an existing cross-cultural sample, or a sub-sample of an existing sample. Five cross-cultural samples are especially useful:

(1) The World Ethnographic Sample (Murdock 1957)
(2) The *Ethnographic Atlas*, both complete and summary forms (Murdock 1967a)
(3) The HRAF Probability Sample Files (HRAF 1967; Naroll 1967; Lagacé 1977, 1979)
(4) The Standard Cross-Cultural Sample (Murdock and White 1969)
(5) The Standard Ethnographic Sample (Naroll et al. 1970; Naroll and Sipes 1973; Naroll 1973b; Naroll and Zucker 1974).

Each of these samples has its strengths and weaknesses. Naroll (1970a) and Otterbein (1976) provide general discussions of cross-cultural sampling.

Coding

We can also collect data in two alternative ways. First, data can be coded directly from the ethnographic sources, or, preferably, from ethnographic reports indexed in the HRAF Files. Or, second, coded data can be taken directly from compendia of coded ethnographic data or from other holocultural studies. Major compendia of coded data are Murdock (1967a); Textor (1967); Levinson and Morgan (n.d.); Barry and Paxson (1971); Barry, Josephson, Lauer and Marshall (1976, 1977); Murdock and Wilson (1972); Murdock and Provost (1973a, 1973b); and Broude and Greene (1976). The prevailing practice these days is to code the dependent variables from ethnographic sources or from the HRAF Files, while collecting the coded data on the independent variables from compendia of coded data.

Analyzing the Data

Computers make the analysis of holocultural data easy. Some, but not a great deal of knowledge of statistical inference is required. Comparativists should no longer be content with chi square analysis. It is now easy to compute measures of association like gamma or tau, and to conduct multivariate analysis with partial and multiple correlations, regression analysis, or factor analysis. HRAFLIB (Naroll, Griffiths, Michik and Naroll 1977) is the most useful set of computer programs for holocultural research. The BMD (Dixon 1964) and SPSS (Nie, Hull, Jenkins, Steinbrenner and Bent 1975) packages are useful also.

Special Methodological Problems

As we have mentioned before, holocultural research is plagued by methodological problems; the literature concerning these problems is broad and complex. Useful summaries of the problems can be found in Naroll and Cohen (1970) and Naroll, Michik and Naroll (1980).

SECTION II. Cultural Evolution

The notion of cultural evolution underlies many of the findings discussed in this book. Thus, it is fitting to begin our review with a discussion of what cultural evolution is and a review of holocultural research bearing on cultural evolution. The study of cultural evolution is alive and flourishing in cultural anthropology. It was not always that way. Anthropology as a science began in the mid-nineteenth century as the study of cultural evolution. Many of our anthropological forefathers—Spencer, Tylor, Morgan, Frazer, Pitt-Rivers, Maine, Bachofen—posited elaborate theories or schemes of sociocultural evolution. These early formulations, familiar to any first-year graduate student in anthropology, suffered from numerous logical and methodological flaws, as did the research used to develop them. Because of these flaws and for other reasons, the theories were discarded and the study of cultural evolution rejected by two generations of anthropologists. For the first fifty years of this century, the concept of cultural evolution was not seen as a viable or useful explanation for the wide variety of beliefs and behaviors ethnographers were reporting on the hundreds of small-scale societies they were studying. Instead, cross-cultural regularities were often explained by diffusion, and cross-cultural variations by the function of the cultural trait within the cultural system.

Carneiro (1973a) has recently demonstrated that, their methodological flaws and ethnocentric biases aside, the nineteenth century theorists were often on the right track. The ideas of these early theorists clearly shape current thinking about cultural evolution. Naroll (1973a) lists three major contemporary ideas about cultural evolution: (1) it reflects development from the simple to the complex; (2) technology and natural selection are the main forces behind cultural evolution; and (3) settlement size plays a central role in the evolutionary process. The first two ideas come from the best known of the nineteenth century evolutionists, Charles Darwin and Herbert Spencer. The third comes from archeology.

In the following chapter we define and describe cultural evolution. Here, we need to point out only that the question of what is cultural evolution is still a matter of debate. The debate goes back a hundred years and continues to focus on the same basic issue. Is

21

cultural evolution a specific process of adaptation of particular cultures to their environment, or is it a progressive sequence of change from the simple to the complex? Dozens of holocultural studies about the measurement and effects of cultural evolution are now in print. These studies take cultural evolution to be the basic cause of the presence or elaboration of specific cultural beliefs and practices. The general conclusions suggested by these studies are summarized in Chapter 4.

Research and ideas about cultural evolution have been reviewed extensively in recent years. Among the basic reviews are those by Harris (1968); Carneiro (1973a; 1973b); Dole (1973); Alland and McCay (1973); Wolf (1977); Naroll (1970b); Sahlins and Service (1960); and Erickson (1977).

Chapter 3
Defining Cultural Evolution

To understand cultural evolution, it is necessary to understand the crucial distinction between specific and general evolution. Specific and general evolution are concepts set forth by Marshall Sahlins (1960) to join the rival evolutionary models of Leslie White (1959) and Julian Steward (1955). We do not take specific and general evolution to be rival processes. Rather, we see them as complementary. The purpose of this chapter is to define specific and general evolution and discuss the relationship between the two.

Specific Evolution

Specific evolution is the process by which specific cultures or cultural institutions adapt to specific environmental circumstances. These circumstances refer to both the physical and sociocultural environments. The goal of specific evolution is survival. The concept of specific evolution is based on Charles Darwin's (1859) model of biological evolution as descent with modification through natural selection. Natural selection, of course, involves random variation and selective retention. Specific evolution takes place through a process of conflict and competition in a particular environment. Specific evolution is a reaction to some environmental change and is the basic source of cultural change. According to Alland and McCay (1973) the study of specific evolution is one especially fruitful approach to the study of the mechanisms that underlie social change.

Divale's (1974a) theory of matrilocal residence, discussed at length in Chapter 9, is one example of a theory based on the notion of specific evolution. Divale argues that a shift to matrilocal residence is an adaptational response of patrilocal societies to the armed conflict that often characterizes their relationship with other societies into whose territory they have migrated. A shift from

23

patrilocal to matrilocal residence is adaptational in that it breaks up fraternal interest groups, thereby reducing the frequency of internal warfare (feuding) and increasing the amount of time and effort men can devote to external warfare. Matrilocal residence, thus, has survival value. When peace is established and maintained for a number of generations, the society reverts to patrilocal residence. Divale's use of the specific evolution model is clear. The specific environmental change is migration into the territory of another society and the resulting warfare. The migration of one small-scale society into the territory of another almost always results in warfare. The adaptational response is a shift from patrilocal to matrilocal residence. Matrilocal residence has a higher survival value than patrilocal residence because it frees men from participation in internal warfare for participation in external warfare.

Some recent thinking about specific evolution has been influenced by cybernetic, systems, game, decision, and information theory. These ideas, while generally ignored by cultural anthropologists, have been used by "new archeologists" to explain change over time. From cybernetics, game theory, and decision theory come the idea of system constraint and the law of requisite variety (Hall and Fagen 1968; Ashby 1964; Luce and Raiffa 1967; Shubik 1964). As applied to specific evolution, the notion of constraint suggests that the greater the selective forces, the smaller and more homogeneous will be the human groups subjected to those forces. The inhibiting effect of constraint on the range of possible variations emphasizes the central role of the environment in specific evolution. The law of requisite variety suggests that only when one system (the culture) has a variety of appropriate responses to the other (the environment), will it be able to decrease the variety of possible outcomes. And, as the number of available responses increases, so does the ability of the culture to control the environment.

The effect of requisite variation on cultural evolution can be seen if we briefly trace the evolution of the relationship between nature and subsistence technology. One million years ago our ancestors were relatively efficient hunters and gatherers. Their tool inventory was limited to no more than a few implements, all used either for food gathering or food preparation. Thus, their repertoire of responses to the environment was so limited that the variety of outcomes was nearly as large as it would have been were there no human beings on earth at all. By 5000 B.C. subsistence technology and social organization had evolved to the point where men were not only hunting in organized groups with a variety of weapons, but also extracting food from crops and livestock whose growth they controlled. While there were still no responses that could neutralize natural disasters such as severe droughts or floods, our ancestors could at least control the amount and types of food they ate. Today, we have such a wide variety of responses that we have the choice of terminating the nature-subsistence technology relationship altogether. The moral: the more choices a culture has, the more control it has over the environment.

From systems theory comes the basic idea that adaptation is a set of relations between two systems—the culture and the environment (Mackay 1968). The attributes of each system provide the boundaries within which their relationship must take place. But the attributes do not determine the system's properties. The properties are determined by the interconnections between the two systems. Thus, the whole is greater than, rather than equal to, the sum of its parts.

Information theory provides two ideas relevant to specific evolution. First, specific evolution is a type of information-flow process (Vickers 1968). Second, specific evolution is a type of behavior information system (Clarke 1968). Specific evolution involves the transfer and processing of information. In terms of information flow, information sent out by the environment is received by the culture, which then changes its behavior accordingly. The culture can change in any one of four possible ways: it can (1) learn new skills or reorganize; (2) alter the environment; (3) withdraw from the environment and seek a more favorable one; (4) alter its basic goals. In Divale's (1974a) matrilocal residence theory discussed above, cultures are seen as learning a new skill and reorganizing as they shift from patrilocal to matrilocal residence.

Information comes to a culture from both external and internal sources. Clarke (1968) lists four effects that new information from external sources (the environment) can have on existing information: it can (1) add to it; (2) provide alternative choices; (3) contradict it and cause disjunction; and (4) confirm what is known. Effects one and three (gain and disjunction) are especially important for specific evolution. Both add new information and, thus, increase the culture's ability to deal with the environment.

We have mentioned only a few ideas from this summary of the relevance of certain cybernetic, systems, game, decision, and information theories that are relevant to the anthropological study of specific evolution. We have grossly simplified some of these ideas to show their relevance. But the key point is that they are relevant and do provide new approaches that may help us better understand specific evolution and cultural change.

Cultural evolution cannot be understood by focussing on specific evolution alone. Specific evolution is but one part of the process. General evolution is the other part. Specific evolution is a necessary condition for general evolution. Change, including evolutionary change, is the result of specific evolution. The grand schemes of general evolution come from the data produced by the study of specific evolution.

General Evolution

Sahlins (1960: 38) defines general evolution as a "passage from less to greater energy transformation, lower to higher levels of integration, and less to greater all-round adaptability." Most scholars take general evolution to be an open-ended, worldwide, developmental process of ever-increasing complexity. General evolution refers to increasing complexity of entire cultures (overall complexity) and particular features of culture, such as the economic or political system or the architectural style. Unlike specific evolution, general evolution is not tied to historical sequences in a particular culture. The concept of general evolution is based on Herbert Spencer's (1862: 216) definition of cultural evolution as "a change from an indefinite, incoherent homogeneity to a definite, coherent heterogeneity." Spencer's definition implies a process of increasing complexity.

Cultural or societal complexity is reflected in differentiation and specialization. Differentiation refers to the separating out or segmentation of cultural features from one another. In relatively simple societies the kinship, political, and economic systems are often intertwined with one another. It is often not at all clear where one system begins and the other ends. But, as a culture becomes more complex, cultural sub-systems tend to separate out or differentiate from each other. Specialization refers to the elaboration of cultural systems and traits. Specialization leads to more different cultural trait types, and more forms of each type. The specific cultural features and practices that are used to distinguish among different levels of complexity are discussed in the following chapter in the section on Measures of Cultural Complexity.

Certain specific patterns of change seem characteristic of the general evolutionary process. Table 3.1 lists some evolutionary trends for four aspects of culture suggested by three different investigators. Lenski and Lenski (1970) and Carneiro (1968) further suggest that the rate of complexity tends to accelerate. Thus, complexity begets complexity.

Not all cultural features follow the pattern of increasing complexity of those listed in Table 3.1. Some multivariate, factor analysis studies suggest that certain traits do not evolve in a linear sequence of increasing complexity at all (Gouldner and Peterson 1962; Sawyer and LeVine 1966; Bowden 1969b; Lomax and Berkowitz 1972; Erickson 1977). Many traits that do not so evolve have to do with kinship rules and practices. For example, the relationship between complexity and family type is curvilinear, not linear (Nimkoff and Middleton 1960). Nuclear families are found in both the simplest and most complex societies, extended families in societies at intermediate levels of complexity. Other related findings are discussed in the section on Kinship, and especially in the chapters on Main Sequence Kinship Theory and Settlement Patterns. See also, the discussion of Lomax's (1968b) research on song style in Chapter 16.

General evolution is an ongoing, open-ended process of ever increasing complexity. What causes cultures and cultural features to become more complex? Leslie White (1959) sees increasing complexity as the result of increasing energy production and utilization. Surprisingly, White's basic formulation has never been formally tested, perhaps because energy production and use are difficult to measure cross-culturally. The idea of energy harnassing does, however, underlie some other theories about the role of agriculture in cultural evolution that have been tested holoculturally. For years many scholars have assumed that the appearance of agriculture as a basic subsistence source, and that increasing agricultural efficiency through technological advancement are two major motivating forces behind cultural evolution. These assumptions seem to be essentially correct. Holocultural research shows that increased reliance on non-human forms of agricultural energy (animal or mechanical-chemical) is associated with increasing complexity (Sheils 1972; Harner 1970). So too are the types of agricultural tools used (wood, stone, bone, iron, steel) and the type of agricultural system (gathering, digging stick, hoe, plow, commercial)—see Sheils (1972). Other theories citing population pressure or popula-

Table 3.1—*Trends in General Evolution*

Aspect of Culture	Evolutionary Trends of the Studies		
	Lenski and Lenski (1970)	Naroll (1970b, 1973a)	Erickson (1977)
1. Relation to Environment	greater impact on biophysical environment	weak to strong control	greater energy extraction
2. Population	overall increase increase in population and geographic size of individual societies increase in size and complexity of communities	rural to urban (dispersed to concentrated)	increase in size and density
3. Economy	technological development development of transportation and communication increase in production of goods and services	wealth sharing to wealth hoarding	increase in energy use technological specialization and bureaucratization exchange goes from reciprocal to redistributive to market
4. Sociopolitical Organization	increase in structural complexity of individual societies increase in size and complexity of communities increase in diversification of individual cultures—both between and within	generalists to specialists simple to complex organizations wealth sharing to wealth hoarding consensual to authoritative leadership responsible to exploitative elite vengeance war to political war	technological specialization and bureaucratization sociopolitical development and social stratification

tion growth as the motivating force of evolution, like White's energy theory, await testing.

As we have said, general evolution is not a process particular to any single society. Rather, it involves all cultures, at all times, in all places. Most cultural features are widespread, that is, they can be found in many different cultures, in many different regions of the world. For example, all cultures have some system of kin terminology, or some rule of post-marital residence, or some belief about the supernatural world. Most traits do not appear in a wide variety of locales because they were independently invented in each. Independent invention is actually relatively rare and is of little importance as an explanation for the widespread distribution of cultural traits (Kroeber 1948; Driver 1970a, 1973). Most traits are distributed by cultural diffusion. So, too, is cultural complexity, as reflected in the spread of more complex traits. Traits diffuse in two ways: through peaceful borrowing; and through migration and warfare and the subjugation of conquered peoples. Recent holocultural evidence suggests that peaceful borrowing is at least as important as warfare as a mechanism for the dispersal of cultural traits and cultural complexity (Naroll and Divale 1976; Naroll and Wirsing 1976).

Not all students of cultural evolution find the concept of general evolution useful and illuminating. Alland and McCay (1973), for instance, take a strong Darwinian-adaptation position and reject the notion of general evolution as cultural evolution. As they see it, evolution is adaptation, nothing more, nothing less. Thus, from their perspective, cultural evolution is specific evolution.

Summary

We disagree with Alland and McCay. Their position is too narrow. Like Sahlins (1960), we find both the concepts of specific evolution and general evolution relevant. They reflect different but inseparably interwoven processes, each of which is measured and studied differently. The ideas of reproductive success and cultural complexity are central to our understanding of cultural evolution. Naroll's (1956) use of population size as an indicator of overall complexity shows that specific and general evolution are not rival concepts but complementary.

Chapter 4
The Effects of Cultural Evolution

Leslie White has reminded us (1960: vii) that "the concept of evolution has proved itself to be too fundamental and fruitful an approach to be ignored indefinitely by anything calling itself a science." The concept of cultural evolution was, of course, ignored and even rejected by most anthropologists for the first forty years of this century. But cultural evolution is ignored no longer. It is certainly not ignored in holocultural studies. Cultural evolution, as measured by the scale of cultural complexity, appears over and over again as a causal variable in dozens of holocultural theory tests. And it appears as a control variable in a substantial number of other studies as well. This chapter is a brief introduction to holocultural research dealing with the measurement and effects of cultural evolution. Many of the substantive findings only mentioned here are discussed in more detail in the appropriate sections of this volume.

Those who study cultural evolution cross-culturally often make two distinctions about the societies in their samples. First, they distinguish between small-scale and complex societies, often using one or more of the characteristics listed in Table 4.1. Holocultural studies, of course, are concerned with small-scale societies. Few include any complex societies in their samples. Second, they distinguish between simple small-scale societies, and complex small-scale societies. Simple small-scale societies are less specialized, less differentiated, and usually smaller than complex small-scale societies.

Measures of Cultural Complexity

Over the past twenty years, seven different measures of cultural evolution or cultural complexity have been proposed, tested, and validated holoculturally. Solid statistical evidence now exists for the convergent validity of each of these measures. In this section we

31

Table 4.1 *Characteristics of Small-Scale and Complex Societies*

Small-Scale Societies	Complex Societies
small population	large population
sparsely settled	densely settled
isolated	incorporated into vast networks
homogeneous	heterogeneous
simple	complex
equalitarian	stratified
inequality simply organized (kin and role ranking)	inequality organized in complex fashion (class and ethnic ranking)
communalistic	individualistic
stable, slow-changing	fast-changing
self-sufficient	depending upon other units
culture	subcultures, contracultures
consensus-based conformity	power-based conformity
total society	part-societies
total visibility of persons	specialized, fragmented social knowledge
total social knowledge	
total accountability	situational accountability
traditional	modern
personal	impersonal or depersonalized
close social contacts	distant social contacts
primary relationships	secondary relationships
individual relations	mass or group relations
sacred	secular
little-traditional	great-traditional
"authentic"	"plastic"
family and kin	status and territory
nonliterate	literate
role integration	role segmentation
status summation	status fragmentation
generalized roles	specialized roles
uniform distribution of social knowledge	uneven distribution of social knowledge
power diffuse	power concentrated
social integration	social disorganization
personal integration	personal disorganization
cooperation	conflict
intensive interaction	extensive interaction
mutual knowledge	anonymity
conformity	diversity
rigidity	mobility
structure	ambiguity
informal controls and sanctions	formal (bureaucratic) controls and sanctions

*Table derived and slightly revised from Gerald D. Berreman, Scale and Social Relations. *Current Anthropology* 19 (1978), 228. Published by University of Chicago.

describe each measure, review the evidence for its validity, and assess its relative usefulness in holocultural research.

(1) Social Development Index (Naroll 1956)
(2) Index of Cultural Accumulation (Carneiro and Tobias 1963; Carneiro 1970)
(3) Guttman Scale of Folk-Urban Variables (Freeman 1957; Freeman and Winch 1957)
(4) Index of Sociocultural Development (Bowden 1969a, 1972)
(5) Index of Differentiation (Marsh 1967)
(6) Settlement Pattern Scale of Cultural Complexity (McNett 1970b)
(7) The SCCS Index of Cultural Complexity (Murdock and Provost 1973b).

A variety of measures of cultural complexity are used in holocultural research. Level of political integration, degree of social stratification, and type of subsistence are three common ones. In fact, any trait found to be strongly associated with cultural evolution can then serve as a measure of cultural evolution. Subsistence type is not an especially precise measure of cultural complexity. The broadest use of a subsistence type measure is Lomax and Arensberg's (1977) attempt to align some 1,300 societies listed in Murdock's (1967a) *Ethnographic Atlas* using a six point scale: (1) collectors; (2) hunters and fishers; (3) incipient producers; (4) animal husbandmen; (5) pastoralists; (6) plow agriculturalists. Their taxonomic scheme is further refined by region and area specializations within each region. We compared this scale with Naroll's (1956) Social Development Index, using a sample of fifteen societies which appeared in both samples. The Spearman's rho of .43 creates some question as to whether both indices are measuring the same phenomena. Since Naroll's measure correlates highly with other measures of cultural complexity, the evidence suggests that subsistence type is not an especially trustworthy measure of cultural complexity.

The movement toward the development of empirically derived, objective measures of cultural evolution began with the publication of Naroll's (1956) "A Preliminary Index of Social Development." Earlier measures of complexity, and especially those used by Nieboer (1900) and Hobhouse, Wheeler and Ginsburg (1915) in their cross-cultural work, were based on a hierarchical ordering of societies according to their primary means of subsistence. Naroll's index is based on three factors: (1) settlement size, (2) craft specialization, and (3) organizational ramification. His indicator of settlement size is the population of the largest settlement; his indicator of craft specialization is the number of craft specialties; his measure of organizational ramification is the number of organizational teams—all carefully defined. Naroll developed the index with a sample of thirty societies, and it was subsequently validated by Schaefer (1969), Tatje and Naroll (1970), Carneiro (1970), and Bowden (1972). Bowden validates only the settlement size measure; he does not deal with the other two. More recently, Naroll and Divale (1976) suggest that settlement size may be the best single indicator of cultural complexity. The statistical evidence for the validity of Naroll's Social Development Index (measure four) and all the other measures is presented in Table 4.2.

Table 4.2—*Evidence of Validity for Seven Measures of Cultural Complexity*

Measure	1	2	3	4	5	6	7
1							
2	.914°						
3							
4	.885†	.969°	.871‡				
5				.782†			
6			.871†	.857† .865†	.899†		
7	.950†						

Measure Codes:

1 = Index of Cultural Accumulation (Carnerio and Tobias 1963; Carneiro 1970)
2 = Index of Sociocultural Development (Bowden 1969a)
3 = Settlement Pattern Scale of Cultural Complexity (McNett 1970b)
4 = Social Development Index (Naroll 1956)
5 = Index of Differentiation (Marsh 1967)
6 = Guttman Scale of Folk-Urban Variables (Freeman 1957)
7 = SCCS Index of Cultural Complexity (Murdock and Provost 1973b)

Correlation Coefficient Codes:

° = correlation coefficient
† = Spearman's rank-order correlation
‡ = Kendall's coefficient of concordance

In 1963 Carneiro and Tobias proposed the Index of Cultural Accumulation (measure one of Table 4.2). Their index has been revised a number of times, with the most recent being Carneiro (1970). Carneiro's index is essentially a list of cultural traits, each of which is likely either to appear or to become more complex or differentiated as the overall level of cultural complexity increases. The 1970 version includes 618 such traits covering: subsistence, settlements, architecture, economics, social organization, stratification, political organization, law, warfare, religion, art, tools, utensils and textiles, metalworking, watercraft, and special knowledge and practices. The index was validated by Carneiro (1970) and Bowden (1969a).

L. C. Freeman (1957) and Freeman and Winch (1957) proposed a Guttman Scale of Folk-Urban Variables (measure six of Table 4.2) based on eleven of Redfield's folk-urban variables: settlement pattern, integration, tool complexity, trade, written language, craft specialization, religious and medical specialists, governmental specialization, money economy, and subsistence. A twelfth variable, stratification, was deleted when it failed to scale. Working with a sample of fifty-two societies, Freeman (1957) reports a coefficient of reproducibility of .96. Additional correlational support comes from Schaefer (1969), Tatje and Naroll (1970) and McNett (1970b). Further support is provided by Hickman's (1972) factor analysis; he identifies a factor called Size-Complexity, which is composed of subsistence group population over 1000, full-time specialization of labor for surplus production, phonetic or alphabetic writing system, and membership in a tribe or nation.

Bowden (1969a, 1972) offers an Index of Sociocultural Development (measure two of Table 4.2). In the 1969 version, his index contains nineteen items: permanency of residence, group life, agriculture, use of grain for food, constancy of food supply, domesticated animals, mining and smelting of metals, metals secured from the outside, pottery, weaving, trade, money, private property in land, power vested in a chief, codified laws, authority of judges, plutocracy, and an organized priesthood. The index was developed through factor analysis and principal-components analysis of Simmons's (1945) data for fifty-five societies included in his study of the aged. Evidence for validity is presented in both of Bowden's papers.

Marsh's (1967) Index of Differentiation is the fifth measure of Table 4.2. It is designed to measure cultural complexity in both nonliterate societies and modern nations. The measure for non-literate societies is the summed ratings of Columns 14 (Social Stratification) and 15 (Political Integration) from Murdock's (1957) World Ethnographic Sample. The measure for modern nations is based on the percentage of males in non-agricultural occupations and gross energy consumption per year. Evidence for validity is provided by Schaefer (1969).

The third measure of cultural evolution in Table 4.2 is McNett's (1970b) Settlement Pattern Scale of Cultural Complexity. McNett presents a five-point scale: (1) band level, (2) village level, (3) town level, (4) city level, and (5) state level. McNett's scale correlates strongly with both Naroll's and Freeman's.

The seventh and final measure in Table 4.2 is Murdock and Provost's (1973b) measure of cultural complexity. For lack of a better name we call it the Standard Cross-Cultural Sample (SCCS) Index of Cultural Complexity. The SCCS measure is based on data for ten individual and one composite scale for the 186 societies constituting the Standard Cross-Cultural Sample. The specific factors considered are: writing; fixity of residence; agriculture; urbanization; technological specialization; land transport; money; density of populations; level of political integration; social stratification. Our own test shows the measure to be highly correlated with Carneiro's (Spearman's rho =.95).

The statistical evidence for the validity of each of these measures, summarized in Table 4.2, shows that all are highly intercorrelated, indicating that all are measuring cultural complexity.

Since all seven measures are valid indicators of cultural complexity, the question of which to use in holocultural research comes down to which one is the easiest to use. Schaefer (1969) argues that Marsh's is easier to use than either Naroll's or Freeman's. The basic advantage of Marsh's measure is the availability of coded data for a large number of societies. Carneiro's and Bowden's indexes seem difficult to use because they require that data be collected for a fairly large number of variables. But, Carneiro's measure offers the choice of measuring the complexity of (1) entire cultures, (2) particular cultural institutions, such as the religious system, or (3) particular cultural features like architectural design. McNett's scale contains only five variables, but they may be difficult to define and measure cross-culturally. Murdock and Provost's measure is tied directly to the Standard Cross-Cultural Sample and, thus, is especially easy to use with the SCCS. One aspect of Naroll's Index—maximum settlement size—seems especially attractive. The only drawback to it is that ethnographers do not always provide accurate census data. However, the maximum settlement size for a number of societies is provided in Tatje and Naroll (1970) and Naroll and Margolis (1974).

The Effects of Cultural Complexity

The effects of cultural complexity on the actions and character-istics of both individuals and cultures is widespread. This section lists some of those effects. The central conclusion suggested by these findings is that cultural complexity influences much of culture. The possible effects of cultural evolution must be considered in any theory that seeks to explain human culture.

All holocultural studies of the effects of cultural complexity make inferences about cultures that existed in the past from data pertaining to cultures that have existed and been described in the past two-hundred years. Some question this approach (see, for example, Berleant-Schiller 1977 or Sherratt 1977). They ask whether the cultures of our ancestors resemble closely those existing today. After all, cultures all have equally long histories and have presumably changed to some extent over time. Drawing inferences about past cultures from contemporary ones is a defensible practice if we take two assumptions to be true (Naroll 1970b). First, that the nervous systems and innate abilities of people alive today are much the same as those of people who lived as much as 25,000 years ago; second, that over the past 25,000 years cultures have increased in scale, as reflected in the size of their largest settlements. If correct, these two assumptions taken together suggest that cultural traits functionally associated with a particular settlement size today would likely have been associated with that same settlement size in the past.

Social and Political Organization

Settlements in more complex cultures tend to be larger, more densely populated, and characterized by rectangular rather than circular dwellings (Osmond 1964; Robbins 1966a; Whiting and Ayres 1968; Goodenough 1969; Murdock and Wilson 1972). Settlement size is probably the best single indicator of cultural complexity. The larger the settlements, the more complex the culture.

Complex cultures often have bilateral/monogamous/nuclear/small families. They tend too towards neolocal post-marital residence (Osmond 1964; M. Ember 1967; Sheils 1971; DeLeeuwe 1971;

McNett 1973). Independent families are the most common family type in both the most and least complex societies (Blumberg and Winch 1972; McNett 1973). Mode of marriage apparently evolves through three distinct phases: (1) bride service, (2) bride wealth, and (3) dowry (Jackson and Romney 1973; Evascu 1975). Inheritance by both males and females is found more often in complex societies, as is deference to certain categories of kin (Goody 1969a; Stephens 1963). And, in general, the more complex a society, the less important are kin ties and kinship organization (Abrahamson 1969).

Complex societies are always more socially stratified than simple ones. Degree of social stratification is, of course, another key indicator of degree of cultural complexity. Social stratification is often reflected in the presence of hierarchically ordered social classes and the presence of widespread socio-economic inequality (Murdock 1949; LeVine 1960; Aberle 1961; Osmond 1964; Spiro 1965; Abrahamson 1969; Stewart and Jones 1972; Pryor 1977).

The level of overall complexity often goes hand-in-hand with the level of political complexity. The number of political power positions increases as a culture becomes complex. And, as the amount of knowledge expands, maintenance of political control tends to depend more and more on the ability of those in power to control key information. In both complex and small-scale societies, economic and political development tend to parallel one another (Befu 1966; M. Ember 1963; Wirsing 1973).

Economics

Pryor (1977) provides some important conclusions about the evolution of economic systems and economic practices in small-scale and peasant societies. Pryor's approach to holocultural research is careful and measured. He successfully combines anthropological data with economic theory and economic methods. The result is the careful testing of important economic theories including some of those proposed by Marx, Engels, Polanyi, and Nieboer.

Market exchange evolves in a clear sequence. Goods markets appear first, followed by labor and credit markets, and finally by land and land rental markets. In societies at the lowest levels of cultural complexity money is often absent. Money here is defined as any item regularly used as a commercial medium of exchange. A distinction is made between commercial money and noncommercial money. Commercial money is money used as a medium of exchange. Noncommercial money is money used as a means of payment—for example, for taxes, sacrifice, tribute, or as a peace offering. Noncommercial use of money often, though not always, appears before commercial use of money.

The reciprocal exchange of goods is most common in both simple hunting and fishing societies and in more complex agricultural ones—in hunting and fishing societies because of a continuous concern about food shortage, in agricultural societies because of temporary food shortages owing to supply problems. In regard to the rise of slavery, Pryor fails to support Marx and Engels. Slavery does not seem to be an inevitable consequence of economic development, nor is slavery strongly associated with any particular stage of economic development. Nieboer (1900), and Baks, Breman and Nooij (1966) suggest that slavery might be associated with open resources. This proposition, too, is discredited by Pryor. Slavery is unrelated to the presence of open resources, either in the form of free land or rental land. Transfers of goods and services to and from a central authority occur in complex societies; non-centric transfers are more often found in less-complex societies.

Work Organization

Work is "any purposive effort to modify man's physical environment" (Udy 1970: 3). At least some kinds of work in all societies are organized. There are four forms of organized work: the first form is production determined work, such as Plains Indian buffalo hunts, where the nature and goals of the work are shaped by the physical setting. The second form is technology determined work, exemplified in some ways by modern industry, where new technology is borrowed from external sources, the organizational structure is then adapted to the new technology, and the technology is then used. The third form is socially determined work, such as is found on the family farm where work is performed in accordance with the social setting. The fourth form is pluralistic work, such as is found in modern industry, where the work organization is divided and subdivided into segregated sub-units.

As shown in Table 4.3, increasing cultural complexity is often accompanied by a shift from production-based to socially determined work in small-scale societies (Udy 1959b, 1970). Type I societies are the least complex, Type V are the most complex.

Socially determined work organizations tend to encourage less efficient manpower allocation, less efficient authority structure, less work requiring undivided attention, and less administrative rationality in decision-making than do production-determined work organizations. Thus, complex small-scale societies tend to have less

Table 4.3—*Type of Society and Type of Work Organization*

Developmental Types of Preindustrial Societies

Type	Characteristics present	Characteristics absent	Frequency
I	None	Exclusive proprietorship Sedentary agriculture Centralized government Complex stratification	12
II	Exclusive proprietorship	Sedentary agriculture Centralized government Complex stratification	12
III	Exclusive proprietorship Sedentary agriculture	Centralized government Complex stratification	42°
IV	Exclusive proprietership Sedentary agriculture Centralized government	Complex stratification	34°°
V	Exclusive proprietorship Sedentary agriculture Centralized government Complex stratification	None	25
	Total societies		125

° Includes nine societies without exclusive proprietorship.
°° Includes eight societies without sedentary agriculture.

Type of Society and Type of Work Organization

Type of Work Organization

Type of society	Production determined	Socially determined
I	31	2
II	15	11
III	28	86
IV	22	82
V	0	78

Table taken from Udy (1970:31,35).

efficient work organizations than do more simple small-scale societies. However, socially determined work organizations do encourage more work continuity and tend to be more permanent. When compared to reciprocal, familial, or contractually based socially determined organizations, politically based organizations tend to be the least efficient of all. Contractually based organizations tend to be the most efficient. Efficiency refers to the amount of organizational activity relative to the amount of physical production from an organization, regardless of the type of technology used (Udy 1959a, 1959b, 1962, 1970).

In order to shift from a non-industrial to an industrially based economy, two changes in the work organizations must take place. First, contractually based work must replace familial, reciprocal, or politically based work as the primary type. Second, and to some extent dependent on the shift to contractually based work, technologically determined work organizations must displace socially determined work organizations as the dominant form of work organization (Udy 1970).

Language

Berlin and Kay (1969) and Hays, Margolis, Naroll, and Perkins (1972) report that the more complex a culture, the more basic color terms one can expect to find in its lexicon. Complex small-scale societies tend to have six or more color terms; simple small-scale societies tend to have five or less. Evidence reviewed later by Brown and Witkowski (in Appendix B) indicates that color terms appear in the following developmental sequence:

Figure 4.1. *Color Term Development Sequence*

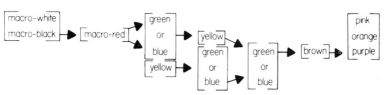

The notion that cultural complexity determines the number of color terms found in a society's lexicon is questioned by Bornstein (1973, 1975) who suggests instead that color terminology is most directly influenced by degree of eye pigmentation. In societies where people have lighter eyes—societies located far from the equator—more color terms are used than in societies located near the equator, where people have darker eyes. These two rival interpretations have been independently tested by M. Ember (1978), who finds both factors—eye pigmentation as measured by distance from the equator and cultural complexity—influencing the number of basic color terms found in a particular society. His general conclusions are that (1) complexity predicts many color terms only in societies located far from the equator, and (2) distance from the equator predicts many color terms only in relatively complex small-scale societies. Thus, the two factors seem to be interrelated and interdependent.

Social Problems

Perhaps individuals in complex societies have more difficulty controlling their aggressive impulses and are more given to acting-out aggression indirectly than are individuals in less complex societies (Bowden 1969b; Allen 1972). Cultural complexity is associated with more frequent external war, warfare for economic or political gain, less feuding, and a more stable peace following the cessation of fighting (Q. Wright 1942; Otterbein and Otterbein 1965; Otterbein 1970; Tefft and Reinhardt 1974). Warfare in politically centralized societies, which are generally more complex than those which are uncentralized, is characterized by professional soldiers, subordination in the military, initiation of hostilities by announcement, and termination by negotiation. In such centralized societies warfare is often waged with cavalry, shock troops, field fortifications, siege operations, and fortified villages (Otterbein 1970).

Suicide rates and theft rates may be higher in more complex societies than in less complex ones (Krauss 1970; Bacon, Child and Barry 1963; Allen 1972). The aged and infirm are more likely to be left to die in small-scale societies, while the aged often enjoy higher status in more complex societies (Simmons 1945; Pryor 1977). But, in industrialized societies the influence of the aged is often reduced (Williams 1972).

Social control in small-scale societies is often maintained through direct retaliation or threat of retaliation by peers. In complex societies social control is more likely to be maintained through formal judicial mechanisms or through the authority of political leaders (J.W.M. Whiting 1960). Responsibility for one's behavior in complex societies tends to reside with the individual (Hobhouse et al. 1915; March 1955; Gouldner and Peterson 1962).

The evolution of legal systems forms a neat Guttman scale from mediation to courts to police to counsel (Schwartz and Miller 1964; Wimberly 1973).

Socialization

Complex forms of economic production are associated with a heightened desire for children and less infanticide (M. Ember 1961). Parents in complex societies are generally less permissive with their children. They expect their children to be obedient, compliant, and responsible, and are more likely to reject them (Barry, Child and Bacon 1967; Rohner 1975; Pryor 1977). Education in complex societies tends to be formal and to take place outside the home (Herzog 1962; Barry, Josephson, Lauer and Marshall 1977). Initiation rites are found more often in tribal level societies (Precourt 1975).

Expressive Culture

Complex cultures are generally restrictive about sexual matters. Modesty and chastity are considered virtuous. Premarital and extramarital sex are discouraged and often punished. Less-complex societies are usually more permissive about sexual matters (Hobhouse et al. 1915; Stephens 1962, 1972; Y.A. Cohen 1969; Unwin 1934; Murdock 1964; Prescott 1975; Maxwell 1967).

Complex societies may taboo fewer foods, both in general and during particular ceremonies, than small-scale societies. But, complex societies taboo more foods during pregnancy (M. Ember 1961; Leary 1961).

The following culture traits are all characteristic of the religious beliefs and practices of more complex cultures: a belief in a high god, calendrical rites, complex religious organization, priests, temples, elaborate funerals, formal religious education, less aid sought from supernaturals in dreams, and possession trance. These traits are often absent from the religious systems of simple societies (Simmons 1945; Swanson 1960; Herzog 1962; McNett 1970a; Binford 1971; Davis 1971; Rosenblatt, Walsh and Jackson 1976; Bourguignon and Evascu 1977).

When games are placed in developmental sequence, games of

physical skill appear first, games of chance second, and games of strategy last (Roberts, Arth and Bush 1959; Roberts and Barry 1976). Riddles, too, are found more often in complex cultures (Roberts and Forman 1971). Complexity of design may be more characteristic of the graphic art of stratified societies than of egalitarian societies. Despite Lomax's earlier pronouncements (see Lomax 1968b; Lomax and Berkowitz 1972), cultural complexity is not a major cause of cross-cultural variations in song style (Erickson 1976).

Summary

We have listed some of the effects (or supposed effects) of cultural evolution on cultural systems and individual behavior. Obviously, the effects are wide and varied. Cultural evolution influences much of culture, sometimes directly, sometimes indirectly. But the influence of cultural evolution must always be considered. The findings mentioned in this chapter make it clear that cultural evolution is a key determinant of the nature of culture.

For those interested in conducting holocultural studies, we suggest that cultural complexity routinely be treated as a hidden factor that may be influencing the relationship between the other variables. Degree of cultural complexity can be easily measured by any of the seven measured described in this chapter; or coded data from Murdock (1969), Murdock and Provost (1973b), or Levinson and Morgan (n.d.) can be used.

SECTION III. Kinship

For over one hundred years kinship has been the major focus of cultural anthropology. and, for over seventy-five years kinship has been the major focus of worldwide cross-cultural research. About one-third of the three hundred or so holocultural studies now in print seek to explain kinship practices (Schaefer and Levinson 1977: 95-96). At least three or four dozen other studies cite kinship practices in their explanations for other phenomena such as alcoholism, child rearing practices, or the treatment of the aged. Some holocultural studies have been widely influential—for example, those by Tylor (1889) and Murdock (1949). Some more recent studies, like those by Divale (1974a, 1974b); Kang (1976a); Ember and Ember (1972); C. Ember (1974, 1975); M. Ember (1975) among others, cannot be ignored by either contemporary or future students of kinship.

While holocultural researchers have been mainly interested in developing and testing theories about kinship, many other anthropologists have been busy describing, conceptualizing, and classifying kinship practices. Almost all ethnographers devote some attention to marriage, residence, descent, kin terminology, the family, inheritance, and kin relations. Perhaps as much as thirty percent of the information contained in the 4,556 sources of ethnographic materials in the Human Relations Area Files is about kinship.

Over the years considerable effort has been devoted to working out universally applicable typologies of various categories of kinship behavior. Kroeber (1909) has given us a list of eight principles upon which kinship distinctions are based. Lowie (1928) and Murdock (1949) have given us two typologies for classifying kin terminological systems. Others have given us typologies for residence rules, rules of descent, and marriage practices.

The availability of this wealth of ethnographic data and the existence of these typologies have encouraged and facilitated the worldwide cross-cultural study of kinship. The importance of typologies cannot be over-estimated. On such topics as residence or descent where relatively clear typologies exist, holocultural research has been very productive—theories have been either clearly supported or clearly discredited. But, on such topics as kin avoidances

47

or inheritance, where clear typologies do not exist, holocultural research has been less productive—the results are often inconclusive or contradictory. We suspect that in some cases, because clear typologies do not exist to guide them, different researchers may operationalize the same variable differently, and thus may be investigating different phenomena.

This section contains seven chapters covering nine broad topics which most anthropologists would agree form the basis of the social structure in kin-based societies: settlement patterns, marriage, the family, incest taboos, residence, descent, kinship terminology, kin relations, and inheritance. As we pointed out in Chapter 1, our choice of topics is governed by the range of subjects included in worldwide cross-cultural studies. So, while we review theories about most aspects of kinship, we do ignore theories like those about age-group systems cited by Stewart (1977), because they have not yet been tested holoculturally.

Chapter 5
Settlement Patterns

How people use space and their physical environment tells us much about their relationships. Although no ethnographer can ignore the settlement pattern of the community in which he or she is working, and Murdock, McNett and others have studied settlement patterns holoculturally, it is archeologists who have provided the basic framework for the comparative study of settlements. Although geographers have also contributed greatly, their theories often need cross-cultural testing.

We begin by outlining a framework for the comparative analysis of settlement patterns. We then review the holocultural research bearing on three key categories of settlement patterns. Finally, we discuss crowding and its effect on human behavior.

Trigger (1968) provides us with a useful and workable typology of settlement patterns; he suggests that we study settlement patterns at three levels: (1) individual buildings, (2) community, and (3) zonal. He defines community as "the manner in which individual buildings are arranged within a single community" and defines zonal as, "the manner in which communities are distributed over the landscape" (Trigger 1968: 55). Different factors may determine the form each type of settlement pattern takes. For example, subsistence, climate and fashion may influence the form of individual structures; kin organization, specialized land use and location of resources may influence the form of communities; and trade, political organization, and warfare may influence the zonal distribution of communities. One key question is left unanswered so far by anthropological research. Which factors are chief determinants of particular settlement patterns? Trigger suggests that one general determinant is population fluctuation, either through extreme changes in birth or death rates, or through migration. Population fluctuations may directly alter settlement patterns by leading to crowding or underpopulation, or they may indirectly alter settlement patterns by introducing technological innovations.

Individual Structures

People live in caves, windscreens, tents, pit-houses, houseboats, huts, houses, castles, and many other types of dwellings. Obviously, there is vast cross-cultural variation in the form, permanence, and construction of dwellings. Rapoport (1969) documents this cross-cultural variation in house form with data for a wide range of nonliterate societies. Whiting and Ayres (1968) detail the differences between rectilinear and curvilinear dwellings:

Dwelling feature	Rectilinear	Curvilinear
roof shape	flat, gabled, hipped or shed	conical, beehive, domed
building materials	rigid—adobe, stone, wood	pliable—grass, felt, hide
size	large (average size of 300 sq. feet)	small (average of 100 sq. feet)
number of rooms	multiple	single

Rapoport (1969) lists seven alternative (or perhaps, interrelated) general factors that influence house form: (1) climate, (2) technology, (3) site, (4) defense, (5) economics, (6) religion, and (7) socio-cultural practices. There is nothing particularly striking about this list, except that there are no empirical studies demonstrating a relationship between any of these factors and house form. As we shall see over and over again, just because a relationship seems obvious does not mean that it is true. For example, Whiting and Ayres (1968: 125-26) report that the availability of building materials does not influence dwelling shape, regardless of the mobility of the population. Common sense suggests that the availability of building material would influence dwelling shape, but apparently it does not.

Rather than test causal theories, most holocultural studies of building form have tried instead to show that certain building features can be used to predict the presence or absence of specific cultural traits. The results of these studies are summarized in Table 5.1; they suggest that people in relatively complex small-scale societies—those with permanent settlements, agriculture, and large community size—tend to live in houses with rectangular floor plans. This practice may be related to the Segall, Campbell, and Herskovits (1966) carpentered world hypothesis. These authors point out that carpentering increases with societal complexity (presumably

Table 5.1—*House Form and Cultural Trait*

House Form Feature	Cultural Trait	Study
one-tenth of the total floor area of the dwellings in square meters (m²)	population of the settlement	Naroll (1962b)
average living floor area of between 14.5 m² and 42.7 m²	patrilocal residence	Ember (1973) Divale (1977)
average living floor area of between 79.2 m² and 270.8 m²	matrilocal residence	Ember (1973) Divale (1977)
circular ground plans	impermanent or mobile settlements	Robbins (1966a)
rectangular, elliptical, and quadrangular floor plans	sedentary or permanent settlements	Robbins (1966a) Whiting and Ayres (1968)
rectangular ground plans	agriculture	Robbins (1966a) Driver (1961)
rectangular ground plans	large community size	Robbins (1966a)
multiple rooms	extended families status distinctions	Whiting and Ayres (1968)
floor area over 200 ft.²	extended families status distinctions	Whiting and Ayres (1968)
curvilinear floor plans	polygynous marriage	Whiting and Ayres (1968)
rectilinear floor plans	monogamous marriage	Whiting and Ayres (1968)

because of the development of specialized carpenter's tools and division of labor) and introduces more and more sharp angles into the previously non-carpentered environment. The relationship, then, is probably not between angular house shape and large community size, but between angular house shape and degree of carpentering. Large community size merely indexes degree of carpentering. The same argument probably holds as well for the Whiting and Ayres (1968) finding, also reported in Table 5.1, between monogamy and houses with rectangular floor plans. This is almost certainly an artifact due to the positive correlation existing between monogamy and societal complexity (discussed in the following chapter). The findings in Table 5.1 may be of special value to archeologists who often have a wealth of data about settlement patterns, but little else to work with. Whiting and Ayres's conclusion that a curvilinear floor plan predicts a polygynous form of marriage also requires further comment. They explain this finding by claiming that father-absent child rearing practices in polygynous societies account for the aesthetic preference for curvilinear dwellings. We think that Whiting and Ayres's data suggests a simpler and more plausible explanation. In nonsororal polygynous societies there are many small, single-room dwellings occupied by a co-wife or a co-wife and her children. Since small dwellings tend to be curvilinear, and co-wives often live in small dwellings, it is not surprising that polygyny is associated with curvilinear dwellings.

Robbins (1966b) and Whiting and Ayres (1968) come to contradictory conclusions about the relationship between dwelling shape and art style. Contrary to his expectations, Robbins finds in two samples that rectangular house shape is associated with a preference for curved lines in art, and circular house shape is associated with a preference for straight lines in art. But Whiting and Ayres find no relationship between curvilinear floor plans and a preference for curved lines in art.

Community and Zonal

Only four holocultural studies deal with community and zonal settlement patterns. For a brief introduction to community settlement patterns we suggest Fraser (1968). Beteille (1971) has written an excellent ethnographic treatment of the relationship between community settlement patterns and other features of the cultural system.

Beardsley, Holder, Krieger, Meggers and Rinaldo (1956) have presented an elaborate though preliminary typology of settlement patterns and related socio-cultural traits. McNett (1970) has used multiple discrimination and linear regression to refine this typology into a five-point settlement pattern scale of cultural complexity, as shown in table 5.2. Each of the five settlement types in the scale is divided into pastoral or non-pastoral. McNett's scale is designed as a measure of cultural complexity or cultural evolution. While researchers may have difficulty using it, the scale does correlate highly with other measures of complexity, most notably Naroll's (1956) and L.C. Freeman's (1957).

Murdock (1949) distinguishes among: (1) *bands*, which are typically migratory and whose members subsist by hunting, gathering,

Table 5.2—*McNett's Settlement Pattern Scale of Cultural Complexity*

Settlement Pattern	Characteristics		Societies
	Non-Pastoral	*Pastoral*	*Example*
Band level	community changes its location more than once a year	more than half of food comes from animals whose movements are not completely controlled	Nipigon Yellow Knife Yukaghir
Village level	communities shift at least once each ten years	domesticated animals are ridden in search of wild animal food that accounts for at least one-half of subsistence	Manus Bungi Abipon
Town level	not normally moved, self-sufficient or center for satellites	half of food from control of domesticated animals, symbiotic relationship with non-pastoral towns	Cuna Lesu Kwoma
City level	political, religious, economic center for surrounding satellites	same as town, except symbiosis is with city	Tswana Somali Ontong Java
State level	cities and lower level communities united by second level political centralization	same as cities, except symbiosis is with states	Aymara Koreans Tahitians

or herding; (2) *villages*, which are concentrated clusters of dwellings, whose members are more or less settled and who subsist mainly on agriculture; and (3) *neighborhoods*, which are semi-isolated dwellings and whose members, according to Goodenough (1969: 292), always subsist on agriculture.

Murdock (1969) and Goodenough (1969) provide the basic cross-cultural data about the relationship between subsistence and settlement patterns. Murdock's main findings are summarized in Tables 5.3 and 5.4. We emphasize Murdock's data because he used a 322-society sample. Goodenough used data on only forty societies. The data in Table 5.3 leads Murdock to question the traditional anthropological practice of categorizing societies as either food collectors or food producers. In regard to settlement patterns, food production

Table 5.3. *Subsistence Economy and Settlement Pattern*

Type of Economy	Nomadic	Semi-nomadic	Semi-sedentary	Sedentary	Totals
Gathering	8	6	3	3	20
Hunting	14	13	3	0	30
Pastoral	10	6	5	0	21
Fishing	4	11	4	22	41
Horticulture	0	1	2	65	68
Extensive cereal cultivation	0	0	5	59	64
Intensive agriculture	0	2	5	71	78
Totals	36	39	27	220	322

Taken from George P. Murdock, Correlations of Exploitative and Settlement Patterns. National Museums of Canada Bulletin 230, *Contributions to Anthropology: Ecological Essays* (1969), 144.

through animal husbandry has the same effects as food collection through hunting and gathering, while food collection through fishing has the same effects as food production through agriculture.

Murdock and Wilson (1972) have refined settlement pattern codes for the Standard Cross-Cultural Sample (SCCS) of 186 societies. Perhaps the most interesting and relevant finding of this study relates to the regional distribution of matrifocal families. Twenty-four of the twenty-eight matrifocal societies are black societies located either in Africa or the New World. They see this pattern as a support for Hersokovits's conception that the matrifocal family is an "Africanism" that has its origin "in the social and economic conditions which give rise to the mother-child household as the predominant indigenous form of family in Africa" (Murdock and Wilson 1972: 278). This conclusion contradicts the more widely held assumption that the matrifocal family is the result of New World slavery and poverty.

Crowding

Urban planners, politicians, journalists and others have made much of the crowded living conditions in modern cities. Disease, crime, mental illness, juvenile delinquency, and even death have been attributed to crowded living conditions. While it is clear that crowding is harmful to other animals (Calhoun 1962; Clough 1965; Marsden 1970), there is no clear evidence that crowding is equally harmful to humans. The findings of case studies and comparative demographic studies are inconclusive. Some studies (Schmitt 1957,

Table 5.4. *Subsistence Economy and Size of Local Community*

(*in percentages*)

Type of Economy	Mean of					Towns of 5,000	Cities of 50,000	Number of cases
	<50	50-99	100-199	200-400	>400 no towns			
Gathering	61	23	16	0	0	0	0	13
Hunting	61	29	0	10	0	0	0	21
Pastoral	59	25	8	0	8	0	0	12
Fishing	40	23	27	5	5	0	0	22
Horticulture	18	18	28	16	10	5	5	39
Extensive cereal cultivation	3	16	36	19	23	3	0	31
Intensive agriculture	0	7.5	11	7.5	9	9	56	54

Taken from George P. Murdock, Correlations of Exploitative and Settlement Patterns, National Museums of Canada Bulletin 230, *Contributions to Anthropology: Ecological Essays* (1969), 145.

1966; J.L. Freedman 1972; Schmid and van Arsdol 1955; Chilton 1964; Wallis and Maliphant 1967; J.N. Morris 1964) find crowding related to such social pathologies as mental illness, suicide, crime, juvenile delinquency, and disease. But, other studies (Schmid 1933; Pressman and Carol 1969; Gillis 1974; and Winsborough 1965) find crowding unrelated to social pathology. The results of experimental and anthropological field research generally show no ill effects of crowding (J.L. Freedman 1973; Anderson 1972; Draper 1973). A holocultural study by Levinson (1979) provides cross-cultural support for the conclusions of the experimental and anthropological field research; in a probability sample of sixty societies there are no statistically significant relationships between residential crowding and homicide, suicide, drunken brawling, male insobriety, witchcraft attribution, sexual anxiety, divorce, infant mortality, or the general mistreatment of infants and children. Thus, it seems that crowded living conditions do not inevitably lead to pathological behavior in humans.

The effect of crowding aside, some cultures do value personal privacy more than others. Privacy is emphasized most often in uncentralized small-scale societies with patrilocal residence, subsistence through agriculture or animal husbandry, and a strong belief in a high god (Roberts and Gregor 1971). Perhaps privacy serves as an alternative to romantic love in that it may keep newlyweds apart from their kin and, thus, protect the couple from kin pressures (Cozby and Rosenblatt 1971).

Summary

We began by pointing out that archeologists and geographers rather than ethnologists have made the major conceptual and theoretical contributions regarding settlement patterns. We have entirely ignored recent theories about urban settlement patterns, ekistics, and proxemics. The contributions of anthropological research in general and holocultural research in particular to the study of settlement patterns have been scanty indeed. The most trustworthy general conclusions are: (1) matrilocal and patrilocal residence can be reliably predicted from dwelling area, and (2) dwellings in permanent (more complex) settlements are usually rectangular. Any researcher who wants to study settlement patterns cross-culturally would do well to begin with works of archeologists and geographers. Some basic archeological works are the collections edited by Chang (1968); Gummerman (1971); Ucko, Tringham and Dimbleby (1972); and Willey (1956). Also of value are essays by Chang (1958, 1962, 1972); Trigger (1963, 1965, 1967); Parsons (1972); and Vogt's (1956) assessment of the Willey (1956) collection. Works by geographers likely to be of value to comparativists are those by Haggett (1965); Jones (1966); Berry (1967); Chorley and Haggett (1967); Hudson (1970); and Haggett and Chorley (1971).

Chapter 6
Marriage

The details of marriage vary from society to society. Nevertheless, most anthropologists feel that a broad, universally applicable definition of marriage is possible. Murdock (1949: 1) defines marriage as "a complex of customs centering on the relationship between a sexually associating pair of adults within the family." Marriage involves common residence, economic cooperation, and reproduction. Murdock further suggests that "marriage exists only when the economic and sexual are united into one relationship and this combination occurs only in marriage. Marriage, thus defined, is found in every known human society" (Murdock 1949: 8). There are, however, subsocietal groups, such as castes, classes and ethnic groups that appear to lack marriage. The most extreme example is the Nayar of south India, who lack any practice that might be considered marriage according to this definition (Gough 1959; see also the discussion of marriage and the nuclear family in Adams 1960).

Goodenough (1970: 12-13) provides a slightly more elaborate definition than Murdock:

> . . . a transaction and resulting contract in which a person (male or female, corporate or individual, in person or by proxy) establishes a continuing claim to the right to sexual access to a woman—this right having priority over rights of sexual access others currently have or may subsequently acquire in relation to her (except in a similar transaction) until the contract resulting from the transaction is terminated—and in which the woman involved is eligible to bear children.

Leach (1961: 105), argues that we can say no more about marriage than that it is "a bundle of rights."

Despite the disagreements over definitions, much of the cross-cultural research on marriage has followed Murdock's, and the questions addressed by ethnographers and comparativists alike are often the same. For the former, these questions provide information about the role of marriage in a particular society. For the latter, these questions provide a framework for the development and testing of general theories of marriage:

(1) Why is marriage universal?
(2) Who may marry whom?
(3) How often can one marry? Once? More than once? Serially? Can one have more than one spouse at a time?
(4) Can a marriage bond be broken? If so, how?
(5) Who decides to form the union?
(6) How does one obtain a spouse?
(7) What is the status of the newlyweds?
(8) Does the marriage create bonds between the affines?
(9) What purpose do the people of the culture feel the marriage serves?

Why Is Marriage Universal?

The question of why nearly all societies at all times have had some sort of marriage is one of the classic concerns of cultural anthropology. A variety of explanations has been suggested. All of these explanations share the common assumption that marriage, because it is universal, is an adaptive response to some widespread human need.

Murdock (1949: 7-10) provides two such explanations. He argues that marriage solves the problems caused by sexual division of labor in subsistence activities. Marriage is the mechanism that enables men and women to share the products of their often mutually exclusive food getting activities. Second, he suggests that marriage may also solve the problem of the very long dependency period of human offspring. Linton (1936: 135-136) offers a third explanation: marriage solves the problem of sexual competition between men. Marriage, by assigning specific women to specific men, reduces competition for those women, and hence, reduces the chance of intra- or intersocietal conflict. None of these theories has been tested cross-culturally. And, because all of the variables involved are nearly universal in distribution, it is not likely that any of them could be tested cross-culturally.

Ember and Ember (1979) have recently presented an indirect, cross-species test of these three theories. Their study is based on ethological data on male-female bonding in a random sample of forty species of birds and non-human mammals. The Embers find little support for any of these theories and suggest a fourth theory instead: "natural selection may favor male-female bonding [marriage] when mothers' feeding requirements interfere with their baby-tending" (Ember and Ember 1979: 43). Regarding humans, the Embers say that "humans may have begun to have male-female bonding when they began to hunt" (Ember and Ember 1979: 44). Their ethological data provides substantial statistical support for this theory, especially as it applies to birds and non-human mammals. So far as we know, the Embers are the first to use a cross-species study to test cross-cultural theories and, while their conclusions are far from definitive, the approach seems to be potentially fruitful.

Who May Marry Whom?

No society leaves unanswered the question of who is an acceptable marriage partner and who is not. The breadth or narrowness of choice varies, but there are always specifications. Anthropological research has largely been confined to explaining two phenomena: (1) exogamy versus endogamy, and (2) cross-cousin marriage.

Endogamy and Exogamy

Endogamy refers to specifications of the group within which one must marry, for example, the caste, the village, the race. Exogamy refers to specifications of the group outside of which one must marry, for example, the nuclear family, the lineage, the clan. The wide range of choice in our society and in Western industrial society in general is in sharp contrast to a culture such as the Tiv of Nigeria who practiced sister exchange because the number of potential spouses was severely limited. But both systems still indicate whom one may and may not marry. In our own society the prescriptions are broad. The only legal barriers are to a limited number of close kin including siblings, parents, and first cousins. Beyond that, legal sanctions rarely apply. Social sanctions, however, operate very strongly to restrict marriage between members of different racial or ethnic groups, or widely divergent socioeconomic and religious groups, or even between persons with different levels of educational attainment. These combinations are neither forbidden nor nonexistent. But the difficulties faced by the partners who chose to form such a union and the pressures brought upon them by family and friends are often sufficiently severe to limit such marriages.

Among the Tiv the traditional marriage system prior to British intervention and prohibition specified that a man should ideally exchange his sister with another man's in another lineage. When individual men did not have sisters to exchange, the daughter of a mother's brother could be substituted. If no female was available to exchange, it was possible to pay bride price for a wife, but this was not the ideal or most prestigious mode. Obviously, this system of direct exchange narrowly limited who could marry whom (Mair 1971: 38-40).

Falling between the rules of groups like the Tiv and our own society, are those like the Australian four- and eight-section systems, which also strictly prescribe the group from which a man may take a wife and to which he gives wives. In these cases, they are different groups, but here the sections cover the whole society, so theoretically the choice is greater. In actuality however, most aboriginal Australian societies are lightly populated and choices are limited.

Most societies thoughout history have been to some extent exogamous. Few have been endogamous. Exogamy can be viewed as a direct consequence of incest prohibitions—men must seek wives from groups other than their own to avoid incestuous matings with near relatives. Although widely ignored, incest theory has yet to be formally discredited. And, on the contrary, M. Ember's (1975) support of the inbreeding theory of incest taboos also indirectly supports the incest theory of exogamy.

The three most popular theories of exogamy are survival value theory, conflicting loyalties theory, and alliance theory. Survival value theory, in its various forms, is most closely associated with Tylor (1889), White (1949), and Service (1971). Survival value theory takes its name from Tylor's (1889) claim that societies must "marry out or be killed out." According to survival value theory, exogamy helps the society survive in two ways: by forging political alliances between neighboring societies and by reducing conflicts within the group.

Conflicting loyalties theory is largely a product of British functionalism. It is most often associated with Colson (1953); Gluckman (1956); Murphy (1957); and Scheffler (1964, 1973). Conflicting loyalties theory argues that exogamy, by creating cross-cutting or divided loyalties, leads to social cohesion.

Alliance theory is associated with, among others, Lévi-Strauss (1956, 1969); Dumont (1966, 1968); Mauss (1967); Leach (1961); Sahlins (1965); Needham (1958, 1962); and Lounsbury (1962). Alliance theory is a form of exchange theory. In alliance theory, women are seen as an exchange product, traded by men. Marriage is, of course, but one form of exchange, but to Lévi-Strauss and others it is the prototypical form, the form that initiates other forms. Like survival value theory, alliance theory predicts that exogamy leads to cooperation and alliances between social units.

Although each of these three theories is widely cited in the anthropological literature, each has been formally tested only once —by Gay Kang (1976a) (see also Kang 1976b and 1979). Kang's test is an especially careful and rigorous one. Her findings cannot be ignored. Kang sees survival value theory, conflicting loyalties theory, and alliance theory as three closely related forms of what she calls solidarity theory. Solidarity theory predicts that exogamy creates cross-allegiances/alliances between exogamous units; these cross-cutting ties established by exogamy promote peace (Kang 1976a: 2). Based on careful tests of nine basic hypotheses, and thirty-six sub-hypotheses, Kang finds *no support* for solidarity theory, and, thus, no support for survival value theory, conflicting loyalties theory, or alliance theory. Kang concludes:

> The implications of this study are that a series of fundamental assumptions, upon which Survival Value, Conflicting Loyalties, and Alliance Theory are based, do not appear to hold true. Exogamy does not appear to create cross-allegiance/alliance between exogamous units; exogamy does not reduce conflict between those units nor within the unit; exogamy does not increase survivability. Furthermore, cross-allegiance/alliance between exogamous groups does not lead to peace or survivability, and peace within or between exogamous units does not increase survivability (Kang 1976a: 178).

Kin group endogamy is quite rare. Only sixty-seven societies listed in Murdock's (1967a) *Ethnographic Atlas* prescribe a form of endogamous marriage within the kin group. The reasons for the use of endogamy in these societies are not clear. Murdock (1949) reports that community endogamy is almost universally found in sedentary, matrilocal communities. Two interpretations are offered for this finding. Murdock reasons:

> A woman can join her husband in another community and continue to carry on without handicap all the technical skills she has acquired since childhood. But a man who goes to a new community in matrilocal marriage has to master an entirely new environment. All the knowledge he has gained as a boy and youth concerning the

location of trails and landmarks, or mineral deposits, of superior stands of timber, of the haunts of game, and of the best grazing or fishing sites becomes largely useless, and must be painfully accumulated afresh for the new territory. These facts discourage a change of community in marriage on the part of the man, whereas they exert no such effect in the case of a woman (Murdock 1949: 213-214).

Kloos (1963) suggests a rival interpretation. In his view, endogamy is related to succession to authority in sedentary, matrilocal communities. In a sample consisting largely of New World matrilocal societies, Kloos finds local endogamy always associated with matrilineally inherited leadership. But, when leadership is achieved rather than inherited, the society could be either endogamous or exogamous. Kloos reasons that when matrilineal succession prevails, endogamy will result, as a mechanism for ensuring the smooth transfer of power.

The sixty-seven endogamous societies listed in Murdock's (1967a) *Ethnographic Atlas* show a striking regional pattern. Endogamous societies in the Old World—Europe, Africa, Asia, Middle East—are often highly complex, stratified societies like the Egyptians, Neapolitans, Turks, and Burmese. In the New World—North and South America—most endogamous societies are egalitarian, lightly populated, and relatively isolated. The few that are not, the Inca, for example, are highly complex and stratified like those in the Old World. According to the control of resources theory, endogamy serves as a mechanism of social and political control in complex societies. Endogamy helps those in power maintain control by preventing potential rivals from gaining access to power or wealth through marriage. No one has as yet explained why some societies choose endogamy as a means of controlling resources while others do not. Endogamy may also foster community cohesion, especially among lower strata groups by keeping heritable property within the local group, by keeping potential political rivals out, and by keeping the divorce rate low (Goody, Irving, and Tahany 1970: 296; Cohen, Schlegel, Felt and Carlson 1968: 142; Ackerman 1968: 471).

Cross-cousin Marriage

Many anthropologists have attempted to explain the complexities and variations of cross-cousin marriage. Any attempt to sort out all the arguments and data easily becomes a project of book-length proportions and we avoid it here. But it is necessary to describe briefly what cross-cousin marriage (ccm) is and how it has been explained. A cross-cousin is the child of a parent's sibling of the opposite sex, either a mother's brother or a father's sister. The children of these relatives will necessarily be outside of one's own kin group, whether matrilineal or patrilineal. Cross-cousins are frequently a class of kin related to ego because of their membership in a particular lineage, not just because of genealogical relations. Thus, an individual may have a large number of classificatory cross-cousins who are not the children of certain aunts and uncles. Cross-cousins are the closest relatives of one's own generation not excluded as marriage partners by kin group incest taboos (exogamy). Marriage to a mother's brother's daughter (MBD) or a father's sister's daughter (FZD) for a man, and to a father's sister's son (FZS) or a mother's brother's son (MBS) for a woman, represents a preferred or even prescribed form in a limited number of societies.

Marriage to parallel cousins, either the children of mother's sisters or father's brothers, is rarer because it involves marriage to a member of one's own kin group. It is found in some societies, such as the Bedouin Arabs of Israel, where it may result from the heavy emphasis placed upon continually recementing alliances within the lineage to maintain solidarity (Mair 1971: 25).

Cross-cousin marriage takes a number of forms and it is this variation that has made it a popular object of study. Variation may occur in the kind of exchange transactions between kin groups. The exchange of women, as Lévi-Strauss sees it, provides a major basis of solidarity between groups within a society. This exchange can be either direct (symmetrical) or indirect (asymmetrical). In direct exchange, only two groups, or multiples of two, are involved. Both give to and receive from the other. In indirect exchange, at least three groups are involved, and the same group cannot be both a giver and a receiver for another. In this system, A gives to B, which gives to C, which gives to A. This second type has numerous advantages over the first in terms of adaptability and flexibility for growth, as well as creating a greater integration of all members of the society, since the entire system has to function in order for anyone to benefit (Homans and Schneider 1962: 208). Related to the form of exchange is the specification of whether all or only certain kinds of cross-cousins are eligible marriage partners. There are matrilateral cross-cousins, and there are patrilateral cross-cousins. If either is an acceptable partner, the system is bilateral; if only one or the other is, it is unilateral.

The often bitter debate about cross-cousin marriage centers on the reasons for the development of these various forms and their relationship with other institutions, such as descent and kin terminology. Most of the recent debate stems from Lévi-Strauss (1969), although he was by no means the first to discuss the implications of cross-cousin marriage. Leach (1961: 64-81) discusses the contributions to the controversy from 1920 to 1951; Lévi-Strauss originally provided a summary of the early literature but dropped it in the revised edition.

Lévi-Strauss argues that generalized (asymmetrical) exchange is superior to direct exchange because it produces greater societal integration. Not only is the generalized form better, but the matrilateral pattern is the most generalized and thus the best of all because it creates continuous and regular relations among all the members of the society. In the patrilateral form, the direction of flow is reversed in each generation. A quick sketch of the kinship diagrams of the two forms shows that this is the case regardless of the descent system (Lévi-Strauss 1969: 452). For that reason, Lévi-Strauss argues that patrilateral cross-cousin marriage is merely delayed direct exchange and creates the same kind of dyadic networks as direct exchange (Lévi-Strauss 1969: 446).

Homans and Schneider (1962) disagree with his analysis and point out that patrilateral cross-cousin marriage can be just as "round-about" (1962: 211) and result in just as much solidarity. But this is not their main criticism. Lévi-Strauss (1969: 438-55) argues that matrilateral cross-cousin marriage is consciously chosen by the people who practice it because they recognize that it is the best form. Homans and Schneider (1962: 213-16) think that choices are made on the basis of short-term individual benefits and because they mesh well with existing institutions, not because the people in a society know what institutions are best for them. These reasons are the efficient causes which a functional theory must explain. According to Homans and Schneider, Lévi-Strauss provides only the final causes, the overall social benefit. Homans and Schneider then provide an alternative theory not necessarily conflicting with Lévi-Strauss, but providing the efficient causes. They argue that the direction of unilateral cross-cousin marriage is a function of the direction of descent linearity in a group. Patrilineal societies will tend to have matrilateral cross-cousin marriages; and matrilineal societies, patrilateral cross-cousin marriages. This is owing to the kinds of relationships parents have with children, and aunts and uncles with nephews and nieces. In a patrilineal society, the father is the authority figure and his relations with his children are likely to be stern and disciplinary. The father's sister will be associated with this same behavior. The mother will be associated with nurturance and warmth, and by association so will her brother. So he is the likely man for a boy to turn to when looking for a wife. From the mother's brother's point of view, his sister's son is a good choice for a son-in-law; he is already likely to have a working relationship with sister's son, who is more likely to submit to the mother's brother's authority and to care for mother's brother in his old age, than would an unrelated man. The opposite situation, between a father's sister and her brother's son in a matrilineal society is felt to hold as well. Homans and Schneider's (1962: 225-46) hypothesis is supported by Murdock's (1949) and by a more informal study of their own.

Needham (1962) criticizes Homans and Schneider, and defends Lévi-Strauss. He finds the Homans and Schneider argument totally "specious," a complete misunderstanding of Lévi-Strauss (Needham 1962: 3-4). But Needham's critique adds nothing of substance to the debate, and has even been rejected by Lévi-Strauss (1969: xxx-xxxv), so it is only noted here in passing.

Leach (1954, 1961) presents a third interpretation of matrilateral cross-cousin marriage. Through his familiarity with the Kachin peoples of Burma, he views matrilateral cross-cousin marriage as characteristic of societies where marriage occurs between hierarchically stratified lineages. In this situation, sometimes wife-givers and sometimes wife-receivers are dominant, but in either case, the exchange of women throughout the system conforms to the "status relations in other (non-kinship) institutions." Leach argues that the assumption of a necessarily egalitarian situation in this sort of marriage system is inaccurate. The exchange of women is part of a whole system of exchanges between lineages and must be viewed as "only one of many possible ways of 'expressing' those relations" (1961: 101).

Three holocultural studies discuss these three rival theories and provide cross-cultural tests. Berting and Philipsen (1960) carefully examine and summarize Lévi-Strauss, Leach, and Homans and Schneider and attempt to test each of their hypotheses. They support Lévi-Strauss's position to some extent, but agree with Homans and Schneider that the key weakness is its lack of an efficient cause. They also feel that Leach's argument is more powerful than Lévi-Strauss's, but see it as a partial explanation because of the many exceptions and because it seems limited to situations in which marriage is closely tied to the political and economic structure. Finally, they find strongest statistical support for Homans and Schneider's hypothesis.

Eyde and Postal (1961) again reviewed this work, this time in relation to the development of Crow-Omaha kinship terminologies. Using Murdock's (1957) World Ethnographic Sample (WES), they test a theory about the development of Crow-Omaha systems and their relation to matrilateral cross-cousin marriage. They find many weaknesses with Homans and Schneider, the most telling being the generality of Homans and Schneider's hypothetical basis—sentimental attachment—and the rarity of the explained phenomenon— unilateral cross-cousin marriage (see Coult 1965: 131-132 for a further discussion of this point). If Homans and Schneider are correct, we would expect unilateral cross-cousin marriage to be far more common. Eyde and Postal (1961: 767) conclude that matrilateral cross-cousin marriage is "a reasonable response to the problems of residential cooperation in unilineal societies," while they find patrilateral cross-cousin marriage to be "an anomaly due to incest extensions which occur under certain limited conditions." These conditions have to do with conflicts between kin terminology and kin behavior.

Coult (1965) is a retest of Eyde and Postal (1961). Also using the WES, he finds little support for their hypothesis—of thirty-three cases relevant to the hypothesis, there are twelve exceptions; and even of the twenty-one cases which are explained, Coult finds that four of those are coded incorrectly. He agrees with Eyde and Postal that a relationship does exist between cross-cousin marriage and Crow and Omaha terminology, but it is not the one they offer. Instead, Coult suggests that cross-cousin marriage is related to Crow and Omaha terminologies because both of these institutions (the marriage system and the kin terminology) are related to particular forms of authority: matrilateral cross-cousin marriage and Omaha terminology to strong patripotestality, or father authority; patrilateral cross-cousin marriage and Crow terminology to avuncupotestality, or mother's brother authority (Coult 1965: 137). So after all this, we are returned to a slightly revised version of Homans and Schneider's hypothesis, for an elaborated but not markedly different set of reasons.

How Often May One Marry?

People may marry once for life. Or, while having that as the ideal, they may find that the marriage is not successful, terminate it, and go on to another. In some cases, marriage is so brittle and divorce so common, that this serial form of marriage is the accepted norm.

Anthropologists have offered little in the way of trustworthy, universal explanations for divorce. The only holocultural study that claims to account for divorce is Ackerman (1968). He finds both consanguine and community exogamy related to frequent divorce. Unfortunately, the non-probability sample contains only eleven societies, too few a number on which to base broad generalizations. Factors that seem to be unrelated to frequency of divorce include the levirate, marriage arrangment, attitudes toward and frequency of homosexuality, and punishment of and frequency of rape (Ackerman 1968: 476; Minturn, Grosse and Haider 1969: 307). Minturn et al. (1969: 308) do report that absence of bride price, dowry, and gift exchange at marriage, and the presence of extended families and matrilocal residence make divorce easier, and presumably, more common. This finding supports the widely held assumption that when a sizeable amount of money or property is exchanged at a marriage, there will be great pressure brought by the spouses' families to keep the couple together.

One major emphasis of cross-cultural research on marriage has been to distinguish between factors that lead to monogamy and to polygamy. Polygamy is found in eighty-three percent of the 862 societies in the *Ethnographic Atlas* (Murdock 1967a). But it is by no means practiced by all members of those societies. The number of individuals who take more than one spouse is often much less than those who do not. Polygyny, one husband and two or more wives, is much more common than polyandry, one wife and two or more husbands. Actual polyandry, as opposed to temporary wife sharing, as a matter of hospitality or for other reasons, has been recorded in only five, possibly six, groups: the Marquesans of Polynesia, the Todas of India, the peasants of Tibet, the Sherpa of the Himalayas (Murdock 1949: 25), the Kandyan Sinhalese of Sri Lanka and, questionably, the Nayar of south India. Since it is debatable whether marriage even exists among the Nayar, their case is ambiguous (Gough 1959). In all cases, except for the Marquesans, polyandry is related to extreme economic conditions and/or female infanticide— where conditions are such that a single husband cannot support a wife and children, and poverty encourages female infanticide, to keep down the population. Murdock (1949: 26) points out that temporary wife sharing, as is found in most Eskimo groups, and especially among brothers, is not polyandry, because it involves only sharing of sexual privileges and not of economic responsibilities.

Interestingly, polygyny occurs both in societies where female economic contribution is significant and in societies where it is insignificant. In both cases, the more wives a man has, the wealthier he is. In the first case, the wives' economic contribution makes him wealthy. In the second, he is wealthy enough to support more than one wife. Thus, their presence is an indicator of his wealth. The relationship between polygyny and the degree of female economic contribution is mediated by the subsistence practices of the society. A significant economic contribution by women is most common in hunting and gathering societies. Thus, men in hunting and gathering societies are often made wealthy by their wives. But, in fact, the wealth distinctions between members of these societies are often slight. In agricultural societies, where wealth differentials are both large and common, men apparently take more than one wife as a show of wealth.

J.W.M. Whiting (1964) points out that polygyny is especially common in societies with a long postpartum sex taboo—one of a year or more in duration. He proposes the following causal sequence: low protein in the diet——➤ long postpartum taboo——➤ polygyny. The long taboo serves to ensure that the mother will have only one nursing infant to feed at a time, and thus can provide the infant with a sufficient amount of protein. Polygyny provides men with an alternative sexual outlet during the long taboo period. Murdock (1967b: 145), however, sees the long taboo–polygyny linkage the other way about. Polygyny, by providing an alternative sexual outlet, makes the long taboo more tolerable. Saucier (1972) questions the linkage between low protein in the diet and long postpartum sex taboo. Basic to Whiting's hypothesis is his contention that low protein-long taboo societies tend to be found primarily in the tropics where the people subsist mainly on roots and fruits. Saucier, in a more careful study based on a random sample of 172 societies, finds no evidence that societies subsisting on roots and fruits have a longer taboo than those subsisting on cereal crops. Thus, Murdock and Saucier give us little reason to accept Whiting's hypothesis.

Obviously, polygyny can operate only so long as the number of marriageable females in a society exceeds the number of marriageable males. M. Ember (1974b) and Witkowski (1977) suggest two mechanisms that help maintain a large pool of marriageable females. Ember finds that warfare, by reducing the number of marriageable males, results in a surplus of marriageable females. Thus, warfare can be viewed as both a reason why polygyny appeared in the first place, and why it continues to be practiced. Witkowski points out that polygynous societies often maintain a pool of excess females by encouraging women to marry at an early age and men to marry when they are considerably older.

The reason why most marriages are monogamous is obvious. In most societies, at most times, the number of men and women of marriageable age is about the same. Thus, there are usually only enough surplus women to enable but a few men to take more than one wife. There has been some anthropological interest in discovering what factors lead to a prescription of purely monogamous marriage. Osmond (1964) provides the broadest search. She reports the following specific relationships between monogamy and indicators of cultural complexity:

Variable	phi	p	n
craft specialization	—	.001	362
large communities	.27	.001	170
plow agriculture	.23	.001	550
average or less economic contribution by women	.04	.10	436
stratification	.21	.001	533
political integration	.11	.01	497
urban settlement pattern	.10	.10	549
overall level of culture complexity	.25	.05	497

Obviously, monogamy is related to cultural complexity, although weakly so. The strongest correlation coefficient is only .27, which accounts for less than nine percent of the variance. A relationship between monogamy and complexity is also found by Sheils (1971: 221), who argues, however, that the relationship is curvilinear, not linear.

Cross-cultural research on marriage has been enlivened by a debate between Spiro (1965) and Chaney (1966a, 1966b) concerning an ambitious study of Spiro's that deals partly with monogamy.

Spiro (1965: 1112) reaches two main conclusions about monogamy: (1) Monogamy tends to appear in a kinship configuration also composed of bilateral descent, independent families, and small households. (2) Food production and social stratification, jointly, comprise a sufficient condition for the existence of monogamy. The first proposition is descriptive, the second causal. Spiro's study was reanalyzed and replicated by Chaney. Using a sample of 565 societies, Chaney finds no evidence to support either of these propositions. And, he explains away Spiro's conclusions on the grounds that Spiro's sample of sixty societies is biased. It was not selected randomly, nor did Spiro recompute his worldwide findings for each region of the world. In his rejoinder to Chaney, Spiro (1966a) conceded that the two propositions were incorrect.

Some societies regulate very carefully the choice of secondary spouses. The levirate prescribes that if a woman's husband dies, she should marry his brother; the sororate, that if a man's wife dies, he should marry her sister. Many societies also practice sororal polygyny, in which a man's prescribed second wife is his first wife's sister. According to Witkowski (1977: 655), sororal polygyny is most frequent in polygynous, matrilocal societies. This is evidently the case because in matrilocal societies marriage to unrelated females is often difficult. Murdock (1961: 219) reports that sixteen percent of plural-marriage societies practice sororal polygyny. Fraternal or adelphic polyandry is practiced by the Toda and the Tibetans.

Who Decides to Form the Union?

A large number of people are potential initiators of a marriage. In a particular society, the actual initiator is often determined by the function of marriage in that society. In patrilineal societies it is often the father or a senior male. In matrilineal societies it is often the mother's brothers. As noted above, Lévi-Strauss and others maintain that the marriage itself is secondary in importance to the alliances created when men exchange sisters or daughters. And, in many societies one sure way to power is the proven ability to provide wives for other men by giving away one's sisters or daughters.

Romantic love as the basis for marriage, in which the potential spouses make the decision to marry, is found in a limited number of societies (Coppinger and Rosenblatt 1968; Rosenblatt 1966, 1967; Rosenblatt and Cozby 1972). Rosenblatt and his associates suggest three reasons why romantic love may be used as a basis for marriage. First, they find romantic love a basis for marriage more often in societies with non-neolocal postmarital residence (Rosenblatt 1967: 476). Rosenblatt reasons that in the non-neolocal situation, romantic love may serve to strengthen the marital relationship and to provide security in the face of little economic dependence between spouses. Second, Rosenblatt (1966: 336) relates romantic love as a basis for marriage to certain child rearing practices. Following Whiting and Child's (1953) negative fixation theory, he suggests that needs which go unmet in childhood will manifest themselves in adulthood. In accordance with this theory, Rosenblatt finds that societies which use romantic love as a basis for marriage often do not meet the oral needs of their children and often use severe oral socialization practices like abrupt weaning. Rosenblatt's third explanation for romantic love as a basis for marriage is reported in Coppinger and Rosenblatt (1968: 310):

> . . .where subsistence dependence between spouses is strong, romantic love is unimportant as a basis of marriage; while where subsistence dependence between spouses is weak, romantic love is important as a basis of marriage.

This interpretation has been questioned by Mukhopadhyay (1979) who finds that the weak relationship (r = .25) between romantic love as a basis for marriage and imbalanced subsistence contribution is reduced to +.10 when the effect of subsistence technology complexity is partialled out.

How Does One Obtain a Spouse?

Murdock (1967a: 47) defines mode of marriage as the "prevailing mode of obtaining a wife." The three most common modes are dowry, bride wealth, and bride theft. Dowry is the transfer of money or property by the wife's family to the husband upon marriage. Bride wealth is the tranfer of property or money by the groom's family to the family of the bride. The participants often view bride wealth as payment in exchange for the wife's sexual, procreative, and economic services. Bride theft is ". . .the forcible abduction of a woman for the purpose of marriage, without the knowledge or consent of her parents or guardians" (Ayres 1974: 238). Obviously, actual bride theft does little to cement intergroup relationships. Rather, it is likely to result in antagonisms and even war. Symbolic or mock bride theft, in which members of the groom's family fight a mock battle with those of the bride's family and carry her off, is not uncommon. In some societies, though, it is possible to compensate the wife's family after the marriage takes place. What is often called bride theft is instead merely a mock fight between affines which always results in the groom capturing the bride.

Ayres (1974) tests three rival theories of bride theft:

(1) Any factors which limit the number of marriageable women or which limit access to a particular woman or class of women may be expected to increase the probability of bride theft occurring.

(2) Bride theft represents a delayed and displaced acting out of the Oedipal conflict.

(3) Such behaviors represent exaggerated attempts to demonstrate masculinity by individuals who have a high level of sex identity conflict and anxiety.

In a series of hypotheses tests inferred from these three theories, Ayres finds no support for theory number one, some support for theory number two, and support for theory number three. In regard to the first theory, Aryes finds no relationship between bride theft and these variables: polygyny, status differentials, a high value placed on virginity, and absolute parental control over daughters. In support of the second theory she finds that in societies which often use bride theft, the father tends to play an important role. In support of theory three, she reports a strong relationship between bride theft and an exclusive mother-child sleeping arrangment. Ayres further suggests that theory three is also the most plausible explanation for bride raiding. Finally, she finds some support for Tylor's (1889) theory that bride theft is associated with patrilocal residence.

It now seems clear that dowry is most generally found in complex societies. Evascu (1975: 168-71) finds dowry strongly related to intensive agriculture, industrialization and societal differentiation. The reported gamma coefficients range from .70 to .93 for his sample of seventy-four societies. Jackson and Romney (1973: 517) also find dowry associated with a high level of cultural complexity.

Evascu (1975: 167-71) finds bride wealth strongly related to a low level of societal differentiation, horticulture, extensive agriculture, and herding. Goody (1973: 51), in an analysis of 857 cultures listed in Murdock's (1967a) *Ethnographic Atlas*, finds bride wealth most often in societies with patrilineal or bilateral descent systems. Heath (1958: 79) reports that bride wealth is dependent on the importance of the female's subsistence contribution—when the contribution is both sizeable and important, bride wealth often accompanies marriage. Evascu (1975: 167-70) finds bride service generally limited to hunting and gathering peoples.

Evascu's work suggests an evolutionary progression in mode of marriage from bride service to bride wealth to dowry. This developmental sequence is partially supported by Jackson and Romney (1973) who find the geographical distribution of dowry rather restricted, and conclude that dowry is probably a fairly recent development. Along the same lines, Rosenblatt and Unangst (1974) report that marriage ceremonies are more common when wealth is transferred at marriage or heritable property is considered important.

What is the Status of the Newlyweds?

As one of the major status changes in a person's life, marriage may be accompanied by many other social changes. Marriage is often a necessary prerequisite for a person to be considered an adult. Once married, a man may participate in the political discussions of the community, join the clubs or associations of the adult men, and participate economically as an adult. A woman may be considered an adult at this point or certainly at the birth of her first child. Frequently in patrilocal societies, however, when women move from the household of their parents to that of their in-laws, they are dominated by a new set of parents. It is often not until much later, when their parents are dead, and their own children grown, that a husband and wife may have some authority in their household.

In addition to the adult status, marriage frequently means a change in kin group membership. In most societies, a wife retains some rights in her natal kin group while going to live with that of her husband. But in some, as in traditional China, the marriage bond effectively cancels her membership in one group and establishes it in another (Levy 1949: 102). In matrilineal societies, men generally retain their interests and authority in their natal kin groups, since it is the mother's brothers who are the authority figures in the lineage. Here there is great variability between how active a part the father plays in the upbringing of his children and how much he is excluded by the lineage members and relegated to the care of his sister's children. The classic case is found among the Trobriand Islanders, where "the mother's brother is considered the real guardian of a boy . . . The real kinship, the real identity of substance is considered only to exist between a man and his mother's relations" (Malinowski 1922: 71). In any event, marriage results in a new set of relationships with a new set of kinsmen—in most cases because, when marriage is with a cross-cousin, one's affines are already consanguines. However, it is the relationship to them that has changed and in that way the individual's status is changed.

Relevant here, also, is the Whiting and Whiting (1975) study of husband-wife relationships. They report that husbands and wives tend to sleep or room apart in societies located in tropical climates, with permanent settlements, at middle levels of social complexity, and when warriors are needed to protect property. They also find that wife beating is more common in independent family households than in extended family households.

Does the Marriage Create Bonds between Affines?

As with the status and relations of the newlyweds, the status and interrelations of the affines are also affected. Especially if the marriage is seen as an alliance between families or lineages, these new relations may be more important than those of the marriage partners. Lévi-Strauss (1969) is chiefly concerned with the importance of these alliances. The marriage of children may create or cement all sorts of relationships. Royal marriages ensuring peace are a common aspect of European political history. In Tudor England, trade or business relationships were often assured by exchanging daughters or sisters (Pearson 1957: 312). And in pre-revolutionary southeastern China, whole lineages were often linked through marriages of their members (M. Freedman 1970: 104-106). Radcliffe-Brown's (1952: 54-60) discussion of mother-in-law avoidance and joking relationships emphasizes the negative aspects of the affinal relationships and examines these behaviors as methods of controlling the conflicts that are possible between new relations.

What Purpose Does the Marriage Serve?

The answer depends on the answers to the previous questions. A couple views a marriage planned by the two fathers differently from one contracted because of their own sexual or emotional attraction to each other. The same differences are likely to be present between monogamous and polygamous marriages. The meaning of marriage cannot be simply stated. It is bound up in all the institutions and behavior patterns affected by interpersonal relations in a particular society. This is one of the reasons marriage is so hard to define. Although it is nearly universal, its forms and functions vary widely. As the structure of interpersonal relations varies, so must the meaning of marriage.

Summary

The literature on marriage is voluminous. As a basic aspect of kinship, it is discussed in every anthropology and sociology textbook and nearly every general ethnography. Two good monographic introductions to the subject are Mair (1971) and Fox (1967). A reader by Bohannan and Middleton (1968) contains various ethnographic accounts and some theoretical articles (including Gough's on the definition of marriage). Regional and individual studies of marriage are far too numerous to mention here and can be easily located in the references in these three books.

Our general impression is that cross-cultural research has been most useful as a means of discrediting widely held theories. For example, Murdock's and Linton's theories of marriages do not survive Ember and Ember's cross-species test; Kang has questioned conflicting loyalties, survival value, and alliance theory as explanations of exogamy; Lévi-Strauss's arguments about cross-cousin marriage have been rejected in every study designed to test them; and J.W.M. Whiting's contention that low protein in the diet leads to polygyny has been questioned by Saucier. Similarly, no powerful explanations for endogamy, divorce, polygyny, or monogamy have been found. However, cross-cultural research on marriage has shown that: (1) warfare and a late age of marriage for men encourages polygyny; (2) monogamy is related to cultural complexity; and (3) dowry tends to be found mainly in complex societies.

A number of other theories concerning endogamy, bride theft and romantic love as a basis for marriage seem plausible, but need rigorous testing.

Chapter 7
The Family

The human family comes in five forms. The *matrifocal* family consists of a mother and her children. The *nuclear* family consists of a wife/mother, husband/father, and their children. The *polygynous* family consists of a husband/father, two or more wives/mothers and their children. The *polyandrous* family consists of one wife/mother, her children, and two or more husband/fathers. And the *extended* family consists of individuals who are recognized as both husband/father and son/brother or wife/mother and sister/daughter at the same time. The nuclear family is by far the most common form. The polyandrous family is the rarest. The family members in each type of family occupy different kinship roles. Thus, each family type faces different interpersonal problems and has different organizational potentials. Table 7.1 lists the roles present in each type.

Some scholars argue that the family is a kinship group and, as such, should not be confused with other social groups based on common residence (household) or function (domestic unit) (Bohannan 1963; Bender 1967). Murdock (1949: 1), however, defines the family functionally, as "a social group characterized by common residence, economic cooperation, and reproduction." Levy and Fallers (1959) also define it functionally and list four universal functions: (1) sexual, (2) reproductive, (3) economic, (4) educational. While there are other institutions in every society that can perform one or more of these functions, no single institution except the family regularly performs them all. Holocultural studies have examined both structure and function, and while the family is a structural unit, the equal importance of function, and the relations between the two, need to be considered.

In this chapter we describe in more detail the five family types listed above. We review the small number of holocultural studies about the determinants of family type. And we discuss the debate over the universality of the nuclear family.

Table 7.1 Kin Roles by Family Type

Kin Roles†	Matrifocal	Nuclear	Polygynous	Polyandrous	Stem	Lineal	Fully Extended
M	+	+	+	+	+	+	+
F		+	+	+	+	+	+
W		+	+	+	+	+	+
H		+	+	+	+	+	+
D	+	+	+	+	+	+	+
S	+	+	+	+	+	+	+
Si	+	+	+	+	+	+	+
B	+	+	+	+	+	+	+
Co-W			+		+/-	+/-	+/-
Co-H				+	+/-	+/-	+/-
½Sb			+	+	+/-	+/-	+/-
GM					+	+	+
GF					+	+	+
GC					+	+	+
A*						+	+
U							+
Ni							+
Ne							+
C						+	+
PL					+	+	+
CL					+	+	+
SL						+	+

Table 7.1, *continued*

M	— mother	Si	— sister
F	— father	B	— brother
W	— wife	Co-W	— co-wife
H	— husband	Co-H	— co-husband
D	— daughter	½Sb	— half sibling
S	— son		

GM	— grandmother	Ni	— niece
GF	— grandfather	Ne	— nephew
GC	— grandchild	C	— cousin
A	— aunt	PL	— parent-in-law
U	— uncle	CL	— child-in-law
		SL	— sibling-in-law

*While we recognize that the use of culture-bound kin terms such as aunt or uncle may be considered ethnocentric, for the summary purposes of this table, we feel that these general terms are sufficiently specific.

†A plus sign indicates that the kin role is present; a plus-minus sign indicates that the kin role may be present or absent.

The Matrifocal Family

A matrifocal family consists of a mother and her children. Although relatively rare, the matrifocal family is described by some as the basic family type. If one views parenthood as the basis of the family, it is then reasonable to take the matrifocal family as the basic family type. There is certainly a parent (always the mother) and one or more children. But, if like Murdock (1961: 83), one sees both marriage and parenthood as the basis of the family, it is no longer reasonable to take the matrifocal family as the basic family type. In the matrifocal family while there is parenthood there is no marriage, or even if there is marriage, the husband/father plays an insignificant role.

Although not the dominant type in any society, the matrifocal family exists as an independent entity among certain groups in the Caribbean, Central America, South America, and increasingly in North America (Adams 1960; Kunstadter 1963; Otterbein 1965). The matrifocal family also existed as part of the matrifocal-matrilineal extended family system of the Nayar sub-caste of south India (Gough 1959).

When the matrifocal family does appear as a distinct family type, it evidently does so only in very specific circumstances. In the western hemisphere, it is mainly found in lower socio-economic groups where the men must travel to find work or where the men have little status or economic security (Adams 1960; Otterbein 1965). Among the Nayar a similar situation existed. Political and military considerations required the men to be mobile. They were mercenaries and were rarely responsible for a family or household.

The concept of matrifocal family should be limited to those situations in which there is no regularly present husband/father. But, Bohannan (1963: 74) wisely cautions against viewing all families as matrifocal units, with a husband/father added. The focus must remain on the entire family unit. And in most societies at most times the entire unit includes a husband/father.

The Nuclear Family

A nuclear (conjugal, elementary) family is a small social group all of whose members, through birth, marriage, or adoption, stand in a relation of parent, child, spouse, or sibling to other members of the group (Murdock 1949: 3-4; Bohannan 1968: 318). Lévi-Strauss (1968) and Adams (1960) make important and related points about the social processes that characterize the nuclear family. Lévi-Strauss (1968: 141) argues that:

> . . .when the family is given a small functional value, it tends to disappear even below the level of the conjugal type. On the contrary, when the family has a great functional value, it becomes actualized much above that level. Our would-be universal conjugal family, then corresponds more to an unstable equilibrium between extremes than to a permanent and everlasting need coming from the deepest requirements of human nature.

The main point here is that the nuclear family as a type of family exists as a result of a compromise between forces. There are always centripedal and centrifugal forces acting on social groups. These forces may come in the form of such diverse phenomena as ideals of individual behavior, social conceptions about the form the family should take, or economic factors that influence family size. It is the interaction of these forces that in some way helps determine the form the family takes.

Adams speaks of relations rather than forces. He sees the nuclear family as a collection of three dyadic relations: the conjugal or sexual; the maternal; and the paternal. The paternal relation is based on the other two. Whether or not a society recognizes a man's role in procreation, his role and status as father are almost always a function of his role as mother's husband. Adams (1960: 40-41) thinks that the sexual and maternal dyad are especially important:

> The conjugal or sexual dyad is particularly significant because it is the reproductive unit of the society, the maternal dyad is the temporal link between successive generations of adult dyads. . .since the mother is the only adult in the maternal dyad, and the wife is the only female in the sexual dyad, they can be joined most readily by identifying the wife with the mother.

Both Lévi-Strauss and Adams make the same basic point. The nuclear family can be viewed as a social product just as easily as it can be viewed as an elementary unit. It is then reasonable to assume that the nuclear family is the result of forces that push and pull in many directions at once.

The Polygynous Family

The polygynous family consists of one husband/father and two or more wives and their children. There is some disagreement over whether to classify the polygynous family as a form of the matrifo-cal family, or whether to classify it as a form of the nuclear family. Murdock (1949: 2) views the polygynous family as a group of nuclear families with a common husband/father. This view conflicts with the position that the polygynous family is a group of matrifocal families sharing one husband/father.

Murdock lists two key characteristics of the polygynous family. First, the marital unions must be contemporaneous. If the marriages are successive, there are no co-wives and the result is a series of nuclear families. Second, the union between the man and the woman must be more than just sexual. Murdock insists that the union also involves residential cohabitation and economic coopera-tion. There are, of course, many examples of polygyny without common residence—such as the Ashanti (Fortes 1950) or the Nava-ho (Kluckhohn and Leighton 1946). There are some societies like the Ashanti again, where there is some economic cooperation between spouses, but it is far less important than the economic cooperation between other kin or associates. Regardless of the criteria for the definition of marriage, if the multiple unions are not socially recognized as marriage by the culture, they are only concubinage.

There are three sets of relations in polygynous families that are not present in nuclear ones: (1) the relationship between co-wives referred to by Bohannan as shared sexuality (all of the wives share sexual relations with the same husband); (2) the relationship between half-siblings, or limited shared descent; and (3) the rela-tionship between children and the wives who are not their mothers. Each type of relationship may lead to feelings of rivalry, jealousy, hostility, and antagonism that each polygynous family must control in order to function and survive. Among those factors that may help maintain social order within the polygynous family are clearly defined roles, equitable distribution of tasks, sororal polygyny, and equitable treatment of co-wives by the husband.

While polygynous families are always in the minority even in societies where they are favored, they tend to be the goal of all men in those societies. They are highly desirable because more wives mean more prestige and more material wealth. Wives also often desire additional wives for their husbands—additional wives lighten their workloads and increase the prestige and wealth of the family. In most polygynous families, wives are an economic asset. Whether they cultivate, or make craft products to sell, their work increases the wealth of the family.

The Polyandrous Family

The polyandrous family consists of one wife/mother and her children and two or more husbands. As with polygyny, it must be based on a relationship which the society recognizes as marriage; for this reason, wife-sharing is not considered polyandry. Additionally, for a family to be considered polyandrous, each of the husbands must be eligible to be considered the jural father of at least one of the woman's children. This conceptualization of polyandry conflicts with that of Hoebel (1966: 362-64) who considers any form of wife-sharing to be polyandry. Hoebel's view seems much too broad, especially since he does not consider the reverse, multiple sexual partners for men, to be polygyny.

Polyandry is quite rare. Bohannan (1963) says that there are ten societies known to have practiced polyandry, but does not list them all. Among the known cases as we said earlier, are the Todas of India, the Sherpa of Nepal, the peasants of Tibet, the Kandyan Sinhalese of Sri Lanka, the Marquesans of Polynesia, and possibly the Nayar of south India. In the first four of these groups, polyandrous marriage is fraternal (adelphic)—groups of brothers marry the same woman. According to Bohannan (1963: 111), one characteristic of polyandrous families is that the husbands had some prior relationship, often as either brothers or business associates.

Why polyandrous families exist is not clear. A number of suggestions have been proposed. Leach (1961: 110) suggests that polyandry is closely tied to a need to keep real property together. Prince Peter (1965: 206) sees polyandry as an adaptation to "a difficult and insecure natural environment." Others have linked to it to female infanticide.

The Extended Family

An extended family consists of individuals who are recognized as both husband/father and son/brother or wife/mother and daughter/sister simultaneously. Extended families combine an individual's family of orientation with his or her family of procreation. Extended families may contain both monogamous and polygamous families. Murdock (1949) views extended familes as composite nuclear families. Linton, however, sees them as multi-generational consanguineal families to which spouses are added. A third view, closer to Linton's than to Murdock's, is expressed by Goodenough (1970) who feels that some groups such as Americans, emphasize conjugal families; some, like the Nayar, emphasize consanguineal families; and some, probably the majority of the world's societies, have important roles for both.

Extended families contain a number of affinal, lineal, and collateral relationships not found in other families. The affinal relationships are those between parents-in-law, children-in-law, and siblings-in-law. Relations between in-laws are often difficult and disruptive, and it is not surprising that they are often handled through institutionalized rules of behavior. These institutionalized rules are discussed in the chapter on Kin Relations. The unique lineal relationship in extended families is that between grandparents and grandchildren. Apple (1956) reports that the grandparent-grandchild relationship seems to be freest and easiest in societies where the grandparents have little authority over their own children. The collateral relationships are those involving cousins, aunts, uncles, nieces, and nephews. Thus there are collaterals in both the same and adjacent generations. There are eight possible sets of relations for adjacent generations and ten for the same generation. Rules of residence and descent largely determine which relationships will be emphasized and which will be ignored. Rules regarding cross-cousin marriage also obviously effect the relationships.

There are a number of kinds of extended families and there are a number of ways to classify them. Nimkoff (1965: 19) classifies four types based on structure:
(1) stem family—two nuclear families in adjacent generations with one son/husband or daughter/wife who is a member of both families
(2) lineal family—one nuclear family in the senior generation and two or more nuclear families in the junior generation
(3) fully extended family—the families of at least two siblings or cousins in each of at least two adjacent generations
(4) joint family—two or more nuclear families who form a corporate economic unit.

Murdock (1949) classifies extended families on the basis of postmarital residence rules; his four types are patrilocal, matrilocal, bilocal, or avunculocal. Most holocultural research follows Nimkoff's rather than Murdock's system, although there is no reason that the two cannot be used together.

Determinants of Family Type

Five holocultural studies demonstrate that family type is closely related to societal scale or complexity. McNett (1973) validates

Spiro's (1965) typology of family types. McNett is also able to place the family types in the following development sequence: (bilateral-polygynous-nuclear-small) ⟶ (unilateral-polygynous-extended-large) ⟶ (bilateral-monogamous-nuclear-small). This sequence indicates that both the least and the most complex societies have small, nuclear families. His finding is in general accord with Blumberg and Winch's (1972) curvilinear hypothesis. The curvilinear hypothesis states that: (1) the independent family is the typical family type in small hunting and gathering societies and in large, industrialized socities; (2) the extended family is the typical family type in settled, agricultural societies. Thus, there is a curvilinear relationship between family type and societal complexity. The curvilinear hypothesis is supported cross-culturally by Blumberg and Winch (1972), McNett (1973), and in part, by Nimkoff and Middleton (1960), and Osmond (1969).

Nimkoff and Middleton (1960) also find that societal complexity (as measured by subsistence complexity) is a determinant of family type. But, their sample does not contain the same range of variation in complexity as does Blumberg and Winch's. Nimkoff and Middleton include no modern, industrialized societies in the sample. Thus, they find a linear relationship between complexity and family type—independent families are found in hunting and gathering societies, extended families are found in agricultural societies. This finding supports point number two of the curvilinear hypothesis. Nimkoff and Middleton also find that the extended family is associated with a higher degree of social stratification than the independent family. This finding is generally supported by Chu and Hollingsworth (1969). With a sample of 531 societies, they find that: (1) fifty percent of independent family societies are socially stratified, (2) sixty percent of extended family societies have social stratification, and (3) seventy-seven percent of stem and lineal family societies are stratified. Table 7.2 shows the breakdown by family and stratification type.

Universality of the Nuclear Family

The nuclear family is a universal human social grouping. Either as the sole prevailing form of the family or as the basic unit from which more complex familial forms are compounded, it exists as a distinct and strongly functional group in every known society (Murdock 1949: 2).

Table 7.2—*Type of Stratification and Type of Family*

Stratification Type

Family Type	Age Grades	Classes or Castes	Hereditary Aristocracy	Wealth Distinction
Independent	0	0	-	0
Extended	0	0	+	0
Lineal and Stem	0	+	0	0

Taken from Hsien-Jen Chu and J. Selwyn Hollingsworth, A Cross-Cultural Study of the Relationship between Family Types and Social Stratification. *Journal of Marriage and the Family* 31 (May, 1969), 326. Copyrighted 1969 by the National Council on Family Relations. Reprinted by permission.

For thirty years researchers have tried to discredit by way of example Murdock's claim that the nuclear family is universal. The Nayar of the Malabar Coast of south India (Gough 1959), the Jamaican lower classes (Clarke 1957), the blacks of British Guiana (Smith 1956), the Black Caribs of British Guiana (Solien 1959), and a whole range of cases from South America (summarized by Adams 1960) have all been cited as examples of groups with matrifocal rather than nuclear families. However, each of these examples has a common weakness. Each group listed is actually a subgroup within a larger society. The Nayar are a subcaste, and the others are either distinct classes or ethnic groups within a larger society with a complex economy (Kunstadter 1963: 63; Nimkoff 1965: 15).

Murdock does not claim that every human family is wholly or partly a nuclear family. His statement is a carefully worded empirical conclusion drawn from a small sample of 250 societies. The presence of matrifocal families in a relatively small number of societies does not discredit the generalization. As the Yiddish proverb tells us, "For example is no proof." A list of deviant intrasociety cases does not discredit Murdock's ideas about the societal universality of the nuclear family. Murdock supports the claim that the nuclear family is "the *basic form* from which more complex familial forms are compounded . . . a distinct and strongly functional group in every known society" (1949:2) with data from his sample. But here, the data supports the claim because Murdock neglected to ask the kind of questions that could have refuted it.

Murdock's interpretation conflicts with Linton's (1936: 139-163) delineation of two basic family types: (1) the conjugal, which is based on the sexual tie between spouses and is equivalent to

Murdock's nuclear family, and (2) the consanguine, which is based upon the asexual tie between siblings, or other blood relatives. Linton suggests that in some societies it is the conjugal family which predominates while in others it is the consanguine. In accordance with this view, in societies characterized by the consanguine family, the family of orientation is the most important kinship unit, and spouses are relatively unimportant. A spouse serves some functions, mainly sexual, but one's consanguines are the source of most aid and support. Children are socialized to expect closer relationships with siblings and other blood kin than they ever expect to have with affines. Levy and Fallers (1959: 649-50) provide four examples of societies which do not emphasize the nuclear family, even though a unit consisting of husband, wife and children can be identified. One of the examples is the Nayar, who are not an independent society. But the other three, the Basoga of East Africa, the Hopi, and the Chinese are all examples of strong unilineally organized societies which promote lineage interests over nuclear family interests in nearly all situations, from child rearing, to the economics of the household, to supporting one's blood kin. There are other examples. Bohannan (1963: 96) describes the loyalty of a Tiv groom to his parents which extends to divorcing his wife if she fails to get along with them. Any society with strong unilineal principles is likely to demand similar behavior. We need a holocultural study bearing on the importance of the nuclear family, its role, and the strength of its bonds—including Bohannan's (1963: 95) question about whom one sides with in a dispute. The mere presence of nuclear families in every known human society is highly suggestive. The debate between Linton and Murdock concerns a basic issue about kinship organization that needs further attention.

Summary

The contributions of holocultural research to our understanding of the family in cross-cultural perspective are meager indeed. The only sound conclusion is that the relationship between cultural complexity and family type is curvilinear, with the independent family predominant at the extremes and the extended family predominant at intermediate levels of complexity. Theoretical work on the family has been hindered, no doubt, by the debates over definition and conceptualization that have yet to be resolved. It is difficult to explain a phenomenon when there is disagreement over what the phenomenon is.

Chapter 8
Incest Taboo

The incest taboo is the prohibition of sexual intercourse between certain categories of kin. In all societies, incest means sexual relations between mothers and their sons, fathers and their daughters, and between brothers and sisters. In all societies incest also means sexual relations between other specific kinsmen, but not always the same ones. Incest taboos regulate sexual behavior. Because our society associates sex with marriage, incest taboos and exogamy are often confused. Exogamic restrictions refer to the establishment of socially recognized bonds between individuals and often kin groups as well. Incest taboos refer only to the regulation of sexual intercourse. Obviously, people between whom sexual intercourse is considered incestuous cannot marry; but between people who cannot marry, sexual intercourse may be perfectly appropriate.

While numerous explanations have been suggested for the universality of incest taboos, few of them have undergone careful cross-cultural testing. We do not review the early and basic theories of Westermarck, Malinowski, and Freud here; they have been discussed widely elsewhere—Durkheim (1898), Fortune (1932), Freud (1938, 1950), Malinowski (1927), Seligman (1929), Sumner and Keller (1927), Tylor (1889), Westermarck (1894), and L.A. White (1948). Summaries and discussions of these early theories can also be found in many of the works we do discuss here, and especially in Aberle et al. (1963: 251-58), Murdock (1949: 289-92), and M. Ember (1975: 251-58).

Cultural and Psychocultural Theories

Murdock (1949: 284-89) lists eight empirical cross-cultural generalizations about incest taboos: 1) incest taboos are universal within the nuclear family; 2) they are never confined to the nuclear family; 3) they do not apply universally to any relative outside the nuclear family; 4) they apply with diminished intensity outside the nuclear family regardless of the use of the same kin terms; 5) they fail strikingly to coincide with biological relations; 6) they are highly correlated with purely conventional groupings of kin; 7) they are characterized by a peculiar intensity and emotional quality; 8) violations do occur. These eight conclusions are used by Murdock to eliminate other hypotheses and to support his own synthetic model. The presence of violations, in Murdock's mind, discredits the instinct hypothesis. Murdock's theory is psychocultural, drawing upon psychoanalysis, sociology, cultural anthropology, and behavioristic psychology.

Psychoanalysis provides answers about the emotional intensity and universality of the taboo by demonstrating the univeral conditions of the nuclear family which affect all individual behavior. It describes the child's attraction to parents and siblings because of his or her dependence on them, and in reaction, the parents discouragement of this attraction for various reasons. But Freud tell us only how children are discouraged. Sociological theory, in the form of ideas about family authority and disruption, tells us why. Malinowski (1927) and Seligman (1929) point out the need to maintain order in the family, an order which incestuous relationships would weaken. Sociological theory accounts for the organizational and reproductive advantages of societies with incest taboos over societies without those taboos. Behavioristic psychology accounts for the spread of taboos beyond the nuclear family through stimulus generalization, owing to the similarity of other relatives to those of the nuclear family. But again this theory explains only the tendency for the general extension of incest taboos. The actual mechanism of extension is provided by anthropological research, which shows that the different directions of extension are related to the social structure and the nature of extended kin groups. Anthropology also explains how the extension of incest taboos benefits lineage and clans in the same way it benefits the nuclear family, especially by enchancing cooperation.

Goody (1969a) and Schlegel (1972) suggest two sociocultural theories which are narrower than Murdock's but provide important concepts and distinctions. Goody's discussion of incest and adultery is relevant only for unilineal societies, but it elaborates a point in Murdock's theory. Goody feels that in societies with unilineal descent groups, incest cannot be viewed merely in terms of the nuclear family, because the unilineal group cuts across the nuclear family. In these societies, incest is the violation of the unilineal group. As an example, he shows that among the patrilineal Tallensi, sexual relations with group wives (wives of men in the lineage), are the most serious sexual crime, while among the matrilineal Ashanti, sexual relations between brothers and sisters are the most serious. The reason is the same in both cases. In matrilineal societies, it is the sisters who continue the lineage, while in patrilineal societies, it is the wives. So it is the violation of the concept of the group which is basically the real crime. Goody opens his article with a perfunctory attack on Murdock. Although he argues against Murdock's assumption of the universal prominence of the nuclear family, Goody's study further demonstrates the correlation between incest taboo extensions and purely conventional groupings of kin, Murdock's sixth empirical conclusion. Goody's sample is limited to four societies. A cross-cultural test on a larger sample would be valuable not only for the study of incest, but for a better understanding of the place of the nuclear family within the larger nexus of kin relations.

Schlegel's (1972) views on the extension of the incest taboo are closely related to Goody's. She finds that it covaries with the direction of domestic authority. In husband dominant (patrilineal) societies, father-daughter incest will be the cause of greatest concern. In societies where husband and brother dominate women equally, both father-daughter and sibling incest will be of equal concern. This position is identical to Goody's but Schlegel provides a slightly different set of reasons for it. She gives two alternative hypotheses, neither of which is carefully tested, but which have some support through analogous examples. The first hypothesis is that "a man who dominates a woman in other spheres of her domestic life is likely to dominate her sexually as well" (Schlegel 1972: 129). Her support here is her previously demonstrated assumption that dominance in one sphere overlaps to others. In this hypothesis the incest taboo is assumed to protect the female. The second hypothesis is that a "subordinate female is not only more accessible to the dominant male, but is more attractive to him as well" (1972: 129). Schlegel means that since the woman's status and welfare are dependent on a man, the woman is attracted to him and is thus seductive. In this explanation the taboo protects the male. The evidence for the second hypothesis is partly based on behavior among nonhuman primates, where dominant and submissive behavior is well documented, and partly on an indirect variable concerning co-wife jealousy, which is greater when the husband controls the welfare of wives and their children and lesser when he does not (Schlegel 1972: 130-131). Both hypotheses are empirically plausible and fit in well with both Goody's and Murdock's more structural explanations. Again cross-cultural tests are necessary to establish their trustworthiness.

Biological Theories

M.K. Slater (1959) and Y.A. Cohen (1964a) provide biological theories of the incest taboo. Each is biological in that a specific universal, physical, inherent trait is seen as the basic cause of incest taboos. Slater argues that specific incest prohibitions are a direct result of specific demographic characteristics of early hominid populations. A short life span of from twenty-five to thirty-four years made parent-child matings unlikely. An infant mortality rate of at least fifty percent, a fifty percent chance of two like-sexed adjacent siblings, and a long spacing between viable offspring made sibling incest unlikely. Slater derives these hypotheses from mathematical models of life spans and comparisons with the most technologically primitive people alive today, whom she assumes must be better off than our ancestors. Slater's argument is faulty. The first problem is the questionable practice of equating today's marginal and highly exploited small-scale societies—which generally live not in ancestral areas, but in regions where they have been placed by their more technologically advanced neighbors—with the small-scale societies of our ancestors (cf. Lee and DeVore 1968). There is no good reason to believe that the two groups are comparable. The second problem is that the theory fails to account for the extension of incest taboos to non-nuclear family kin (M. Ember 1975). It can only *account* for the absence of incestuous relations among nuclear family members. The third problem, and perhaps the most serious one, is that the models of the average life span cannot be tested. They are postulated figures and we can only quibble with the mathematics. The key question is whether the model reflects a situation that ever really existed. And without age and sex statistics for a large sample of early hominid populations, the model remains untestable.

Y.A. Cohen (1964a) has proposed a complex psychobiological explanation for the universality of the incest taboo, which although based on an impressive array of information from ethology, psychoanalysis and ethnography, has not been tested. His discussion and analysis of the incest taboo is nevertheless stimulating. He presents two reasons for, or actually functions of, incest taboos within the nuclear family. He refers to these as core incest taboos. The first is the need for privacy, defined as "freedom from extreme emotional and physical stimulation, especially from other people" (Cohen 1964a: 161-72). Cohen maintains that some degree of privacy is a necessity for almost all animals. For human beings, it is necessary in order to maintain a strong concept of self. Sex, especially sex leading to orgasm, tends to blur the concept of self by encouraging identification with the sexual partner. For a not yet mature adolescent, this can be an overwhelming experience. When sexual activity is with a member of one's nuclear family, and especially a parent, the effect can be devastating and is likely to have severe psychological consequences.

Boundary maintenance is an important aspect of the need for privacy. Cohen argues that as the closeness of interpersonal relations increases, greater limits must be placed on behavior. A boundary maintainance system, such as one composed of consanguineal kin, leads to very strong emotional attachments. Thus within the family, limits on emotional interaction are necessarily great because so many forces cause closeness (Cohen 1964a: 176-179). The prohibition of sex between consanguines in a boundary maintenance system is necessary to define the limits of their interaction. Cohen's argument is difficult to evaluate because it rests on ideas for which he claims great generality, but which lack clearly demonstrable features, such as a need for privacy, or the necessity of limiting emotional interaction. Cohen relates the universality of core incest taboos to certain universal elements of human interaction and human needs. The interaction is observable, but how can we measure these unobservable needs?

We think that Aberle et al. (1963) and M. Ember (1975) have provided the two best explanations for the universality of incest taboos. They are best both on logical and empirical grounds, and, most important, both are testable. Aberle et al. (1963: 259-261) integrate both sociocultural and biological genetic ideas. They look at mating patterns in animals in order to select a sample within which the occurrence of incest varies, because as has been already noted, its universal prohibition among humans makes it difficult to find correlations. Looking at mating patterns and family structure among wild geese and mammals, they conclude that " . . . there seems to be an empirical tendency for barriers against close inbreeding to be found where inbreeding would otherwise occur.

The more intelligent, slower-maturing animals living in family groups, where stable attachments are likely, and human beings, who also live in family groups where stable attachments are likely, mainfest patterns which limit familial inbreeding: asexual imprinting, intergenerational competition and the familial incest taboo" (Aberle et al. 1963: 261). Asexual imprinting, found in geese, is not known to occur in mammals, including human beings. Intergenerational competition, in the form of expulsion of the sexually mature young is also not possible with humans because sexual maturity precedes the individual's ability to survive independently.

The authors mention two basic problems which incest creates: the disruption of familial order or authority, and the deleterious genetic effect of mutations. There are only two possible solutions to these problems, given the previous limitations. The authority problem may be dealt with through institutionalized sexual access within the family, wherein some orderly form of sexual relations might be developed within the context of the already-established parental authority patterns. However, this does not solve the problem of inbreeding. The prohibition of incestuous relations altogether solves both problems. This prohibition does not require the individuals who practice incest prohibition to be aware of its benefits for breeding; it solves the problems of intrafamily competition without such awareness. However, these people would have had a genetically selective advantage over people who did practice in-breeding. The consequences of the incest prohibition, such as the linking of families through marriage alliances, are then seen as later advantages which reinforced this behavior pattern. Their explanation has considerable merit—it is simple and does not require the broad assumptions and essentially untestable models of Slater or the complex psychological formulations of Cohen. It is also in line with Murdock's empirical conclusions.

M. Ember's (1975) study is the only one which systematically tests incest taboo theories. Since the incest taboo is universal for the nuclear family, there is no way to test it by means of correlations (Ember 1975: 249). Ember is thus forced to employ indirect variables concerning dimensions which do vary in order to support or reject the hypotheses. He does this by looking at the distribution of first-cousin marriage and the kinds of societies within which it occurs. He reasons that "if a given theory is correct about why natural selection should have universally favored the prohibition of familial mating, then that theory should also predict the conditions under which the incest taboo extends to first cousins" (M. Ember 1975: 250). The only hypothesis which does this is inbreeding theory. Westermarck's childhood familiarity and Tylor's (1889) and L.A. White's (1948) cooperation theories do not.

Ember's study also employs demographic models, which he uses to generate and organize data for further testing. Ember's ideas are based on genetics and especially on recent knowledge about the mechanisms of inbreeding and mutation. The standard argument against the inbreeding theory of incest prohibition is that primitive people, with little or no idea of the biology of reproduction, are unlikely to connect inbreeding with the appearance of lethal or deleterious recessive traits. Ember counters this argument first by citing recent findings on the effects of mutations and inbreeding and second by demonstrating through a genetic model, just how frequent such traits might be. He claims that the genetic literature shows that "the percentage of early deaths is consistently greater among the offspring of tertiary relatives (first cousins) than among the offspring of unrelated spouses. Moreover, there are data which show that marriages between secondary relatives (such as uncle-niece) entail even greater risks of premature death in the offspring, and that marriages between second and more distant cousins entail fewer risks" (M. Ember 1975: 265).

Ember compares the reproductive rates of familial versus non-familial matings under various conditions by assigning different values in his model for: the number of offspring who do or do not (for genetic reasons) survive to reproductive age; the genetic risks of familial marriages divided by nonfamilial marriages; and the number of offspring from nonfamilial marriages divided by familial marriages. He concludes that "the differences in reproductive rates between familial and nonfamilial matings may have been great enough for people to have recognized the disadvantage of inbreeding and to have consciously prohibited it" (Ember 1975: 279). Since first cousin (tertiary) matings are also shown to be disadvantageous, but not so much as primary matings, he also demonstrates that in the majority of cases, they are found in societies with large genetic isolates where mating with an actual first cousin is rarer; and that the incest taboo is extended to first cousins in societies where the genetic isolate is small and mating with an actual first cousin is more likely. The exceptions, where first cousin marriage is found in small size populations, can be explained by either the depopulation of a middle-sized society which thus causes the relaxation of taboos, or by the presence of a very small population whch allows first cousin marriage in order to provide enough mating possibilities.

One final point. Much has been made over whether or not people in small-scale societies recognized the deleterious consequences of inbreeding. Whether they did or did not is really beside the point. Even if there were no overt recognition, the strong selective disadvantage of close inbreeding would favor societies which prohibited it and disfavor those which did not prohibit it. Thus, societies with a strong incest taboo are likely to have survived, those lacking a strong taboo are likely to have disappeared.

Summary

From these studies, we can conclude that there are genetic, psychological, and sociological advantages to the prohibition of sexual relations. These advantages are especially important for the nuclear family and kin groups (or small-scale cooperating groups) in general. However, we still lack rigorous, large scale replications of Murdock's findings and trustworthy cross-cultural tests of the hypotheses of Goody, Cohen, Aberle, and Schlegel. Natural and social science syntheses, like those of Aberle and his associates, provide a strong basis for supposing the incest taboo to be a singularly advantageous solution to universal human problems. But the very variety of explanations which have been proposed over the last hundred years should warn us that the absence of cases which would permit falsification of the hypotheses make the dependability of any of them tenuous (cf. Hempel 1965: 39, 106; Popper 1968: 40-42). The use of ethological data by Aberle et al. is an attempt at such a formulation, but the lack of human data is the real problem.

Chapter 9
Residence, Descent, and
Kinship Terminology

Aside from those interested in general culture theory, most anthropologists with theoretical inclinations have been interested in the causes, functions, and effects of certain kinship practices. Three categories of kinship practices are of concern to them—post-marital residence, descent, and kinship terminology.

Many scholars now believe that residence, descent, and kin terminology form a developmental sequence called main sequence kinship theory (Naroll 1970b; Divale 1974a; Witkowski 1977; Levinson 1977a). Proponents of main sequence theory argue that post-marital residence influences rules of descent, and that descent, in turn, influences kin terminology. In this chapter we restrict our review to holocultural studies bearing either directly or indirectly on main sequence theory and ignore many descriptive and conceptual studies that have played a central role in the development of anthropology as a scientific discipline.

This chapter is divided into three sections. The first defines residence, descent, and kinship terminology. The second reviews main sequence theory. And the third reviews alternatives to main sequence theory.

Residence, Descent, and Kinship Terminology

The definitions that follow are necessarily brief and deal with only the bare essentials. They are not intended to provide an exhaustive summary of the conceptual literature on kinship.

Residence

To anthropologists residence means post-marital residence, the place in which a couple lives following their marriage. The post-marital residence rule for a particular couple or an entire society is usually described in terms of the relatives the couple resides near or with following their marriage. Divale (1974a) restates Murdock's (1967a: 48) definitions of the eight basic residence patterns as follows:

1A.	Patrilocal:	Normal residence is with or near the husband's patrilineal kinsmen.
1B.	Virilocal:	Equivalent to patrilocal but patrilineal kin groups are absent.
2A.	Matrilocal:	Normal residence is with or near the wife's matrilineal kinsmen.
2B.	Uxorilocal:	Equivalent to matrilocal but matrilineal kin groups are absent.
3.	Avunculocal:	Normal residence is with or near the maternal uncle or other male matrilineal kinsmen of the husband.
4.	Bilocal: (Ambilocal)	Residence is established optionally with or near the parents of either spouse.
5.	Matrilocal-Avunculocal option:	Like bilocal, except that the option is limited to either matrilocal or avunculocal residence.
6.	Avunculocal-Virilocal option:	Like bilocal, except that the option is limited to either avunculocal or virilocal residence.
7.	Neolocal:	Normal residence is apart from the relatives of both spouses.
8.	Duolocal:	There is no common household. Spouses remain in their natal groups.

There is some confusion in the literature over the use of the terms virilocal and uxorilocal as alternatives for patrilocal and matrilocal, respectively. So far as residence is concerned, patrilocal and virilocal and matrilocal and uxorilocal refer to the same practices. According to Murdock (1957, 1967a) and Divale (1974a) the difference in usage is related to the type of descent associated with the residence pattern. When descent is patrilineal, residence with the husband's patrilineal kinsmen is called patrilocal. When descent is any form other than patrilineal, residence with the husband's kinsmen is called virilocal. When descent is matrilineal, residence with the wife's matrilineal kinsmen is called matrilocal. When descent is any form other than matrilineal, residence with the wife's kinsmen is called uxorilocal.

There is a striking and theoretically significant difference in the frequency with which these residence patterns occur throughout the world. Table 9.1 summarizes this distribution.

Table 9.1—*Frequency of Occurrence of the World's Residence Patterns*

Residence Pattern	Numerical Frequency	Percent
Patrilocal	576	50%
Virilocal	229	20%
Matrilocal	52	4%
Uxorilocal	82	7%
Avunculocal	51	4%
Bilocal	80	7%
Matrilocal-Avunculocal option	5	1%
Avunculocal-Virilocal option	11	1%
Neolocal	60	5%
Duolocal	7	1%
Totals	1,153	100%

°Based on the 1,153 societies of the 1,179 societies in the IBM card version of the *Ethnographic Atlas* (Barry 1967) for which information on residence patterns are available. Taken from Divale (1974a: 25).

The overwhelming predominance of patrilocal-virilocal residence suggests that these two forms are the typical ones in nonliterate societies. Although relatively rare in the non-industrialized societies, neolocal residence is the dominant form in the contemporary world.

Descent

In many societies, and especially in non-industrial ones, relations between kinsmen influence many spheres of life including, among others, subsistence practices, religious beliefs, political behavior, and child rearing practices. Thus, most societies which organize their activities and beliefs around kin ties need a set of rules which relate each person to a specific set of kinsmen. Anthropologists have identified five such rules of descent:

1. Bilateral   An individual is affiliated with both his or her mother's and father's relatives.

2. Patrilineal   An individual is affiliated with kin of both sexes through men only.

3. Matrilineal   An individual is affiliated with kin of both sexes through women only.

4. Ambilineal (cognatic)   An individual is affiliated with kin through either men or women. In societies with ambilineal descent, some individuals affiliate with kin through their mothers and others through their fathers. Certain kinds of relations may exist on one side (land inheritance) and certain on the other (succession to office).

5. Double   An individual is affiliated with both his father's patrilineal kin and his mother's matrilineal kin.

From the perspective of kinship theory, the key point about rules of descent is that they are systematically related to rules of residence. Table 9.2, taken from Coult and Habenstein (1965: 391), shows a strong relationship between certain types of residence and certain types of descent. For main sequence theory, the most important relationships are those between patrilocal residence and patrilineal descent, between matrilocal residence and matrilineal descent, and between neolocal and bilocal residence and bilateral descent.

Table 9.2—*Cross-Tabulations for Residence and Descent*

Residence	Descent			
	Patrilineal	*Bilateral*	*Matrilineal*	*Ambilineal*
Patrilocal	.571	-.319	-.438	.116
Bilocal	-.198	.307	-.087	-.048
Neolocal	-.208	.284	-.047	-.038
Matrilocal	-.349	.099	.391	-.062
Avunculocal	-.180	-.130	.442	-.012

Underlined correlation coefficients (Yule's Q, N=565) are significant at the .05 level.

Adapted from Coult and Habenstein (1965: 391).

Kinship Terminology

Kinship terminology is the third and final link in the main sequence chain. To many non-anthropologists the study of kinship terminology—the way people organize and identify their kin—seems like little more than an esoteric intellectual exercise. But, anthropologists have long known that to understand a kinship system one must understand the terminological system. Stated more strongly, understanding the terminological system is the key to understanding the kinship system. Given this strong feeling among anthropologists, it is not suprising to find that at least one-half of the studies on kinship are studies of kinship terminology.

Anthropologists alternatively rely on two criteria to describe terminological types or systems. First, they describe the system in terms of the merging or differentiating of cousins and siblings. Second, they describe the system in terms of the classification of members of the parental generation. Description based on classification of cousins and siblings generally produces more refined results and is the one frequently used in worldwide comparative research.

Murdock (1949) lists six terminological systems based on the classification of cousins and siblings (see Murdock 1968 for a categorization and distributional study of sibling terminology):

1.	Hawaiian	This type is the simplest. All male cousins are referred to by the same term used for one's brother and all female cousins are referred to by the same term used for one's sister.
2.	Eskimo	This is another simple system, the one used in contemporary American society. Cousins are distinguished from brothers and sisters, but no distinction is made between cross-cousins and parallel cousins.
3.	Sudanese	This is a third relatively simple system. There is a distinct term for each category of cousin and sibling, and for aunts, uncles, nieces and nephews.
4.	Iroquois	This type is more complex. Parallel cousins are referred to by the

		same term used for brothers and sisters. But cross-cousins are identified by a different term.
5.	Crow	This type is typical of matrilineal societies. Matrilateral cross-cousins are distinguished from each other and from parallel cousins and siblings. But patrilateral cross-cousins are referred to by the same terms used for father or father's sister.
6.	Omaha	This type, which is typical of patrilineal societies, is the opposite of the Crow type. Here, female matrilateral cross-cousins are referred to by the same term used for mother, while female patrilateral cross-cousins are referred to by the same term used for sister's daughter.

Kinship descriptions based on classification of members of the parental generation are of four types:

1.	Generational	All kin of the same generation and sex are referred to by the same term. Thus, father, father's brother, and mother's brother are identified by the same term.
2.	Lineal	This type distinguishes between kin who are direct ascendants or direct descendants and collaterals. Thus, there are separate terms for mother and mother's sister.
3.	Bifurcate-merging	This sytem distinguishes between members of the two descent groups. For example, father and father's brother are assigned the same term, but mother's brother is assigned a different one. Bifurcate-merging systems are unilineal.

4. Bifurcate-collateral In this system all collaterals of the same generation are distinguished from one another. Thus, father, father's brother, and mother's brother are all assigned different terms.

Main Sequence Kinship Theory

The development, testing, and revision of main sequence kinship theory has been and continues to be one of the major activities and achievements of worldwide cross-cultural research. Main sequence theory is not entirely the work of comparativists. Important contributions have been made by Lowie (1920), Linton (1936), Eggan (1950), Service (1971), and others.

The developmental sequence was first suggested in its entirety by Murdock; his main argument runs as follows:

> When any social system which has attained equilibrium begins to change, such change regularly begins with modification of the rule of residence. Alteration in residence rules is followed by development or change in form of descent consistent with residence rules. Finally adaptive changes in kinship terminology follow (1949: 221-222).

Murdock's methods and main sequence theory have been widely discussed (Nadel 1955: 364; DeLint and Cohen 1960; Leach 1966: 1518; Harris 1968: 618-625; Murdock and White 1969; Naroll 1970b; Barnes 1971: 1-199). Critics have suspected that the data of Murdock's (1949) *Social Structure* is inaccurate, and that the sample of 250 societies over-represents North America and is influenced by cultural diffusion (Tatje n.d.). Given the large number of correlation coefficients computed, we would expect a certain percentage to be statistically significant by chance alone. In spite of these shortcomings, no holocultural study has had as great an impact as *Social Structure*. It has served, and continues to serve for some, as the model for holocultural research. And, over the past four years, it has been cited in the social science periodical literature twice as often as any other holocultural study, except for McClelland (1961), which is only partly holocultural. If, as is commonly assumed, the number of times a study is cited by others is a measure of its impact, *Social Structure* is the most important holocultural study published so far. But the best measure of Murdock's contribution to kinship theory is

not the number of times his works are cited, nor their methodological shortcomings. Rather, the best measure is whether they
survive empirical testing. Let us look at these tests of main sequence
theory beginning with Driver (1956). In a study limited to North
American societies, he finds general support for Murdock's main
sequence. Following Murdock, and also Lippert (1931: 237) and
Linton (1936: 168-69), Driver suggests that the relative importance
of male or female subsistence contributions is the key determinant
of residence rules.

When men make the major subsistence contribution, residence
will be patrilocal, descent will be patrilineal,and cousin terms will
be of the Omaha type, while bifurcate merging aunt and uncle terms
will predominate. When women make the major subsistence contribution, residence will be matrilocal, descent will be matrilineal, and
cousin terms will be of the Crow type, while bifurcate aunt and
uncle terms will predominate. When both sexes make a major
subsistence contribution, residence will be bilocal or neolocal,
descent will be bilateral, cousin terms will be of the Hawaiian or
Eskimo type, and lineal or generational aunt and uncle terms will
predominate. Over the past twenty years various aspects of main
sequence theory have been tested in a number of cross-cultural
studies. The results of these studies have called into question some
of the basic assumptions of main sequence theory. At the same time,
these studies have suggested some new, plausible rival hypotheses.

Murdock's and Driver's contention—that the relative importance
of male versus female subsistence contributions determines post-
marital residence rules—has now been tested seven times. No study
supports this hypothesis for the world as a whole. On the contrary,
D.R. White (1967), Hiatt (1970), Ember and Ember (1971), and
Divale (1974a, 1974b) fail to find a relationship between sexual
division of labor and post-marital residence in six different worldwide samples. Tables 9.3 and 9.4, taken from Ember and Ember
(1971) and based on the first 455 societies listed in Murdock's
(1967a) *Ethnographic Atlas*, show just how weak the relationship is.
However, six studies (Driver 1956; Driver and Massey 1957; D.R.
White 1967; Ember and Ember 1971; Divale 1974a; M. Ember 1975)
show the relationship between sexual division of labor and residence
holding true for aboriginal North America. Evidently, sexual differentiation in the importance of subsistence contributions does influence post-marital residence in North America, but not in the world
as a whole. The division of labor by sex hypothesis holds in North

Table 9.3 *Division of Labor and Matrilocal Residence*

Division of Labor	Pattern of Residence		
	Matrilocal	Other	Total
Women do more than men	4	27	31
Other	51	206	257
Total	55	233	288

phi = .05; n.s.

Taken from M. Ember and C. Ember (1971). Reproduced by permission of the American Anthropological Association, from the *American Anthropologist* 73(1971), 574.

Table 9.4 *Division of Labor and Patrilocal Residence*

Division of Labor	Pattern of Residence		
	Patrilocal	Other	Total
Men do more than women	100	73	173
Other	71	44	115
Total	171	117	288

phi = .04; n.s.

Taken from M. Ember and C. Ember (1971). Reproduced by permission of the American Anthropological Association, from the *American Anthropologist* 73(1971), 574.

America because North America contained a large percentage of food gathering societies. And, as C. Ember (1975) shows, in gathering societies, subsistence activities are related to post-marital residence practices in the direction predicted by Murdock and by Driver.

One assumption underlying main sequence theory is Murdock's and Driver's contention that it is residential localization of certain groups of kinsmen which leads to the formation of unilineal kin groups and which is reflected in a society's kinship terminology. Three holocultural studies test this proposition. While all three find a relationship between residence and descent or terminology, none supports the contention that it is residential aggregation of certain categories of kin which leads to the formation of specific kinds of descent groups or the use of certain kin terms. The broadest of these three studies is Witkowski's (1972) test of the proximity hypothesis. The proximity hypothesis (Tylor 1889; Titiev 1943, 1956; Murdock 1949; Diebold 1966) suggests that residential proximity influences the development of certain kin avoidance and terminological practices. Witkowski finds no evidence of this. The correlations between various measures of residential proximity and avoidance, degree of collateral merging, degree of terminological merging, and degree of terminological bifurcation are weak and statistically insignificant.

Divale (1974a) and Ember, Ember, and Pasternak (1974) question whether unilineal descent is a predictable result of unilocal residence. As Table 9.5 indicates, not all unilocal societies show unilineal descent present. This finding suggests to Ember et al. (1974) that unilocal residence is a necessary but not a sufficient cause of unilineal descent. Likewise Divale (1974a) finds that some societies have had unilocal residence for as many as one thousand years without also having unilineal descent.

To summarize: main sequence kinship theory, which postulates a causal chain involving sexual division of labor, post-marital residence, descent, and kinship terminology, is largely the work of Murdock and Driver, although they clearly acknowledge the contributions of others. Tests of various aspects of the main sequence suggest that (1) there is a developmental sequence involving residence, descent, and terminology; (2) sexual division of labor alone is not a determinant of post-marital residence rules; and (3) residential proximity does not explain the relationship between unilocal residence and unilineal descent or between residence and kin terminology.

Table 9.5 *Unilocal Residence and Unilineal Descent*

Unilocal Residence	Unilineal Descent		Total
	Absent	Present	
Present	135	350	485
Absent	65	10	75
Total	200	360	560

$\emptyset = .42$ $X^2 = 97.92$ P = .0005 (one-tail)

Taken from Ember, Ember, and Pasternak (1974: 71).

Let us turn to an examination of studies which seek to revise main sequence theory. Most experts on kinship now agree that patrilocal residence and other male-centered institutions are the typical kinship structures in nonliterate societies (Service 1971; Divale and Harris 1976; Pasternak 1976; Witkowski 1977). It follows then that matrilocal residence and other female-centered institutions (such as matrilineal descent) are exceptions or special cases. Much of the recent holocultural research on main sequence theory seeks to explain these special cases. The key variable is now believed to be warfare. The basic studies are those by Ember and Ember (1971), Divale (1974a, 1974b), and C. Ember (1975). These three studies have produced two rival theories of matrilocal residence. The Embers also claim to explain patrilocal residence, Divale does not.

The Embers describe their theory, which we call warfare theory, as follows:

> Patrilocal residence is favored by the presence of at least some internal warfare (that is, warfare within the society), whether or not such warfare interferes with a patridominant division of labor; and matrilocal residence is favored by purely external warfare if such warfare compels the division of labor to become matridominant (Ember and Ember 1971: 593).

Warfare theory assumes that patrilocal residence is the usual form. Matrilocal residence arises only when the nature of external warfare is such that it causes women to replace men in the key subsistence activities. C. Ember (1974) re-examined warfare theory in the light of Divale's (1974b) research. After considering some new data on societal size and success in warfare, she rejected Divale's migration theory and revised warfare theory. The data suggest that the matrilocal societies are only those small societies (with populations less than 21,000) which usually defeat their enemies. Other societies (small ones which usually lose and large ones, whether they win or lose) have some internal as well as external warfare. Thus, these societies are usually patrilocal. Her 1974 version of warfare theory is diagrammed in Figure 9.1.

Warfare theory has been given broad play, both in Ember and Ember (1973) and Pasternak (1976). The Embers expand on warfare theory to explain polygyny, avunculocal residence, and unilineal descent as well. M. Ember (1974a) argues that frequent warfare leads to high male mortality rates, which leaves a surplus of marriageable women, and thus encourages polygyny. In another article, M. Ember (1974b) argues that matrilocal/matrilineal soci-

Figure 9.1. *Warfare Theory of Post-Marital Residence*

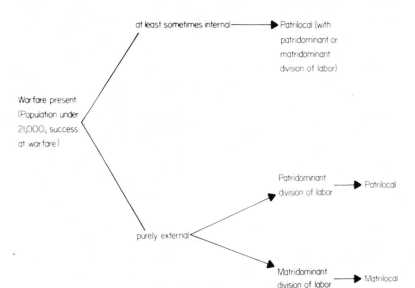

Adapted from Ember and Ember (1971: 573) and C. Ember (1974).

eties, which are pressured by high male mortality rates when they switch from external to internal warfare, are the ones most likely to adopt avunculocal residence. They do so to maintain their unilineal descent system. In regard to unilineal descent, Ember, Ember and Pasternak (1974) argue that, in the face of warfare, unilineal descent arises as a means of ensuring group solidarity and cohesiveness. Each of these three hypotheses has been tested rather casually. They are best viewed as tentative hypotheses in need of more careful testing.

Divale's migration theory of matrilocal residence (Divale 1974a, 1974b; Divale, Chamberis and Gangloff 1976) contradicts warfare theory. Divale does not claim to explain patrilocal residence; he is concerned only with matrilocal residence:

> It is suggested that matrilocal residence is an adaptive response to the disequilibrium that occurs when a virilocal or patrilocal society migrates into an already inhabited region. The sudden immigration will result in external warfare between the migrating and indigenous societies. Most of the world's societies (approximately seventy per

cent) practice patrilocal residence and are characterized by the presence of fraternal interest groups, which have been shown to be conducive to the frequent feuding and internal warfare that also characterizes these societies. In face of severe external warfare, the chances of successful adaptation would be increased if these societies cease their feuding and internal war and instead concentrate all their resources against the other society. Matrilocal residence accomplishes this, because the dispersal of males from their natal villages upon marriage results in the breakup of fraternal interest groups (Divale 1974b: 75).

Divale argues that matrilocal residence physically disperses the men who would form fraternal interest groups if residence were patrilocal. Witkowski (1977) disagrees. Matrilocal societies are usually endogamous—the men marry women from their own community. Thus, the men are not physically dispersed, but, rather, continue to reside in the same community, but with their wife's family instead of their own. While it may not physically disperse men, matrilocal residence may disperse their interest. Once married and residing with his wife's family, a man's interests are split between those of his wife's family and those of his own. So, matrilocal residence breaks up fraternal interest groups by dispersing the loyalties of its members.

Warfare and migration theory differ in a number of crucial ways. Most important, they postulate opposing causal connections. Warfare theory suggests that the type of warfare determines the type of residence. Migration theory suggests that the type of residence determines the type of warfare. A second key difference concerns the relative importance of male versus female subsistence contribution. The Embers think that it matters; Divale thinks it is irrelevant. Otterbein (1977: 702-03) finds that both studies suffer from the same serious methodological problem. Otterbein points out that one crucial piece of evidence for both theories rests on the interpretation of data organized in the following two-by-two contingency table:

	Residence	
Warfare	matrilocal	patrilocal
purely external	A	B
internal or internal and external	C	D

Those cases falling in either box A or box D support both

migration and warfare theory. They indicate that internal warfare is associated with patrilocal residence, and external warfare with matrilocal residence. But, Otterbein points out that in five of the six tests of these theories, over fifty percent of the cases fall in box D. Thus, the relationship between matrilocal residence and external warfare can be explained as an artifact of the strong association between patrilocal residence and internal warfare.

Migration theory and warfare theory share the same theoretical roots although they suggest contradictory causal sequences. Both are based on fraternal interest group theory (Thoden van Velzen and van Wetering 1960; Otterbein and Otterbein 1965; Paige 1974), which predicts that patrilocal residence will aggregate related men into fraternal interest groups. These fraternal interest groups will then engage in feuding and internal warfare with other groups. Divale accepts this developmental sequence, the Embers reverse it and argue that internal warfare leads to patrilocal residence.

At this time it is impossible to choose between these two rivals. Tests of migration theory are more careful, and are based on both ethnographic and ethnohistorical data. But, tests of warfare theory are careful enough so that the findings cannot be questioned on methodological grounds alone. Similarly, neither suffers from logical errors serious enough to cause it to be rejected. The basic question is one of sequence. Which changes first: warfare or residence?

So far, our discussion has been limited to theories about societies with unilocal residence. But a fair number of societies practice multilocal residence. That is, two different residence rules are optional, or one prevails, but the other is a viable alternative. Thus, for example, newlywed couples may have the option of choosing between living with the husband's family or with the wife's mother's brother's family. Among factors thought to explain multilocal residence are: migratory band life; little dependence on agriculture; male and female equality as reflected in female inheritance rights; depopulation following European contact; and a closed environment (Murdock 1949; Eggan 1966; Service 1971; Goodenough 1955; M. Ember 1962). As shown in Table 9.6, Ember and Ember's (1972) holocultural test most strongly supports the depopulation theory suggested by Service, although further analysis restricts its applicability to relatively sedentary societies with at least fifteen percent dependence on agriculture.

Table 9.6 *Tests of Theories of Multilocal Residence*

Causal Variable	phi	p	N
Migratory Bands	.16	.01	688
Dependence on Agriculture	.23	.01	687
Equality of Inheritance	.22	.01	381
Depopulation	.42	.05	31
	.56	.01	27
Closed Environment		NOT TESTED	

Table constructed from data in C. Ember and M. Ember (1972).

Alternatives to Main Sequence Theory

Not all students of kinship believe that there is a main sequence nor do they all believe that the relative importance of subsistence contributions or warfare or migration have anything to do with post-marital residence. Service (1971: 120-22) and Aberle (1961: 668) argue that uxorilocal/matrilineal residence and descent are found mainly in tropical rain forest environments. Divale (1974b: 108) tests this proposition. He finds no support for it. Matrilocal societies are no more likely to be found in tropical rain forests than in any other environment. Nor does it seem that matrilocal residence or matri-lineal descent are likely to be characteristic of any particular environment.

Service (1971), Aberle (1961) and Gough (1961) suggest that matrilineal societies usually subsist by means of horticulture rather than agriculture. Aberle in a study of 564 societies finds a statistically significant relationship between matrilineality and horticulture. But Divale, using a 1106 society sample and somewhat different mea-sures, finds no association between horticulture and matrilocal residence or matrilineal descent.

Zern (1972) sees kin terminological practices as one indicator of how a society differentiates its social environment. Specifically, he finds that in societies where the nurturant agent is often absent, there is no separate kin term for mother. But, when the nurturant agent is usually present, mother is identified by a distinct term. Also, early separation of a mother and her child is associated with differenti-ation of nieces from daughters.

Many nineteenth century evolutionists believed that rules of descent evolved in an orderly sequence from matrilineal to patrilineal to cognatic descent; they also believed that unilineal descent preceeded bilateral descent. Both of these ideas have been tested cross-culturally. Murdock (1937), Murdock and Wilson (1972), and Divale (1974a) all find no evidence that matrilineal descent predominates in simple societies or that cognatic descent predominates in the more complex ones. On the contrary, Murdock and Provost (1973b) find that bilateral descent predominates in both the simplest and most complex nonliterate societies. Patrilineal descent is found most often in societies at middle levels of complexity, and matrilineal descent most often among societies at the stage of incipient agriculture. Regarding the appearance of unilineal descent, Murdock and Wilson (1972) report that eighty-four percent of contemporary hunters and gatherers have cognatic, not unilineal descent. These four studies indicate that nineteenth century ideas about the evolution of descent systems were wrong. Still, these ideas die slowly. DeLeeuwe (1971) published a cross-cultural study supporting the notion that matrilineality precedes bilaterality. The studies by Murdock and by Divale are more careful than DeLeeuwe's, and so we are inclined to dismiss his findings and to accept theirs. But, in one key way DeLeeuwe's work is better—his sample is broader. He includes data on preindustrial societies, preindustrial civilizations, contemporary nonindustrialized societies, and contemporary industrialized societies. He looks at a much broader range of sample units than Murdock or Divale, who restrict their sample to preindustrial societies. So, we can not completely dismiss DeLeeuwe's conclusions, even though all the other evidence points in the opposite direction.

Along somewhat different lines, Dole (1972) suggests a developmental sequence for kinship nomenclature. As shown in Table 9.7, bifurcate merging, cross-generation, lineage, and modern isolating are each found generally in societies of different levels of cultural complexity, as measured by Carneiro's (1970) Complexity Index. (For a further discussion of the evolution of lineage type nomenclature, see Dole 1965).

Neolocal residence, the predominant form in the contemporary world, is not explained by the sexual division of labor hypothesis, migration theory, or warfare theory. The two cross-cultural studies of neolocal residence by DeLeeuwe (1971) and M. Ember (1967) suggest that it is a product of industrialization and commerciali-

Table 9.7. *Relationship between Kinship Nomenclature Patterns and Cultural Complexity*

Nomenclature	Society	Complexity Score
Modern Isolating	Anglo-Saxon	186
Lineage	India (250 B.C.)	336
	Rome	323
	China	229
	Batak	119
	Masai	71
	Chiga	52
	Nuer	28
Cross Generation	Creek	77
	Thonga	68
	Lango	50
	Omaha	45
	Trobriand	45
	Hottentot	44
	Menomini	43
	Gururumba	36
	Canella	23
	Mundurucú	18
	Sirionó	7
Bifurcate Merging	Tuareg (Ahaggar)	76
	Iroquois	64
	Island Carib	46
	Toda (Cross-Cousin)	36
	Barama R. Carib (Cross-Cousin)	18
	Campa (Cross-Cousin)	17
	Yaruro	16
	Yanomamö (Cross-Cousin)	16
	Akwe Shavante	15
	Amahuaca	11
	Ojibwa	10
	Vedda (Cross-Cousin)	7
	Naskapi	6
	Murngin (Cross-Cousin)	5

Table adapted from Dole (1972). Reproduced by permission of the Anthropological Society of Washington, from Priscilla Reining, ed., *Kinship Studies in the Morgan Centennial Year* (1972), 155.

zation. Industrialization and commercialization allow people to sell their labor for money. By selling their labor, they reduce the need for support from kinsmen, while also increasing their standard of living.

Summary

Holocultural research on residence, descent, and kinship terminology has produced four reasonably trustworthy propositions:
(1) There is a developmental sequence involving post-marital residence, rules of descent, and kinship terminology.
(2) The relative importance of male versus female subsistence contribution is not an important determinant of post-marital residence.
(3) Type of warfare is related to residence practices either as cause or as effect.
(4) No alternatives to main sequence theory have been convincingly supported by cross-cultural research.

More research is needed on the rival migration and warfare theories, on the Embers' theories of unilineal descent and avunculocal residence, on nineteenth century evolutionary theory, and on the causes of neolocal residence.

Chapter 10
Kin Relations

Western anthropologists from non-kin based societies have been quick to note the frequent ritualization of relations between kinsmen in kin based societies (Gluckman 1962: 24-28). We do not mean to imply that ritualized interpersonal relations are non-existent in industrialized societies. On the contrary, they are quite common, although they seem more elaborate in regard to strangers than kinsmen. Lofland (1973), for example, provides a brilliant analysis of the ritualized poses people use to deal with one another in modern cities. In nonliterate societies ritualization of interpersonal interaction is especially common among certain categories of kin, and particularly so among those related by marriage. Avoidance, formality, informality, joking, and license are five such behavior patterns. They form a continuum from avoidance, where there may be no interaction at all, to license, where even sexual relations are condoned. The worldwide distibution of each of the five patterns of kin behavior varies to some extent by region, by type of descent, and by extent of marriage prohibitions (Goody and Buckley 1974). For example, cross-sex sibling relations are more informal in patrilineal than in matrilineal or bilateral societies, whereas mother-in-law avoidance is more common in Africa and America than in Eurasia and the Insular Pacific. A variety of explanations for these behavior patterns have been suggested and debated over the years. But, after at least fourteen worldwide comparative studies and many more case studies, no viable explanations have been found.

One relationship not discussed at length here is the avunculate— the special relationship between mother's brother and sister's son in matrilineal societies. Radcliffe-Brown (1952) suggested that the avunculate should be studied in the context of the relationships between father's sister and brother's son, a man and his maternal kin, and a man and his mother's kin as a whole. Unfortunately, Radcliffe-Brown did not follow his own advice, and his avunculate theory has been criticized and rejected by Goody (1959). Lévi-Strauss (1963) takes the avunculate to be a set of kin terms and attitudes characteristic of and distinguishing among four pairs of kin— mother's brother/sister's son, brother/sister, father/son, and husband/wife. Of the societies sampled in Ryder and Blackman's (1970) holocultural test, one-half have the mother's brother/sister's son relationship but lack the other three relationships. Thus, Lévi-Strauss's avunculate theory, like his alliance theory of marriage, is not supported holoculturally. For a discussion of whether Lévi-Strauss's ideas are amenable to empirical testing see Barnes (1971); Köbben, Veripps and Brunt (1974); and Scholte (1966). In general, though, it seems that the mother's brother's role is most elaborated in societies where the unilineal kin group is active in organizing social relationships as reflected in the presence of exogamous clan communities, exogamous unilineal descent groups, and unilocal residence (Sweetser 1966b, 1967).

Avoidance

Avoidance between kin was defined by Murdock as "complete avoidance of speech and physical contact" (1949: 272). He later revised this to "observance of a strict taboo against sex relations and against all but the most restricted physical and social contact" (Murdock 1971: 360). Murdock's definitions emphasize sex restrictions because he sees a relationship between avoidance and maintenance of incest taboos. Sweetser (1966a) considers avoidance present if any of the following are prohibited: proximity, touch, nakedness or undress, eating together, looking directly at each other, or speech. Stephens and D'Andrade (1962: 133) provide a more precise 5-point Guttman scale: (5) can't eat together and can't look eye-to-eye; (4) *either* eating together or eye contact is avoided, but not both; (3) can't talk directly; (2) can't talk about sex; (1) no avoidance. The value of their scale is that it provides a framework for testing avoidance theories. Each of these definitions has in common the prohibition of sexual relations and social and physical contact.

Avoidances most commonly occur between three categories of kin—wife's mother and daughter's husband; husband's father and son's wife; brother and sister. Avoidance between wife's mother and daughter's husband (mother-in-law avoidance) is the most common form. The second is between husband's father and son's wife (father-in-law avoidance) and the third is between brother and sister, which is less common than either form of in-law avoidance. Stephens and D'Andrade (1962) conclude on the basis of their own and Murdock's data that these three kin relations represent the focal avoidances of which all others are extensions.

Two brief examples of avoidance indicate the particular forms the behavior may take. Radcliffe-Brown (1952) interprets these ritualized kin relationships as conflict mediating devices. When his students honored him with the collection on American Indian social organization (Eggan 1955b), they applied Radcliffe-Brown's own interpretation. Eggan's (1955a: 76-77) study of the Cheyenne and the Arapaho of the Great Plains illustrates avoidance in the context of matrilocal residence:

> By the general rule of matrilocal residence he must reside in his parents-in-law's camp and must help support them economically, though to begin with he may feel as an intruder. The mother-daughter relationship is a respect relationship; this respect is intensified in the case of the son-in-law by the difference in sex. There is a further factor in the rivalry of the mother-daughter and husband-wife relationships; in order that the affairs of the camp may run smoothly, the son-in-law and the mother-in-law avoid each other completely, though manifesting the highest respect for each other. It is significant, in this connection, that the restrictions may be removed when a satisfactory adjustment has been reached by a public exchange of gifts.

The temporary mother-in-law avoidance described by Eggan is common. That the relationship may change when "a satisfactory adjustment has been reached" is a significant piece of evidence which conflicts with the view that mother-in-law avoidance is a means of maintaining the incest taboo. If that were the case, we would expect the avoidance to be permanent. The temporary nature of the avoidance accords with Radcliffe-Brown's (1952) and Eggan's (1955a) ideas about reducing conflict, which would no longer be necessary if and when the two affines had gotten to know each other.

In his analysis of the social organization of the Kiowa-Apache of southwestern Oklahoma, McAllister (1955: 130) gives the following account:

> The most marked restriction is that between affinal relatives of the opposite sex and the relationship that one hears the most about is

between son-in-law and mother-in-law, though the avoidances between a man and his daughter-in-law are equally strict. A man would
never touch his mother-in-law, look at her, talk to her, call her name,
or be alone with her in a tipi. The attitutude is one of utmost respect
and avoidance. In a similar manner a woman avoids her son-in-law.

Both of these descriptions emphasize the ambiguous nature of
relations between parents-in-law and children-in-law and show how
avoidance allows the smooth functioning of the community by
avoiding conflict from competing sources of authority—parents
versus spouses.

The views of Murdock, Stephens and D'Andrade, Eggan, and
Radcliffe-Brown suggest two rival theories of kin avoidances. These
two theories have come to be known as (1) the incest-phobia
hypothesis, and (2) the proximity hypothesis. The incest-phobia
hypothesis is derived from Freudian psychoanalytic theory. Stephens
and D'Andrade (1962) suggest the following sequence: (1) The long
postpartum sex taboo intensifies the son-to-mother sex attraction (2)
which makes phobic attitudes toward incest more likely (3) which
contributes to the severity of kin-avoidances. Their major underlying assumption is that the Oedipal sex attraction between son and
mother, and father and daughter leads to the phobic attitude toward
incest. Stephens and D'Andrade test the hypothesis by correlating
length of the postpartum sex taboo with son's wife avoidance,
brother-sister avoidance, and mother-in-law avoidance. They report
the following results:

Type of Avoidance	p	n
son's wife	.05	33
brother-sister	.01	36
mother-in-law	.01	49

Thus, they conclude that the incest-phobia hypothesis explains
avoidance practices. Sweetser (1966a) and Nerlove and Romney
(1967) replicate portions of the incest-phobia hypothesis. Sweetser
reports a Yule's Q of only .12 between a long postpartum taboo and
parent-in-law avoidance in a sample of one hundred societies.
Similarly, Nerlove and Romney report only a weak relationship ($p <$
.10) between the length of the postpartum taboo and brother-sister
avoidance. These two retests suggest that the incest-phobia hypothesis is not an especially viable explanation for kin avoidances.

Tylor (1889) initiated the holocultural method with a study

pointing to a relationship between avoidance practices and post-marital residence rules. Specifically, he found mother-in-law avoidance associated with matrilocal residence. The general notion that kin avoidances are associated with residence rules has come to be known as the proximity hypothesis. Witkowski´ (1972: 124) summarizes the proximity hypothesis as follows:

> . . . the proximity hypothesis . . . asserts that residential propinquity influences the possession by a society of certain kin avoidance and kin terminological practices.

In addition the proximity hypothesis has also been tested by Murdock (1949), Stephens and D'Andrade (1962), Jorgensen (1966), Sweetser (1966a), and Witkowski (1972). These studies have generally been restricted to parent-in-law avoidance—son-in-law/ mother-in-law avoidance (SM) and daughter-in-law/ father-in-law avoidance (DF). If the proximity hypothesis is correct, SM avoidance should be associated with matrilocal residence, and DF avoidance should be associated with patrilocal residence. Murdock (1949), Jorgensen (1966), and, of course, Tylor (1889) find the SM-matrilocal residence pattern holding true. And Stephens and D'Andrade (1962) support the DF-patrilocal residence pattern. But Stephens and D'Andrade and Sweetser (1966a) reject the SM-matrilocal association and Jorgensen (1966) and Sweetser reject the DF-patrilocal one. Thus, these studies neither support nor discredit entirely the proximity hypothesis. Witkowski (1972) provides the broadest test of the proximity hypothesis. He defines residential propinquity in two ways: community coresidence, where the in-laws reside in the same community; and household coresidence, where the in-laws reside in the same household. Witkowski reports the following findings (all correlations $p > .10$):

Type of Avoidance	Residence	gamma
DF	community coresidence	.12
DF	household coresidence	.04
SM	community coresidence	-.10
SM	household coresidence	-.05

Apparently, the proximity hypothesis has no more validity than does the incest-phobia hypothesis. Thus, holocultural research has proposed, tested, retested, and discredited the two best known explanations for kin avoidances.

Holocultural research has also produced some explanations for kin avoidances that do withstand empirical testing. In a careful study of male control over females, Schlegel (1972) finds brother-sister avoidance most often in societies where the husband has authority over his wife. She reasons that in these societies sibling avoidance is a mechanism for preventing the wife's brother from interfering in her marriage. This hypothesis seems intuitively sound but needs more testing. Jorgensen (1966) finds that cultural diffusion accounts for the spread of avoidance practices more often than psychological and functional explanations. Jorgensen's conclusion is supported by Driver (1966), whose sample, however, is restricted to North America. Thus, the function of kin avoidance, if there is a single function, which Lowie doubted (1920: 104), remains unexplained empirically.

Formality

Murdock (1971: 360) defines formality or respect as "the observance of a taboo against sex relations and of cultural restraints which, though they do not entirely prevent social interaction, inject a definite element of formality into the relationship." Like avoidance, formality is characteristic of relations between affines, often parents-in-law and children-in-law where actual avoidance is not found. Formality also characterizes relations between adjoining generations, presumably as an acknowledgement of the authority of the senior generation. Goffman's (1961, 1967) work on deference and demeanor, which is a general theoretical formulation and is in no way concerned with the behavior of kinsmen in small-scale societies, is still relevant to this sort of interaction.

Examples of formality may be found among the Fox of Iowa, where according to Tax (1955: 259), between parents-in-law and children-in-law:

> especially when these relatives are of the opposite sex, there seems to be a feeling between them of uncomfortable restraint that keeps them from speaking to one another except on business matters. They would never just sit down and gossip or indulge in small talk.

Among the Tikopia of Polynesia relations between parents and children, especially father and son, father's sister and her brother's children, and above all affinal relatives, involve the use of kinship terms instead of personal names, the use of special polite pronouns, and social practices—such as not reaching over the head or passing directly in front of an affine, and not standing when the other is sitting (Firth 1957). Obviously, these are mechanisms for recognizing the separate status of another individual. It may be noticed that Stephens and D'Andrade's (1962) intermediate forms of avoidance may be seen as forms of respect, since below their most extreme form, physical avoidance is not required. Hence, what they were really examining was both avoidance and formality—which may be seen as alloforms, since the two are alternative relations which generally occur between the same kinds of relatives and, while connoting many things, universally indicate differentiation as opposed to indentification.

Informality

Informality is defined by Murdock (1971: 360) as "the absence of both avoidance and respect restraints and of prescribed joking, coupled in nearly all instances, with a prohibition of sex relations." Thus, informality is the intermediate point on the continuum between avoidance and formality at one end, and joking and license at the other. An example of these combinations of closeness and distance, of respect without formality, and intimacy without license, is the relation of brother and sister among the Tikopia (Firth 1957). Brother-sister relations in many societies are frequently subject to severe restrictions and their interaction may be even completely curtailed (Murdock 1949: 277). However, among the Tikopia, while there are certain restrictions, the two are in many ways allowed a great deal of freedom in their dealings with each other. Firth (1957: 178) indicates the presence of what appears to be friendly joking and criticism, such as "it is as common to hear a sister call her brother a fool, as contrariwise." They work together in the home, eat and sit together, spend time together with friends and even sleep together under the same blanket, which in many areas of the world would be unthinkable. The one area which should be avoided however, is conversation with "any obscene or sexual reference. The love affairs of a sister are likewise supposed to be outside the purview of a brother and vice versa" (Firth 1957: 179). So, while bodily contact, even in sleeping, is not avoided, explicit talk about sex is. Firth points out, however, that this may have to do with avoiding interference in the sex life of the sibling, rather than the desire to maintain incest prohibitions. Thus, the brother-sister relation among the Tikopia appears to be generally free and easy. It lacks the avoidance or formality found in many societies and the prescribed joking found in a few (Murdock 1949: 277). Firth's description indicates a general lack of tension between the two, which is in keeping with the style of patrilineal societies, since it is the husband rather than the brother who has an interest in the sister's reproductive functions and, by extension, her sex life.

Joking

Joking relationships are "the observance of a pattern of pre-scribed or obligatory joking when not reported to be accompanied by privileged sex relations" (Murdock 1971: 360). Joking relation-ships are fairly common and are widely described in the ethno-graphic literature. Radcliffe-Brown (1952) explains the behavior in terms of the need to regulate the potentially hostile (disjunctive) relations between affines. He sees two ways to do this, either through extreme respect or avoidance, or through institutionalized joking in which "the playful antagonism of teasing . . . is a constant expression or reminder of that social disjunction [i.e., the divergent interests of the different kin groups] which is one of the essential components of the relation, while the social conjunction [i.e., their relation through marriage] is maintained by the friendliness that takes no offense at insult" (Radcliffe-Brown 1952: 92). Murdock has criticized this "Radcliffe-Brownian verbalism" (1949: 275) for over-simplifying the need to avoid conflict within the household organi-zation and for being incapable of objective application. In other words, Radcliffe Brown does not tell us how to measure the alleged effect of joking and avoidance on conflict within the household.

Murdock, on the other hand, interprets joking relations as rela-tions which tend to occcur between potential spouses. This idea is supported cross-culturally by his own findings (Murdock 1949: 276), as well as Brant's (1972). Murdock provides a separate explanation of joking between grandparents and grandchildren. He feels that it is based on their mutually ambivalent feeling about the intervening relative and their positive feelings toward each other, since the need for discipline of the child and the expectations of the parents are both excluded. Here joking is based on "warm congeniality" (Murdock 1949: 278). While Murdock thus explains joking between grandparents and grandchildren, and between opposite sex-same generation affines, he fails to explain the sort of rough joking which is often found between individuals of the same sex, especially brothers-in-law. This sort of joking is a frequently described pattern which has been ignored by cross-cultural theory.

Among the Eastern Cherokee of North Carolina, the roughest joking is found between an individual and the husbands of the women in his father's clan, his father's sisters' husbands (Gilbert 1955). The joke which Gilbert describes as characteristic of this relation involves the children asking their father's sister's husband for tobacco. If he refuses them, they will "set upon him, throw him to the ground, and strike, kick, and otherwise maltreat him without effective resistance on his part" (Gilbert 1955: 298). While this joke sounds to us rather humorless, the obvious inversion of the standard generational respect seems to be at the core of the interaction. Most joking is not so violent and involves such things as name calling, mutual insulting, and practical or obscene jokes. Among the Navaho, Kluckhohn and Leighton (1946: 99) tell of the relations between a grandfather and grandson where the grandfather steals the boy's clothes while he is taking a sweatbath and in return the grandson, during the grandfather's sweatbath, puts a piece of cactus in the old man's moccasin. Both jokes occasioned laughter by all involved and there were no hard feelings.

Eggan argues that joking is used in these situations to structure relations where cooperation is necessary, and conflict is likely. Where differences in generation are involved, the joking will be mild and will serve to smooth over rough spots. This mild joking usually characterizes the relations between grandparents and grandchildren as well as aunts and uncles with nephews and nieces. But between affines of the same generation where respect or avoidance are unlikely because of the lack of generational deference, joking may be a necessity to avoid the high potential for conflict when they must cooperate. This is a plausible but untested explanation.

License

The cross-sex joking that Brant (1972) and Murdock (1949) discuss is a frequent occurrence and its strong sexual component, including both verbal suggestiveness and physical contact, indicates its relations between the joking individuals. In this case also, the line between joking and license becomes blurred. Murdock bases his distinction on the presence or absence of approved sexual relations between the pair. When approved sexual relations are part of the interaction, Murdock (1971: 360) calls the behavior license. Associated with license in nearly all reported instances is a pattern of prescribed joking, especially of heavy joking or sexual horseplay.

The Tarahumara of northern Mexico (Bennett and Zingg 1935: 222), exhibit this sort of behavior:

> The relationship is a humorous one and consists of rather obscene play and speech between the parties concerned, which increases in boisterousness at the Tesguinadas (cooperative work parties). The play consists of obscene jokes, attempts to lift the woman's skirts, touching of private parts, pulling off clothes, wrestling, and numerous other tricks which would never be tolerated in other relationships, even that of man and wife.

The Tarahumara practice both sororal polygyny and the sororate, so sisters and brothers-in-law are potential future spouses. Passin's (1943: 490) discussion of the Tarahumara notes that sexual relations between opposite sex siblings-in-law "are rarely publicly questioned. As a channel for the regularized expression of non-marital sex desires, it appears to be a convenient device."

Brant (1972) found that there are statistically significant associations between the presence of joking relations (equivalent to Murdock's license) and the presence of sororate, levirate, and cross-cousin marriage in a sample of 220 societies. However, he found in all cases large numbers of exceptions, where sororate, levirate, and cross-cousins marriage were present and joking relations were absent. So the two need not always coincide and the frequent absence of joking relations in these circumstances is a finding worth considering.

Summary

The complexity of ritualized kin relationships has been suggested, but hardly elaborated here. While we are in a better position than Lowie (1920: 101) was sixty years ago to evaluate the varieties of avoidance and privilege that are found, and while we may seriously question his dictum that "we renounce once and for all a theory that shall embrace all the data cited," that theory is not yet at hand. Murdock's (1949) interpretations are certainly valuable but their concentration on incest taboos to the neglect of other clearly important factors lessens their value. Similarly, Driver's (1966) and Jorgensen's (1966) diffusionist interpretation tells us something about intersocietal borrowing of various kinds of behaviors and relationships, but little or nothing about the functions of these relationships. The incest-phobia and proximity hypotheses of kin avoidances have not survived empirical testing. Radcliffe-Brown's (1952) explanation, concerned with avoiding conflict, is suggestive but not only requires testing; it must be put into a much more specific form. Ritualized kin relations involve authority, cooperation, and competition, in both intergenerational and interfamily settings. They also involve sexual desires and sexual relations between various persons. That a single satisfying theory has not been developed is not surprising. That none exists is of course another question.

Chapter 11
Inheritance

In any society inheritance patterns are to some extent the result of the interplay of two systems: kinship relations and the property system. Variation in these two systems, themselves dependent on other socioeconomic conditions, influences the pattern of inheritance in a particular society. Hoebel (1966: 431) suggests that property is composed of two components: "(1) an object (material or incorporeal) and (2) a web of social relations that establishes a limiting and defined relationship between persons and that object." The objects can be tools, domestic animals, farmland, a hunting territory, or sacred songs. The web of social relations is composed of legal and ethical norms. These norms regulate interpersonal behavior. It is this web of social relations that Radcliffe-Brown (1952: 32) was speaking of when he employed the legal distinction between rights "in personam," rights "in rem," and rights over a thing. Rights "in personam" involve the relation between two individuals, A and B, covering the obligations of each to the other. Rights "in rem," and rights over a thing involve the relation between all others toward A and B as a unit, whether B is a person or an object, or toward either A or B as a part of that unit. These rights constitute the relations of the property system.

Kinship relations vary widely from one society to another. This variation cannot be tied to a single cause, such as variation in the subsistence economy, but is the result of the interaction of a number of factors. The central kinship distinctions employed by a society are basic to the inheritance system. When the kin group is a corporate unit, the shared use and intragroup transmission of property will be basic to that unity. When kin ties have been replaced by economic relations, inheritance will still be one of the few property transaction supplying contiguity to the group. While it is analytically possible to separate kinship from property relations, in reality each affects the workings of the other and cannot be understood in isolation.

The distinction between patrilineal and matrilineal systems, one emphasizing the husband-wife bond, and the other the brother-sister bond, is relevant to inheritance patterns. But because different kinds of property are likely to be transmitted through different lines, many scholars (Lowie 1920: 255; Murdock 1949: 38) have recognized that this distinction is inadequate for the description of inheritance systems. Lowie (1948) pointed out that sexual division of labor and property have a great deal to do with inheritance. As a matter of simple practicality, women's tools and clothing most frequently pass to women and men's to men. Even in a matrilineal system, some property will pass only between men and some between women. Among the Hopi, houses are women's property and pass from mothers to daughters. Sacred offices, however, are the property of men, and an office such as that of the Snake priest passes from brother to brother or mother's brother to sister's son.

Property may also be classed as either heritable or nonheritable. The more intimate objects of a person's life, whether tools, clothing, a favorite horse, or even a house, may be considered so heavily imbued with the spirit of the deceased that these objects may have to be buried with him or destroyed. Very valuable property, like farmland or hunting territory, may belong to the corporate group and not be inheritable at all. The right to use this property is not inherited but is a benefit of membership in the corporate group, which usually passes to some of the children of group members only—for example, to sons in a patrilineal system. When these rights are passed on, the continuity of the corporation is assured. But it is group membership, with all that it involves, and not property, which is inherited (Cole 1932; Radcliffe-Brown 1952: 34). How property is transmitted may also depend upon how it was acquired. Inherited property is often more stringently controlled than property that an individual acquires by himself.

Besides type of property, type of status also influences inheritance. Hoben (1973: 146) notes that an individual's position in the domestic cycle, such as his age, marital status, or residence, affects inheritance decisions. Primogeniture and ultimogeniture introduce birth order as an aspect of inheritance (see Lowie 1920: 248-254, for specific examples of these forms). Agricultural peoples often favor one particular child. By so doing, they keep from breaking up the family estate into units too small to be of economic value (Lowie 1948: 150).

Inheritance and Subsistence

The basic subsistence economy is a major determinant of inheritance patterns. People in simple hunting and gathering societies vary little in the quality and quantity of their material possessions. Thus, the transmission of particular items or rights of use have little importance to an individual's standard of living. Clothes and tools may be passed on to others upon an individual's death, but their intimate connection with the deceased is likely to prompt the survivors to bury them with the deceased or destroy them. In any case, their commonness hardly encourages others to desire them strongly. Ritual items, especially since they may be symbols of the group and less intimately connected with a specific person, are more likely to be passed on at death. Among the Aranda of central Australia, *churinga*, the sacred stones possessing the ancestral spirits, were a major item of inheritance. The Aranda's materially poor existence, and subsistence based on the collection of plants and small animals, produced little else worth inheriting (Spencer and Gillen 1927: 118).

Among pastoral and horticultural peoples subsistence is more complex. The upkeep of animals and fields often requires a large amount of physical energy. Large herds may be important not only for subsistence but also for status and political authority. Fields may also be status and power symbols, as well as sources of sustenance for a family. The possession of large herds or plots of land represents unevenly distributed resources which play a major role in the social system. These sorts of resources are not willingly given up by those who benefit from them at the death of the owner. What Lowie (1948: 147) referred to as their economically imbecile treatment (either their destruction, abandonment, or in some way, their loss to the community), is unlikely to be tolerated in most situations, as it is in simpler economies.

Linton's (1936) account of how the Comanche adjusted their inheritance rules to accommodate the possession of large herds of horses is a classic example. Before the Comanche became pastoral plains dwellers, most of a man's possessions were buried with him or destroyed. Even his tent and everything in it were burned. His dependents voluntarily impoverished themselves and became dependent on the rest of the community for their support until they could recover. With the advent of horses, however, a man's possessions might include a herd of as many as two thousand horses, many of which might be used by others. Hunting and status became closely connected with the possession of horses. To destroy a resource on which so many depended became not only imbecilic but unthinkable. The Comanche quickly developed a system in which a few of a man's favorite horses were destroyed and the rest redistributed to other kin. Thus, a change in their subsistence economy forced a change in their inheritance patterns.

Among intensive agriculturalists who rely on the plough and/or irrigation, the energy invested in producing food is greater yet. The farmland is permanently improved and becomes a resource of tremendous value. Its productivity can create large differences in wealth and status within a society. Concern about the transmission not only of this land but also the wealth derived from it over a lifetime, is necessarily great. Goody (1969a, 1969b, 1970b, 1976; Goody, Irving, and Tahany 1970) and his associates have produced the only formal cross-cultural research on inheritance. Goody is chiefly interested in diverging devolution, the passing of property to both males and females. Goody, Irving and Tahany (1970: 306) provide us with a broad model of diverging devolution as shown in Figure 11.1. This model was developed through path analysis of four samples of societies representing Africa and Eurasia. Goody sees inheritance as occupying a key position in the development of social systems—directly influencing marriage practices, sexual behavior and kinship terminology. We expect that others would take a more cautious view than Goody, especially since the correlation coefficients between the variables are low, ranging from .09 to .31, although low coefficients are expected in path analysis.

Goody (1970b: 634) also tells us something about the direction in which property is transmitted. He finds a striking difference in direction of inheritance between societies in Africa and those in Eurasia. Inheritance tends to be lateral and matrilineal in Africa. In Europe it is more likely to be vertical and patrilineal. Goody reasons that in the more economically complex Eurasian societies, vertical transmission of property ensures that the propety will remain in the family. In Africa, the corporate nature of many kinship systems encourages the transfer of property to siblings and collateral relations.

In industrial economies, the differences in wealth are still greater, as is the case in which wealth is transmitted to heirs. Cole (1932) emphasizes the role of private property in inheritance. In an industrialized society, large amounts of capital investment are required to produce many important commodities. Many have

Figure 11.1. *Goody's Model of Diverging Devolution*

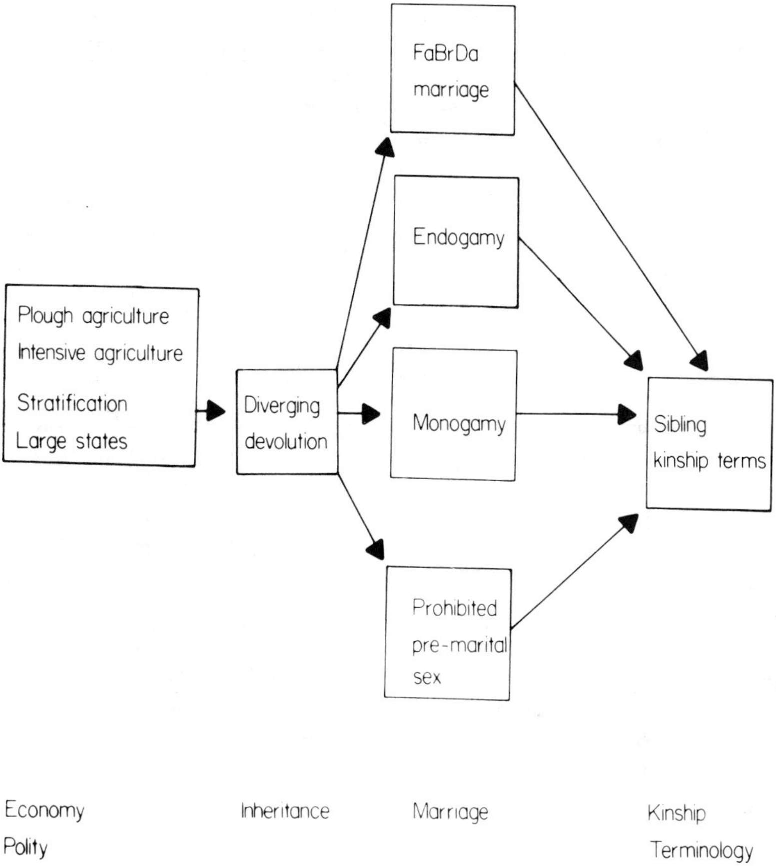

Taken from Goody, Irving and Tahany 1970.

argued that in nonsocialist economies, the inheritance of large sums of wealth is a key source of capital for production. In the United States and Great Britain especially, laissez-faire, non-interference (or very limited interference) by the state in the market economy, allowed the inheritance of very large fortunes and the perpetuation of vast differences in wealth in order to encourage the investment of substantial quantities of capital in the economy (Cole 1932). In socialist economies it is the state which acquires and invests the capital.

The basic point about inheritance and subsistence is that the more complex and productive the economy, the greater the concern with the systematization of inheritance. It may seem self-evident that the more people who are affected by an individual's estate (and the more they are affected), the more concern there will be with seeing that the estate is carefully and systematically distributed upon his death. But it is important to remember that inheritance systems are intimately connected with the property system and the economy of a particular society.

Conceptualizing Inheritance

There is a minor controversy about the concept of inheritance which requires mention. The basis of the debate is the distinctions first made by Rivers (1924: 85-87) among: descent, the transmission of group membership; inheritance, the transmission of property; and succession, the transmission of office. Some theorists, such as Lowie (1948) and Hoebel (1966), feel that inheritance is the same as succession or at least a form of succession. Lowie (1948: 147) finds no reason to contrast inheritance and succession. Since property is not wealth, but only the title to it, office then is just another title which may be inherited. Hoebel argues that inheritance is not a transfer of possessions, but a transfer of statuses. But not all transfers of status are inheritance. For one thing, some kinds may take place while the transferor is still alive. So inheritance is one kind of status transfer. Other kinds include the transfer of a chieftainship from father to son. Hoebel then (1966: 431-432) also lumps inheritance and succession, since both are transfers of status.

If we study society solely from the point of view of status, this merging is valid. But other points of view require other mergings and contrasts. It is important to remember that all three of these systems are aspects of social status. Each may vary independently of the others; there may be different rules for each kind of transfer. For this reason, it would seem more useful to treat the three as separate systems whose interrelations are problematic rather than taken for granted. To combine the three concepts may mask subtle variations in the relationship of group membership, politics, and property.

Summary

Murdock (1949:39) stated that "a really adequate study of property rights and inheritance in cross-cultural perspective still remains to be made." It is surprising to find that some thirty years later, the situation has hardly changed. Pospisil (1974) points out that Murdock's (1949) and Lowie's (1920) discussions prompted more detailed ethnographies. But there is still no full-scale cross-cultural study. Pospisil (1974: 303ff), making use of these detailed ethnographies, demonstrated the value of the native categories of property in analyzing patterns of inheritance. His formal analysis provides an interesting, but so far as we know, untested model for dealing with the study of property and inheritance.

Aside from Goody's (1976) stimulating work, there is little else; his summary of the relationship between subsistence economy and inheritance patterns should generate some controversy (cf. the review by Gudeman 1977), further hypotheses, and cross-cultural tests. But its focus is Africa and Eurasia, and it stands alone. We hope that Goody's efforts will stimulate others to replicate and expand research on property rights and inheritance.

Section IV.   Expressive Culture

Religion, taboos, rules governing sexual behavior, games and the fine arts are five examples of expressive culture. Expressive culture refers to two related phenomena: first, to the function of cultural activities and practices as mechanisms for the release or expression of emotions; and second, to the role of these activities as models, reflections or expressions of the themes or structures characteristic of instrumental features of culture. For example, Swanson (1960) argues that the social system of the supernatural world is modeled on the social system of the world of the believers. J.L. Fischer (1961), for another, finds the degree of social stratification present in a society reflected in the design in its graphic arts.

Expressive culture has been relatively ignored by holocultural researchers—perhaps because some types of expressive culture like the arts, religion or games are more often thought of as being within the realm of the humanities than the social sciences. However, the Lomax group's (1968a, 1968b) approach to the cross-cultural study of music, called Cantometrics, demonstrates clearly that expressive culture is amenable to empirical social science analysis.

Chapter 12
Religion

In the beginning, anthropologists were interested in the origin of religion. Tylor (1871), Frazer (1959), Marett (1909), H. Spencer (1876-1896), and Schmidt (1931), among others, proposed universal, evoluntionary theories of religion. These men also added to the anthropological vocabulary terms like animism, animatism, reanimation, and magic. But the ideas of these early theorists were soon disproved and abandoned, and many of their concepts, though still used, are not yet clearly defined. In fact, anthropologists do not yet agree on what religion is. Three definitions of religion appear regularly:

> ... (1) a system of symbols which acts to (2) establish powerful, pervasive, and longlasting moods and motivations in men by (3) formulating conceptions of a general order of existence and (4) clothing those conceptions with such an aura of factuality that (5) the moods and motivations seem uniquely realistic (Geertz 1966: 4).

> Religion may be described as a system of beliefs and practices directed toward the 'ultimate concern' of a society (Lessa and Vogt 1972: 1).

> ... an institution consisting of culturally patterned interaction with culturally postulated superhuman beings (Spiro 1966b: 96).

Spiro's definition is the one followed most often in holocultural research; it is an etic definition, and, as such facilitates cross-cultural comparison; and, it can easily be operationalized. Ethnographic accounts are usually detailed enough so that the presence, absence or nature of supernatural beings can be determined.

The anthropological study of religion encompasses a wide range of topics. Here we are mainly interested in theories about the origin, development, and nature of religious practices and beliefs. We also look briefly at cross-cultural research on reactions to death and dying, evil eye beliefs, and altered states of consciousness. We ignore altogether topics like religion and social change, symbolic analysis, and structural analysis—because there has been no holocultural research on them, even though they interest some contemporary anthropologists. Recent research on these topics is reviewed by Justinger (1977).

Anthropological thought about religion has been strongly influenced by the views of Freud, Durkheim, Malinowski, and Radcliffe-Brown. Interestingly, Max Weber's ideas on religion have been largely ignored by anthropologists (Gerth and Mills 1958). Some of Freud's and Durkheim's ideas have been tested holoculturally and are discussed in more detail further along in the chapter. Malinowski's and Radcliffe-Brown's ideas have not been so tested and should be mentioned briefly here. Malinowski (1954) emphasized the needs religion meets. Subsequent research by others suggests that religion: helps explain human existence; provides emotional support and release; creates and maintains social solidarity; validates cultural norms and values; and helps human groups adapt to the natural environment. Barber (1941), Linton (1943), and Wallace (1956) suggest another function—an agent of social change. Cargo cults in Melanesia and revitalization movements among Native Americans are two well documented cases where religious movements facilitated social change. However, most scholars would argue that religion is more likely to foster stability than change. These functions are basically a list of benefits. Religion may also be harmful and disruptive, perhaps by causing anxiety and guilt in believers, or by creating social disorganization and conflict. Radcliffe-Brown (1952, 1964) emphasized the relationship between religion and other cultural systems and institutions; he saw religion primarily as a mechanism of social control and solidarity. This approach has strongly influenced the ethnographic study of religion and is exemplied by DeWaal Malefijt (1968).

The past twenty years have seen the birth of a renewed interest in explaining the origins, development, and nature of religion. Three different theoretical approaches dominate the scene. First, the Freudian model of religion as an extension of childhood experiences. Second, the Durkheimian model of religion as a reflection of the social system. And, third, the neo-evolutionary models of Swanson, Bellah, Wallace, and Davis. We begin with Freud.

Freud and Religion

Freud's ideas about religion (1928, 1950, 1955, 1961) have been roundly criticized. They are often little more than fantasy backed up by a misreading of the then-available ethnographic record. Few, if any, anthropologists take these ideas seriously. But it is not these ideas that underlie some recent holocultural research on the relationship between socialization and supernatural beliefs. Rather, researchers have drawn upon Freud's more general personality theories to explain cross-cultural variation in supernatural beliefs. The basic model followed by these researchers can be paraphrased from Spiro and D'Andrade (1967) as follows: (1) fantasy, which represents a child's perception of the world, arises from childhood experiences; (2) religious beliefs are a product of human fantasy; (3) religious beliefs are passed on from one generation to the next; (4) these beliefs constitute projective systems (Kardiner 1939) and, as such, are shared by the group members but often differ from one group to another.

Five holocultural studies demonstrate a clear and consistent relationship between child rearing practices and attitudes and the perception of supernatural beings (Spiro and D'Andrade 1967; Lambert, Minturn and Wolf 1959; J.W.M. Whiting 1967; Rohner 1975; Prescott 1975). The Rohner study is especially careful, the others less so. Spiro and D'Andrade report that assistance from supernaturals is contingent on the performance of rituals in societies where there is much concern about dependency and orality in childhood. And, they further report that supernaturals are perceived as punishing in societies where children are little indulged and encouraged to be independent. Lambert, Minturn, and Wolf (1959) report similar findings. Absence of pain during infancy is associated with benevolent supernaturals, but the presence of only a limited number of caretakers and little indulgence are associated with a belief in aggressive deities. These patterns of relationships are supported by two more recent and more rigorous studies. Rohner (1975) finds supernaturals perceived as hostile and evil in societies where children are rejected, and Prescott (1975) finds pain infliction on infants associated with a belief in aggressive deities. J.W.M. Whiting (1967), too, reports a relationship between socialization and religious beliefs. Infant neglect and punishment are strongly related to a fear of ghosts at funerals. Ghost fear is seen as a projection of the mourners' own feelings about their neglectful caretakers. These five studies point to a relationship between socialization and religious beliefs. They say very little about religious practices. They say nothing about causal direction, although it is usually assumed that socialization practices are the cause and religious beliefs the effect. But, it does seem that when caretakers are warm and accepting, so too are supernatural beings. And, when caretakers are seen as cold and rejecting, supernaturals are seen as aggressive and punishing, and ghosts are feared.

Durkheim and Religion

Durkheim has contributed as much to the study of religion as any other social scientist. His definitions, conceptualizations, and theories are still widely cited. Here we are interested in his theory of religion. As Parsons (1949: 66) tells us, Durkheim (1915) argued that "society is always the real object of religious veneration." According to Swanson (1960), Durkheim's proposition suggests that the supernatural world is organized or modeled on the social structure of the world of the believers. Swanson (1960) and Davis (1971) have tested this proposition holoculturally. The findings are summarized in Table 12.1. They are largely contradictory. Davis fails to replicate Swanson's results for four of the six hypotheses tested. Why these two studies fail to agree is not clear, but the main point is that they do not. Swanson supports Durkheim's formulation, Davis rejects it. Thus, we do not know whether people model the supernatural world after their own. What is needed is a third study controlling for the possible influence of Galton's Problem, regional variation, and data inaccuracies.

One of the two hypotheses that Swanson and Davis do agree on is that the presence of numerous sovereign kin groups leads to a belief in active ancestral spirits. This finding is explained somewhat differently by Tatje and Hsu (1969) in a typological study of twelve religious systems. While acknowledging the importance of social structure, Tatje and Hsu attribute cross-cultural differences in ancestor beliefs to the type of kinship dyad or dyads that dominate in a particular society. A dyad is composed of two persons who stand in some kind of role relationship to one another. Typical dyads within a family are husband-wife, father-son, or mother-son. Each dyad type has a specific set of characteristics or attributes. According to Tatje and Hsu, in any particular society one or possibly two

Table 12.1. *The Relationship between Social Structure and Religious Beliefs*

Social Structure Variable	Religious Belief	Support	
		Swanson	Davis
three or more sovereign groups ordered hierarchically	high god (monotheism)	yes	yes
numerous occupational specialties compatible with the ultimately sovereign group	superior gods (polytheism)	yes	no
many sovereign kin groups	active ancestral spirits	yes	yes
small, continuing residence units	reincarnation	yes	no
restricted membership in sovereign groups	immanence of the soul	yes	no
unlegitimized social contacts	witchcraft	yes	no

dyad types dominate. As shown in Table 12.2, they predict that certain dyad types will be related to certain types of ancestor beliefs. It is the nature of the dyad attributes that tie the two together. This formulation strikes us as an important refinement of Durkheim's original proposition, But, before it can be accepted with any confidence, a careful holocultural test is needed.

The presence or absence of ancestral shrines and the frequency of rituals for deceased ancestors in peasant societies may also be a function of social structural factors (Michaelson and Goldschmidt 1976). Shrines and frequent rituals are found most often in peasant communities with patrilineal land inheritance. The rituals, the shrines, and family owned land all may serve as symbols of solidarity and continuity in these communities.

These studies present no clear picture of a relationship between social organization and religion, but it seems likely that social organization somehow influences religious beliefs and practices.

Table 12.2. *Kinship Content and Ancestor Beliefs*

Dominant Dyad	Dyad Attributes	Ancestor Belief Type
husband-wife	discontinuity, volition, exclusiveness, sexuality	none, or no role in human affiars
mother-son	discontinuity, dependence, inclusiveness, libidinality, diffuseness	unimportant in human affairs
mother-daughter	inclusiveness, dependence, diffuseness, continuity	malicious or capricious, or punishing
brother-brother	discontinuity, rivalry, equality, inclusiveness	punishing or rewarding-punishing
father-son	continuity, authority, inclusiveness, asexuality	rewarding-punishing or benevolent-rewarding

Table constructed from data in Tatje and Hsu (1969).

Neo-Evolutionary Theory

We have noted that nineteenth century evolutionary theories of religion were abandoned long ago. Only within the past ten to fifteen years has there been,a revival of interest in the evolution of religion. At least four different models of religious evolution have found their way into the literature. While these four models differ from one another, they are not necessarily contradictory, as each attempts to explain the development of religion at a different level of abstraction.

Swanson (1960) suggests a four-stage model of the evolution of religious patterns: ancestor worship ⟶ animism ⟶ polytheism ⟶ monotheism. Each stage is seen as corresponding to a particular attribute of social organization. Thus, for example, monotheism is associated with the hierarchical ordering of social groups. The evolution of religious patterns is seen as paralleling the evolution of social structure. The trustworthiness of this model then depends on the validity of Durkheim's social organization theory, which has yet to be proven cross-culturally.

Bellah (1964) suggests a five-stage model of the evolution of broad religious trends: primitive ⟶ archaic ⟶ historic ⟶ early modern ⟶ modern. In developing this scheme, Bellah emphasizes the increasing elaboration of religious forms, and the increasing importance of freedom, individualism, and objective reasoning. This model has yet to be tested holoculturally.

Wallace (1966) suggests a five-stage model of the evolution of what he calls religious cults: individualistic ⟶ shamanistic ⟶ communal ⟶ Olympian ⟶ monotheistic. Each cult type is characterized by a specific set of theological beliefs and a particular type of religous organization. This model also needs to be tested holoculturally.

Davis (1971) suggests the only evolutionary model that has been tested, point by point, holoculturally; he argues that societal complexity, as measured by type of subsistence economy, determines the nature of religious beliefs and practices. Table 12.3 shows that religious practices do scale well with subsistence types. McNett (1970a), too, finds religious practices related to societal complexity as measured by community type. These findings are summarized in Table 12.4. Additional support for this model comes from the findings that ritual specialists appear more often in complex societies, and that status distinctions in burial rituals reflect the level of status distinctions within the society (Rosenblatt, Walsh and Jackson 1976; Binford 1971).

Thus, there is convincing cross-cultural evidence that societal complexity shapes the nature of religious practices. But, there is no similar evidence that cultural complexity shapes the nature of religious beliefs. Here, Davis found only three—animism, high god, and superior gods—of the eleven beliefs studies associated with a specific level of societal complexity.

Death and Reaction to Death

Until recently, most social scientists, anthropologists included, were little interested in death and reactions to death. In the last few years, though, the situation has changed markedly. The major anthropological contribution is Rosenblatt, Walsh and Jackson (1976). Their approach combines methodological rigor with theoretical caution. The conclusions reached cannot be ignored; they can be summarized as follows:

(1) There is general similarity among cultures in the emotions expressed during bereavement.

(2) Women tend to internalize grief, men tend to externalize it.

(3) Guidance provided by ritual specialists, marking, and isolation

Table 12.3. *Relationship between Subsistence Economy and Religious Practices*

	Religious Practices			
Subsistence Type	A	B	C	D
Agrarian	4	4	4	4
Advanced horticulture	3	4	3	3
Simple horticulture	2	2	2	2
Hunting and gathering	1	1	1	1

Religious practices are rated for complexity on a 1-4 scale:
A = extent of religious organization
B = type of religious functionary
C = number of calendrical rites
D = locus of participation

Table constructed from data in Davis (1971).

Table 12.4. *Community Patterns and Religious Practices*

	Community Pattern				
Religious Behavior	Band	Village	Town	City	State
Magic	1.00	1.00	.63	.33	.00
No ethical supernatural	1.00	1.00	.63	.50	.00
Vague supernatural	1.00	.83	.57	.33	.00
Spirits	1.00	1.00	.63	.42	.00
Shamans	1.00	1.00	.75	.42	.00
No religious hierarchy	1.00	1.00	.88	.30	.00
Individual ritual	.86	.83	.57	.36	.00
Infrequent group ceremony	.86	.50	.14	.10	.00
Simple funeral	.86	.00	.38	.17	.07
Simple paraphernalia	1.00	.67	.50	.27	.00
No temples	1.00	.83	.86	.18	.00

Table revised from McNett (1970a: 205).
The numbers indicate the probability of a trait being present; 1.00 means the trait will always be present, and .00 that it will always be absent.

of the bereaved tend to control the anger and aggression associated with grief.
(4) Ghost beliefs, ghost cognitions, and fear of ghosts are universal responses to death; they seem to be normal responses to the termination of close interpersonal relationships.
(5) Remarriage of the survivor is facilitated by change of residence,

a taboo on the name of the deceased, and the discarding of property of the deceased.

(6) Final funeral rites tend to limit the length of bereavement.

(7) Christianity has had little influence on the death customs practiced in primitive societies.

Lester (1971, 1975) relates fear of death to high rates of suicide and love-oriented techniques of punishment. He also finds fear of death and fear of the dead associated with a high need to achieve (Lester 1969). He presents the plausible argument that people who have a strong need to achieve will view death as an end to their achieving and thus, will fear it. However, his samples are small, ranging in size from fifteen to thirty-three cases, and the methodological analysis is limited.

The Evil Eye

The evil eye belief is a widespread, though not universal, belief "that one's eye power can cause sudden harm to another's property or person" (Maloney 1976: vi). The evil eye belief does not occur in all regions of the world. It is found most often in northern Mesoamerica, the Near East, northern Africa and Europe. It is found only sporadically in North America, South America, Asia, and Oceania. Many scholars think that the evil eye belief originated among the complex urban-peasant cultures of the Near East and then spread elsewhere. Other rival explanations focusing on functional, ecological, and psychodynamic factors are briefly discussed by Spooner (1976).

As yet there are no theories of the evil eye that have been tested holoculturally. Roberts (1976), however, in a broad study based on Murdock and White's (1969) Standard Cross-Cultural Sample and interviews with 257 American college students, provides a framework for future theoretical research. For Roberts, the evil eye belief is closely related to feelings of envy—envy about wealth, power, or prestige. Societies with the evil eye belief tend to be characterized by (1) unequal distribution of material goods; (2) social and political inequality; (3) milking, animal husbandry, and intensive agriculture; (4) transfer of wealth at marriage; and (5) child rearing practices characterized by father-child separation, dependence, and pain infliction. Roberts's preliminary analysis is both broad and cautious. It should stimulate more holocultural research on the evil eye belief. Holocultural research concerning witchcraft and sorcery is discussed in Chapter 29, Social Control.

Altered States of Consciousness

Altered states of consciousness come in a wide variety of forms. Dreams are by far the most common. In our own culture, altered states are often associated with psychotic personality disorders such as schizophrenia, or with drug use. Bourguignon's (1972) continuum shown in Figure 12.1, gives some idea of the form altered states take in small-scale societies. Eighty-nine percent of 488 societies sampled have some form of institutionalized dissociational state—either trance, possession trance, or both. Trance is defined as "an altered state of consciousness in which contact with self and others is modified in some particular way, ranging from total unconsciousness to a very shallow modification" (Bourguignon 1972: 417). Possession trance differs in that a person's actions and words are attributed to a spirit who has taken temporary possession of the person's body.

Thirty-three percent of the societies sampled have trance, twenty-seven percent have possession trance, and twenty-four percent have both. The presence of trance and possession trance is clearly related to the level of cultural complexity for the world as a whole, although there are significant regional variations (Bourguignon and Evascu 1977). Trance alone is found in the least complex societies, trance and possession trance in societies at a mid-level of complexity, and possession trance alone in the most complex societies.

Summary

Holocultural research has produced two clear findings about the development of religion: child rearing practices are in some way related to beliefs about supernatural beings; and, societal complexity influences religious *practices*. But there is little evidence that societal complexity influences religious *beliefs*. And, the question of whether specific social organizational factors shape religious beliefs and practices is left unanswered. Swanson says they do. Davis says they do not. More research is needed. Four evolutionary models of religion have been suggested, but only one has been tested and then only partially supported.

The findings of Rosenblatt and his associates about reactions to death are interesting and informative; they show that anthropological research in general and holocultural research in particular can be timely and socially useful. Two exciting topics ripe for

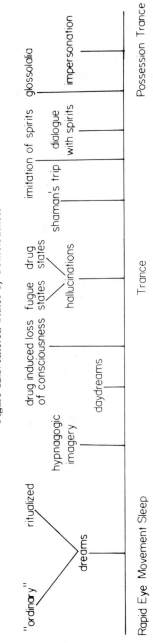

Figure 12.1. *Altered States of Consciousness*

Taken from Bourguignon (1972).

further holocultural study are evil eye beliefs and altered states of consciousness. Roberts and Bourguignon have laid the groundwork.

The finding that childrearing practices may influence beliefs about the supernatural is somewhat surprising. Anthropologists have long assumed that religion is a group rather than individually determined social institution. Apparently, though, both individual personality and social factors shape religious beliefs.

Chapter 13
Taboos

A taboo (tabu) is a prohibition. All taboos contain two elements: the action that is prohibited; and, the object to which the action applies. Taboos may be temporary or permanent, or they may apply only to certain categories of people, but not to others.

In strict anthropological terms, taboo refers to specific behaviors, usually associated with certain Polynesian societies, that are strictly sanctioned by the threat of supernatural reprisal. But over the years, taboo has been used in a more general sense to refer to many strongly prohibited actions regardless of whether or not supernatural sanctions apply. A taboo may apply to a particular act at all times, to a particular act occasionally, or to a particular category of persons all of the time or only occasionally.

Some ethnographic descriptions make clear the forms a taboo may take. Reynolds (1968: 54) describes a Tonga occasional taboo associated with subsistence activities:

He must refrain from sexual intercourse the night before going fishing, and on the morning of the fishing must also refrain from washing.

Gorer (1935: 52-53) describes a name taboo:

There is a curious relic of totemism among the Wolof. Nearly all family names are the names of animals (*M' Benga* is the name of the jackal, *Dragne* of the snake) and the animal whose name a man bears is taboo to him; if he eats its flesh he will be very ill, and should he merely touch it his skin will break out in a rash and blisters.

And, Underhill (1946: 253) details Papago beliefs about menstruation:

The mysterious power which descended periodically upon women was thought to be entirely incompatible with the life and activities of men. A male who touched a menstruating woman might die, and even to see her would cause weakness. Contact with her would take the strength from his weapons and poison his food. For the sake of the community, therefore, she must be segregated whenever the magic came upon her, and every family had a hut where its women could be sent at the proper time.

Taboos are often conceptualized as ritual symbols that help to maintain boundaries between different categories of objects in the universe (Douglas 1957, 1966; Leach 1964). Taboos are a mechanism for excluding objects that do not fit neatly into a particular society's scheme of the universe. Thus, taboos are seen as helping to maintain moral order by helping to order the universe. This conceptualization of taboos as ordering mechanisms is but one of many explanations that have been suggested over the years. Theories about taboos in general have been suggested by Marett (1909), Wundt (1916), Lévy-Bruhl (1926, 1931), Radcliffe-Brown (1952, 1964), Freud (1950), Frazer (1959), and Malinowski (1954). Many of these theories are critically reviewed by Steiner (1956), although none has been tested holoculturally.

Investigators who rely on the holocultural method have chosen to study specific though widespread taboos—incest, menstrual, post-partum sex, food, and pregnancy—rather than taboos in general. The underlying assumption of these studies seems to be that particular types of taboos exist in the context of and can be explained by a limited number of psycho-cultural factors. So, for example, menstrual taboos are explained in terms of specific child rearing practices and the status of women. And a long postpartum sex taboo is analyzed in the context of family organization. To some extent we follow this line of reasoning in assigning the incest taboo a separate chapter in the Kinship Section. Here, we discuss menstrual, postpartum sex, food and pregnancy taboos.

Menstrual Taboos

Most cultures have some type of restriction placed on menstruating women, although the intensity of the restriction varies widely. Young and Bacdayan's (1967) Guttman scale indicates the range of cross-cultural variation of menstrual taboos:

Revised Scale of Elaboration of Menstrual Taboos

Step No.	Item content
0	Concern for menstruation is informal
1	Explicit rule that menstruants should not indulge in sexual intercourse
2	Personal restrictions or requirements on menstruants, such as food taboos, no scratching of body, no loud laughing
3	Menstruants not allowed to have contact with male things, especially such capital equipment as bows or fishing gear
4	Menstruants not allowed to cook for men
5	Menstruants must spend their menstrual periods in menstrual huts

Menstrual taboos have been explained both psychogenically and sociogenically. Stephens (1962) proposes the following psychoanalytic theory: certain child rearing practices lead to male castration anxiety which manifests itself in menstrual taboos. The more severe the castration anxiety, the more extensive the menstrual taboo. Stephens's statistical results are in the predicted direction, although weakly so. Thus, he concludes that castration anxiety is a real phenomenon—this conclusion is supported by Fisher and Greenberg's (1977) review of empirical tests of psychoanalytic theory—and that castration anxiety determines the extensiveness of the menstrual taboo. Young and Bacdayan (1967) also support the castration anxiety hypothesis weakly, but suggest that it be replaced by a rival sociogenic theory. Here, the menstrual taboo is seen as a device used by men to control women. This hypothesis is supported statistically, although the degree of support is no greater than that for Stephens's castration anxiety hypothesis. Obviously, we have much left to learn about the causes of menstrual taboos.

Postpartum Sex Taboo

The postpartum sex taboo prohibits a mother from engaging in sexual intercourse for a set period of time following the birth of her child. The postpartum taboo is generally described as either long—over one year in duration—or short—less than one year in duration

(Whiting, Kluckhohn and Anthony 1958; Stephens 1962; J.W.M. Whiting 1964; Saucier 1972). Saucier's data from a random sample of 172 societies (see Table 13.1) indicate that 33.7 percent of the world's societies have a long taboo, and 66.3 percent have a short taboo. Here we are mainly interested in the long postpartum sex taboo.

Of all taboos, the long postpartum taboo is the most burdensome. It must be very frustrating for women and men in monogamous societies and monogamous men in polygynous societies to go without sexual intercourse for a year or more. Thus, it is not surprising that the long postpartum taboo is more often than not found in societies with some form of polygnous marriage (Stephens 1962; Whiting 1964; Saucier 1972). In polygynous societies, some men, although not women, have access to alternative sexual partners. Polygyny can be seen as either a cause or an effect. Either way, polygyny certainly makes the long postpartum taboo more tolerable for some men.

Whiting (1964) suggests that the long taboo exists for health reasons. A long taboo often occurs in tropical societies which receive a substantial portion of their nutrition from root crops. Root crops are not an especially good source of protein, and infants in these societies are especially susceptible to the protein deficiency disease, kwashiokor. The long taboo ensures that the nursing mother will have only one child to nurse at a time, and thus, will have enough protein for herself and her child. Saucier (1972), in a broad study of possible causes of long taboo, finds Whiting's interpretation overly simplistic and suggests (in Figure 13.1) a model for future research. This model is a good starting point. Future research should be able to narrow the list to those factors that best predict the occurrence of a long postpartum sex taboo.

The length of the postpartum taboo is a variable that appears with some regularity in holocultural studies. It has been used as an indicator of castration anxiety, mother-child closeness, and father-child distance, or, in short, as an indicator of a child rearing environment that will likely lead to an unresolved Oedipus complex in boys. A long taboo is also cited as a cause of male initiation rites, sorcery as an explanation for illness, menstrual taboos, and mother-in-law and sister avoidance. As discussed elsewhere, there is no convincing empirical evidence that a long taboo causes any of these practices. Despite its popularity in holocultural research, we know very little about the causes or effects of a long postpartum sex taboo.

Table 13.1. *World Distribution of the Postpartum Taboo*

Duration of Postpartum Taboo	Geographic Regions							World Total (%)	
	Sub-Saharan Africa	North Africa	Mediter-ranean	East Eurasia	Insular Pacific	North America	South and Central America		
No taboo	0	0	1	1	0	0	0	2	(1.1%)
1 month	2	0	2	8	6	7	8	33	(19.2%)
2-6 months	9	4	2	7	7	20	9	58	(33.7%)
7-12 months	7	0	0	0	5	4	5	21	(12.3%)
13-24 months	13	3	0	1	5	5	4	31	(18.0%)
25 months +	12	1	0	2	4	5	3	27	(15.7%)
0-12 months	18	4	5	16	18	31	22	114	
13 months +	25	4	0	3	9	10	7	58	
% Long Postpartum	58.1°	50°	0	15.7	33.3	24.3	24.1	33.7	
Ranking	1	2	7	6	3	4	5		

°Here the frequency is particularly high.

Table taken from Jean-François Saucier, Correlates of the Long Postpartum Taboo. *Current Anthropology* 13(1972), 243. Published by the University of Chicago.

Figure 13.1. *Saucier Model for the Long Postpartum Taboo*

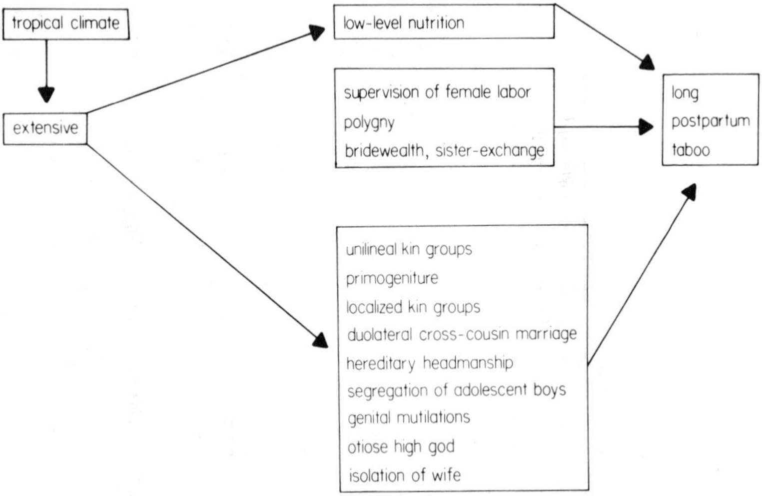

Taken from Saucier (1972: 248).

Food Taboos

All cultures prohibit the eating of certain types of food. Some foods are prohibited altogether, others are prohibited on certain occasions, and still others may not be eaten with certain other foods. Occasional food taboos are often associated with rites, stages, or events in the life cycle. Food taboos are a common element in initiation, marriage, and funeral rites, and are often followed during menstruation and pregnancy. Specific food taboos may also apply only to certain categories of people like women, children, shamans or the aged.

The number of foods either generally or occasionally tabooed in a society seems dependent on the level of cultural complexity of that society (Leary 1961). As Tables 13.2 and 13.3 show, there is a direct, linear relationship between the number of foods tabooed and the level of political integration. However, during pregnancy the reverse may be true. Complex societies taboo more foods during pregnancy than do less complex ones (M. Ember 1961).

Table 13.2. *General Food Taboos and Cultural Complexity*

	Level of Political Integration				
	Absence of Political Integration	Autonomous Local Communities	Minimal States	Little States	States
Average Number of Food Taboos	9.50	7.52	7.16	5.83	3.90

Table taken from Leary (1961: 11-12).

Table 13.3. *Occasional Food Taboos and Cultural Complexity*

	Level of Political Integration				
	Absence of Political Integration	Autonomous Local Communities	Minimal States	Little States	States
Average Number of Life Cycle Food Taboos	5.2	3.47	2.38	2.00	.55

Table taken from Leary (1961: 11-12).

Pregnancy Taboos

All cultures have taboos specifically associated with pregnancy. The eating of certain foods is prohibited, sexual activity may be limited, and other activities may be curtailed altogether. In our own culture these restrictions are explained in terms of the health benefits for the mother and her unborn child. This same line of reasoning may also explain food taboos during pregnancy in small-scale societies. Ayres (1967) draws upon Freud's (1950) contention that "the basis of taboo is a forbidden action for which there exists a strong inclination of the unconscious," and upon Whiting and Child's (1953) fixation theory to explain food taboos during pregnancy. Ayres (1967: 114) suggests the following causal sequence: "pregnancy ——→frustration and anxiety——→increased need for nurturance and affection——→demands on relatives and husband in the form of food cravings——→ increase in food consumption ——→ excessive weight gain with discomfort and the threat of toxemia ——→social sanctions in the form of taboos..."

In accordance with the fixation theory, women are more likely to develop this pattern of dependency during pregnancy in societies where dependency during childhood is rewarded. And penalties for food taboo violations should be severe in societies where dependency is punished. These propositions are supported, as shown in Tables 13.4 and 13.5. Food taboos during pregnancy are seen as a method of weight control, and hence a means of protecting the health of the mother and her unborn child. Ayres's findings concerning sex taboos during pregnancy are less enlightening, although they are evidently not due to the over-indulgence of sexual desires during childhood.

Table 13.4. *Food Taboos and Reward for Dependency*

Number of Foods Tabooed	Reward for Dependency	
	Low	*High*
High	Azande	Arapesh
	Chenchu	Chagga
	Comanche	Chamorro
	Flathead	Dusun
	Lesu	Kurtatchi
	Paiute	Kwoma
	Tanala	Pukapuka
		Sanpoil
		Siriono
		Trobriand
		Venda
		Wogeo
Low	Alorese	Andamanese
	Ainu	Kutenai
	Baiga	Thonga
	Chiracahua	Witoto
	Hopi	
	Ifugao	
	Kiwai	
	Kwakiutl	
	Lakher	
	Lepcha	
	Manus	
	Marshallese	
	Seniang	

Fisher's Exact Test   p = .019
Taken from Ayres (1967: 116).

Table 13.5. *Penalties for Food Taboo Violations and Punishment for Dependency*

Penalties for Food Taboo Violations	Punishment for Dependency	
	Low	High
High	Andamanese Marshallese Tanala Wogeo	Ainu Baiga Chiracahua Ifugao Kutenai Kwoma Pukapuka Sanpoil Siriono Thonga Trobriands
Low	Arapesh Chagga Chamorro Flathead Hopi Kurtatchi Lepcha Paiute Venda	Alorese Azande Dusun Kwakiutl Lesu

Fisher's Exact Test p = .048
Taken from Ayres (1967: 118).

Summary

We know very little about the origin of taboos. Quite possibly, they do symbolize features of the environment that do not fit neatly into a society's organizational scheme of the universe. But this idea has not been tested holoculturally, and probably cannot be, given the nature of existing ethnographic materials. Holocultural studies have demonstrated that the importance of the long postpartum sex taboo as a cause of other cultural practices has been grossly over-estimated. It is interesting that the taboos which have drawn the most attention—menstrual, postpartum sex, food, pregnancy, incest —generally have something to do with human reproduction. Our understanding of taboos might be enhanced by research exploring the relationship between taboos and population growth. The long postpartum sex taboo, for example, is often seen as controlling the birth rate by increasing the time interval between births. And, Montgomery (1974) in a study of forty-one societies relates the degree of male participation in procreation to the intensity of menstrual taboos. Societies with little in the way of menstrual taboos are often ones where there are: pre and postpartum taboos; men present at birth; men present at female initiation rites; and myths with men involved in creation.

Chapter 14
SEXUAL BEHAVIOR

Cultural regulations may either prohibit, permit, or make obligatory certain categories of sexual behavior. Cultural regulations also
control sexual relations between certain categories of individuals,
and especially between certain categories of kin. Murdock (1949)
makes the important point that sex regulations do not exist in a
cultural vacuum. Rather, they are closely tied to specific institutions
and practices, most importantly marriage, ethnic differences, social
stratification, events in the reproductive cycle, ceremonies and
kinship. Ethnic differences and social stratification, for example,
prohibit relations between certain categories of people, while
encouraging relations between others. Stephens (1963: 245) tells us
that regulations govern four general categories of sexual behavior:
(1) occasional sex in specific circumstances such as during menstruation or following birth; (2) sex relations between kin; (3) premarital
sex; and (4) extra-marital sex. Holocultural research bearing on
occasional sex and sex relations with kin is reviewed in the chapters
on the Incest Taboo, Taboos, and Kin Relations.

Cultural Patterning of Sexual Behavior

Societies differ widely from one another in the degree to which
they prohibit or permit sexual activity in general. At one extreme are
the Rural Irish who do not discuss sex in the home, keep the sexes
separate, see sexual intercourse as debilitating, abhor nudity, and
prohibit all premarital sex (Messenger 1971). Near the other extreme
are the Mangaia of the Cook Islands who permit extramarital sex by
men and women, encourage premarital sex, permit autoeroticism by
children, and indulge in sexual intercourse as often as possible
(Marshall 1971).

The fascination of anthropologists with exotic behavior (in this
case total sexual restriction or total freedom) and with the notion of

cultural relativism has led some to assume that sexual practices are patterned consistently within cultural units. Broude (1976), for example, assumed that if a culture was restrictive about premarital sex it would be restrictive about sexual matters in general. But her research convinced her otherwise. Broude's work and the results of three other independent holocultural studies suggest that there is some, but certainly not total consistency in the patterning of sexual attitudes and practices both within and across cultures. There are some sexual practices and attitudes that regularly appear together, but there are probably a larger number that are not consistently associated with one another.

These holocultural studies suggest specific configurations of sexual practices and attitudes. Julia Brown (1952) reports that when the first of the behaviors in the following pairs is punished, so usually is the second:

(1) premarital sex for males and extramarital sex with another man's wife
(2) premarital sex for females and extramarital sex for females
(3) premarital sex for males and rape of an unmarried girl
(4) premarital sex for males and premarital sex for females
(5) extramarital sex for males and extramarital sex for females
(6) extramarital sex for males and rape

Stephens (1972) identifies two factors: a modesty-chastity factor, consisting of modesty in speech and dress, and restrictions on premarital and extramarital sex for women; and a taboo factor, consisting of kin avoidances, sex taboos during menstruation and following birth, and some other sex taboos.

Minturn, Grosse, and Haider (1969) report the following statistically significant positive associations for their sample of 135 small-scale societies:

Associated Variables	Pearson's r
sex charms and sex anxiety	.48
homosexuality accepted and marriages arranged	.31
homosexuality accepted and sex anxiety	.20
frequent homosexuality and marriages arranged	.26
frequent homosexuality and sex charms	.31
frequent homosexuality and homosexuality accepted	.39
frequent rape and severe punishment of rape	.47

Broude (1976), in perhaps the most careful of these four studies, uses a correlation matrix and Johnson's clustering solution to identify three clusters of sexual attitudes and practices:

Cluster 1	*Cluster 2*	*Cluster 3*
Premarital restrictiveness for girls	Double standard in extramarital sex	Impotence present
Premarital sex for boys infrequent	Extramarital restrictiveness for wives	Homosexuality present
Extramarital sex for husbands infrequent	No wife sharing	Extramarital restrictiveness for husbands
Arranged marriages		

Each cluster contains a list of specific sexual practices that are likely to appear together. While clusters one and three are interesting, cluster two is not. It seems obvious that if there is a double-standard in extramarital sex, there will be extramarital restrictions on wives and no wife sharing. Furthermore, it is important to keep in mind that the clusters are not entirely independent. Certain variables in clusters one and three are strongly related to variables in cluster two.

Given the large number of sexual practices and attitudes that these four studies have attempted to relate to one another, and the relatively few that do cluster together, we can only conclude that cultures are neither entirely consistent nor entirely inconsistent in their patterning of sexual behavior and attitudes.

Sexual Prohibition and Sexual Freedom

The best predictor, and perhaps the major cause of sexual restrictiveness, appears to be a high level of cultural complexity. Large-scale societies are almost always more restrictive about sexual matters than small-scale ones. The results of five independent holocultural studies summarized in Table 14.1 all support this conclusion.

Broude (1975) too finds complexity related to premarital sex restrictions, but suggests that the availability of caretakers during

Table 14.1. *Relationship between Cultural Complexity and*
Sexual Restrictions

Measure of Cultural Complexity	*Sexual Behavior*	*Source*
economic development	chastity	Hobhouse et al. (1915)
community size class stratification	punishment and repression of pre-marital sex	Prescott (1975)
political complexity technological complexity subsistence complexity community size belief in a high god	restriction of premarital sex	Murdock (1964)
rectangular and quadrangular floor plan	sanctions on premarital sex	Maxwell (1967)
Christianity, Islam, Buddism, Hinduism	chastity	Stephens (1972)
political development	modesty, chastity	Stephens (1972)

infancy and childhood is an even more important factor. And, Rosenblatt and Hillabrant (1972) find adultery less punished where divorce for childlessness is not allowed.

Y.A. Cohen (1969: 676) explains the association between complexity and restrictiveness in terms of political control:

> The control of sexuality is one of the most common elements in [the] legitimization of distant and centralized authority. Its stimulus is political . . . its goal [to] subvert local corporate groups.

In support of this hypothesis, Cohen finds that incorporative states are more restrictive and institute more severe sanctions for adultery, incest, and violation of celibacy than do other states. By incorporative state, Cohen means the centrally ruling bodies of incorporative nations. Incorporative nations are culturally similar, geographically contiguous societies. The incorporative state is the dominant society. Cohen's reasoning is the reverse of Unwin's (1934); whereas Cohen argues that the nature of the political system determines the degree of sexual restrictiveness, Unwin sees it the other way about:

> The cultural condition of any society in any geographical environment is conditioned by its past and present methods of regulating the relations between the sexes (Unwin 1934: 340).

Clearly, both hypotheses cannot be correct. They suggest opposing causal sequences. The key question is whether a change in the form of government precedes a change in the level for sexual repression or vice versa. The only solution to this controversy is a third study using diachronic data to establish the causal sequence.

A variety of other explanations have been offered for sexual repression. While no holocultural study that tests these ideas is notable for its methodological rigor, the hypotheses are interesting and deserve further study. Rosenblatt, Fugita and McDowell (1969) support the widely held belief that the amount of sexual freedom allowed engaged couples is partially determined by the amount of wealth to be transferred at marriage. As shown in Table 14.2, the more wealth to be transferred, the greater the restrictions. Zern (1969) argues that the importance of group membership leads to restrictions on premarital sex and premarital pregnancy. He finds that strongly lineal societies use severe sanctions against premarital sex.

Maxwell (1967) suggests that premarital sexual restrictions tend to be more severe when considerable opportunity exists for clandestine sexual encounters. Lastly, K. Eckhardt (1971: 7) sees sex as an exchange commodity possessed by women but controlled by men. Thus, sexual permissiveness for women is determined by the amount of control males exert over females and the strength of the male sex drive.

In regard to the antecedents of sexual freedom, the only finding that has been supported by more than one study is the relation between a warm climate and sexual permissiveness for both men and women (Maxwell 1967; Robbins, DeWalt and Pelto 1972: 337). DeLeeuwe (1970: 12-19) sees subsistence practices and political oppression as the key determinants of sexual freedom. He finds that people with the greatest degree of sexual freedom often reside in communities above the lowest subsistence level and without internal oppression such as slavery and social stratification. And Munroe, Whiting and Hally (1969; 88) suggest that societies which do not emphasize sex differences will be more likely to have institutionalized male transvestism.

Table 14.2. *Wealth Transfer and Change in Restrictions on Sexual Relations*

Restrictions following Onset of Betrothal	Magnitude of Wealth Transferred	
	None or Token Bride Wealth	Bride Wealth, Dowry, or Substantial Gift Exchange
More Restrictive	Rotuma	Burmese Chagga Fang Ganda Lakher Manus Monguor Siuai Thonga
Unchanged	Ainu Hano Iban Japanese Koreans Trumai	Ila Lau Lolo Somali
Less Restrictive	Lapps Merina Ona Tanala—Menabe Yokuts	Araucanians Mongo

Taken from Rosenblatt, Fugita and McDowell (1969).

Summary

Holocultural research has been confined largely to testing theories about the patterning of sexual behavior and about sexual restriction and freedom. The two most trustworthy conclusions are: societies are neither especially consistent nor inconsistent in the patterning of the various aspects of sexual behavior; and cultural complexity is closely related to sexual restrictiveness. More research is needed to explain this relationship between complexity and restrictiveness. Additionally, a number of intriguing theories suggested by Zern, Maxwell, and Eckhardt need careful testing. As mentioned above, additional ideas about sexual behavior can be found in the chapters on the Incest Taboo, Taboos, and Kin Relations. Theories about human reproduction are reviewed in the chapter on Over-population.

Chapter 15
Games and Game Involvement

Games have traditionally been viewed and studied by social scientists as symbolic representations or models of interpersonal interaction. Games, too, are sometimes interpreted as reflections of the dominant themes or patterns underlying other cultural institutions and activities.

The major body of empirical cross-cultural research on games and game involvement has been produced by John M. Roberts, Brian Sutton-Smith, their associates and students. Roberts and his group define games as recreational activities characterized by "organized play, competition, two or more sides, and criteria for determining the winner" (Roberts, Arth and Bush 1959: 597). This definition is somewhat narrower than those suggested by others who prefer to lump rather than distinguish among games, amusements, and play (Caillois 1961; Barnouw 1971). Perhaps the major limitation of Roberts's definition is that it effectively excludes from consideration a number of children's games; however, it is the one followed in all holocultural research on games, so we follow it here.

Games are relatively well described in the ethnographic literature. Most, but not all, cultures have games of some type. Two cultures without games are the Murngin of northern Australia and the YirYoront of Queensland, Australia. The Murngin probably never developed games of any kind. The YirYoront probably did have games at one time, although they disappeared following Western contact. But most other cultures have games, and the more complex the culture, the more games it will have.

All games can be classified as either games of physical skill, games of chance, or games of strategy. The outcome of games of physical skill is determined by the relative physical strength and dexterity of the participants. Those who are strong, fast, or agile usually win. Those who are weak, slow, or clumsy usually lose. Games of physical skill may require skill only (weightlifting, racing), skill and strategy (football), skill and chance (musical chairs), or skill, strategy and chance (steal the bacon). The outcome of games of strategy is determined by rational choices made by the participants. Those who make the wiser or better choices usually win. Games of strategy may involve strategy alone (chess) or strategy and chance (poker). The outcome of games of chance is beyond the direct control of the participants. Neither physical skill nor strategy influences the outcome. Winning is a matter of luck, as in dice, roulette, or bingo.

Games may serve any number of functions within the cultural system. In general, the more complex a culture, the more functions a game serves. Games have both sociogenic and psychogenic functions. Thus, games benefit both individuals who participate in or observe them and entire cultural systems.

Games are a major source of pleasure, recreation, and entertainment for both participants and spectators. Games also help foster a feeling of group solidarity and may provide some individuals with an emotional release from the tensions and frustrations of everyday life. In our own culture, athletic sports are often lauded for their function as character builders. It is commonly assumed that athletic success leads to success in life. Participation in athletic competition, it is suggested, encourages ambition, assertiveness, determination, dedication, leadership, respect for authority, toughness, cooperation, and self-confidence. Too often, though, assertiveness turns into destructiveness, dedication into narrow-mindedness, cooperation into self-gain, and self-confidence into arrogance (Tutko 1979: 108). Whether they build character or not, games do figure in the socialization process. Spelling bees, lotto, and other educational games are often used as teaching aids in elementary and secondary schools. The consensus of researchers is that educational games are more useful as attention getters than as learning aids (Avedon and Sutton-Smith 1971: 321). In all cultures, game involvement helps children learn the rules, values, and interpersonal coping techniques appropriate to their cultures.

From an economic perspective, it can be argued that gambling games are a means of redistributing goods and money. Often, though, redistribution takes the form of the rich getting richer and the poor getting poorer. In modern, industrialized nations, games are used in other ways as well—for the diagnosis and treatment of physical and emotional illness, in military exercises, and for fundraising, among others.

Cultures differ from one another in both the number and types of games found in their trait inventories. Some, like the Siriono of

Bolivia or the Mbuti Pygmies of central Africa, have only games of physical skill. Others, like the Chiricahua Apache of the southwestern United States or the Trukese of Micronesia, have games of physical skill and chance. And, still others, like the Azande of the Congo Basin, have games of physical skill, chance and strategy. When placed in developmental sequence, we find that games of physical skill appear first, games of chance second, and games of strategy last (Roberts, Arth and Bush 1959; Roberts and Barry 1976).

As we said earlier, Roberts and his associates have produced the major body of empirical cross-cultural research about games. Let us look at the results of their research.

Games as Expressive Culture

Roberts and his associates take games to be expressive models of other cultural activities. The themes or patterns found in other activities manifest themselves in or help determine the types of games found in a culture. Roberts also uses the conflict-enculturation hypothesis to explain cross-cultural variations in game types and game involvement. The conflict-enculturation hypothesis suggests that child rearing practices inevitably produce conflicts in the child. Involvement in games helps to reduce the conflict and socialize the child.

Games of Strategy

Games of strategy are expressive models of the kind of social interaction found in cultures with highly stratified social systems (Roberts, Arth and Bush 1959; Roberts, Sutton-Smith and Kendon 1963). As shown in Table 15.1, games of strategy are most often found in societies organized as states which have clear social class distinctions.

Games of strategy are also strongly associated with socialization for obedience—a goal of many parents in complex, small-scale societies (Roberts and Barry 1976; Roberts and Sutton-Smith 1962). The cross-cultural relationship between games of strategy and obedience training is replicated in a study of the game preferences of 1,900 school children in the United States (Roberts and Sutton-Smith 1962). Table 15.2 shows that girls, who are more likely to be raised to be obedient, more often participate in games of strategy than do boys, who are less likely to be raised to be obedient.

Table 15.1. *System Complexity and Games of Strategy*

		Games of Strategy Present	Games of Strategy Absent
Low Political Integration	Social Classes Absent	3 (Hopi, Woleaian, Zuni)	13 (Baiga, Copper Eskimo, Kiwai, Lesu, Murngin, Navaho, Papago, Siriono, Wapishana, Warrau, Witoto, Yaruro, Yungar)
	Social Classes Present	2 (Aleut, Nauru)	5 (Alor, Buka, Chukchee, Kwakiutl, Malekula)
High Political Integration	Social Classes Absent	2 (Achewa, Masai)	4 (Ainu, Gros Ventre, Maricopa, Menomini)
	Social Classes Present	12 (BaVenda, Chagga, Dahomey, Jukun, Korea, Lakher, Lamba, Mbundu, Siwa, Tanala, Vietnam, Yap)	2 (Kababish, Rwala Bedouin)

Table taken from Roberts, Arth and Bush (1959). Reproduced by permission of the American Anthropological Association, from the *American Anthropologist* 61(1959), 600.

Thus, the cross cultural and intra-cultural evidence suggests that games of strategy are models of social interaction between individuals in stratified social systems.

Games of Chance

Games of chance are expressive models of an uncertain, unpredictable world (Roberts, Arth and Bush 1959; Roberts and Sutton-Smith 1962, 1966; Barry and Roberts 1972). Games of chance occur most often in societies where life is insecure and infants are made to feel dependent. Specifically, games of chance are associated with a belief in active and benevolent gods, unreliable means of food preparation, frequent food shortages, frequent warfare, and feelings of anxiety. All of these factors are either likely sources or indicators of insecurity. In societies with these characteristics, the locus of control is often external rather than internal. Furthermore, in societies with games of chance, infants are often reared in such a way that as adults they will have problems managing their own feeling of dependency; infants are socially isolated, sleep apart from

Table 15.2. *Number of Games Differentiating between the Sexes at p = .05 or Better*

Game Classes	Nonsignificant	Favoring Girls	Favoring Boys
Strategy	Beast, Birds & Fish, Dominoes, Chess, Parcheesi, Scrabble, Tic Tac Toe, Clue, Monopoly	I've Got a Secret, Name That Tune, Checkers, Twenty Questions, I Spy	
Chance	Coin-Matching, Forfeits, Cards, Seven-up	Bingo, Spin the Bottle, Post Office, Musical Chairs, Letters, Colors, Initials	Dice
Pure Physical Skill	Quoits	Hopscotch, Jump Rope, Jacks, Tiddleywinks	Bowling, Horseshoes, Racing, Tug of War, Darts, Shuffleboard, Bows & Arrows, Throwing Snowballs, Shooting
Physical Skill and Strategy	Handball, Tennis, Volleyball Prisoner's Base, Fox & Hounds, Ping Pong	Pick up Sticks	Marbles, Wrestling, Boxing, Basketball, Football, Capture the Flag, Punt Back, Pool, Billiards, Baseball, Soccer

Taken from Roberts and Sutton-Smith (1962).

their mothers, are carried in rigid carrying devices, and rarely held or fondled. But they are neither neglected nor abused and their needs are met. This pattern of child rearing tends to produce adults who are often passive and submissive, but at the same time perceive themselves to be omnipotent and of central importance to those around them. Participation in games of chance reduces the inherent conflict caused by the conflicting feeling of dependency and omnipotence. Thus, it seems that games of chance reflect a view of the world as an uncertain place beyond direct human control.

Games of Physical Skill

Unlike games of strategy and chance, it is not clear what features of culture games of physical skill are modeled after. Roberts, Arth and Bush (1959) initially suggested that games of physical skill are somehow related to the nature of the physical environment. But no evidence has yet emerged to support this interpretation. It seems clear, though, that games of physical skill are most prominent in societies which value and encourage individual achievement. As shown in Table 15.3, games of physical skill are most numerous in societies which reward childhood achievement. Games of physical skill are also especially common in societies where children are made to feel anxious about not achieving. Table 15.2 shows that the association between achievement and games of skill holds in the United States as well. Achievement oriented boys are more likely to prefer games of physical skill than are obedience oriented girls.

Table 15.3. *Reward for Achievement and Number of Games of Physical Skill, Including Games of Physical Skill and Strategy*

	High	*Low*
9 or more games	Crow, Chagga, Comanche, Kwakiutl, Ojibwa, Aranda, Maori, Papago, Aleut, Gikuyu, Omaha, Pukapukans, Thonga, Chukchee	Nauruans, Hopi, Samoans, Koryak, Zuni, Kaska, Trukese
8 or fewer games	Araucanians, Mandan, Ganda, Bena	Venda, Konde, Masai, Muria, Navaho, Chewa, Balinese, Siriono, Tallensi, Tanala, Murngin, Woleaians, Ainu, Azande, Mbundu, Aymara, Wogeo, Lepcha, Lesu

Median number of games = 8
Median rating = 11
p. = .01

Taken from Roberts and Sutton-Smith (1962)

Riddles

A riddle is "a mystifying, misleading, or puzzling question posed as a problem to be solved or guessed often as a game" (Roberts and Forman 1971: 510); riddles may be expressive models of the kind of oral interrogation that takes place between subordinates and superordinates in complex societies. Some common subordinate-superordinate dyads are parent-child, student-teacher, employee-employer, and enlisted soldier-officer.

The presence of riddling in a culture (many cultures do not have riddling) is associated with childhood training for responsibility, political integration, jurisdictional hierarchy, oaths, ordeals, and games of strategy (Roberts and Forman 1971). Roberts's research is only preliminary. More study is needed on the effect of oral socialization practices, responsibility training, oral interrogation, and strategic competence on the development of both riddling and riddling competence.

Summary

Games serve as expressive models of specific themes that underlie other cultural activities and institutions. Roberts and Sutton-Smith's cross-cultural and intra-cultural investigations show games of strategy to be models of social interaction, and games of chance to be models of an uncertain world. The expressive roles played by riddles and games of physical skill are not yet clear.

The anthropological literature on games is fairly rich. Avedon and Sutton-Smith (1971) provide a broad bibliographic guide to the social science literature on games. Schwartzman (1976) is a review and extensive bibliography of anthropological studies of children's play. Huizinga (1955) is generally considered to be the classic interpretation of games and play.

Chapter 16
Fine Arts

All cultures have fine arts—painting, drawing, sculpture, carving, music, dance, architecture, and literature (Boas 1955). As perhaps the most obvious form of expressive culture, the arts serve any number of readily identifiable functions within a culture. Merriam (1964: 334), referring to Hallowell's interpretation, suggests that fine arts are mediative factors in human adaptation and create a "world of common meanings" for human societies. Art styles also may reflect and help promote feelings of group solidarity and ethnic identity (cf. Erickson 1976 on music). The fine arts evidently bring pleasure to both the artist and his or her audience, serve as a medium of communication both between individuals and between individuals and the supernatural world, and serve as a means for the expression of both positive and negative feelings.

For an activity of such acknowledged universality, anthropological interest in the arts has been surprisingly uneven, with much interest in oral literature, music, and the graphic arts, and much less interest in drama, architecture, and, until recently, dance (Merriam 1964: 333). One problem facing any cross-cultural investigator interested in the arts is that people in small-scale societies do not conceive of the arts as separate activities, as do people in complex societies. In small-scale societies, artistic activities are not differentiated from other activities like religious practices, subsistence activities, or warfare. Instead, art is seen as an integral part of those activities.

Only a small number of holocultural studies bear on the fine arts: three on painting and drawing, seven on music, one on dance, and none at all on drama and architecture. Nor are there any published holocultural studies on either oral or written literature that are devoted to forms or aesthetics for their own sake. Those that do exist use the content of folk tales as indirect measures of other traits that are often difficult to measure directly, as anxiety or fear

(McClelland, Davis, Wanner and Kalin 1972) or castration anxiety (Stephens 1962). For a discussion of the trustworthiness of these folk tale theme measures see Chapter 25 on Alcoholism.

A more general approach is Naroll, Benjamin, Fohl, Hildreth and Schaefer's (1971) pilot holohistorical study of creativity. A holo-historical study takes distinct time periods for particular cultures or civilizations as its sample units, in this case twenty-eight periods of ninety-nine years for civilizations in Europe, India, the Middle East, and China. Creativity is defined as "that quality in an artist or thinker which results in his art or thought being valued by succeeding generations. The greater a person's posthumous reputation among experts in his own field, the greater his creativity is taken to be" (Naroll et al. 1971: 182). Naroll and his associates ask: What socio-cultural factors tend to produce a greater number of creative people in one civilization than in another? Their analysis provides tentative support for Toynbee's (1957) claim that political fragmentation within a polity leads to increased creative output. For example, the arts flourished in renaissance Italy as princes and city-states sought to outdo one another. However, Naroll et al.'s analysis fails to support Banks and Textor's (1963) ideas concerning amount of wealth, Toynbee's (1957) concerning geographical expansion and degree of challenge, and Quigley's (1961) concerning governmental centralization.

Graphic Arts

While the three holocultural studies bearing on the graphic arts (Barry 1957; Fischer 1961; Robbins 1966a) offer some suggestive conclusions, all suffer from methodological flaws serious enough to render their findings untrustworthy—that is, they need further, more rigorous testing. The basic flaw in these three studies is the same. Each is based on the same judgemental sample of thirty small-scale societies, a sample which badly over-represents North America and the Insular Pacific, with twenty-two of the thirty coming from these two regions alone. Because of this sampling bias, these studies do not permit generalization to the world as a whole.

The most instructive of these studies is Fischer's on art style. Like Roberts on games and Swanson on religion, Fischer tests the proposition that art style will in some way reflect or be modeled on the social organization of the society of the artist. As shown in Table 16.1, Fischer finds that egalitarian societies—those with little or no social stratification according to Murdock's (1957) World Ethnographic Sample—have art styles characterized by simple design, empty space, symmetry, and figures without enclosures. Presumably, these art style features reflect the equality, comradeship, and lack of social boundaries that characterize social relations in egalitarian societies. On the other hand, hierarchical societies—those with social stratification—have art styles characterized by complex design, crowded space, asymmetry, and enclosed figures. These art style features presumably reflect the differentiation, control, and boundaries that characterize social relations in stratified societies. Fischer's other findings concerning the relationship between straight and curved lines, male solidarity, and polygyny are less clear. Not surprisingly, Fischer also supports Barry's (1957) earlier findings relating complexity of art design to severity of socialization. Barry also suggests that it is socialization for independence through punishment for dependence and reward for self-reliance that is most strongly related to complexity of design.

Robbins (1966a) suggests that art style (straight versus curved lines) may be reflected in house shape. Societies which prefer straight lines should have rectangular dwellings. Those with a preference for curved lines in art should have circular dwellings. Robbins, again using the Barry (1957) sample, finds the opposite. Curved lines go with rectangular dwellings; straight lines with circular dwellings. Aside from failing to confirm the hypothesis,

Table 16.1. Relationship of Social Stratification to Art Style

Art Style	Stratification of Peers		
	Low	High	
Simple design	16	1	p then becomes .000045
Complex design	3	8	
Space empty	12	2	p is less than .05
Space crowded	7	7	
Design symmetrical	12	2	p is less than .05
Design asymmetrical	7	7	
Enclosed figures	7	7	p is less than .05
No enclosed figures	12	2	

Fisher-Yates test used for probabilities.

Taken from Fischer (1961). Reproduced by permission of the American Anthropological Association from the *American Anthropologist* 63(1961), 83.

Robbins's findings conflict as well with those of Whiting and Ayres (1968), who find no relationship between line preference and dwelling shape. Dwelling shape seems to be mostly a matter of cultural complexity. As we mentioned in Chapter 5, the more complex the society, the more emphasis on straight lines and angles in architectural design.

A more sophisticated, though regionally limited study of art style is Wolfe's (1969) analysis of the social structural basis of African art. Through multivariate analysis, Wolfe attempts to determine what makes for high quality versus low quality art in fifty-three African societies. His measure of art quality is the subjective ratings of twenty-five Africanist scholars. Of the 105 independent variables studied, quality of art design is most parsimoniously predicted by four—large settlements, castes, nucleated settlements, and fixed settlements. The association between these four traits and art design suggests that cultural complexity has something to do with the quality of art produced by a culture. This interpretation is supported cross-culturally by Carneiro (1968, 1970) and McNett (1970a). Evidently, full-time painters, architects, sculptors and specialized craftsmen are found only in the most complex nonindustrialized societies such as ancient Rome, Egypt, and the Inca and Aztec Empires.

Music

A person's cultural background invariably affects his or her understanding and appreciation of the music of other cultures. Thus, until the fairly recent development of sensitive recording equipment that could be transported easily to and from the field, it was difficult to study the music of small-scale societies objectively. The music of small-scale societies often differs from Western music in a number of ways (Nettl 1956; Taylor 1973): (1) pitch or concern with pitch is often absent; (2) a five-point rather than a seven-point scale is often used; (3) monophonic rather than polyphonic sound is the rule; (4) melodies are often free-floating rather than ascending; (5) rhythm rather than tunes is emphasized; (6) percussion instruments are mainly used.

The major holocultural study of music is Lomax's (1968b) careful analysis of the song and performance styles of some 233 small-scale societies; it is the major product thus far of the Cantometrics Project at Columbia University. Cantometrics is the term coined by Lomax and Victor Grauer for the descriptive system they use to measure song performance features from recordings. The Cantometrics measure assesses twenty-seven performance features including, among others, the composition and nature of the singing group, instrumentation, tonal and rhythmic characteristics, phrase length, scale interval, vocal range, degree of embellishment, tempo, volume, and voice characteristics. Table 16.2. shows the worldwide regional variation for some of these cantometric features.

The holocultural phase of the Cantometrics Project produced two general conclusions about song style: first, that song and performance style reflect the overall level of cultural complexity of the society. Among those song features found associated with cultural complexity, as measured by subsistence type, were text wordiness and precision, narrowness of melodic interval, degree of melodic embellishment, and rhythmic freedom (Lomax 1968a, 1968b; Lomax and Berkowitz 1972). This general conclusion has not survived subsequent testing. It has been effectively discredited by Erickson; regional analysis of the cantometric data through factor and path analysis convinces Erickson (1976: 305) that:

> The song features posited to be correlates of such an evolutionary process can be explained exclusively by regional location (hence, prima facie, by history alone). There is a universal pattern of correlation linking population size, productive range, and sociopolitical complexity, but, in the same universal sense, song styles are not part of this nexus. On the other hand, certain vocal qualities and polyphony do appear to have universal cultural correlates. These correlates, however, are essentially independent of the presumed indicators of evolution.

The second general conclusion of the Cantometrics Project has not been subsequently discredited: that certain features of song style reflect themes which characterize the sociocultural system of the musicians and the listeners. For example, societies which restrict premarital sex for women have restricted—nasal and narrow—singing. Or, when females participate in subsistence activities, indicating economic cooperation between the sexes, there tends to be multiparted rather than just solo singing. Thus, it seems that in some ways song performance style reflects themes characteristic of other cultural activities.

The Cantometrics Project also points to a relationship between child rearing practices and song style (Erickson 1968; Ayres 1968,

Table 16.2. *Percent Frequency of Cantometric Traits by World Region*

Region	Polyphony	Good Tonal Blend	Repetitious Text	One-phrase Melody	Wide Singing Voice	Precise Articulation	Wide Melodic Intervals
South America	28	11	58	58	35	6	64
North America	8	17	69	26	35	5	79
Arctic Asia	13	0	52	72	50	14	64
Australia	6	3	22	44	10	13	3
Pacific	41	47	27	58	58	33	32
Africa	49	61	34	63	69	8	48
Tribal India	26	52	21	59	11	53	58
Old High Culture	6	5	7	36	17	57	24
Europe	28	28	7	19	51	50	21

Taken from Lomax (1968b: 119).

1973). Although the findings of these studies are suggestive, more research is needed, especially in regard to the measurement of the mediating psychodynamic mechanisms. The most striking finding is the one reported by Ayres regarding infant stress. Following Landauer and Whiting (1964) and others, Ayres finds that in societies where infants are stressed through piercing, molding, shaping, circumcision, clitoridectomy, cauterization, scarification, tooth evulsion, and injury leading to bleeding, songs tend to be in a regular rhythm, vocal range is generally one minor sixth or more, and accenting in singing is forceful.

Despite the problems with his evolutionary theory of song style— the regional patterns highlighted by Erickson and the untrust-worthiness of the complexity measure as discussed in Chapter 4— the Lomax group's contribution to ethnomusicology will long be felt. For as Harold Driver (1970b: 117) tells us:

> Lomax and his fourteen collaborators have made a significant salta-tion toward greater objectivity of expression of the similarities and differences in song styles among societies around the world. They have shown again that *scientific method* is applicable to any and all kinds of *human behavior,* whether conventionally subsumed under the sciences or the humanities by academicians. This book is a major achievement in ethnomusicology and cross-cultural method, regard-less of the amount of criticism that may be leveled at the details.

Dance

Dance style, like art style and song style, presumably reflects themes characteristic of other cultural activities. Using films and choreometric assessment sheets, Lomax, Bartenieff, and Paulay (1968) show that movement in dance is much like and thus reflects the most common, everyday movements found in the culture of the dancers. This similarity holds true for both the dance postures and the organization of the dance group. Furthermore, the Lomax group finds that the dances of complex cultures tend to involve many body parts, full use of movement, the use of various forms in many combinations, and three-dimensional transitory loops. Kaeppler (1978: 41-43) offers a lengthy critque of Lomax's conclusions and his entire approach. But, since her critique rests on intellectual pref-erence rather than empirical testing, it warrants no further dis-cussion here.

Summary

Like games and religion, certain aspects of art style are probably modeled on other features of the sociocultural system. The studies point to relationships between social organization and choral organization, between sexual restrictions and vocal restrictions, between dance movement and work movement, and between social complexity and design complexity. Holocultural research on the fine arts is just beginning and the Cantometrics data is among the most precise used in holocultural research. The sophistication of Lomax's work on music and dance, and Wolfe's on art offer a substantial base on which to build.

Section V. Socialization

Socialization is the process that turns infants into children and children into adults; it takes place in the context of a social group, either an entire society, or a sub-group within a society. Here we are interested only in socialization in a specific society or cultural group. Socialization starts during infancy and, in fact, continues throughout the whole life cycle. Infancy ends at about one and one-half to two years of age or when the infant first talks. Childhood is often divided into early and late: early childhood runs from about two years of age to six or seven years of age; late childhood begins around seven or eight and ends at puberty. The adolescent period is difficult to define temporally. Generally, it begins at puberty, but may last for only a few weeks or for as long as ten years. Adolescence, as a concept, is not widely recognized cross-culturally.

A large and varied group of researchers have been attracted to the study of socialization. Educators, demographers, home economists, political scientists, economists, jurists, historians, psychologists, sociologists, anthropologists, physicians, biologists, all study socialization. The list of specific topics studied is equally long and varied. Among those given the most attention are: learning; personality development; perceptual and cognitive development; internalization of norms; child-caretaker relations; the educational process; sex role socialization; and physical growth and development. The scope of the questions addressed by holocultural researchers is just as broad: (1) Why do cultures differ from one another in the way they raise their infants and children? (2) Do child rearing practices influence adult personality and the expressive systems of a culture? (3) Why do some cultures use initiation ceremonies during adolescence? (4) Does Freudian psychoanalytic personality theory survive cross-cultural testing? In the four chapters in this section we survey what has been discovered about these four questions through holocultural research.

Many anthropologists would argue with our use of the term socialization to identify the process that turns infants into adults (see, for example, J.W.M. Whiting 1968a). Over the years a number of alternative labels have been suggested. Kluckhohn (1939) preferred culturalization, Herskovits (1948) preferred enculturation, and Whiting and Child (1953) chose the more limited concept of child training. More recently, Burnett, Gordon and Gormley (1974) and Gearing and Tindall (1973) have been speaking of cultural transmission, especially in regard to education. Many anthropologists prefer Margaret Mead's (1963) distinction between socialization and enculturation. For Mead and for Rohner (1975) socialization means the universal process of learning, while enculturation means the learning process in a particular culture. Because it is the broadest label, we prefer to call the process that turns infants into adults socialization. So, when we say socialization we are referring to the same process that others may call enculturation or cultural transmission.

We do not equate socialization with education. We see education as only one part of the entire socialization process. Education is that part of the process that results in a person acquiring specific knowledge or skills through deliberate instruction or formal schooling. In most small-scale societies, a child learns specific skills and information through informal training or through an apprenticeship. Formal schooling is often absent. Modern industralized societies rely almost exclusively on formal education. The extent to which a small-scale society uses formal schooling or deliberate instruction outside the home is a function of the overall complexity of the society. The more complex a society, the more likely that children will be taught through formal schooling outside the home (Herzog 1962; Barry, Josephson, Lauer and Marshall 1977).

Much of the holocultural research discussed here is strongly influenced by what may be best called the Social Systems Model for Psychocultural Research shown in Figure 17.1. This model is also called the Whiting Model for Psychocultural Research (J.W.M. Whiting 1977). The Social Systems Model is complex and controversial; we will be referring to it often. In the summaries to Chapters 17 and 18 we review what we have learned about the trustworthiness of this model from holocultural research.

The anthropological literature on socialization is broad and complex. It is impossible to list all noteworthy books and articles. Instead, we mention only those works that, taken together, will lead the beginner to most of the relevant literature. The place to begin is with Margaret Mead (1928, 1930). Her two books made the cross-cultural study of socialization a legitimate anthropological enterprise. They also represent a theoretical position still held by many. Williams (1972) provides a book-length review of socialization, including an excellent bibliography of ethnographic studies. Burnett, Gordon and Gormley (1974) is a bibliographic guide to anthropological studies of education. Henry (1972) provides a useful checklist for the cross-cultural study of education. And, Gearing and Tindall (1973) emphasize the study of cognitive maps, hidden curriculums, and transactions in their review of research on cultural transmission. Draper (1974) touches upon the socialization of language, cognition, and sex roles. Munroe and Munroe (1977) and Munroe, Munroe, and B. Whiting (1981) review cross-cultural research on human development. Harrington and Whiting (1972) provide a lengthy though not entirely objective review of tests of the Social Systems Model. Finally, Rohner and Nielsen (1978) review the literature on parental acceptance and rejection.

We need to begin this chapter with a warning. Many of the holocultural studies of psychoanalytic theory, initiation ceremonies, and the effects of child rearing practices on adult personality reported in Chapters 18, 19, and 20, *are not direct tests of the hypotheses they claim to test.* These studies often suggest a causal sequence—involving a cause (long postpartum sex taboo, for example), and mediating psychodynamic mechanism (castration anxiety, for example), and an effect (male initiation ceremonies, for example). The cause and effect are measured, the mediating variable is not—it is simply assumed to be operating. Thus, they do not test the hypothesis. At best, these studies show only that specific child rearing circumstances and the postulated outcome are related. More about this and other shortcomings of holocultural tests of socialization theory in Chapter 20.

Chapter 17
Cross-Cultural Variations
in Child Rearing

Caretakers are people charged with meeting the physical and emotional needs of an infant child. In most societies, an infant or child is cared for to a large extent by his or her parents. Parents, or at least one parent, are usually the primary caretakers, disciplinarians, decision-makers, and teachers (Barry et al. 1977). But, as shown in Table 17.1, others—grandparents, siblings, playmates—may play a significant role in a child's life.

Table 17.1. *Percentage of Non-Parental Socialization Agents in Late Childhood*

	Agent			
Role	Grandparent	Mother's Brother	Sibling	Other Relative
Residence	11	6	0	21
Caretaker	46	4	65	21
Authority	41	19	54	34
Disciplinarian	38	19	51	31
Educator	20	9	31	23

	Agent			
Role	Teacher	The Child	Another Child	Non-Relative
Residence	0	4	22	27
Caretaker	2	28	5	29
Authority	10	4	11	27
Disciplinarian	15	16	14	29
Educator	41	0	27	50

Table revised from data in Barry, Josephson, Lauer and Marshall (1977). Data is from the Standard Cross-Cultural Sample.

Individual caretakers differ from one another in how they raise their children. For the most part, parents raise their children the way they were raised by their parents. Like individuals, entire cultures also differ from one another in how they raise their children. Some cultures stress independence and self-reliance, some compliance and cooperation. Some cultures punish children by withholding love and affection, some by beating and isolation. Some cultures accept their infants and children, some reject theirs. And, in some cultures parents are the primary caretakers, while in some, grandparents, siblings, or others fill that role. The extent of cross-cultural variation in child rearing is richly documented in the ethnographic literature. Few ethnographies ignore the subject of child rearing altogether. Barry and his associates have published a series of codes on child rearing variables for the 186 societies in Murdock and White's (1969) Standard Cross-Cultural Sample (Barry, Josephson, Lauer and Marshall 1977). This data and others like it by Whiting and Child (1953) and Barry, Bacon and Child (1967) have been used to test a number of theories about the causes of cross-cultural variation in child rearing. Many of these studies test ideas about the degree to which infants and children are *indulged.* By indulgence researchers usually mean how often and how quickly an infant's or child's demands are met. Degree of indulgence in a family, community or entire society is often measured on a continuum from neglectful at one extreme to lenient and affectionate at the other. Most societies are indulgent with their infants and children. Rohner (1975) has been studying child rearing in terms of parental acceptance/rejection of their children; acceptance is demonstrated by love, warmth, and affection, rejection by physical and verbal abuse, indifference, and neglect.

The Social Systems Model shown in Figure 17.1 predicts that cultural maintenance systems directly influence an infant or child's learning environment. Maintenance systems are defined as the "economic, political, and social organizations of a society surrounding the nourishment, sheltering, and protection of its members" (Harrington and Whiting 1972: 471). Many of the theories reviewed here operate within this model. A few do not. We review those that do first; then we review the alternative theories.

Maintenance Systems and the Learning Environment

The household structure and the nature of the subsistence economy are two maintenance systems that clearly influence an

Figure 17.1. *Social Systems Model for Psychocultural Research*

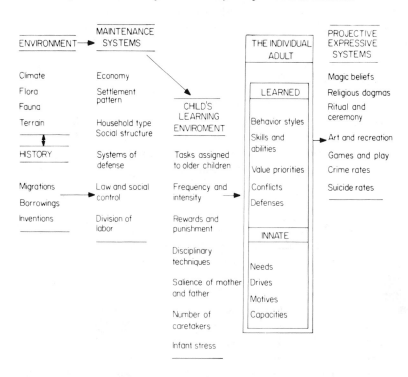

Taken from J.W.M. Whiting (1977: 30).

infant or child's learning environment. The household structure is often the more important of the two.

The best assurance that an infant or child will be treated warmly and affectionately in nuclear, joint and lineal family households and have his or her needs met, is the availability of alternative caretakers in the household (J.W.M. Whiting 1960; Minturn and Lambert 1964; Rohner 1975; Levinson 1979). The presence of multiple caretakers in the home almost guarantees that an infant or child will be indulged and accepted, although who the caretakers are makes a difference. Siblings, for example, are not especially warm and loving, but fathers and grandparents in the home on a day-to-day basis help ensure that a child will be held and treated warmly. On the other hand, an infant or child is more likely to be rejected or neglected when raised by his or her mother alone. A woman in continual contact with her child is more likely to abuse that child emotionally than a woman who has other adults in the home or nearby to help her. Mothers who are often away from the home do not tolerate insubordination from their children, but are not much concerned about irresponsible behavior.

Household type seems to affect child rearing practices. In extended family households where multiple caretakers are readily available, infants are frequently indulged. In nuclear family households where only two caretakers are generally available, infants may or may not be indulged. And, in mother-child households where the mother is the only caretaker, children run a fair risk of being neglected, and sometimes rejected in the form of physical and verbal abuse.

The subsistence economy also influences child rearing practices. Food accumulating societies (agriculturalists and pastoralists) raise their children to be responsible, obedient, and compliant; non-accumulating societies (hunters, gatherers, fishers) raise their children to be independent, self-reliant, and achievement-oriented (Barry, Child and Bacon 1967). Why subsistence practices and child rearing practices are related is not yet clear. A number of rival explanations have been suggested. Barry, Child and Bacon (1967) argue that parents will encourage the development of the personality traits in their children that are most likely to enable those children to become functioning members of the society. Thus, in accumulating societies where food is shared, people fare best if they are cooperative, compliant, and responsible. But, in non-accumulating societies where food is often scarce and people must fend for themselves, people fare best being independent, self-reliant, and achievement oriented. This interpretation is disputed by Romney (1965) who suggests instead that: in accumulating societies the father is often absent from the home; so the mother is the primary caretaker; and since women tend to emphasize compliance more than men, accumulating societies emphasize compliance. The key weakness of Romney's argument is his assumption that in accumulating societies men and not women are often absent from the home. In fact, as J.W.M. Whiting (1977) points out, in agricultural societies it is often women who spend most of their day working the fields. Whiting goes on to argue that in agricultural societies responsibility is stressed in children because women are often outside the home and their children must perform the household chores and care for their younger siblings.

Along the same lines as Barry, Child and Bacon (1967), Rohner (1975) finds that hunters accept their children while pastoralists tend slightly to reject theirs. In Rohner's sample, no hunting society—not even one—rejects its children. This finding is explained by Rohner in terms of Darwinian natural selection. He reasons that, in order to survive, hunters must be emotionally stable people who can fare well on their own. And, since parental acceptance leads to emotional stability, those hunting societies which accept their children have a selective advantage over those which reject theirs. According to this reasoning, hunting societies which accept their children survive, hunting societies which reject their children die out.

The level of societal scale or complexity may also influence child rearing practices. Rohner finds that people in complex societies— those with high levels of political integration and social stratification and a fixed settlement pattern—tend to reject their children to a somewhat greater extent than people in less complex societies. Hines and Martindale (1974), in a less rigorous study than Rohner's, find no evidence that cultural complexity influences maternal behavior towards infants. It seems likely to us that cultural complexity influences child rearing practices, although perhaps indirectly through some intervening variable such as household structure or type of economy. But, more cross-cultural research is needed before we can say that this is the case, and if so, how and why.

Alternatives to the Maintenance System Model

Hines and Martindale (1974) offer an intriguing alternative to the maintenance system model. Drawing upon the findings of laboratory research with rodents, they suggest that the degree of maternal behavior exhibited by a woman is a function of the degree of rhinencephalon or smell-brain activity within her central nervous system. Using the frequency of references to odors in folk tales as their proxy measure of rhinencephalic activity, they find that in societies where odor references are frequent, infants are weaned and trained for independence late, and children are generally protected from socialization anxiety and painful experiences. This rhinencephalic theory would be powerful and convincing were it not for one serious and potentially fatal flaw. There is no empirical evidence supporting the validity of frequency of odor references in folk tales as a proxy measure of rhinencephalic activity. We find no reason to believe that odor references are a manifestly valid measure. Convincing empirical evidence is needed.

Birth order certainly influences child rearing practices. Cross-culturally, first borns are treated different from last borns (Rosenblatt and Skoogberg 1974). First borns often have more elaborate birth ceremonies, more duties, more authority over siblings, and receive more respect from siblings. Last borns are more often spoiled and indulged to the point of dependence. In general, first born males fare better than first born females.

Climatic conditions may also influence child rearing practices. J. W. M. Whiting (1964) and the Social Systems Model predict that environmental conditions do directly influence child rearing practices. For example, mother-child households are most common in warm climates—and in mother-child households children are less often indulged. Robbins, De Walt and Pelto (1972) draw a direct link between climate and child rearing. They report that in societies where the average winter temperature exceeds 50°F, aggressive behavior in children tends to be indulged.

Another possible determinant of child rearing practices is suggested by Rohner's (1975), and Minturn and Lambert's (1964) research. It seems plausible to view the indulgence/non-indulgence of infants and the acceptance/rejection of children as one aspect of a wider cultural pattern of acceptance or rejection. We are suggesting that some cultures view the world as open and accepting while others view the world as closed and rejecting. This idea is supported tangentially by some holocultural research. Rohner, for example, finds that children are more loved when they are planned for and when their parents are concerned about their needs for food, drink, and comfort. Additional support for this acceptance/rejection model comes from the work of Y.A. Cohen (1961) and Stewart and Jones (1972). Cohen reports that children who are fed on demand tend to share food and wealth as adults. And, Stewart and Jones find childhood indulgence related to high general indulgence, display of affection, drive reduction, and satisfaction of an infant's needs. Thus, there is tentative support for the notion that some cultures are characterized by a general pattern of acceptance and concern for others—either children or adults.

Summary

Holocultural research on the causes of cross-cultural variation in child rearing has produced some clear results. First, as the Social Systems Model predicts, two maintenance systems—the household structure and the nature of the economy—influence child rearing practices. Alternative caretakers living in the household help ensure that an infant or child will be indulged and accepted. An infant raised by the mother alone is far more likely to be rejected. The nature of the subsistence economy helps determine whether a child will be accepted or rejected, or pushed toward self-reliance and independence or compliance and cooperation. It is not always clear why the economy influences child rearing practices. Birth order also matters, with first borns almost always treated differently from last borns. The level of cultural complexity of a society and the amount of rhinencephalic activity in a woman's brain may also matter; more research is needed to support the validity of the rhinencephalic theory.

Chapter 18
Child Rearing, Adult Personality, and Expressive Systems

Psychological anthropology is the study of the relationship between the individual and the wider cultural system. The study of the effects of child rearing practices on adult personality and cultural expressive systems is one type of psychological anthropology research. The broad field of psychological anthropology is somewhat fragmented and disorganized. At least four rival theoretical models compete for dominance. One of the models, and the one most often followed in holocultural research, is the Social Systems or Whiting Model. J.W.M. Whiting (1977) suggests that the learning environment influences adult personality and behavior, which in turn influences cultural expressive systems. This model has been diagrammed by LeVine (1973) as $C_1 \longrightarrow P \longrightarrow C_2$. Levine discusses three other models. First, the personality-is-culture model (P=C) of Mead (1953), Benedict (1946), and Gorer (1948). Here, individual personality is seen as a reflection of the cultural system. Little attention is paid to causation or causal direction. Second, the psychological reductionism model ($P \longrightarrow C$) where individual behavior or personality traits are seen as the basic cause of cultural institutions. McClelland (1961) follows an elaborated form of this model in his widely influential research on achievement motivation. Using cross-cultural, cross-national, and case study materials, McClelland makes a case for the proposition that a strong need to achieve in individuals leads to a high level of societal economic achievement. Third, the two systems model ($P \rightleftharpoons C$) followed by Inkeles and Levinson (1954) and Spiro (1961). Here, the typical personality configuration of the members of a group and the cultural system are seen as separate systems. For a society to function and survive, the two systems must change to accomodate one another. Only then can stability be achieved.

As we said, the Social Systems Model of Whiting is the one most followed in holocultural research. With the exception of McClelland's use of psychological reductionism, the other models have so far escaped holocultural testing.

The Social Systems Model

The right side of the Social Systems Model predicts that the learning environment influences adult personality which in turn influences the systems of a culture. The learning environment is presented as a direct cause of adult personality and behavior. This idea is, of course, not new. It underlies the thinking of many personality theorists, including psychoanalysts and behaviorists who disagree over most other matters. The hypothesized relationship between the learning environment and expressive systems is more complex:

> All the cultures we have thus far studied make rather heavy demands on their children, many of which demands have been described in our discussion of learning environments. Such demands, we believe, produce enduring conflicts that would be intolerable and would soon be replaced by neurotic symptoms unless there were culturally approved modes of defending against them. We assume, then, that a given culture's projective-expressive systems arise out of these defensive struggles—partly consist, in fact, of these necessary and socially accepted defenses—and differ from those of other cultures to the degree that its members have distinctive conflicts to defend against (J.W.M. Whiting 1977: 39).

Dozens of studies operating within the theoretical boundaries of the Social Systems Model test this. The results of these studies are listed in Table 18.1. Many of these findings are discussed in more detail in other sections of this book. For example, the relationship between religion and child rearing practices is discussed in the chapter on religion.

Column One of Table 18.1 lists the specific child rearing practice or condition which the author cites as the causal factor. These child rearing practices and conditions are divided into nine categories: (1) Indulgence and Acceptance, (2) General Parent-Child Relationships, (3) Physical Treatment and Discipline, (4) Sex Training, (5) Oral Training, (6) Anal Training, (7) Independence Training, (8) Achievement Training, (9) Aggression Training. Column Two lists the personality traits or cultural practices that are found associated

Table 18.1. *Child Rearing, Adult Behavior, and Expressive Systems*

Child Rearing Practices and Conditions	Adult Behavior and Expressive Systems	Source
1. Indulgence and Acceptance		
indulgence	frequent drunkenness	Field 1962:66
		Davis 1964:72
	not related to drunkenness	Bacon, Barry and Child 1965:35
	aggression	Allen 1972:263
	crime	Allen 1972:265
	undifferentiated	Zern 1976:15
	sense of time	Zern 1970:206
	alcohol use by adults only	Blum 1969:162
lack of indulgence	aggressive deities	Lambert, Triandis and Wolf 1959:168
	punishment of aggression in folk tales	Child, Storm and Veroff 1958:489
	jurisdictional hierarchy	Zern 1976:8
fed on demand	share wealth	Cohen 1961:318
not fed on demand	amass and hoard wealth	Cohen 1961:318
acceptance in childhood	generous, responsible	Rohner 1975:170
rejection in childhood	negative world view	Rohner 1975:97, 101, 103, 168
	negative self-evaluation	
	problems with management of hostility	
	dependency	
	emotional instability	
	supernatural seen as hostile	
	fear of ghosts at funerals	Whiting 1967:155
2. Parent-Child Relationships		
mother-child household (father-absent)	couvade	Munroe et al. 1973
	males segregated at puberty	Kitahara 1975:6
	deliberate instruction	Herzog 1962:319
mother-child sleeping arrangement	bride theft	Ayres 1974:247
	bride raiding	Ayres 1974:249
	sexual restraint	Stewart and Jones 1972:62
	male initiation ceremonies	Whiting et al. 1958:364
	painful initiation	J.K. Brown 1963:843
infant carried by mother	songs in regular rhythm	Ayres 1973:395
mother-child closeness	narcissism	Slater and Slater 1965:255
mother-child separation	early menarche	Whiting 1965:228
mother-infant separation	taller adult males	Gunders and Whiting 1968:199
father-child closeness	games of chance	Barry and Roberts 1972:300
less important role for parents	weak superego	Whiting and Child 1953:246

Table 18.1. *continued*

Child Rearing Practices and Conditions	Adult Behavior and Expressive Systems	Source
father not the disciplinarian	male initiation ceremonies	Whiting et al. 1958:369
father important	bride-theft	Ayres 1974:248

3. Physical Treatment and Discipline

infant stress	early menarche	Whiting 1965:226
	taller adults	Landauer and Whiting 1964 Gunders and Whiting 1968
	more accent and wider range in songs	Ayres 1968:213
	witchcraft accusations	Whiting and Child 1953
pain infliction	slavery	Prescott 1975:12
	polygyny	
	inferior status for women	
	aggressive deities	
	tobacco use by both sexes	Blum 1969:162
rigid carrying device	games of chance	Barry and Roberts 1972:300
physical punishment	long menstrual taboo	Stephens 1962:104
frustrating discipline practices	military glory and sadism	Eckhardt 1975:7
absence of pain infliction	benevolent deities	Lambert, Triandis and Wolf 1959:168
love-oriented punishment	fear of death	Lester 1975:229
discipline practices	not related to aggression	Lester 1967b:735
severe socialization	complex and representative art design	Barry 1957:383
physical protectiveness	games of chance	Barry and Roberts 1972:300
general socialization anxiety	fear of others	Whiting and Child 1953:267
	patient responsibility for illness	Whiting and Child 1953:234
	not related to aggression	Palmer 1970:64

4. Sex Training

severe sex training	homosexuality accepted	Minturn et al. 1969:309
	long menstrual taboo	Stephens 1962:102 Stephens 1967:69
	long sex taboo during pregnancy	Ayres 1967:119
sexual repression	narcissism	Eckhardt 1971:9
	militarism	Eckhardt 1971:9
sexual anxiety	ego strength	Allen 1967:60

Table 18.1. *continued*

Child Rearing Practices and Conditions	Adult Behavior and Expressive Systems	Source
	sexual explanations for illness	Whiting and Child 1953:159
	love magic	Shirley and Romney 1962:102-8
castration anxiety	long menstrual taboo	Stephens 1967:89
sexual permissiveness	oral and dependency explanations for illness	Prothro 1960:152
sexual satisfaction	crime	Allen 1972:265
	sexual therapies for illness	Whiting and Child 1953:196

5. Oral Training

inadequate oral satisfaction	anal and dependency explanations for illness	Prothro 1960:152
	concern with affection romantic love as a basis for marriage	Rosenblatt 1966:336-338
oral anxiety	ego strength	Allen 1967:60
	oral explanations for illness	Whiting and Child 1953:130
	drug use	Blum 1969:161
oral satisfaction	religious rituals	Spiro and D'Andrade 1967:200
	oral therapies for illness	Whiting and Child 1953:203

6. Anal Training

anal anxiety	ego strength	Allen 1967:60
	anal explanations for illness	Whiting and Child 1953:203-204

7. Independence Training

independence training	aggressive deities	Lambert, Triandis and Wolf 1959:164
	not related to aggression	Allen 1972:263
	marriage arrangement by the couple	Minturn et al. 1969:309
	patient activity during illness	Kiev 1960:199
assertiveness	individual singing	Ayres 1968:191
self-reliance	aggressive deities	Lambert, Triandis and Wolf 1959:166
	aggressive achievement	Stewart and Jones 1972:60
	not related to aggression	Allen 1972:263
	alcohol use by males stimulant use by males of all ages	Blum 1969:161

Table 18.1. *continued*

Child Rearing Practices and Conditions	Adult Behavior and Expressive Systems	Source
obedience	drunkenness	McClelland et al. 1972:27
	games of strategy	Roberts et al. 1963:189
	autonomic oaths and ordeals	Roberts 1967:188
	drug use	Blum 1969:160-61
	achievement in folk tales	Child et al. 1958:485
compliance	cohesive singing	Ayres 1968:191
	sobriety	Barry 1969:31-2
	group initiation with masks and/or whips	Granzberg 1973a:5
responsibility	games of chance	Roberts and Sutton-Smith 1962:173
	riddling	Roberts and Forman 1971
	autonomic oaths and ordeals	Roberts 1967:188
	tobacco not used	Blum 1969:161
dependency satisfaction	religious rituals	Spiro and D'Andrade 1967:200
	food taboos	Ayres 1967:115
	dependency explanations for illness	Whiting and Child 1953:209-211
dependence anxiety	patient activity during illness	Kiev 1960:196
	oral and dependency explanations for illness	Prothro 1960:152
	ego strength	Allen 1967:60
	personal crime	Bacon et al. 1963:298
	not related to crime	Allen 1972:265
punishment for dependency	severe sanctions for food taboo violations	Ayres 1967:117
responsibility anxiety	games of chance	Roberts and Sutton-Smith 1962:173
responsibility and self-reliance anxiety	theft	Bacon et al. 1963:296
	not related to crime	Allen 1972:265
	military glory and sadism	Eckhardt 1971:7

8. Achievement Training

pressure to achieve	theft	Bacon et al. 1963:296
	not related to crime	Allen 1972:266
	narcissism	Slater and Slater 1965:255
	drunkenness	McClelland et al. 1972:67
	aggressive achievement	Stewart and Jones 1972:60
	achievement in folk tales	Child et al. 1958:485
	games of physical skill	Roberts and Sutton-Smith 1962:174
achievement anxiety	narcissism	Slater and Slater 1965:255

Table 18.1. *continued*

Child Rearing Practices and Conditions	Adult Behavior and Expressive Systems	Source
9. Aggression Training		
aggression	warfare	Russell 1972:295
aggression anxiety	displaced aggression	Wright 1970:352
	fear of others	Whiting and Child 1953:281
	aggression therapies and	Whiting and Child 1953:161
	explanations for illness	Kiev 1960:200-204
		Prothro 1960:152

with these child rearing practices. Column Three provides citations to the studies.

All of the relationships listed in Table 18.1 are ones between specific child rearing practices and specific adult behaviors or cultural practices. Taken as a group these findings support the idea that childhood experiences influence adult personality and behavior, although no study draws a direct link between the two. All of the evidence is correlational and inferential. The studies by Whiting and Child (1953), Prothro (1960) and Kiev (1960), among others, claim to support the general assumption that exaggerated adult behaviors reflect development phases which were either over- or under-indulged in infancy and childhood. But, Whiting and Child's findings have been questioned by Guthrie (1971: 319); using computer technology unavailable to Whiting and Child and borrowing from Campbell and Fiske (1959), Guthrie argues:

> Just as a test should correlate highly with its own criterion variables and lowly with criteria for other traits, so an index of a socialization variable should relate as highly as possible with an index of its predicted behavior sequelae, and lowly with indices of behavior which are theoretically related to other socialization antecedents. In short, experiences predisposing to oral behavior should correlate highly with later oral manifestations but lowly with manifestations theoretically related to sexual or anal dynamic features.

Guthrie computes just such a matrix of correlations for Whiting and Child's data. He finds that the off-diagonal correlations—for example, those between anal training and oral explanations for illness—are often as high as those predicted by Whiting and Child's theory. This re-analysis, of course, casts doubt on the validity of the negative fixation theory tested by Whiting and Child. Additionally, these studies fail to measure the key psychodynamic mechanisms—fixation and anxiety—that supposedly link the childhood and adulthood variables. But, more about this in the chapter on psychoanalytic personality theory.

The findings linking child rearing practices with expressive systems listed in Table 18.1 are not especially trustworthy either. Many of the cultural practices listed in the table can be accounted for equally well by rival sociogenic theories. And many of these rival sociogenic theories have been tested and supported holoculturally. For example, some of the psychogenic theories of religious beliefs listed in Table 18.1 are challenged by the sociogenic explanations of Swanson (1960) and Davis (1971). Likewise, as we will see in the next chapter, some of the psychogenic theories of initiation rites listed in the table are challenged by the sociogenic ones of Y.A. Cohen (1964a), Young (1965) and Precourt (1975).

However, one set of findings reported in the table requires further comment. Landauer and J.W.M. Whiting (1964), J.W.M. Whiting (1964) and Gunders and J.W.M. Whiting (1968) in a series of holocultural studies, and J.W.M. Whiting, Landauer and Jones (1968), Gunders and J.W.M. Whiting (1964, 1968) and Landauer (n.d.) in a series of longitudinal and case studies report a reasonably strong and consistent relationship between infant stimulation (stress) and physiological development. Both cross-culturally and intraculturally, infants who are stressed before the age of two years by piercing, molding, or separation from their mothers are likely to be taller adults by two to two and one-half inches and the stressed girls are likely to have their first menarche at an earlier age. Along the same lines, Rohner (1975) finds that adults are larger in societies where children are accepted than in societies where children are rejected.

Chapter 19
Initiation Rites

Initiation rites are ceremonies that mark the transition from childhood to adulthood in many societies. A particular society may have rites for both men and women (although they are always held separately), for men only or women only, or no rites at all. About one-half of all known small-scale societies have initiation rites of some type. Apparently, initiation rites for women are more common, but rites for men are usually more intense and more dramatic. The general discussions of van Gennep (1960) and Y.A. Cohen (1964a) suggest seven universal characteristics of initiation rites:

(1) Elders preside over the rite, and are often members of a male initiate's descent group who have some role in his upbringing.

(2) Parents of initiates usually have no role in the rite.

(3) The rite involves education in the basic rules and practices of the group.

(4) The rite often involves physical hardship including scarification, circumcision, clitoridectomy, severe punishment, and denial of food or sleep.

(5) All boys or girls of the appropriate age must be initiated; if one must go through the rite, all must go through it.

(6) The rite is focussed on the group of initiates, not on any single initiate.

(7) The opposite sex is prohibited from viewing the rite.

Like other rites of passage, including those for birth, marriage, and death, initiation rites tend to proceed through stages of separation, transition, and incorporation. During separation the initiate is removed from the childhood home and segregated with other initiates. Once so isolated, the initiates are between statuses, neither children nor adults. During the transition stage, the initiates are introduced to or learn the basic rules and practices of the society through memorization, instruction by elders, physical coercion, and other like techniques. When the transition stage ends, the initiates are ready to assume their new role as adult members of the community. During the incorporation stage the new, adult status of the initiates is dramatized and given public recognition.

Initiation rites vary widely from one society to another in intensity, duration, and importance in the overall socialization process. At one extreme are societies like our own which have no formal rites to mark the transition from childhood to adulthood. At the other extreme are societies like the Thonga and Kwoma which use painful hazing, seclusion from women, and circumcision in their male initiation ceremonies. The variation in initiation rites has made it difficult to define and measure initiation rites cross-culturally. As shown in Table 19.1, those who have tried have often come up with different measures. The measures used in the six major holocultural studies of initiation rites listed in Table 19.1 differ in some important ways. First, Young (1962, 1965) is the only investigator to use an ordinal (Guttman) scale; the others all rely on simple yes/no dichotomies. Secondly, J.W.M. Whiting et al. (1958) and Y.A. Cohen (1964a, 1964b) include seclusion in their measures, but Young purposely omits it. He finds that it does not scale with the other items in his scale. And, third, Granzberg (1973a) measures only one type of initiation rite while the others look at all forms. There is no empirical evidence that any one of these measures is superior to any other, although Young's seems to be the most careful and useful.

A wide variety of explanations have been offered for initiation rites, and for such practices as circumcision and segregation of males at puberty—which are often important elements of the rite (Freud 1918; Benedict 1946; Bettelheim 1954; Eliade 1958; Whiting et al. 1958; Read 1960; Gluckman 1962; Young 1962, 1965; Burton and J.W.M. Whiting 1963; Judith Brown 1963; Y.A. Cohen 1964a, 1964b; Weiss 1966; Harrington 1968; Granzberg 1973a; Kitahara 1974, 1975; Precourt 1975). The twelve theories that have been tested holoculturally can be loosely classified as either psychogenic or sociogenic (Young 1965; Y.A. Cohen 1964b; Naroll 1970b). In this chapter we first review the psychogenic theories, then the sociogenic ones, and we close the chapter with a methodological critique of the studies testing these theories.

Psychogenic Theories

In their most elaborate form, psychogenic theories follow the Social Systems Model in its most elaborate form; none of these

Table 19.1. *Measures of Initiation Rites*

Study	*Variable*	*Measure*	*Scale*
Whiting et al. (1958)	male initiation	Presence of one or more of: painful hazing, genital operations, seclusion from women, tests of manliness	dichotomy
Burton and Whiting (1963)	male initiation	Presence of one or more of: painful hazing, genital operations, seclusion from women, tests of manliness	dichotomy
Young (1962; 1965)	initiation	Guttman scale: (4) affective social response, (3) organized social response, (2) personal dramatization, (1) minimal social recognition, (0) undramatic recognition only	ordinal
J. K. Brown (1963)	female initiation	one or more ceremonial events for girls between eight and twenty years of age	dichotomy
Cohen (1964a, 1964b)	initiation	physical pain, isolation from family	dichotomy
Granzberg (1973a)	Hopi type initiation	rites with masks and/or disciplinary whippings	dichotomy

theories is trustworthy, as none measures the mediating variable—the psychodynamic mechanism. Most, however, are not so complex and follow a simpler model, shown in Figure 19.1.

Five psychogenic theories of initiation rites or some component of initiation rites have been tested holoculturally. Some of these theories overlap, and some are contradictory. All are best conceptualized by diagramming the causal sequence.

In the first study to formally test a psychogenic theory of initiation rites, J.W.M. Whiting et al. (1958) predicted the following sequence that was later replicated by Stephens (1962)—see Figure 19.2.

Burton and J.W.M. Whiting (1963) and Judith Brown (1963) working on painful female rites, revised the information in Figure 19.2, as shown in Figure 19.3.

And, J.W.M. Whiting (1964) followed with an elaborate theory for circumcision, shown in Figure 19.4.

Kitahara (1974, 1975) disagrees with Whiting. He sees polygyny as a cause, not an effect, and too little father-son contact as being more important than too much mother-son contact—see Figure 19.5.

And, Granzberg (1973a) offers a psychogenic theory for what he calls Hopi type initiation rites, rites characterized by the use of masks and whippings—see Figure 19.6.

These are the five psychogenic theories of initiation rites that have been studied holoculturally. Each is claimed to have been supported. Actually, none has been tested. At best, the tests do no more than demonstrate a weak relationship between certain child rearing practices and the presence, absence, or form of initiation rites.

Sociogenic Theories

Sociogenic theories do not view the individual personality as an intervening variable mediating between one cultural factor and another. Rather, the individual is seen as operating within the context of the social system. Most sociogenic theories endorse the model shown in Figure 19.7. The best known sociogenic explanation is Young's (1962, 1965) status dramatization theory—see Figure 19.8. Closely related to Young's theory, are Judith Brown's (1963) explanations of female rites—see Figure 19.9. Y.A. Cohen (1964a, 1964b) conceptualizes the transition from childhood to adulthood somewhat differently; he sees the transition as a two-stage process, with stage one occurring between eight to ten years of age and stage two at the time of physiological puberty—see Figure 19.10. For Cohen extrusion (casting out and forbidding the child to sleep in the parents' house) and brother-sister avoidance are more important and more common tie-breaking practices than initiation rites.

Harrington (1968) offers sociogenic explanations for circumcision and supercision—see Figure 19.11. And, Precourt (1975) in a discussion of education in general, relates initiation rites to the level of societal complexity—see Figure 19.12.

Figure 19.1. *Model for Psychogenic Theories of Initiation*

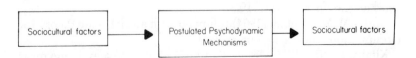

Figure 19.2. *Model for a Psychogenic Theory of Initiation Rites*

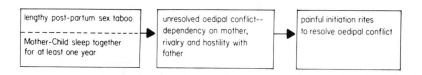

Figure 19.3. *Model for a Psychogenic Theory of Painful Initiation Rites*

Figure 19.4. *Model for Whiting's Theory of Circumsicion at Puberty*

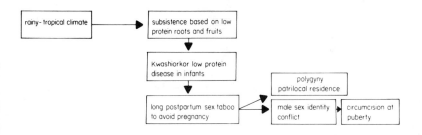

Figure 19.5. *Model for Kitahara's Theory on Circumcision at Puberty*

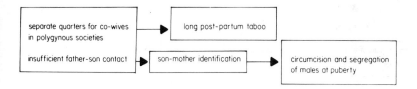

Figure 19.6. *Model for Granzberg's Theory of Hopi-Type Initiation*

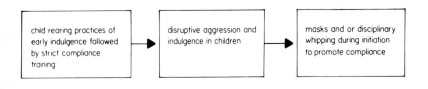

Figure 19.7. *Model for Sociogenic Theories of Initiation*

Figure 19.8. *Model for Status Dramatization Theory of Initiation Rites*

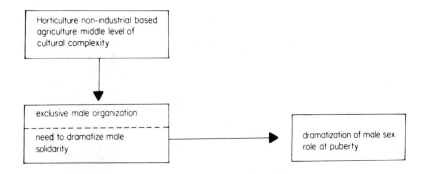

Figure 19.9. *Model for Brown's Theory of Female Initiation Rites*

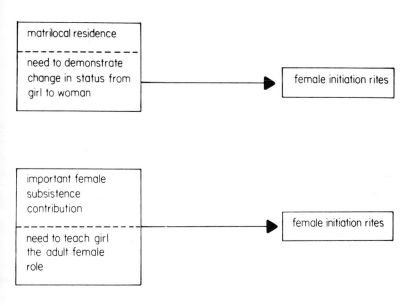

Figure 19.10. *Model for Cohen's Concept of Transition to Adulthood*

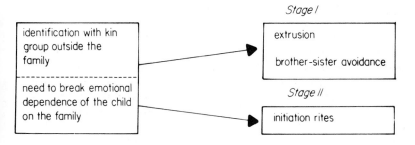

Figure 19.11. *Model for Harrington's Theory of Circumcision and Supercision*

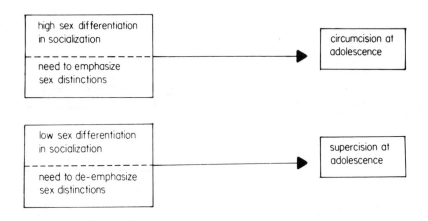

Figure 19.12. *Model for Precourt's Theory of Initiation Rites*

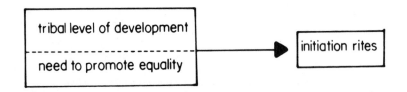

Summary

The basic elements of five psychogenic and seven sociogenic theories of initiation rites have been tested holoculturally. Each theory has been tested at least once. We are left with a long list of plausible, rival theories. Our analysis of the research used to test each theory leads to the conclusion that none of these theories is trustworthy because none has been tested rigorously, none has been retested carefully. Additionally, a number of these studies suffer from specific methodological shortcomings: (1) Norbeck, Walker and M. Cohen (1962) question the accuracy of some of the data of J.W.M. Whiting et al. (1958); (2) Saucier (1972) fails to replicate the long postpartum sex taboo, fruit and root crops association reported by J.W.M. Whiting (1964); (3) Driver (1969) reanalyzes Brown's data and attributes the association between matrilocal residence and female initiation rites to the joint effect of matrilocal and bilocal residence; and (4) Y.A. Cohen (1964a), Granzberg (1973a) and Kitahara (1974) ignore the technical requirement that there be at least five cases in each cell of two-by-two chi-square contingency tables.

Putting aside these methodological problems, the studies as a group seem to suggest the following general conclusion: initiation rites exist to help ensure a smooth transition from childhood to adulthood in those societies where either individual personality or social structural factors are likely to interfere with a smooth transition.

Chapter 20
Psychoanalytic Theory

Psychoanalytic theory—that body of concepts, methods, and propositions pertaining to human psychological functioning which was set forth by Sigmund Freud in the early twentieth century and subsequently revised and expanded by his supporters and critics—rests on two basic principles that tend to set it apart from other personality theories. The first is psychic determinism, the belief that psychic events do not occur randomly, but are influenced by psychic events that precede them. The second is the principle that unconscious mental functioning is the typical state of mental activity; conscious functioning is an exceptional state (Brenner 1957: 1-15).

No system of thought has so greatly influenced psychological anthropology as psychoanalytic theory. Kroeber, Sapir, Malinowski, and Rivers spent substantial portions of their careers studying, testing, and discussing the theories of Freud and his followers. Mead, Linton, DuBois, Spiro, Kluckhohn, Marvin Opler, and Murdock in anthropology and Kardiner, Sullivan, Horney, Fromm, and Erickson in psychiatry have pointed to the mutual relevance of anthropology and psychoanalysis.

Fisher and Greenberg (1977) have reviewed the empirical evidence for the validity of many of Feud's theories. By empirical evidence they mean theory tests through formal experiments or quasi-experiments like holocultural studies.

It is important to keep in mind that holocultural studies bear on only a small portion—about ten percent—of the entire body of Freudian theory. Holocultural studies do, however, bear on hypotheses relating to the key concepts of fixation, anxiety, the Oedipus complex, narcissism, symbolism, ego strength, and dreams.

Holocultural studies are generally an inadequate method for testing theories dealing with unconscious psychodynamic mechanisms and, at best, provide indirect or remote tests. First, they do not constitute direct tests, because the underlying mechanisms are not directly measured. No study directly measures fixation, sexual anxiety, castration anxiety, identification, and other like concepts. Instead, the mechanism is either simply assumed to be operating, or is measured indirectly through the analysis of folk tale themes or some other questionable means. These studies show only that specific parenting behaviors or sociocultural traits are related to the postulated outcome. Second, they say nothing about causal direction, and in some cases the causal direction can be plausibly reversed. Third, the ethnographic literature on child rearing and personality development is not rich enough for researchers to develop precise measures of the relevant variables. So, the findings in this chapter are far from definitive, and, in some cases, are nothing short of questionable.

Fixation

Fixation is one of the psychic mechanisms linking child rearing practices to the adult personality. Whiting and Child (1953: 130) define fixation:

> . . . events occurring in childhood with respect to a particular system of behavior, e.g., oral or sexual behavior, may bring about a continued importance or preportance of that system of behavior, in comparison with the importance it would have had in the absence of those events.

Fenichel (1945: 65) suggests two major causes of fixation:

> 1. The consequence of experiencing excessive satisfactions at a given level is renounced only with reluctance; if, later, misfortunes occur, there is always a yearning for the satisfaction formerly enjoyed.
> 2. A similar effect is wrought by excessive *frustrations* at a given level.

Fixation manifests itself in two forms. There can be a total halt in development at the level of over-satisfaction or over-frustration. Or, there can be a retention of certain characteristics of a particular developmental level. Psychoanalytic theory lists three development levels at which a person may be fixated: the oral, the anal, and the sexual.

The key holocultural study bearing on fixation is Whiting and Child (1953). They revise Freud's fixation hypothesis in two key ways. They list five development foci at which a person can become fixated: oral, anal, sexual, dependence, and aggression. And they question the notion that both satisfaction and frustration lead to the same form of fixation. Citing learning theory, they suggest two alternative forms of fixation: positive fixation and negative fixation. Gratification leads to positive fixation, which leads, in turn, to acquired reward. Frustration leads to negative fixation, which leads, in turn, to acquired drive. They test the fixation hypothesis with a series of what can no longer be considered carefully developed and defined measures of the antecedent child rearing practices and the consequent adult behaviors. For each of the five developmental stages they measure the degree of initial indulgence, severity of socialization, and age of socialization. Their questionable indirect measure of adult fixation is the explanations for illness and the techniques of therapy used by each society in their sample. They collect data for five aspects of the illness and therapy measures: the agent responsible; the degree of patient responsibility; the degree of patient activity; treatment materials used or deemed important; and the manner in which the materials are used. They claim strong support for the negative fixation hypothesis, especially in regard to the oral, dependence, and aggression modes. For example, oral socialization anxiety is found to be related to oral explanation for illness. They claim little support for positive fixation as it applies to early childhood, but some support for its importance in later socialization. Thus, they suggest that a fixation mechanism does operate, but that it is a far more complicated process than traditional psychoanalytic theory suggests.

Prothro (1960), Kiev (1960), and Guthrie (1971) provide the broadest replications of Whiting and Child's work. Kiev and Prothro also claim to support the fixation hypothesis; Guthrie does not. Kiev finds aggression socialization anxiety associated with the use of sacrifice and bloodletting as medical treatments. He also reports that early socialization of independence is associated with patient activity during illness. Prothro provides a factor analysis of data from thirty-six societies. He isolates three primary factors: aggression-hypochondria, independence-anxiety, and orality-sexuality. The variables he finds highly loaded on each of these factors are in general accordance with the fixation hypothesis. For example, the major components of the independence-anality factor include indulgence about the infant's anal activity, late toilet training, early independence training, and anxiety during independence training. As discussed in the previous chapter, Guthrie (1971) questions the validity of the fixation hypothesis. He finds that no developmental stage is a more powerful predictor of adult personality than any other stage. For example, early toilet training and early weaning are both strongly related to the use of oral medical treatments. The fixation hypothesis would predict, of course, that early weaning and the use of oral medications would be more strongly associated.

Additional support for the fixation hypothesis is claimed in a series of studies which indirectly test propositions inferred from the fixation hypothesis. Bacon, Barry and Child (1965), Blum (1969), and McClelland, Davis, Wanner and Kalin (1972) all provide evidence bearing on the widely held psychoanalytic assumption that alcoholism is caused by a fixation at the oral stage. Bacon et al. find that a concern with food storing is associated with drunkenness, and Blum finds oral anxiety related to drug use in general. Rosenblatt (1966: 336-338) finds an inadequate satisfaction of oral needs in infancy associated with a concern for affection. Ayres (1967: 119) finds high reward for dependency in childhood associated with many food taboos, and severe sex training associated with a long sex taboo during pregnancy. Shirley and Romney (1962: 1029) find that societies with much sexual socialization anxiety tend to use love magic.

Taken as a group, these ten studies fail to disprove the fixation hypothesis, although it is questionable whether they really test it. The findings of all these studies (except for Guthrie's) are in the predicted direction. However, we find it difficult to argue that these studies strongly support the fixation hypothesis. In fact, it can be argued that none of these studies even tests the fixation hypothesis. Fixation is simply assumed to be operating; no study measures it. All that is measured are the hypothesized antecedents of fixation and the hypothesized results of fixation. Of course, this is the central problem confronting any researcher interested in testing psychoanalytic theories. The key concepts are often inferences that cannot be observed and, thus, cannot be measured directly. Still, these studies suggest that there is some mechanism linking adult behavior with child rearing practices. Fixation has yet to be ruled out as that mechanism.

Anxiety

If fixation is the mechanism linking child rearing practices with adult behavior, anxiety is said to be the agent that calls fixation and other such mechanisms into action. Anxiety is one of the central concepts of Freudian psychoanalytic theory. Anxiety plays an important role in personality development, personality functioning, psychopathology, and treatment.

Anxiety is a conscious state comprised of symptoms that are both psychological and physiological. Anxiety is similar to fear but differs from tension, pain, and unhappiness. Freud proposed two theories of anxiety. In the first theory Freud (1924) suggested that anxiety was caused by the build-up and inadequate discharge of libidinal (sexual) energy. He abandoned this theory and proposed a second theory (1936). The key features of this second theory are summarized by Brenner (1957: 82,87):

(1) Anxiety develops automatically whenever the psyche is overwhelmed by an influx of stimuli too great to be mastered or discharged.

(2) These stimuli may be either of external or of internal origin, but most frequently they arise from the id, that is, from the drive.

(3) When the anxiety develops automatically according to this pattern, the situation is called a traumatic one.

(4) The prototype of such traumatic situations is birth.

(5) Automatic anxiety is characteristic of infancy, because of the weakness and immaturity of the ego at that time of life, and is also found in adult life in cases of so-called actual anxiety neuroses. . . .Let us now recapitulate this second part of the new theory of anxiety:

(1) In the course of development the ego acquires the capacity to produce anxiety when a danger situation arises (threat of a traumatic situation) and later in anticipation of danger.

(2) Through the operation of the pleasure principle this signal anxiety enables the ego to check or inhibit id impulses in a situation of danger.

(3) There is a characteristic set or sequence of danger situations in early and later childhood which persist as such to a greater or less degree throughout life *unconsciously*.

(4) Signal anxiety is an attenuated form of anxiety, it plays a great role in normal development, and it is the form of anxiety which is characteristic of the psychoneuroses.

Holocultural research relating to anxiety focuses exclusively on signal anxiety. These studies are of two types. First are those which relate presumed childhood anxiety to adult behavior. The basic assumption of such studies is that fixation occurs in infancy and childhood, and when anxiety occurs in adulthood, the person reacts in accordance with the stage at which he or she may be fixated.

Second, are studies which see anxiety producing situations as the basic cause of certain behaviors. These studies make no claim that the resulting behaviors are influnced by fixation.

Many of the propositions relating childhood anxiety to adult behavior are already listed in Table 18.1. The studies of interest are Whiting and Child (1953), Roberts and Sutton-Smith (1962), Shirley and Romney (1962), Bacon, Child and Barry (1963), Bacon, Barry and Child (1965), Stephens (1962, 1967), Wright (1970), Kiev (1960), Prothro (1960), Field (1962), Minturn, Grosse and Haider (1969), Allen (1972), and Prescott (1975). These studies suffer from many methodological deficiencies, not the least of which is the all-too-common practice of using data on the key variables from other studies. As a group, these studies claim a relationship between anxiety in childhood and adult behavior. More specifically, they argue that anxiety in childhood is related, and perhaps even leads to pathological behavior in adulthood. The adult behaviors found associated with childhood anxiety are often those such as crime, alcoholism, displaced indirect aggression, and warfare.

Horton (1943) introduced the concept of anxiety to holocultural research with his finding that anxiety leads to alcoholism. His anxiety theory of alcoholism has been retested six times. Four studies fail to support it, one study partially supports it, and one study supports it entirely. Bacon, Barry and Child (1965) and Schaefer (1973) are more careful and more rigorous than the others. And, interestingly, Bacon et al. partially support the anxiety theory, and Schaefer supports it entirely. Additionally, Horton's measures of anxiety are more careful and more plausible than the measures used in the four discrediting studies. Thus, it seems reasonable to conclude that anxiety is associated with alcoholism.

Russell (1972: 295) finds that insecurity and anxiety are fairly typical of societies which often go to war. And Allen (1972: 263) reports that aggression tends to be handled directly when anxiety is low. Thus, it seems that anxiety in adulthood may be associated with pathological behavior, just as is anxiety in childhood.

Oedipus Complex

The Oedipus complex is the third major psychoanalytic hypothesis to be tested holoculturally. Freud's (1953) Oedipal hypothesis is one of the few major psychoanalytic concepts that has not been substantially revised. The following summary of the

Oedipus complex hypothesis is taken primarily from Fenichel (1945), Hall (1954), Brenner (1957), and Stephens (1962):

(1) During the psychosexual stage (ages four to six) young boys typically develop a strong sexual and emotional desire for their mothers.

(2) At the same time they develop strong feelings of hostility and envy toward their fathers.

(3) Fear of the father leads to castration anxiety in the boys.

(4) In order to control the castration anxiety, the boys repress both the desire for mother and the envy of father. This repression is aided by the mother's attitude, the unreality of the boy's actually engaging in sexual intercourse with his mother, and maturation.

(5) After the feelings are repressed, psychological development can take one of two courses. The boy can identify either with his father or mother.

(6) The specific course followed partially determines the nature of the boy's moral standards, unconscious fantasies, and his attitude toward sex. It even influences the development and nature of mental illness.

Holocultural research does not test this entire sequence; rather, it relates almost exclusively to steps number one and number six.

Stephens (1962) is primarily interested in documenting the existence of the Oedipus complex and its effects. The studies offering psychogenic theories of male initiation rites discussed in the previous chapter also relate to the Oedipus complex, and a number of other studies treat the Oedipus complex as the basic cause of a variety of adult behaviors. The key weakness of all of these studies is their measure of the Oedipus complex. Most of these studies use either mother-child households, mother-child sleeping arrangements, or a long postpartum taboo as their measure of the mother-son attachment and father-son rivalry that supposedly characterize the Oedipus complex. These are imprecise and entirely problematic measures of so complicated a concept and process.

Stephens (1962: 17) claims to test the following hypothesis:

> Young boys—at least under optimal conditions—become sexually attracted to their mothers. This generates lasting sexual fears and avoidances. These fears are (at least in one instance) mediated by unconscious fantasies.

Stephens reports twenty-four correlations as his test of this hypothesis. All but one coefficient are in the predicted directions, although most are relatively weak, ranging from -.04 to .47. Stephens concludes that the hypothesis is supported and that the Oedipus complex, or at least that part of it he claims to test, does actually exist. Stephens's findings concerning menstrual taboos summarized in Table 20.1, also suggest to him that a phenomenon approximating Freud's concept of castration anxiety exists cross-culturally and influences male behavior. We are more skeptical, for the reasons mentioned above.

Table 20.1. *Summary of Evidence on the Castration Anxiety Interpretation of Menstrual Taboos*

Measures Correlated with Menstrual Taboos	Trend in Expected Direction	Probability of Chance Occurrence
Intensity of Sex Anxiety		0.01
Duration of Postpartum Sex Taboo	Yes	0.02
Diffusion of Nurturance	Yes	0.28
Severity of Punishment for Masturbation	Yes	0.01
Over-all Severity of Sex Training	Yes	0.05
Severity of Aggression Training	Yes	0.18
Importance of Physical Punishment	Yes	0.07
Pressure for Obedience	No	0.65
Severity of Punishment for Disobedience	Yes	0.18
Strictness of Father's Obedience Demands	Yes	0.20
Whether or Not Father is Main Disciplinarian	Yes	0.02
Composite Predictor of Castration Anxiety		0.000001
Frequency of Severing in Folk Tales		0.30
Frequency of All Types of Physical Injury in Folk Tales		0.001

Table taken from Stephens (1962:118)

As noted earlier, the five questionable psychogenic studies of male initiation rites (J.W.M. Whiting et al. 1958; Burton and J.W.M. Whiting 1963; Granzberg 1973a; Kitahara 1974, 1975) all suggest that male initiation rites serve to resolve certain personality problems resulting from specific child rearing practices, particularly mother-child households and sleeping arrangements. Additional support for the interpretation comes from Stewart and Jones (1972) and Saucier (1972). Thus, it may be that the repression of the Oedipal feelings and identification with one parent at the age of five or six is not the only manner in which the Oedipus complex can be resolved. Assuming that the Oedipus complex exists cross-culturally, these initiation rites studies suggest that the complex may also be resolved at puberty through the use of structural mechanisms that encourage the boy to identify with his father and other men.

A number of studies claim that the Oedipus complex and, particularly, the unresolved Oedipus complex may nor may not lead to certain adult personality traits. Many of the supposed effects of the Oedipus complex relate to adult sexual behavior. Prescott (1975) and Stewart and Jones (1972) find mother-child sleeping arrangements associated with sexual restrictiveness. Stephens (1962) and Young and Bacdayan (1967) both find some support for Stephens's contention that castration anxiety leads to extensive menstrual taboos. J.W.M. Whiting (1967) suggests that a long postpartum sex taboo leads to sexual anxiety, which leads to paranoia, which manifests itself in sorcery. His chi square analysis of data from thirty-six societies points to a strong relationship between a long postpartum taboo and a strong belief in sorcery. But, Minturn et al. (1969) find a lengthy postpartum taboo unrelated to rape and homosexuality, and Stephens and D'Andrade's (1962) incest-phobia hypothesis of kin avoidances has been discredited.

Ayres (1974) attributes the practice of bride theft to an acting out of unresolved Oedipal feelings. However, the Oedipus complex does not appear to be a viable explanation for bride raiding. Bacon, Child and Barry (1963: 298) report a relationship between mother-child sleeping arrangements and personal crime. Davis (1964), however, finds mother-child households unrelated to levels of drunkenness. In all these studies note the indirect measures, such as long postpartum taboo or mother-child sleeping arrangements. These imprecise measures make it impossible to say if any process closely approximating Freud's Oedipus complex exists cross-culturally.

Narcissism

Narcissism, the fourth major Freudian concept dealt with holo-culturally, occupies a position of less importance than fixation, anxiety, or the Oedipus complex in psychoanalytic theory; but it has gained increased attention in recent years, particularly in reference to the pursuit of pleasure. According to psychoanalytic personality theory, in infancy all libidinal energy or pleasure seeking is self-centered. As the infant matures, the libidinal energy tends to become both self- and other-centered. Narcissism refers to the situation wherein libidinal energy is still almost exclusively self-centered. In infancy this is the normal state of affairs, but in adulthood it is not.

The basic holocultural study of narcissism is Slater and Slater (1965). Using concepts suggested by Stephens (1962) and data from J.W.M. Whiting (1964), they claim to test the following causal theory:

> (a) that in societies with a structural pattern which tended to weaken the marital bond, maternal ambivalence towards sons would be high.
> (b) that such ambivalence would generate in that society a modal personality of a narcissistic type (Slater and Slater 1965: 243).

Their key measure of structural mechanisms that weaken the marital bond is the long postpartum taboo. Their measures of adult narcissism are sensitivity to insult, invidious display of wealth, pursuit of military glory, bellicosity, bloodthirstiness, institutionalized boasting, and exhibitionistic dancing. Their sample is based on ninety cases, and their statistical analysis is based on chi-square, phi, and factor analysis. They also include in their analysis variables relating to maternal treatment of infants. Their major conclusion is that in societies high on the narcissism scale, mothers underindulge their infant sons, put pressure upon them to achieve, and share sleeping quarters for a relatively long time. To Slater and Slater this suggests that narcissism in adult males is caused by mothers who see their sons as husband surrogates and alternately seduce and reject them. To us, it suggests, just as plausibly, that adult male narcissism causes mothers to seduce and reject their sons alternately.

Additional findings about narcissism come from Stewart and Jones (1972: 60), who find aggressive achievement behavior associated with male narcissism; Russell (1972: 292), who finds narcissism most often in warlike cultures; and Swanson (1971: 608), who relates narcissism to unitary and simple centralist governments.

Other Topics

Kaplan and Lawless (1965) provide an interesting test of the universality of responses to the Rorschach test. Their study is based on the Rorschach responses of subjects in eleven different societies in Asia, North America, Oceania, and South America. They find a general similarity in responses in the eleven different cultures. However, they also find substantial regional differences, both within and between geographical areas. Thus, it seems that factors associated with geographic location influence both perception and psychic reality.

Allen (1967) investigates the sources of ego strength. The concept of the ego is, of course, attributable to Freud himself, although the notion of ego strength was a later development. According to Allen, ego strength is the ability to deal with reality. Working with questionable measures of ego strength, Allen finds high levels of ego strength most often in societies with average levels of childhood indulgence, anxiety, and frustration. Low levels of ego strength seem to occur more often in societies which either over- or under-indulge their infants and children.

Minturn (1965) and Colby (1963) examine aspects of Freudian theory concerning dreams and dream symbolism. Minturn tests the proposition that nouns representing male and female sex symbols will be assigned gender in accordance with the symbolism gender. Her sample is composed of nouns from ten different languages, six Indo-European and one each from the Semitic, American Indian, Khosian, and Chad-Hamitic language families. Her analysis of the assignment of gender to sexual symbol nouns supports the proposition entirely. Colby (1963) tests the proposition that there are differences in the contents of the dreams of men and women. He had previously supported this proposition in case studies of the dream content of American students and hospital patients. In this holocultural study he examines the dream content of a probability sample of 549 dreams from persons in seventy-five different societies. He finds that men dream predominately about their wives, weapons, coitus, death, and animals; women dream more often about their husbands, their mothers, clothes, and female figures. There are no sex differences concerning father, child, grass, the color red and home.

Summary

At best, the holocultural studies reviewed in this chapter provide indirect, imprecise, and partial tests of a few core elements of Freudian psychoanalytic personality theory. The weaknesses of these studies are their lack of or imprecise measurement of the key variables and their inability to link cause and effect directly. These studies suggest that the psychodynamic processes examined are complex and their effects more varied than indicated by psychoanalytic theory.

How do the conclusions of holocultural research—tentative as they may be—compare with Fisher and Greenberg's (1977)? They actually mesh quite well. Both sets of findings suggest that there are certain personality types which can be labeled as either oral or anal. Both suggest that under certain conditions a young boy may become sexually attached to his mother. And, both suggest that under certain conditions males may display various amounts of castration anxiety. So, these imprecise holocultural tests do support the findings of more careful experimental and clinical tests of Freudian psychoanalytic theory.

Section VI. Social Problems, Deviance and Social Control

Social problems and deviant behaviors are actions of individuals or groups of individuals that are seen by a sizeable number of people as threatening to certain basic group values or institutions. This definition will not please many of those currently involved in the debate over what constitutes a social problem or a deviant act. But it is the definition most often followed by holocultural investigators, so it is the one we follow here. In this section we review the findings of holocultural research about eight specific social problems: aggression; war; suicide; crime; alcoholism; role, status and power of women; role and status of the aged; overpopulation. We close the section with a chapter on social control.

The study of social problems has long been the domain of sociologists, psychologists, and psychiatrists. Anthropologists are thought to have little interest in social problems. And, in fact, few basic cultural anthropology texts say much about social problems; for example, Hunter and Whitten's (1976) *Encyclopedia of Anthropology* has no entry labeled "social problems." So it seems that anthropologists have not paid much attention to social problems and deviance. While this may be true for anthropology in general, it is certainly not true for holocultural anthropology. Fully one-third of all hypotheses tested holoculturally are hypotheses about social problems and deviance. Major theories about aggression, suicide, war, alcoholism, and the status of women have been tested. A surprisingly large number have been discredited. A lesser number have been supported, either partially or fully. Additionally, some of the best holocultural research—the most rigorous and careful—is research about social problems. Studies by Schaefer (1973) on alcoholism; Sipes (1973, 1974) on overpopulation and aggression; Otterbein (1970) and Naroll, Bullough and Naroll (1974) on warfare; Naroll (1963), Krauss (1966) and Masamura (1977b) on suicide; and Schlegel (1972) and Whyte (1978b) on women's status, are among the most carefully reasoned and most rigorously carried out studies published to date. Thus, many of the conclusions discussed here are conclusions we can trust.

Chapter 21
Aggression

Reasons for the widespread violence and aggression so common in the modern world have long perplexed social and behavioral scientists. Political scientists, economists, psychologists, sociologists, anthropologists, psychiatrists, and others have suggested dozens of explanations for human aggression in general and for such specific forms of aggression as homicide or war. In this chapter we review some of these theories about aggression in general, with special attention given to theories tested holoculturally. In later chapters we review theories about suicide, warfare, and homicide.

An almost endless list of behaviors have at one time or another been considered to be forms of aggression. In Table 21.1 we list only a few of the forms aggression may take. Given the wide range of behaviors encompassed by aggression, no single study can hope to measure all forms of aggression. Most studies of aggression look only at a small number of aggressive behaviors and then often generalize their findings to all forms, or all related forms.

Table 21.1. *Forms of Human Aggression*

Group Aggression	*Individual Aggression*
warfare	arson
riots	rape
strikes	murder
lynchings	assault
demonstrations	suicide
capital punishment	drunken brawling
human sacrifice	wife beating
	satirical humor
	sibling jealousy
	gossip
	stubbornness

Most holocultural researchers seem to base their definition of aggression on Dollard, Doob, Miller, Mowrer and Sears's (1939) conception of aggression as an act whose goal-response is injury to an organism (or an organism-surrogate). By organism, most researchers mean a human being. A few researchers expand this basic definition to include behaviors like entrepreneurial activity that do not manifestly seem to be forms of aggressive behavior (Greenwood and Stini 1977; Steward and Jones 1972).

Since aggression is a complex, multifaceted topic, many researchers have sought to classify aggressive behaviors into systems of more easily manageable sub-categories. Three such classification schemes predominate. First is the distinction often made between individual aggression and group aggression we followed in Table 21.1; group aggression is carried out by a number of people for a common purpose and directed against a common target; individual aggression is carried out by a single individual. Second is the distinction often made between internal aggression and external aggression. Internal aggression is violent behavior by members of one social group directed either at other members of the group or at themselves. External aggression is violent behavior by members of one social group directed at members of another social group or groups. Third is the distinction often made between aggression that is acted out directly and aggression that is acted out indirectly. Aggression acted out directly is aimed at the perceived, appropriate target of that aggression. Aggression acted out indirectly is aimed at someone or something other than the perceived appropriate target of that aggression.

In this chapter we review four general categories of theories of aggression. We examine the controversy over the rival instinctual and culture pattern models of aggression. We then review the cross-cultural evidence for Dollard et al.'s (1939) frustration aggression formulation. We discuss the relationship between child rearing practices and conditions and adult aggression. Finally, we review cross-cultural studies that suggest environmental and cultural explanations for aggression.

Instincts, Culture Patterns and Aggression

For the past fifteen years or so a substantial number of scholars have debated the question of whether human aggression is instinctual, that is, inherited genetically and passed on from one generation to the next, or whether it is controlled by cultural practices and processes. Sipes (1973: 64-5) summarizes these two rival viewpoints:

> Instinct and Aggression: Individual and group aggressive behavior is the result of an innate drive in the individual human. This drive, although somewhat responsive to the environment, normally generates tension in the individual. There is a certain basal level of aggression pressure in every individual and society.

> Instinct and Aggression: Individual aggression behavior primarily is learned. Although perhaps utilizing some innate characteristics, its intensity and configuration can be considered predominately cultural characteristics.

The most widely publicized proponents of the instinctual model are Lorenz and Ardrey. Lorenz's (1966) conception of humans as basically aggressive is derived from his research with greylag geese. He draws close analogies between aggressive behavior in humans and pair-bonding, dominance, and fighting behavior in geese. Few would dispute the care and value of Lorenz's research on non-human animals. But many dispute the practice of drawing analogies between animal behavior (and particularly non-anthropoid animal behavior) and human behavior, and criticize Lorenz's ideas about the instinctual basis of human aggression. Goose behavior is interpreted in human terms, then presented as evidence that humans act like geese whose behavior is largely instinctually derived.

Ardrey's views of human aggression (1961, 1966, 1970) have been aimed at the general public. Ardrey sees human aggression as based on an instinct for territoriality. He views man as having an innate drive to acquire, maintain, and defend territory. Ardrey's theories, conceptions, and data have been challenged by many anthropologists and human biologists. Few, if any, anthropologists accept his theories.

Lorenz and Ardrey are by no means the only scientists who subscribe to the instinctual model. They are merely the two best known. Among others who subscribe to some form of instinctual theory are Morris (1967, 1969), Tiger (1969), and Eibl-Eibesfeldt (1970). Major critics of the model include Andrew (1971), Becker (1962), and the contributors to Montagu (1968).

These rival instinctual and culture pattern theories have been tested holoculturally four times. In each test the instinctual model has been discredited and the culture pattern model supported. The findings summarized in Table 21.2 suggest two general conclusions:

Table 21.2. *Summary of the Findings of Holocultural Tests of the Instinctual and Culture Pattern Models of Aggression*

Associated Aggressive Behaviors	Sample Size	Source
suicide, homicide	58	Palmer (1970)
bellicosity, military glory, boastfulness, warfare, personal crime, full-time entrepreneurs	98	Stewart and Jones (1972)
military glory, bellicosity, torture and kill enemy, warfare, crime	400	Russell (1972)
warfare, combative sports	20	Sipes (1973)

human aggression does not appear to be the inevitable result of an innate drive that exists in all people and societies and which must be discharged in some way; cultural factors and patterns strongly influence the amount of aggressive behavior displayed by an individual or group of individuals.

Of the five studies cited in Table 21.2, those by Sipes (1973) and Russell (1972, 1973) are the most significant. Sipes's work measures up especially well to 1970 standards for holocultural research (see Naroll, Michik, and Naroll 1976; Levinson 1977b; and Rohner et al. 1978 for statements about current standards for holocultural research). As shown in Table 21.3, Sipes finds that warfare and combative sports frequently appear together. Warlike societies generally have combative sports, peaceful societies generally lack combative sports. Russell's (1972) factor analysis of seventy-eight traits taken from Textor (1967) suggests that aggressive cultures have considerable amounts of internal and external aggression, while peaceful cultures have little of either. Both of these studies strongly support the culture pattern model. It seems that cultures either exhibit many forms of aggression or few forms. That is, they are usually either generally aggressive or generally peaceful. It does not appear that cultures rely upon alternative forms of aggression to discharge pent-up aggressive tensions.

Frustration and Aggression

This relatively simple and elegant formulation proposed by John Dollard and his colleagues in 1939 has been widely influential. Frustration causes aggression: (1) frustration leads to hostility and anger which manifest themselves in aggressive acts; (2) the amount

Table 21.3. *Relationship between War and Combative Sports*

	Combative Sports	
Warlike	Yes	No
Yes	Tibetan Thai Sema Naga Ila Comox Aztec Tehuelche Abipon Timbira	Mundurucu
No	Copper Eskimo Tikopia	Semang Bhil Toda Hutterite Lapp Dorobo Kung Bushman Montagnais

phi = .6035   p = .028
Table constructed from data in Sipes (1973).

of frustration felt by a person depends on the strength of the frustrated response, the amount of interference with the response, and the number of frustrated responses; (3) aggression tends to be inhibited by the anticipation of punishment for the aggressive act; (4) the greatest feeling of aggression will be directed against the perceived agent of aggression; (5) inhibited aggression tends to be displaced to indirect objects of aggression; (6) aggression against oneself tends to occur when aggression against other objects is inhibited; and (7) the expression of any aggression reduces the need to express other acts of aggression.

The idea that frustrating experiences produce aggressive responses has influenced the thinking and attitudes of political scientist, economists, psychologists, psychiatrists, historians, sociologists, anthropologists, social workers, educators, and others. The current standing of the frustration/aggression theory in the scientific community was summed up by May in his foreword to the 1969 reprint of Dollard et al.:

Although psychologists may not be agreed on the causal relations between frustration and the manifold forms of aggressive behavior, yet they are agreed that when one sees aggression it is well worth while to look for a thwarted desire, aspiration, promise, hope, or some other motive.

Nammour (1974: 48-50) criticized the frustration-aggression theory on the following grounds. Since frustration is seen as the cause of all aggression, "we cannot ask what it would be like *not to be* frustrated." Actually, the frustration-aggression theory is testable. A study which fails to find a relationship between certain frustrating acts and certain aggressive acts that we would expect to be associated calls into question some part of the general theory. The two holocultural studies presented as tests of the frustration/ aggression formulation do just that. As shown in Table 21.4, Naroll's (1963) correlation matrix for eleven measures of frustration and six measures of aggression produced only three statistically significant positive correlations. Furthermore, thirty-one of the sixty-six correlation coefficients are negative, suggesting that certain frustrations lead to less aggression. While Naroll's findings clearly dispute the general frustration/aggression formulation, his study does support one specific formulation. He finds a strong relationship between seven frustrating interpersonal situations and suicide. Similarly, Rosenblatt, Walsh and Jackson (1976) find that frustrations resulting from the death of a friend or relative often lead to anger and aggression. These findings will be discussed further in subsequent chapters. Palmer (1970), using a worldwide sample of fifty-eight societies, also questions the frustration/aggression theory. He finds no relationship between an index of aggression based on eighteen aggressive behaviors and an index of social anxiety. Thus, there is no empirical cross-cultural evidence that supports the general theory that frustration always leads to aggression.

Triandis and Lambert (1961), Wright (1970), and Allen (1972) provide some tentative cross-cultural generalizations about the manner in which aggression is typically acted out. Triandis and Lambert (1961) classify aggression into three types: intrapunitive, exptrapunitive and impunitive. Operationally, they define intra-punitive aggression as frequency of sacrifice; extrapunitive aggression as aggression to initiates, frequent warfare, and coercion of the gods; and impunitive aggression as the absence of either extra or intrapunitive aggression. Extrapunitive aggression is typically aimed

Table 21.4. *Frustration Aggression Correlations*

Aggressions

Frustrations	Protest Suicide Wordage	Defiant Homicide Wordage	Witchcraft Accusations	Drunken Brawling	Wife Beating	Dog Beating
Marriage Restrictions	.34	.03	.06	-.38	.05	-.18
Child Beating	.01	.01	-.03	-.02	.35	-.29
Severe Weaning	.03	-.33	.01	-.20	.13	.10
Extramarital Children Penalized	.07	-.17	-.04	-.16	.11	-.17
Arbitrary Capital Punishment	-.39	-.20	.10	.07	.15	0.0
Famine	.18	.40	-.12	.08	.22	0.0
Natural Catastrophes	.11	-.04	.04	-.02	.21	0.0
Epidemics	.07	.04	-.06	.04	-.27	.10
Men's Divorce Restrictions	-.60	-.32	-.05	-.04	-.03	-.27
Occupational Restrictions	-.12	.10	.09	-.17	-.04	.13
Castes	.59	.01	-.03	-.06	-.09	-.35

underlined coefficients, $P < .05$
Taken from Naroll (1963).

at the appropriate agents of aggression—those outside the social group. But, intrapunitive aggression is not necessarily aimed at persons within the social group, even when they are perceived as the source of frustration.

Working within a psychoanalytic framework, Wright (1970) examines the effect of aggression anxiety in childhood on the position of objects of aggression, of agents of aggression, and the intensity of aggression in the folk tales of thirty-three societies. He suggests that aggression anxiety in childhood may influence the displacement and projection of aggression in four ways: objects of displaced aggression are less well known to the aggressor; agents of displaced aggression are less well known to the aggressor; the intensity of the aggressive response increases in situations that are unlike the original one; and the hero triumphs less often in folk tales.

Allen (1972) provides a broad correlational analysis of the direction of aggression (indirect versus direct) for some forty-eight variables about ego strength, childhood experience, and social structure. The eleven statistically significant correlation coefficients he reports are listed in Table 21.5.

Table 21.5. *Correlates of Direct Aggression*

Variable	Pearson's r	n
work productivity	.50	58
functional vs. disfunctional activity	.78	58
anxiety	.29	58
creativity	.36	45
incidence of mental illness	.33	46
incidence of crime	.53	53
incidence of suicide	.31	49
high deviance or conformity	.34	53
infant indulgence	.36	46
childhood indulgence	.28	48

Table condensed from Allen (1972:264-66)

These studies by Triandis and Lambert, Wright, and Allen give us some clues about how aggression is acted out. Obviously, these hypotheses need further, more rigorous testing.

Child Rearing and Aggression

It seems clear to many observers that child rearing practices and experiences are in some way related to adult aggression. The results of the thirteen holocultural studies that suggest or question this conclusion are summarized in Table 21.6. Only those by Lester (1967b) (based on nine cases), and Palmer (1970) fail to find a relationship between child rearing practices and some form of adult aggression. The other eleven studies all report some such relationship. Variables such as socialization anxiety or aggression anxiety are indicated in these studies with only remote and problematic measures; thus, their trustworthiness is suspect. The results in Table 21.6 show no clear pattern. A wide variety of child rearing practices are tied to an almost equally wide variety of aggressive behaviors or thoughts. While most of these studies imply a causal relationship, with the child rearing practices as the cause and the aggressive behaviors as the result, none empirically demonstrates such a relationship. They give us some hints about the causes of aggression, but tell us nothing definitive. However, these studies and dozens of others like them on other topics do tell us something about the general effects of childhood experiences on adult behavior.

Table 21.6. *Child Rearing Practices and Adult Aggression*

Child Rearing Practices and Conditions	Aggression	Source
lack of indulgence	aggressive deities	Lambert et al. (1959)
low indulgence	punishment of aggression in folk tales	Child et al. (1958)
diffusion of nurturance	aggressive deities	Lambert et al. (1959)
rejection	problems with management of hostility	Rohner (1975)
	supernatural seen as hostile	Rohner (1975)
stress	witchcraft accusations	Prescott (1975)
control through punishment	aggressive deities	Lambert et al. (1959)
pain inflictions	aggressive deities	Prescott (1975)
independence training	aggressive deities	Lambert et al. (1959)
pressure to achieve	aggressive achievement	Stewart and Jones (1972)
self-reliance	aggressive deities	Lambert et al. (1959)
	aggressive achievement	Stewart and Jones (1972)
dependence anxiety	personal crime	Bacon et al. (1963)
aggression training	warfare	Russell (1972)
aggression anxiety	displaced aggression	Wright (1970)
	aggression explanations and therapies for illness	Whiting and Child (1953) Kiev (1960) Prothro (1960)
discipline practices	unrelated to aggression	Lester (1967b)
general socialization anxiety	unrelated to aggression	Palmer (1970)

Table condensed from Levinson (1977a: 771-73).

Culture, Environment and Aggression

We have reviewed four major explanations for human aggression—the instinctual and culture pattern models, frustration aggression theory, and hypotheses based on child rearing practices. Holocultural research has also uncovered a number of other factors that are related to aggression, although these findings are tentative and in need of further testing. Robbins, DeWalt and Pelto (1972), Whiting and Whiting (1975), J.W.M. Whiting, Chasdi, Antonovsky and Ayres, (1974) and Levinson (1979) test hypotheses about the influence of certain environmental conditions on aggression.

Robbins and his associates work from the premise that people living in warm climates are more emotionally expressive than those living in cool or temperate ones. In accord with this general assumption, they find a relationship between a warm climate and human aggressiveness; and between a warm climate and humans more often portrayed in folk tales as the aggressor than non-humans. Whiting and Whiting (1975) suggest that rooming apart from one's wife tends to make men hyperaggressive. They find that societies which need warriors often have separate rooming for husbands and wives.

Whiting et al. (1974) and Levinson (1979) provide evidence that crowded living conditions are either unrelated or negatively related to homicide and suicide rates, witchcraft accusations, drunken brawling, and pain infliction on infants. Levinson also reports that societies with crowded living conditions tend to indulge both their infants and children. Whiting et al. (1974) argue that tight living conditions require an emphasis on harmony and the control of aggression.

Finally, Watson (1973) reports that deindividuation (a change in the warrior's appearance before battle through masking, hair-cutting, ornamentation, or painting) is associated with increased killing, torturing, and mutilating of the enemy.

There is considerable cross-cultural evidence that the amount and kind of aggression displayed varies widely from one culture to another. More research is needed on the cultural and environmental factors that may effect aggression. We need to begin searching for those factors which cause this variation.

Summary

Like many holocultural researchers, we have tended to portray aggressive acts as harmful. Certainly war, homicide, or assault do cause destruction, injury and death. But, aggression can also be beneficial. Warfare has speeded cultural evolution. Warfare and peaceful borrowing are the main mechanisms by which cultural traits, practices, and beliefs have been passed from one culture to another. Successful warlike cultures expand and grow at the expense of their neighbors. And Simmel (1955), along with others, sees conflict as the mechanism that draws people together as well as apart.

The findings of holocultural research on aggression are important for two reasons. First, they question many of the leading theories of aggression. Second, as a group they are more rigorous and careful than holocultural studies on most other topics. Thus, many of these findings cannot be dismissed on methodological grounds alone.

Holocultural research suggests four major conclusions about the causes of human aggression:

(1) There is no empirical cross-cultural evidence that human aggression is an innate drive that must be discharged in some way.

(2) Frustration does not invariably lead to aggression, although certain frustrations seem to produce certain aggressive responses.

(3) The cross-cultural variation in the amount of aggression displayed by different societies is best explained as an example of cultural patterning.

(4) Child rearing practices may be related to adult aggression, although the nature and direction of the relationship is unclear.

Chapter 22
Warfare

In this chapter and the two which follow, we shift our focus to theories about specific forms of aggression. In this chapter we will focus on aggression manifested in external warfare, internal warfare, and feuding. In the following two chapters we will deal with suicide and crime.

Otterbein distinguishes among external war, internal war and feuding. He defines external war as "warfare between culturally different political communities . . . which are not members of the same cultural unit"; he defines internal war as "warfare between political communities within the same cultural unit" (Otterbein 1973: 924). Feuding is defined in Otterbein and Otterbein (1965: 1740):

> A society is considered to have . . . feuding if after a homicide, the kin of the deceased was expected to take revenge through killing the offender or any member of his kin group.

The relationships between and the differences among three forms of combat are shown in Figure 22.1.

Anthropological studies of warfare come in three forms. First are a substantial number of descriptive accounts of the methods, organization, and results of warfare in specific societies. Chagnon (1968) and Gardner (1964) are two well-known studies of this type. Divale (1971) lists many of these descriptive studies. Turney-High (1949) remains the classic survey of warfare in nonliterate societies. Turney-High reviews the functions, forms, tactics, strategies, and weapons of war and presents some tentative hypotheses about the cause of war. Second are studies that develop or test theories about war. It is this category of studies that interests us here, although a more comprehensive review is presented in Otterbein (1973). Third are studies which cite warfare or some form of warfare as the cause of some other cultural trait or practice. Examples of this kind of study are Divale (1974a) and Ember and Ember (1971)—on main

Figure 22.1. *Types of War*

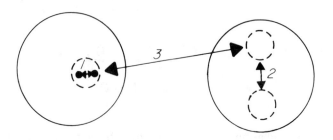

Key:

    Circles

Solid circles represent military organizations

Broken-line circles represent political communities

Solid-line circles represent cultures

    Double-headed arrows (◀━━▶)

1 feuding

2 internal war

3 external war

Taken from Otterbein (1972: 83).

sequence kinship theory—and Naroll and Wirsing (1976) and Naroll and Divale (1976)—on cultural evolution. Here we are mainly interested in the second category of studies—studies about the causes of war that test their hypotheses holoculturally.

External Warfare

How warfare is carried out varies widely from one society to another. It now seems clear that much of this variation is due to differences in societal scale or complexity. Turney-High (1949) goes so far as to argue that small-scale societies lack true war, participating instead only in various forms of combat. Turney-High (1949: 23) speaks of the military horizon:

> It is now necessary to discuss the concept of the "Military Horizon." This means that there are tribes with social control adequate enough for all other purposes, and certainly making such tribes happy enough

in their daily relations with their fellows, but which is so ineffective, so lacking in authority, team work, cohesion, and cooperation that they could not indulge in a fight which could be called a battle. It is also stated herewith that there are tribes which have such capacity for military organization. It is furthermore alleged that the tribes lacking in such organization would have been or have been defeated by those who had it.

For Turney-High (1949: 30) true war depends on five conditions. If any of these conditions are absent, then true warfare is also absent:

1. Tactical operations.
2. Definite command and control. Without definite military authority in control throughout the action, there exists only a bloody brawl.
3. Ability to conduct a campaign for the reduction of enemy resistance if the first battle fails. This is a much higher condition than that of the mere raid, and implies more self-discipline and social organization.
4. The motive must have some clarity. The war must have a group motive rather than an individual one, or even one based on kinship. True war is above the plane of feuds; it is a political device, properly so-called.
5. An adequate supply.

This view of warfare in small-scale societies is disputed by Otterbein (1973), who points out that some of Turney-High's examples of societies that have reached the military horizon are indeed small-scale, nonliterate societies. Additional ideas about the relationship between societal scale or complexity and warfare appear in the works of Sumner (1911), Davie (1929), Childe (1941), Malinowski (1941), White (1949), Service (1971), and Fried (1967).

Theories about cultural complexity and warfare have been tested cross-culturally by Hobhouse, Wheeler and Ginsburg (1915), Wright (1942), and Otterbein (1968, 1970, 1971). The Hobhouse and the Wright studies are methodologically unsophisticated by today's standards. Otterbein's work is more careful than most, especially in regard to sampling and the operational definition of key variables. In their early study, Hobhouse and his colleagues report that as food production technology becomes more sophisticated, the number of captives killed declines. Wright suggests that societal complexity influences the reasons for going to war, that as societies increase in complexity the reasons for going to war shift from defense to social to economic and finally to political motives. The major cross-cultural study of the relationship between societal complexity and warfare is Otterbein (1970). As shown in Table 22.1, societies with uncentralized political systems wage war very differently from societies with centralized political systems. Political centralization is one widely used indicator of societal complexity.

Table 22.1. *Distribution of Military Practices by Level of Political Centralization*

	Political Level	
	Uncentralized Political Systems	*Centralized Political Systems*
1. Military organization	nonprofessionals	professionals
2. Subordination	low	high
3. Initiating party	anyone	official
4. Means of initiation	surprise	announcement or arrangement
5. Diplomatic negotiations	absent	present
6. Tactical systems	ambushes or lines	lines and ambushes
7. Weapons	projectile	shock
8. Protection	absent	present
9. Field fortifications	absent	present
10. Cavalry	absent	present
11. Fortified villages	absent	present
12. Siege operations	absent	present
13. Causes of war	defense, plunder, or prestige	political control

Table 22.1 suggests quite clearly that military complexity tends to accompany overall societal complexity. Complex societies wage war in a far more sophisticated manner than simple ones. Otterbein (1970: 102) further reports that:

> . . . the political communities of a cultural unit which wage war in a sophisticated manner are likely to have high casualty rates, to frequently attack the political communities of neighboring cultural units, to be militarily successful.

However, in this study and in others, Otterbein (1968, 1971) questions the basic assumption made by many evolutionists that small-scale societies do not wage war effectively and that the frequency of offensive external warfare is unrelated to the degree of political centralization in a society. Otterbein's data make it clear that military sophistication is related to military success and territorial expansion. So, too, is the degree of aggressiveness or ferocity of a society (Russell 1973). Societies such as the Aztec, Jivaro, or Somali who attack others frequently or continually, tend to expand the amount of territory under their control.

Two studies test the deterrence theory of war. Proponents of the deterrence theory argue that nations or societies which are well prepared for war are less likely to engage in war than societies which are ill-prepared for war. This general theory, which has many adherents among today's political leaders, is tested holoculturally by Otterbein (1970) and holohistorically by Naroll, Bullough, and Naroll (1974). Otterbein tests the relationship between measures of military efficiency and warfare frequency in a probability sample of non-literate societies. He finds no support for the deterrence theory. Naroll et al. test the relationship between three warfare measures and twenty-seven other variables in a sample composed of twenty conspicuous states and their leading rivals for twenty different historical periods. One of their sample units, for example, is England and its rival, France, for the years 1376-1385. And Naroll et al. also discredit the deterrence theory. These two studies suggest that preparedness for war begets war.

Among other factors found to be associated with frequent warfare are frustrating discipline of children, sexual repression, narcissism, a warm climate, anxiety, insecurity, an emphasis on military glory, and torturing and killing the enemy (Wright 1942: 66; Young 1965: 90; R. Cohen et al. 1968; Russell 1972: 295; Eckhardt 1975: 7).

Regarding the resolution of war, military victory appears to come to societies whose leaders are strong enough to control feuding and who are wise enough to attack first (Otterbein 1970: 95, 1971: 114; Russell 1973: 205). It is the militarily sophisticated society fighting for land, tribute, or power which can establish peace only through military conquest. Politically complex societies, at war with societies whose value systems differ considerably from their own, tend to end war through negotiation or other nonviolent means. The best assurance of a stable peace seems to be economic, religious, and social contact between societies (Tefft and Reinhart 1974: 157; Naroll et al. 1974).

Internal War and Feuding

As we mentioned earlier, internal war is armed combat between political communities, while feuding is armed combat between members of one political community. Feuding is revenge. In small-scale societies feuding is often a direct consequence of homicide. The relatives of the victim avenge the death by killing the murderer or a close relative. Of course, not all small-scale societies handle homicide through feuding. Two other alternatives are frequently used. Some societies have formal judicial procedures which ensure that the murderer will be punished and/or the victim's family compensated. Other societies use a combination of feuding and compensation. In these societies the victim's relatives may choose either compensation or revenge through feuding.

The holocultural research of Thoden van Velzen and van Wetering (1960), Otterbein and Otterbein (1965), and Otterbein (1968) indicates that the presence of fraternal interest groups is a major determinant of feuding. Fraternal interest groups are aggregates of related men who fight alongside and for each other against other like groups. Tables 22.2 and 22.3 show that polygyny and patrilocal residence are both associated with feuding; both are thought to be trustworthy indicators of the presence of fraternal interest groups. However, since the statistical relationships are weak (phi = .32 and .31), factors other than the presence of fraternal interest groups must also be operating. Otterbein and Otterbein (1965: 1480) suggest that frequency of war and the level of political integration may be two such factors:

> . . . feuding is predicted in a high level society if the society does not engage in continual war and has fraternal interest groups; feuding is predicted in a low level society if it has fraternal interest groups.

In a later study, Otterbein (1968) finds that fraternal interest group theory partially explains internal warfare as well. It seems that in societies with uncentralized political systems, fraternal interest groups lead both to feuding and internal war. But, in societies with centralized political systems, fraternal interest groups do not lead to internal war.

The best explanation for feuding and internal war produced by holocultural research so far is fraternal interest group theory. Still, fraternal interest group theory has two serious shortcomings. First, statistical support for it is weak. Although statistically significant, phi coefficients of .32 and .31 are small and explain only a small percentage of the variance. Correlation coefficients of this size suggest that the presence of fraternal interest groups is not the only factor influencing the frequency of feuding or internal war. Second, fraternal interest group theory is only a partial theory. It imme-

Table 22.2 *Relationship between Feuding and Patrilocal Residence*

Residence	Feuding		
	Frequent or Infrequent	Absent	Total
Patrilocal	15	10	25
Other	7	18	25
Total	22	28	50

·phi = .32   .02 < p < .05

Taken from Otterbein and Otterbein (1965). Reproduced by permission of the American Anthropological Association, from the *American Anthropologist* 67 (1965), 1473.

Table 22.3. *Relationship between Feuding and Polygyny*

Polygyny	Feuding		
	Frequent or Infrequent	Absent	Total
absent	9	20	29
present	13	8	21
Total	22	28	50

phi = .31   .02 < p < .05

Taken from Otterbein and Otterbein (1965). Reproduced by permission of the American Anthropological Association, from the *American Anthropologist* 67 (1965), 1474.

diately begs the question of what causes fraternal interest groups. Otterbein's research and some of that reviewed in the chapter on Residence, Descent, and Terminology suggest that the presence of fraternal interest groups is part of a causal sequence which also includes post-marital residence, type of warfare, migration, descent, and kinship terminology. The exact sequence has yet to be worked out, with Divale (1974a) and Ember and Ember (1971) suggesting rival interpretations.

Summary

Warfare is the most common form of aggressive behavior in small-scale societies. Holocultural research has tested and supported three conclusions about war that can be accepted with some degree of trust:

(1) The manner in which war is carried out is influenced by societal scale or complexity.

(2) Preparedness for war begets war.

(3) The presence of fraternal interest groups predicts feuding.

Chapter 23
Suicide

Sociologists on one hand, and psychologists and psychiatrists on the other, have long disagreed about the causes of suicide. World-wide cross-cultural research, as reflected in the work of Naroll (1963, 1969), Krauss (1966, 1970), Lester (1967a, 1971), and Masamura (1977b) has done much to reconcile the differences between these two groups. Researchers also disagree about what suicide is. Menninger (1938) sees suicide as any self-destructive act. Durkheim (1951) sees only a purposive act on the part of the victim as suicide. Naroll (1963, 1969) focuses on protest suicide, which he defines as voluntary suicide committed in such a way as to come to public notice.

In addition to defining carefully what is meant by suicide, it is also important to distinguish among suicide threats, suicide gestures, and suicide attempts. A suicide threat is simply a verbal statement by an individual indicating that he plans to take his own life. A suicide gesture is an actual attempt by an individual to take his own life, but the attempt is carried out in such a way that it will very likely fail and the individual will not die. Usually the attempt is thwarted because it is carried out in such a way that it will be discovered by a second person in time to render the necessary medical assistance. A suicide attempt is an actual attempt by an individual to take his own life, carried out in such a way that it will very likely succeed or, if it is thwarted, it will be thwarted by accident rather than by design. Suicide research has suffered because it is impossible to study directly the suicide victim himself. Rather, researchers have been forced to deal mainly with those who have made threats, gestures, or attempts; or they have tried to reconstruct the lives of those who have succeeded.

Sociological Explanations

Many sociological explanations for suicide are based on Durkheim's (1951) contention that suicide frequency is related to social integration. Durkheim distinguished among egoistic, altruistic, and anomic suicide. Each is related in a different way to the nature and degree of social integration found in a particular society. The general propostition linking integration and suicide has been re-tested many times, in a variety of ways, and with a variety of indicators of social integration. The proposition has generally been supported (Henry and Short 1954; Bohannan 1960; Dublin 1963; Gibbs and Martin 1964). The major cross-cultural test was published by Masamura (1977b). Using three measures of social integration—group life versus atomism, elaboration of ceremony and ritual, and presence of an organized priesthood—and a sample of thirty-five non-literate societies, Masamura finds a direct rather than an indirect relationship between suicide and social integration. He suggests that this finding does not necessarily call for the rejection of Durkheim's theory, but instead calls for its revision along the following lines: socially alienated individuals in highly integrated societies are those most likely to commit suicide.

A number of holonational studies point to a strong relationship between economic development and suicide rates. Suicide rates, the world over, tend to increase with rapid economic development, industrialization, and urbanization (Quinney 1965: 403-04; Haas 1967: 243; Barrett and Franke 1970: 350-06; Whitt, Gordon and Hofley 1972: 195-97).

Psychological Explanations

The causal theories championed by psychologists and psychiatrists have their genesis in the works of Freud (1956, 1959, 1960), Menninger (1938), and Dollard et al. (1939). The current thinking of many clinically oriented psychologists and psychiatrists can be summarized in somewhat oversimpled form: (1) an individual is thwarted (frustrated) by another individual; (2) the thwarted individual becomes aggressive and angry; (3) for reasons having to do with socialization experiences and personality development, certain individuals displace this anger, turn it inward, and kill themselves.

Studies of this general proposition or portions of it provide general support. Unfortunately, many of these studies are clinical case studies which do not readily allow one to distinguish truth from fiction.

Thwarting Disorientation Theory

Naroll (1963, 1969) has suggested his thwarting disorientation theory of suicide, a theory that does much to integrate the essential elements of both sociological and psychological theory. Naroll (1963:1) argues that "thwarting disorientation situations, in which a victim blames a person for the victim's loss of social ties, tend to cause suicide." Thwarting disorientation theory has been tested and supported holoculturally by Naroll (1969). The results of Naroll's study are summarized in Table 23.1. In addition, the theory has been tested and supported by Krauss and Krauss (1968), Lester (1970), and Krauss and Tesser (1971). Further, Krauss (1966) provides a content analysis of the suicide cases reported for Naroll's sample units which refines and provides additional support for thwarting disorientation theory.

Table 23.1. *Thwarting Disorientation Situations and Suicide Wordage*

Thwarting Disorientation Situations	*Point Biserial Correlations*
Wife Beating	.69
Marriage Restrictions	.34
Men's Divorce Freedom	.60
Witchcraft Accusations	.34
Drunken Brawling	.30
Defiant Homicide Cases	.45
Warfare Frequency	.41

All correlations are significant at the .05 level.
Taken from Naroll (1969).

Because few ethnographers provide any statistics, let alone trustworthy statistics, about the frequency of suicide in primitive societies, Naroll (1963) developed an indirect or proxy measure of suicide frequency, the suicide wordage ratio: a score computed by dividing the total number of words the ethnographer devotes to suicide by the total number of words in the ethnography—indirectly measuring suicide frequency. The underlying assumption is that the more words about suicide, the more suicide there is. What troubles some scholars is the possibility that the suicide wordage ratio may be measuring ethnographer interest in suicide, and not suicide frequency. This does not seem to be the case, however. The studies of Naroll (1963, 1969), Krauss (1966), and Naroll, Michik and Naroll (1976) provide statistical evidence of the convergent validity of the suicide wordage ratio as a measure of suicide frequency. Evidently ethnographers write more about suicide when there is more suicide in a society, not just because they are interested in it.

Other factors linked to high rates of suicide in a wide range of cultural contexts are the need for power, fear of death, a cold climate, and social complexity (Lester 1967a, 1968, 1971, 1975; Robbins et al. 1972; Krauss 1970)

Chapter 24
Crime

Anthropologists have shown little interest in crime. Only a few of the leading cultural anthropology textbooks even mention crime in their indexes. And, while there are general anthropological works about law (Hoebel 1954; Nader 1965; Pospisil 1974), there are no like anthropological works about crime. Perhaps this is so because there is some question of whether we can talk about crime in small-scale societies. Those who take crime to be a product of state organization prefer to speak only of violations of norms or mores in reference to small-scale societies. On the other hand, sociologists and social psychologists who study people in complex cultures have been very interested in deviant behavior in general and criminal behavior in particular. They have developed a variety of competing theoretical models which claim to explain deviance in general. Among the better known of these models are social disorganization, value conflict, anomie, labeling, and class or conflict theory. And, there are other models based on physiological and genetic factors. Since none of these models has been tested cross-culturally, we merely list them. General discussions of each can be found in the following sources: Faris (1948); Fuller and Myers (1941); Merton (1957); Becker (1963); Cavan (1969); Matza (1969); Taylor, Walton and Young (1973); and McCord and McCord (1977).

There are no holocultural studies of deviance in general. Two broad and a handful of more narrow holocultural studies of crime are now in print, Bacon, Child and Barry (1963) and Allen (1972); both are designed to develop hypotheses about crime. Neither should be viewed as a definitive test of any hypothesis about crime. Bacon, Child and Barry's research is based on a non-probability sample of forty-eight societies. They distinguish between theft and personal crime—rape, assault, murder, suicide, sorcery designed to cause illness, and making false accusations. Allen's research is based on a non-probability sample of fifty-eight societies. He does not distinguish between personal crime and theft. There is considerable overlap between the two samples. Over fifty percent of the same societies appear in each. Thus, in no way can Allen's research be seen as a replication of Bacon, Child and Barry's. Any agreement between the two studies can be explained as an artifact of the more than fifty percent overlap between the two samples.

Bacon, Child and Barry find support for J.W.M. Whiting's (1960) status envy-masculine protest theory. B. Whiting (1965: 126-127) provides the clearest statement of this theory:

> In simplest terms, the theory states that an individual identifies with that person who seems most important to him, the person who is perceived as controlling those resources that he wants. If during the first two or three years of life a child is constantly with his mother and infrequently sees, and is handled by, his father, he will identify strongly with his mother and not with his father; in short, if he is a boy he will have a cross-sex identification. If, later in life, he is involved in a world that is obviously dominated by men, a world in which men are perceived to be more prestigeful and powerful than women, he will be thrown into conflict. He will develop a strong need to reject his underlying female identity. This may lead to an overdetermined attempt to prove his masculinity, manifested by a preoccupation with physical strength and athletic prowess, or attempts to demonstrate daring and valor, or behavior that is violent and aggressive. These types of behavior will be referred to as "protest masculinity."

Consistent with the status envy theory, Bacon, Child, and Barry find societies with much personal crime having mother-child households, and societies with much personal crime and theft having little contact between fathers and their children. Allen, however, does not support the hypothesis. He fails to find a relationship between type of household and crime in general or aggression. Similarily, Minturn et al. (1969: 309) find no relationship between rape and another measure of father-child contact, the length of the postpartum sex taboo.

Allen (1972) and Bacon, Child and Barry (1963) do agree on some other matters. Both suggest that theft may be caused in part by a feeling of being unloved. Factors associated with theft include child training for responsibility, obedience, achievement, and self-reliance; low erogenous and sexual satisfaction in childhood; and low childhood indulgence. Along the same lines, Lester (1967a, 1967b) finds discipline practices in childhood unrelated to either suicide or homicide rates. In a later study Lester (1968) relates homicide to a need for power. Bacon, Child and Barry and Allen also agree that a high level of cultural complexity and social stratification are associated with theft. Bacon and her associates also report that theft is associated with a high level of socialization anxiety, while personal crime is associated with a general distrust of the environment.

Perhaps the most trustworthy proposition produced by these studies is that deprivation of love in childhood is associated with theft in adulthood. This proposition is supported by both Bacon, Child, and Barry (1963) and Allen (1972), and coincides with the standard psychoanalytic interpretation of theft (Fenichel 1945) and Glueck and Glueck's (1950) conclusions regarding the causes of juvenile delinquency. The validity of J.W.M. Whiting's status-envy hypothesis as an explanation for crime is unclear. Bacon and her associates and B. Whiting (1965) in a study of six cultures support it, but Allen and the Minturn group do not. Obviously, more cross-cultural research is needed not only on the status-envy hypothesis, but on crime and deviant behavior in cross-cultural perspective.

Chapter 25
Alcoholism

A series of Harris surveys conducted from 1972 to 1974 found nine percent or twenty million Americans to be heavy drinkers. In 1972 the average American consumed 2.63 gallons of alcohol (Efron, Keller and Gurioli 1974)—forty-six percent through beer, forty-two percent through distilled alcohol, and twelve percent through wine. Epidemiological studies have regularly shown an increasing rate of alcohol use in the world (Keller and Efron 1959; Efron et al. 1974).

The pattern of alcohol use in nonliterate societies is much the same as in literate ones. Blum (1969) provides the relevant statistics. Sixty-five of 132 societies sampled use alcohol frequently or excessively. Twenty-nine other societies use alcohol moderately. Both persons inside and outside the culture describe more societies as having an alcohol abuse problem than as not having one. And, alcohol use is seen as increasing in nonliterate societies, although data are lacking for many societies. The effects of alcoholism on both the individual and the society are often harmful and sometimes even devastating. One study, by R. Berry, Boland, Laxson, Hayler, Sillman, Fein and Feldstein (1974) estimates that the economic cost of alcholism in the United States in 1971 was above $25 billion. Over $9 billion was lost in economic production. The cost of health and medical expenses approached $8.5 billion. Auto accidents directly attributable to drunk driving cost $6.4 billion. And more than $1 billion was spent on treatment, research, criminal justice, and social welfare.

Alcoholism also has disastrous effects on the physical health of the alcoholic. Alcohol consumption has been tied to cancer of the mouth, pharnyx, and larynx (Rothman and Keller 1972); esophagus (Wynder and Bross 1961; Wynder, Bross and Feldman 1957); pancreas (Hirayama 1970); and liver (Davidson 1970; Prince, Leblanc, Krohn, Maseyeff and Alpert 1970). No one, however, suggests that alcohol directly causes any form of cancer. Rather, it is now generally assumed that cancer is caused by a variety of interacting factors. In some forms of cancer, alcohol may be one of those factors. Alcohol may induce cancer in four ways: by enhancing the cancer-inducing effects of carcinogens such as tobacco smoke; by irritating and making body tissues vulnerable; by encouraging malnutrition which also may weaken body tissue; by producing cirrhosis of the liver, which often precedes hepatoma (cancer of the liver).

Heavy alcohol consumption has also been tied to liver diseases such as hepatitis and cirrhosis and to birth defects in the offspring of alcoholic women. But there is no evidence linking alcohol consumption to coronary heart disease, and in the elderly, moderate drinking may have beneficial effects. Beyond the economic and health consequences are the hundreds of thousands of broken families, wrecked lives and abused children which result from alcoholism.

Despite the obvious harmful effects of alcohol, most people in the world use it regularly, and a substantial number use it excessively. This widespread use of alcohol suggests that for some people and some societies, alcohol has beneficial effects as well as harmful ones. Worldwide comparative studies suggest four such beneficial effects—although the benefits are often short-lived: alcohol reduces feelings of anxiety or fear; alcohol makes men feel more powerful; alcohol relieves the distress caused by competing intrapsychic needs for nurturance and independence; alcohol relieves the stress that often characterizes life in unstructured communites. Thus, the consumption of alcohol may temporarily make life easier and more pleasant.

One of the major stumbling blocks in research on alcoholism has been the lack of a widely accepted definition for it. A variety of definitions and classification schemes have been proposed, but none has been widely accepted. Operationally, we find the following most serviceable: the use of alcoholic beverages which seems to any scientific investigator to constitute some kind of personal or social problem. Thus, we include, among other things, so-called problem drinking, situational drinking, excessive drinking, drunkenness, periodic alcoholism, drunken brawling, drinking bouts, and insobriety.

The number of different explanations proposed for alcoholism rivals only the number of different types of alcoholic beverages consumed around the world. Theories of alcoholism can be loosely placed in seven groups: biological, psychological, sociocultural, psychosocial, ecological, demographic, economic. Cross-cultural investigators have looked only at psychological and sociocultural theories. A few cross-national studies have looked at economic and ecological theories as well.

The leading theory of alcoholism supported by worldwide comparative research is the anxiety-reduction hypothesis. It was first suggested by Horton (1943), although its roots lie within the framework of Freudian psychoanalytic personality theory. Horton argues that people drink excessively to reduce feelings of anxiety—especially anxiety about not having enough food to eat. He states the hypothesis as follows: "The strength of the drinking response in any society tends to vary with the level of anxiety" (Horton 1943: 230). He uses degree of male insobriety as his measure of drinking response, and subsistence type, availability of food, warfare frequency, and sorcery as his measures of anxiety. Obviously, then, anxiety is measured indirectly and imprecisely. Through a chi-square analysis of samples ranging in size from thirty-seven to fifty-six societies, Horton finds consistent, statistically significant relationships between male insobriety and his anxiety measures. The anxiety-reduction hypothesis has been retested by Field (1962), Klausner (1964), McClelland, Davis and Kalin (1972), Bacon, Barry and Child (1965), Kalin, Davis and McClelland (1966), and Schaefer (1973). Working with relatively small samples of from fourteen to twenty-seven cases, Field (1962) finds drunkenness unrelated to sex anxiety and fear of supernatural beings and rejects the anxiety-reduction hypothesis. Klausner (1964) provides a second retest of Horton. He finds anxiety—as measured by fear of blood—associated with sobriety, not insobriety, as the anxiety-reduction hypothesis predicts. Likewise, both Kalin and his associates (1966: 581) and the McClelland team (1972: 59), using references to fear in folk tales as their measure of anxiety, find insobriety unrelated to anxiety. It should be noted that neither of these studies provides substantial empirical evidence for the validity of references to fear in folk tales as an indirect measure of anxiety. Schaefer (1976: 301-307) provides a lengthy critique of McClelland's folk tale theme measures. He summarizes the major weaknesses as follows:

> His cross-cultural folk tale work, however, is not convincing. In his 1972 book, *The Drinking Man*, McClelland (1972: 52) devotes only one paragraph to the description of the folk tale selection process. He fails to discuss the shortcomings of his sample with respect to folk

tales. Moreover, he fails to discuss the internal consistency or lack of consistency as to folk tale representativeness. He does not sample randomly from folk tale collections nor does he assure us that the collections are anything like complete (Schaefer 1976: 303).

Bacon, Barry and Child's (1965) massive study of drinking practices provides a fifth, independent test of the anxiety-reduction hypothesis. They do find anxiety associated with drunkenness, but cite conflicts over unmet dependency needs as the key determinant, not anxiety-reduction. The most recent and most careful test of the anxiety-reduction hypothesis is Schaefer (1973, 1976). His study is far more rigorous and comprehensive than any of the earlier ones. He uses probability sampling, multivariate analysis, and tests for the biases that may result from untrustworthy data, interdependence of sampling units, regional variation and group insignificance. Schaefer (1973: 287) supports the anxiety-reduction hypothesis entirely. He finds that societies which believe in capricious and fearful supernatural spirits have high rates of aggressive drunkenness.

As an alternative to the anxiety-reduction hypothesis, Bacon, Barry and Child (1965) offer the dependency-conflict hypothesis. They argue that people drink excessively to temporarily resolve (or forget) conflicts caused by competing intrapsychic needs for dependence and independence. The dependency-conflict problem is especially common in societies which fail to meet childhood dependency needs, but demand that adults act in a responsible and independent manner. Bacon et al. test this hypothesis through a series of tests, most of which show a consistent though weak relationship between low indulgence in childhood and frequency of drunkenness. The dependency-conflict hypothesis is supported by Barry (1968: 31-32); Bacon (1974); and Davis (1964), who suggests that sex identity conflicts may play a key role.

The third general psychological theory of alcoholism tested holoculturally is McClelland et al.'s (1972) power-motivation theory. McClelland and his associates argue that men drink to feel stronger. They drink to feel more like men. Both McClelland et al. (1972) and Davis (1964), working with folk tale theme indicators, support this theory. More reliable support is provided by Schaefer (1973), who however, sees the power-motivation hypothesis as little more than a restatement of Horton's anxiety-reduction hypothesis.

Field (1962) offers a fourth theory of alcoholism, one citing sociocultural rather than psychological factors as the key causal variables. Field suggests that people with drinking problems tend to live in relatively unstructured societies where there is little respect for authority. Field's basic point is that social disorganization causes alcoholism. Additional support comes from McClelland et al. (1972), working again with folk tale theme measures, and Schaefer (1973). Schaefer reports that societies characterized by father-son authority patterns tend to have controlled drinkers.

It is important to keep in mind that each of these theories, so far as the cross-cultural evidence is concerned, explains alcoholism only in men. Largely because there is so little cross-cultural data about drinking by women, no cross-cultural study testing any of these theories looks at alcoholism in women. Child, Barry and Bacon (1965) do, however, suggest some tentative hypotheses about sex differences in drinking behavior. They find sex differences most pronounced when alcoholic beverages are widely available, and when the society is characterized by hostility.

Thus, worldwide comparative research supports in varying degrees four ostensibly rival theories of alcoholism in men: anxiety-reduction, dependency-conflict, power-motivation, and social disorganization. But, we submit that these four theories need not be considered rivals at all. Rather, each can be viewed as an alternative form of Horton's anxiety-reduction hypothesis—if we assume that there is such a phenomenon as anxiety—since none of these studies directly measures it. The reduction of feelings of anxiety is the common thread running through these four theories. Each of these theories and each of the studies supporting them can be interpreted as supporting the general hypothesis that people become intoxicated to alleviate stress or, in psychoanalytic terms, to relieve anxiety: anxiety over not enough to eat, anxiety over dependence-independence-conflicts, anxiety over feeling weak and powerless, and anxiety over loss of control.

The studies of anxiety-reduction show it to be a precipitating cause of alcoholism. That is, people may drink excessively to reduce feelings of anxiety they are experiencing at a particular moment in time. But what causes them to feel anxious in the first place? Horton suggests that in nonliterate societies it is an uncertain food supply. McClelland et al. suggest that in men, it is a feeling of powerlessness. And Field suggests that it is social disorganization. There are, of course, many other potential sources of anxiety that go unmentioned here: diet, a poor climate, urbanization, and unemployment are a few obvious ones (Graves 1967; Seeley 1962; Haas 1967).

If our goal is to cure or prevent alcoholism we need to know more than that anxiety may lead to excessive drinking. We need to know what factors are causing the anxiety. Is it a lack of economic opportunity? Or a hot climate? Or racial discrimination? Or even boredom? We need also to investigate cross-culturally, theories that are not based on anxiety reduction. What is the cross-cultural evidence for genetic theories or physiological theories? Such questions are often difficult to address cross-culturally. The necessary data is often scarce or non-existent. Field work can be expensive and time-consuming. These are not questions often asked by anthropologists and clinically-oriented psychologists, but they are the very questions that need to be examined cross-culturally. Comparative research has given us some clues that may help prevent alcoholism. Among factors that characterize societies with moderate drinking are family disapproval of immoderate drinking, government control of alcoholic beverages, interpersonal respect, community solidarity, and loyalty and cooperation.

Chapter 26
Role and Status of Women

In virtually all societies men fare better than women. Men exercise more power, have more status and enjoy more freedom. Men usually head the family, exercise considerable force in legal, political, and religious matters, take alternative sexual partners, may often take more than one wife, have greater freedom in the choice of a spouse, usually reside near their own kin, and have easier access to alcoholic beverages and other drugs. Women, on the other hand, are often segregated or avoided during menstruation, must often share their husbands with one or more co-wives, are blamed for childlessness, and are often forced to defer to men in public places. Child rearing is the only domain where women regularly exert more influence than men.

While men have far more public status and power, the situation is more balanced within the domestic unit. Within the household women can and do use a variety of techniques to increase their power. The sexual division of labor affords them considerable control over their own subsistence activities and over the types of food their families will eat. Often, women can rely on the support of their children or their kin in power struggles with their husbands. And, they can also exercise some control over their mate by withholding sexual access.

The current worldwide interest in equality for women has stimulated holocultural research about the role, status and power of women in small-scale societies. Since 1968, ten new holocultural studies about women have appeared. We review here only those studies which explicitly claim to be about women's role, status, or power. Other related findings may be found in the chapters on marriage, taboos, sexual behavior, and child rearing. Of all the subjects investigated holoculturally, the study of women may be the most difficult. The researcher immediately faces two pressing methodological problems: the problem of developing valid and reliable measures of women's status and power; and the problem of collecting trustworthy data about women from published ethnographic reports. We begin with an examination of how different researchers have measured female status and power. We then discuss the issue of male bias in ethnographic reports about women. Finally, we review holocultural studies testing theories about female role, status, and power.

Measuring Female Status and Power

Status and power are subjective concepts. They exist in the minds of those being judged and doing the judging, of those in control and being controlled. Status and power are difficult to measure and operationalize; and, they are even more difficult to measure when data is culled from ethnographic reports or from compendia such as Murdock's (1967a) *Ethnographic Atlas*.

Comparativists have followed two strategies in trying to measure female status and power. Some, like Simmons (1937) and Divale (1976) have used general measures based on the ethnographer's judgment as to the situation in each particular society. Others, like Schlegel (1972), Sanday (1973) and Whyte (1978a, 19789b) have used more precise measures based on the presence or absence of specific cultural practices and beliefs.

We would not recommend that researchers use the measures that Simmons and Divale have used. Simmons neither defines the concept being measured nor supplies his coding rules. Divale is imprecise. Divale's (1976: 178) measure of female status is the "ethnographer's assessment of the overall prestige, esteem, power, or recognition given to the 'average' woman in comparison to the 'average' man in a society." As we point out in the next section, broad measures like these seem to lead inevitably to a male bias problem with the data. Additionally, since the measure failed to produce the theoretical relationship between cultural complexity and female status predicted by Divale, there is no evidence of construct validity. Sanday (1973: 1694-1695) provides us with a four point Guttman scale which purports to measure the "number of economic and political rights which accrue to women":

IV   Presence of Female Solidarity Groups
III   Female Participation in Political Activities
II   Demand for Female Produce
I   Female Control over Produce

This measure troubles us for two reasons: it is based on a non-probability sample of only twelve societies; and as in Divale's measure, there is no evidence of construct validity. Sanday predicted that female status would be related to female participation in production. She found the opposite.

Measures that strike us as being more careful are those used by Schlegel (1972), Whyte (1978a, 1978b) and Munroe and Munroe (1969). Schlegel's measure is based on two dozen or so specific variables about deference, control over person, control over property, and degree of female autonomy. Schlegel's measure seems to control the male bias problem. Whyte's measure is the most elaborate; he examined eighty-seven variables relating to women's role, status, and power in a sample of ninety-three societies selected from Murdock and White's (1969) Standard Cross-Cultural Sample. He then reduced these variables into nine general scales measuring: property control; kin group power; value of women's lives; value of women's labor; domestic authority; sexual solidarity; control of sex; ritualized insecurity between sexes; joint participation. Like Schlegel's measure, Whyte's is specific enough to control the male bias that may exist in the ethnographic record.

Munroe and Munroe (1969) provide a different approach. They are interested in structural sex bias rather than female status. The two concepts are related, of course. They measure sex bias by rating form of post-marital residence, type of kin groups, and inheritance as either patri- or matri- centered. They then correlate the sex bias rating with the percentage of male versus female gender nouns in nine different language groups. The resulting Spearman's rho of .81 ($p < .01$) indicates a strong relationship between structural sex bias and male gender nouns. It further suggests that the percentage of male versus female nouns in a society's lexicon is a measure of sex bias and female status.

Female status and power are difficult concepts to measure and should be based on careful coding of specific cultural practices and beliefs. Researchers interested in studying women's status cross-culturally would do well to consider Whyte's measure.

The Question of Male Bias

Many anthropological students of the status of women believe that the existing ethnographic literature is badly biased in favor of the male viewpoint (Westermarck 1905; Evans-Pritchard 1965; Friedl 1967, 1975; Linton 1971; Hochschild 1973; Rosaldo and Lamphere 1974). Some argue that the data are so severely biased that the development and testing of trustworthy theories is impossible. The question of whether male ethnographers report data about women with a bias has three related aspects. First, some argue that since male ethnographers may be prevented from speaking with or observing women, they cannot possible present an accurate or complete picture of women's role and status. Second, a number of anthropologists argue that male ethnographers and even some female ethnographers arrive in the field with certain male biases that lead them to view all women as subservient to and less important than men. Third, some argue that a woman's world view is somewhat different from a man's, and therefore, can be completely understood only by another woman.

Although common sense tells us that they are true, and many believe them to be true, there is almost no empirical support for points one and two above. Five holocultural studies test for male bias in ethnographic reports. Martin (1978) found, not surprisingly, that the majority of the data reports about women included in the Human Relations Area Files are written by male ethnographers. But, when she compared the reports of male and female ethnographers in a random sample of ten cultures, she found that in their general reports the male ethnographers reported more data about women than the female ethnographers. In an early study of data quality control, Naroll, Naroll and Howard (1961) find no significant difference between the reports of male and female ethnographers regarding the position of women in childbirth (upright versus reclining). Schlegel (1972: 49-50) finds only two statistically significant associations among the more than fifty she computed between sex of the ethnographer and various measures of women's status and role in matrilineal societies. Because two out of fifty is less than one would expect to find by chance alone she concludes that the sex of the ethnographer is not a source of systematic bias in her data. Divale (1976) does report a male bias effect. The relationship he found between low cultural complexity and high female status either disappeared completely or was reversed when he controlled for sex of the ethnographer. An analysis of the data suggests to Divale that the most accurate data about women came from female ethnographers or from male ethnographers who spoke the native language and spent more than one year in the field. Divale's problem may be more one of imprecise measurement than of male bias. As we mentioned above, Divale's broad definition based on the ethnographer's judgement is too imprecise a measure for such an elusive and complex concept as status. Whyte (1978a) provides the broadest test of the male bias problem. He correlates sex of the ethnographer with ninety-six measures of female role and status. Nine of the correlation coefficients are statistically significant at the .10 level, six are significant at the .05 level. Fifty-six correlations are positive, thirty-six are negative, and suggest that ethnographic reports about women do not have a male bias problem. However, the large number of positive correlations indicates that female ethnographers do report the status of women somewhat more favorably than male ethnographers. We agree with Whyte (1978a: 70) that "male bias problems may be largely avoided if the customs and behavior coded are fairly concrete and specific, and will be reflected primarily when overall statements about the degree of male superiority and female subservience are coded."

Men and women the world around often live in different worlds. Women interact mostly with other women and children; men interact mostly with other men. Women often gather plant foods and cultivate crops; men often hunt and wage war. Women work mostly in or around the home; men work mostly outside the home. Women dream about their husbands, mothers, clothes and female figures; men dream about their wives, coitus, death and animals (Colby 1963: 1116).

These and many other differences in life style and world view have important implications for the question of male bias in ethnographic data. These differences suggest that because women's lives differ from men's, men cannot accurately describe women's view of the world. They cannot accurately describe it because they cannot understand it fully. Ardener (1972, 1975) argues that much of social theory is invalid because it is based on the world view of male informants. Theory based on the world view of female informants may be quite different. A number of ethnographic reports about women by female ethnographers suggest that women's world view may indeed differ from that of men (Kaberry 1939; Goodale 1971; M. Wolf 1972). The issue of male versus female world view is one that needs to be considered by comparitivists interested in the role of status of women. Unfortunately, it has not been considered very often. No holocultural study examines the issue in any detail. Perhaps when more data about women are gathered by women the issue can be addressed empirically.

Women's Role

Anthropologists have devoted considerable effort to cataloging cross-cultural sex differences in behavior. In Table 26.1 we list eight areas where sex differences are well documented. For more detailed discussions of cross-cultural sex differences see C. Ember (1981) and Rosenblatt and Cunningham (1976).

Table 26.1. *Cross-Cultural Sex Differences*

1. *Subsistence Activities* (Murdock and Provost 1973a)

Males Predominate	*Females Predominate*	*Neither Predominates*
hunting	gathering wild plants	agriculture
trapping	preparing drinks	milking
herding large animals	dairy production	
fishing	food preparation	
collecting honey	cooking	
clearing land	preserving	
working the soil		
butchering		

2. *Crafts and Manufacturing* (Murdock and Provost 1973a; White, Burton and Brudner 1977)

Males Predominate	*Females Predominate*
mining	spinning
smelting	weaving
metal working	basketry
lumbering	mat making
carpentry	clothes making
working with stone, bone and shell	pottery
house building	hide preparation
net making	
rope making	

3. *Household Tasks* (Murdock and Provost 1973a)

Males Predominate	*Females Predominate*
house building	fuel gathering
	water fetching
	clothes laundering

Table 26.1. *continued*

4. *Child Care* (Weisner and Gallimore 1977; Raphael 1969)

Males Predominate	*Females Predominate*
	all activities
	midwifery

5. *Warfare* (Ember and Ember 1971)

Males Predominate	*Females Predominate*
participation in	
armed combat	

6. *Social Structure* (D'Andrade 1966; Divale and Harris 1976)

Males Predominate	*Females Predominate*
post-marital residence	
descent	
inheritance	
freedom to take	
multiple spouses	

7. *Social Relations* (Schlegel 1972; Stephens 1963)

Males Predominate	*Females Predominate*
key political positions	
household leadership	
deferred to by spouse	

8. *Sexual Behavior* (Ford and Beach 1951; Broude and Green 1976)

Males Predominate	*Females Predominate*
take initiative	
premarital and extra-	
marital freedom	

Why is There a Division of Labor by Sex?

The nearly universal pattern of division of labor by sex shown for activities one through five in Table 26.1 is currently explained by anthropologists in three ways. First, Murdock and Provost (1973a) suggest that men perform such tasks requiring superior strength as hunting, herding, hurling weapons, lifting stones and working metals. Women perform such tasks requiring less strength as child care, cooking, and gathering. It is difficult to argue that this is not both a plausible and parsimonious explanations for the division of labor by sex. But, Judith Brown (1970) provides an equally plausible rival explanation. She argues that work is assigned in accordance with its compatibility with child rearing responsibilities. Women perform tasks that can be interrupted, that keep their children away from danger, and that can be performed near the home. Men perform tasks that are incompatible with these three child rearing requirements. In a related study, Nerlove (1974: 210) shows that women participate more in basic subsistence activities if they begin supplementary feeding of their infants before the infant reaches one month of age. D. White, Burton and Brudner (1977) provide a third explanation. They argue that the differential assignment of certain tasks can be explained as economies of effort. That is, certain tasks are performed by the same sex because they either follow in the production sequence or because they are carried out in the same location as other tasks. For example, men make nets because they also fish, women do the housework because their husbands are often away from home hunting or fighting. The evidence for each of these theories is largely based on data about the distribution of certain cultural practices in the ethnographic universe. None of them has been tested through careful holocultural research. Independent measures of strength, incompatibility, and economy of effort need to be devised.

Related to the division of labor by sex in a society is the division of responsibilities or roles in the family. Sociologists have long distinguished between instrumental and expressive roles. The person who plays the instrumental role sees that things get done. The person who plays the expressive role maintains emotional equilibrium within the group. Parsons and Bales (1955) argued that within the family (read nuclear family) men will always take the instrumental role, women the expressive role. Zelditch (1955) supports this proposition in a sample of thirty-seven nonliterate societies, regardless of the rule of residence. Even in matrilineal societies it is the husband, not the wife's brother, who takes the instrumental role. Aronoff and Crano (1975: 17) indicate that the relationship may not be so clear cut. For example, they report that even when men take the instrumental role, women still may make an important subsistence contribution.

Female Status and Power

As discussed at length above, methodological problems make the empirical testing of theories about female status and power difficult. The key dependent variables are often difficult to measure precisely, and the possible confounding effects of male bias in the ethnographic record must be measured and, if necessary, controlled statistically. Most holocultural studies ignore these two problems. Still, these studies provide us with a general appraisal of some of the leading theories of women's status and power.

Subsistence Contribution, Status and Power

Early theorists like Engels, Morgan and Schmidt argued that the importance of female contribution to basic subsistence activities is the key determinant of female status and power. Their basic argument runs as follows: A substantial subsistence contribution leads to ownership of property, which leads to increased political power. D'Andrade (1966: 201) uses the same general line of reasoning to explain male dominance over females—the sex which controls the basic subsistence activities also controls the property used for those activities and, thus, dominates the other sex. Since in most societies men control the basic subsistence activities, males the world around generally dominate females.

Although many still believe that female contribution to subsistence activities is the key determinant of increased female power and status, there is no empirical evidence that supports this proposition. Oliver (1972), Zelman (1975) and Sanday (1973, 1974) all test this proposition cross-culturally. None support it. Zelman's is the most rigorous of these four studies. Her analysis is based on a sample of sixty societies selected from Naroll and Sipes's (1973) Standard Ethnographic Sample. She finds no relationship between female power and an important subsistence contribution by women, and a weak one between female power and female status. Two years earlier Oliver (1972) reached much the same conclusion. With two samples she found negative (-.16, -.28) correlations between female status and importance of female subsistence contribution. Since the relationship between these two variables has been found to be either weak, non-existent or negative, subsistence contribution cannot be viewed as a major determinant of female status or power. But, despite these findings, the proposition has not been abandoned. Instead it has been elaborated. Subsistence contribution is now seen as a necessary though not a sufficient cause of female status and power. Zelman (1975: 67) suggests that in technologically simple societies an important female subsistence contribution combined with male sharing of child rearing responsibilities leads to equal power and prestige for men and women. A weakness of this hypothesis is that the causal sequence can logically be reversed. One could argue just as convincingly that it is equal status for men and women that leads to the sharing of child care responsibilities. Sanday (1973) presents us with another theory also based on female subsistence contribution. She argues that in those societies where status and contribution are linked, female status increases when women produce valuable goods. Unfortunately this theory tells us little about female status in general—in most societies status and contribution are not linked.

A number of researchers suggest that trading is an important source of power and status for women (Rosaldo 1974: 34; Lamphere 1974: 108; Sanday 1974: 193-94; Leis 1974: 230-233; Friedl 1967). Actually the relationship between male versus female dominance in trading and female power is quite weak. We computed a *phi* coefficient of only .25 for Zelman's measures of female participation in trading and female power. Still, it seems obvious that female participation in trading can increase female power in a variety of ways. It can increase their control over the production of trade goods. It can give them more freedom to travel and be outside the domestic unit. It can give them more freedom from their husbands. And, it can enable them to interact at a professional level with other women traders. Levinson and Swanson (n.d.) speculate that it is not who does the trading but rather, who trades whose products, that is the key determinant of female power. They find female power greatest in societies where women trade items produced by both men and women. Female power is lowest in societies where men trade products produced by both men and women. And, female power is at an intermediate level in societies where women trade only their own products or assist male traders in the trading of all products. They test these propositions with Zelman's sample and her measure of female power as shown in Table 26.2

Female Pollution

The concept of female pollution and the rituals associated with female pollution are commonly seen as means used by men to control women. The notion of female pollution is a pervasive one in nonliterate societies and, to some extent, in modern, industralized ones as well. Menstruating women are often thought of as unclean and are avoided or segregated; various taboos are place on pregnant women; men rarely assist at childbirth; and many societies enforce a lengthy postpartum sex taboo.

For Young and Bacdayan (1967) mentrual taboos are a form of

Table 26.2. *Relationship between Female Power and Female Trading*

	Female Power		
Trading	*High*	*Medium*	*Low*
Women Trade Women's and Men's Products	Navajo Crow Yoruba Yahgan Pomo		
Women Trade Women's Products or Assist Male Traders	Jivaro	Azande Tlingit Fox Tallensi Warao Aleut Lapp Nyakyusa	Ganda Araucanians Papago Lau
Men Trade Women's and Men's Products		Iban Ifugao Micmac	Nambicuara Kapauku Yakut Yanoamo Chukchee Rwala Santal Bambara Winnebago Thonga

Pearson's r = .765 (p. < .001)

male control of females. They find that menstrual taboos occur most often in communities where men dominate women and where men are tightly organized; this interpretation runs counter to the one offered by Stephens and D'Andrade (1962) who see menstrual taboos as an institutionalized form of defense against male castration anxiety.

Douglas (1966: 140-157) interprets the function of a belief in female pollution slightly differently. In her view, the notion of female pollution is especially pronounced in societies where men dominate women, but where they are prevented from physically coercing women. This interpretation meshes well with the more general theory that pollution rituals and a belief in the idea of pollution help maintain interpersonal boundaries in ambiguous social contexts (Douglas 1968: 200; Turner 1969: 107-109).

Husband versus Brother Dominance

In a carefully thought out and rigorous study of sixty-six matrilineal societies, Alice Schlegel classifies male authority over adult women into a five-point scale:

Type   I — strong husband authority; no brother authority

Type II — some brother authority but husband authority predominant

Type III — authority of husband and brother about equal

Type IV — some husband authority but brother authority predominant

Type V - strong brother authority; no husband authority

Schlegel finds that it is in type III societies where men have the least amount of control over women. In these societies women are able to play their brothers off against their husbands in order to maintain their own autonomy. This model applies only to matrilineal societies (about ten percent of the world's known societies), since it is only in matrilineal societies that brothers are in a position to interfere in the lives of their sisters.

Summary

Holocultural research has produced two firm methodological and two firm theoretical propositions about female role, status, and power:

(1) Measures of female status and power which are based on ethnographic descriptions of specific behaviors are more likely to be valid indicators than measures based on general statements.

(2) The male bias problem can be controlled by using precise measures of female status and power. The issue of the possible confounding effects of differences in male and female world view and life experiences has not yet been tested empirically.

(3) The relative importance of female subsistence contribution is unrelated to female status and power.

(4) In matrilineal societies female autonomy is greatest when brothers and husbands hold an about equal degree of control over women.

Two tentative findings suggest:

(5) When women trade products produced by men, female power will increase.

(6) The concept of female pollution and the ritual associated with it are often used by men to control women.

Chapter 27
Role and Status of the Aged

Old age is a difficult concept to define. In the United States today, when people are sixty-five years of age they become eligible to receive social security benefits and usually retire from full-time employment. But there are many people over sixty-five who do not feel old and are not seen as old by others. Clark (1973: 80) points out that aging is conceptualized in at least six different ways: as dying, as decrement of disengagement, as disease, as dependency and regression, as minority group status, as development. This list makes it quite clear why aging and the aged are widely seen as a social problem. They are alternately described as dying, withdrawn, sick, dependent, or as members of an out-group. Only occasionally is the aging process seen as a normal developmental phase in the life cycle.

Gerontology, the study of the aged and the aging process, is a relatively new and expanding discipline. Many hypotheses about the role, status, or treatment of the aged are really little more than suggestions in need of rigorous testing. Botwinick (1973) reviews many of these ideas. Cultural anthropology has contributed relatively little to our understanding of the aged and the aging process. Clark (1973: 79) offers two reasons why anthropology has lagged behind sociology and psychology in studying the aged:

> First, relatively few individuals in subsistence economies tend to live to 'old age' as we define it in industrial society. Second, those who do survive to later years often retain relatively good physical and mental faculties and pursue many of the activities of earlier adulthood until shortly before death; they must, to survive under the demanding conditions of tribal or peasant life.

LeVine (1978) indicates that anthropology is still largely involved in defining concepts and collecting primary data about the aged.

Apparently, we are not yet ready to develop and test broad theories about the role, status, and treatment of the aged in cross-cultural perspective. Two recent works by Silverman and Maxwell (1978) and Maxwell, Krassen-Maxwell and Silverman (1978) give some indication of future trends in cross-cultural research on the aged.

Simmons (1945) is still the basic anthropological study of aging. With a worldwide sample of seventy-one societies and data for 234 variables, Simmons produced a correlation matrix of 1146 correlation coefficients. This early study is methodologically unsophisticated and suffers especially from the group significance problem. Of the 1146 reported correlation coefficients only a small number are statistically significant. The number of significant correlations is no more than the number of significant correlations one would expect to find by chance alone; that is, by computing correlations between batches of meaningless data. But, in spite of their methodological shortcomings, Simmons's findings are worth considering when treated as suggestions in need of further testing rather than as firm conclusions. The dozens of hypotheses he tested and found support for can be lumped together into five broad propositions:

(1) The aged in most societies are afforded considerable prestige, but this prestige ends quite abruptly once the aged are no longer able to care for themselves.

(2) Aged females tend to fare best in hunting, gathering, and fishing societies with matrilineal descent systems. Aged males fare best in more advanced societies with patrilineal descent systems.

(3) Aged men and aged women tend to be treated about equally when it comes to the sharing of food.

(4) Because of their role as repositories of knowledge, the aged often hold important social and political positions.

(5) Increasing status for the aged is associated with social stability, an advanced economic system, and a high level of societal complexity.

Proposition four has been retested by Maxwell and Silverman (1970: 381). They find that esteem for the aged is directly related to the amount of control the aged have over key information. Working with a sample of twenty-six societies they report a gamma of $+.68$ $(p.<.01)$ between treatment of the aged and control of informational resources by the aged. Thus, Simmons's proposition number four is supported.

Williams's holocultural study (1972: 155) reports the effect of industrialization on family relationships. He finds that the grandparents' role, "as guides to the ethos and eidos of a culture" declines with industrialization. Thus he calles into question Simmons's proposition number five.

Chapter 28
Overpopulation

There are now four billion people on the earth. The world's population has not merely steadily increased. The rate of increase is far more rapid today than at any time in the past. Many people consider that four billion inhabitants of the earth is far too many, and the threat of eight billion inhabitants by the year 2015 strikes many more as disastrous. Thus, it is not surprising that overpopulation and rapid population growth are widely seen as two of the leading social problems of our time. Overpopulation is seen as the basic cause of a wide variety of other problems, including environmental pollution, poverty, hunger, illness, death, unemployment, child neglect, and crime. These problems, or the fear of them, have resulted in the appearance of a variety of programs, movements, and organizations devoted to controlling population growth. Many of these programs have been directed at population growth in underdeveloped nations, although often with little success.

For any population control program to succeed, the planners, administrators, researchers, and practitioners need to know what factors affect population growth rates. We now know with some degree of certainty that the history of the growth of the world's population is basically one of changes in the death rate. The birth rate has remained fairly constant, at about fifty live births per 1000 people per year. But the death rate has declined substantially. Technological and intellectual advances arising from the agricultural and the industrial revolutions and urbanization have lowered death rates in all regions of the world. Certainly warfare, famine, and disease have led to population fluctuations, but their effects have generally been short-lived. Currently, it is the death rate reduction in underdeveloped nations that is causing rapid worldwide population growth. For the past thirty years or so, the birth rate (although not the growth rate) has been decreasing in industrialized nations.

People interested in controlling population growth are caught in a dilemma. On the one hand, they know that decreasing death rates are the major cause of population growth. But, for moral and ethical reasons, nothing can be done to manipulate death rates artificially. Thus, the major cause of population growth throughout human history is beyond direct human control. Instead, planners and researchers must direct their efforts at finding factors that influence the birth or fertility rate. As mentioned above, the birth rate is the number of live births in a set time period. The fertility rate—the number of live births to women between the ages of fifteen and forty-four in a set time period—is a more precise measure of birth trends. The fertility rate controls for sex ratio and sociocultural, economic, psychological, and physiological factors which have been tied to both increasing and decreasing growth rates. Sipes (1974: 134-139), for example, lists some sixty propositions that link sociocultural factors to decreasing growth rates. But, while there is no shortage of ideas about population growth, there is a severe shortage of ideas that have been tested cross-culturally. Most propositions about the causes of population growth have been tested only in case study research on specific groups of people. Of the seven major cross-cultural surveys, four are basically descriptive studies which may propose but do not test causal hypotheses (Carr-Saunders 1922; Krzywicki 1934; Ford 1945; Devereux 1955). The three theory-testing studies are Lorimer et al. (1954), Nag (1962), and Sipes (1974). All three are book-length monographs, with the Sipes and Nag studies being rigorous enough so that we can accept their findings with some trust.

Following Davis and Blake (1956), we divide variables about population growth into three categories: causal factors; intermediate factors; and population change. The casual sequence runs as follows:

sociocultural factors ——▶variation in reproductive practices ——▶variation in population growth rates.

In Table 28.1 we summarize the findings from Lorimer et al., Nag, and Sipes which bear on this model. Obviously, the findings are somewhat meager. We suspect that the results of these three studies are disappointing for two main reasons. First, it is extremely difficult, time-consuming,and expensive to find trustworthy data about population growth variables in the ethnographic literature. Sipes (1974) discusses this problem at length, and Levinson (1979) could find information on infant mortality rates for only twenty-two of the sixty societies used in his study of population density. Second, because they are interested in decreasing or stabilizing population growth, researchers have tended to ignore the basic factor that increases population growth—a decrease in the death rate. Perhaps a holocultural study that examines the effect of missionary or colonial contact, disease, famine, warfare, or degree of acculturation on population growth will produce more substantial findings.

Infanticide is one practice that can artificially inflate the death rate and, thus, reduce the population growth rate. Infanticide in a variety of forms is practiced in a number of small-scale societies, although its frequency is probably less than is commonly assumed.

Table 28.1. *Determinants of Population Growth*

Sociocultural Trait	*Reproductive Practice*	*Population Growth*	*Source*
unilineal and corporate kin groups		high fertility rate	Lorimer et al. (1954)
social disorganization		high or low fertility rate	Lorimer et al. (1954)
polygyny		high fertility rate	Lorimer et al. (1954)
		unrelated to fertility rate	Nag (1962)
economic contribution by children		high population growth rate	Sipes (1974)
women subservient to men		unrelated to population growth rate	Sipes (1974)
frequent separation or divorce	sterility	unrelated to fertility rate	Nag (1962)
	lack of effective contraception	high fertility rate	Lorimer et al. (1954)
	use of primitive means of contraception	unrelated to fertility rate	Nag (1962)
	frequency of abortion	unrelated to fertility rate	Nag (1962)
	age of women at entry into regular sexual union	unrelated to fertility rate	Nag (1962)
	long postpartum sex taboo	low fertility rate	Nag (1962)
	sterility	low fertility rate	Nag (1962)
	venereal disease	low fertility rate	Nag (1962)
	high child mortality rate	low fertility rate	Nag (1962)

Divale (1970, 1971) sees infanticide as a mechanism for balancing the sex ratio. He presents statistical evidence that when the pool of marriageable men in a society is reduced through warfare, female infanticide is used to reduce the number of marriageable females. In another holocultural study, M. Ember (1961) suggests that people facing food shortages are the ones most likely to practice infanticide. And, in a third study, Granzberg (1973b) argues that when only one twin is killed in twin infanticide, it is often because the mother has neither the time nor the help needed to rear two infants at the same time.

Additional studies dealing indirectly with overpopulation are reviewed in the chapters on Marriage, Sexual Behavior, and the Role and Status of Women.

Chapter 29
Social Control

Social controls are specific practices or processes which limit the actions of individuals or groups in accordance with the general rules, values and practices of the group. The major mechanism of social control in any group is the socialization process during which the group members internalize the rules and norms of the group. There are two main types of social control. The first, coordinate control, is based on retaliation or the threat of retaliation by peers. The second, superordinate control, is based on the authority of some third party to adjudicate the dispute. Most societies rely on a combination of six primary sources of control (B. Whiting 1950: 11-12): the superego or conscience; public opinion; reciprocity; supernatural sanction; retaliation; institutionalized agencies of authority.

The specific mechanisms used to maintain social control vary widely from one society to another. But, in general, nonliterate societies tend to rely more on mechanisms of coordinate control. The cross-cultural evidence suggests that as societies become more complex, stratified, and autonomous, the responsibility for the control of individual behavior shifts from the individual to the group or to representatives of the group (Gouldner and Peterson 1962: 36, 61; March 1955: 322; Hobhouse et al. 1915: 61,75). Additionally, Moore (1942: 230) notes that an increase in the number of structural control positions in stratified societies is often accompanied by increased control for those in the upper strata at the expense of those in the lower strata.

It is commonly assumed that life in nonliterate societies is more harmonious than life in advanced societies because of the direct, informal nature of interpersonal relations and the use of informal mechanisms of social control. A second assumption arising out of this first one is that nonliterate societies, because they are harmonious, have little need for mechanisms of superordinate control. Masamura (1977a) tested this proposition in a holocultural study;

287

while not disputing the importance of informal control mechanisms, he finds that formal ones are also important. As shown in Table 29.1 and 29.2, both superordinate justice and punishment are associated with lower rates of internal violence.

Table 29.1. *Internal Violence and Superordinate Justice*

	Justice			
Internal Violence	*Coordinate*		*Superordinate*	
high	Apache	Lango	Azande	Tonga
	Arunta	Lesu	Chagga	Venda
	Buka	Maori	Kazak	
	Chukchee	Murngin	Kwakiutl	
	Dobu	Orokaiva	Masai	
	Ifugao	Paiute	Riff	
	Jivaro	Trobriands	Samoa	
	Kiwai	Witoto	Tiv	
low	Barama River Caribs		Ashanti	Japan
	Polar Eskimo		Bali	Lamba
	Delaware		Cayapa	Lepcha
	Kutchin		Cheyenne	Ontong Java
	Kwoma		Crow	Sanpoil
	Yurok		Lau Fiji	Tanala
	Zuni		Maria Gond	Tikopia

tau = .38, p < .001, N = 47
Taken from Masamura (1977a:393).

A key control mechanism in nonliterate societies is witchcraft and sorcery. Both B. Whiting (1950) and Swanson (1960) demonstrate that, in the absence of formal control mechanisms or unlegitimized social contacts, the threat of retaliation through witchcraft or sorcery serves as a means of social control. Swanson finds witchcraft especially prevalent in societies where interpersonal relationships are important but are uncontrolled and often unlegitimized. And, as shown below in Tables 29.3 and 29.4, B. Whiting reports an equally strong relationship between sorcery and coordinate control and punishment. Similarly, LeVine (1962) reports that sorcery tends to accompany co-wife proximity in polygynous societies. These three

Table 29.2. *Internal Violence and Superordinate Punishment*

Internal Violence	Superordinate Punishment			
	Absent		Present	
high	Apache	Kwakiutl	Riff	
	Arunta	Lango	Samoa	
	Azande	Lesu	Tonga	
	Buka.	Maori	Venda	
	Chagga	Masai		
	Chukchee	Murngin		
	Dobu	Orokaiva		
	Ifugao	Paiute		
	Jivaro	Tiv		
	Kazak	Trobriands		
	Kiwai	Witoto		
low	Barama River Caribs		Ashanti	Lepcha
	Polar Eskimo		Bali	Ontong Java
	Delaware		Cayapa	Sanpoil
	Maria Gond		Cheyenne	Tanala
	Kutchin		Crow	Tikopia
	Kwoma		Lau Fiji	
	Yurok		Japan	
	Zuni		Lamba	

tau = .44, p < .001, N = 47
Taken from Masamura (1977a:394).

independent studies suggest that sorcery and witchcraft help maintain social order by instilling the fear of retaliation in persons who are about to break social rules.

Related to these findings about the function of sorcery and witchcraft as mechanisms of social control is Roberts's (1967) preliminary study of oaths and autonomic ordeals. Roberts finds that oaths and ordeals are mechanisms of social control in relatively complex societies that lack a centralized authority.

So far, we have looked only at control mechanisms which exist at the group level. But, in any society it is the rules and norms that are internalized during socialization which are the most important mechanisms of social control. J.W.M. Whiting (1967), working within a Freudian framework, lists three basic sources of individual or internal social control: paranoid fear of retaliation by others;

Table 29.3. *Relationship between Sorcery and Superordinate Justice*

Sorcery	Superordinate Justice				
	No			Yes	
important	Arunta	Apache	Barama	Ashanti	Hill Maria
	Buka	Chukchee	Caribs	Azande	Gonds
	Dieri	Copper Eskimo	Delaware	Chagga	Kwakiutl
	Dobu	Ifugao	Jivaro	Fiji	Lamba
	Kiwai	Kutchin	Witoto	Kamilaroi	Sanpoil
	Kwoma	Mala		Tiv	
	Lesu	Maori		Venda	
	Murngin	Paiute			
	Orokaiva	Yurok			
	Trobriands	Zuni			
unimportant	Lango			Bali	Cayapa
				Japan	Cheyenne
				Kazak	Crow
				Lepcha	Samoa
				Masai	Tikopia
				Ontong Java	Tonga
				Riff	
				Tanala	

Taken from B. Whiting (1950:85).

sense of sin over fantasized punishment by ghosts or gods; and sense of guilt for one's own behavior. He relates each of these internal control mechanisms to specific childhood experiences. Fear of others arises from childhood conflicts over sexual permissiveness versus sexual repression. A sense of sin develops from parental neglect and severe punishment for aggressive acting out. And guilt arises from competition between the male child and his father for the mother's affection. Whether all of this is true or not is highly problematic, as we do not have the cross-cultural measures or data with which to assess feelings of retaliation, sin or guilt.

Summary

This small number of studies suggests two conclusions. First, holocultural researchers have been far more interested in the causes of social problems than in their cure or prevention. Second, the threat of retaliation through witchcraft or sorcery may operate as a social control in the absence of superordinate controls.

Table 29.4. *Relationship between Sorcery and Superordinate Punishment*

Sorcery	Superordinate Punishment			
	No		Yes	
important	Arunta Buka Dieri Dobu Kamilaroi Kiwai Kwoma Lesu Mala Maori Murngin Orokaiva	Apache Chukchee Copper Eskimo Delaware Ifugao Kutchin Kwakiutl Paiute Trobriands Yurok Zuni	Azande Barama Caribs Chagga Hill Maria Gonds Jivaro Tiv Witoto	Ashanti Fiji Lamba Sanpoil Venda
unimportant	Kazak Lango Masai		Bali Japan Lepcha Ontong Java Riff Samoa Tanala	Cayapa Cheyenne Crow Tikopia Tonga

Taken from B. Whiting (1950:87).

SECTION VII.
CONCLUSIONS

Chapter 30
What Have We Learned?

What have we learned about human culture and behavior from holocultural research? What have the more than three hundred studies discussed throughout this volume taught us? And, what have they failed to teach us? Where is more research needed? We answer these questions by briefly listing the most trustworthy conclusions produced by holocultural research and by mentioning those areas or topics where more research is clearly needed.

Cultural Evolution

We know that the level of cultural complexity of a society or of a particular cultural trait or practice can be accurately and reliably measured. Seven validated measures of cultural complexity are now available for use by interested researchers. We know that cultural complexity is related to many aspects of culture and many types of human behavior. As Table 30.1 shows, complex small-scale societies differ from simple ones in many ways. We know, too, that complexity tends to diffuse as much through peaceful borrowing as through warfare. And, it seems that increasing agricultural efficiency is a factor that fuels the evolutionary process. Untested as yet are ideas about the effects of energy transformation, population pressure, and population density on evolution.

Kinship

We know that dwellings in matrilocal societies are generally larger than those in patrilocal societies. So, archeologists now have a valid measure of residence. Dwellings in permanent settlements are often rectangular, while those in nomadic settlements are often circular. And, we know that crowded living conditions do not necessarily lead to social ills such as suicide, homicide, anxiety, or child neglect.

Table 30.1. *Effects of Cultural Complexity*

Cultural Feature	Complex	Simple
Settlements	large, densely populated	small, lightly populated
Marriage	monogamy, dowry	monogamy or polygyny, bride service/bride price
Kinship	neolocal residence, small, independent families, kin ties less important	matrilocal/patrilocal residence, small, independent families, kin ties important
Social and Political Stratification	high	low or absent
Expressive Culture	sexually restrictive, complex religious organization and practices, games of all types and riddles	sexually permissive, simple religious organization and practices, games of physical skill or physical skill and chance
Social Control	mostly superordinate	mostly coordinate
Warfare	for economic and political gain, complex tactics and strategy	for revenge and retaliation
Socialization	restrictive, rejecting, emphasis on compliance, responsibility, formal education outside the home	permissive, accepting, emphasis on independence, achievement, self-reliance, informal education in or near the home

We know that the three major explanations of exogamy set forth to date—conflicting loyalties, alliance, and survival value theory—do not withstand holocultural testing. Nor do Lévi-Strauss's ideas concerning the causes of cross-cousin marriage. We need to know more about endogamy, divorce, polygyny, mode of marriage, and the basis of marriage. For all these topics the groundwork has been laid. What is needed is expansion, revision, and testing of existing ideas.

We know that the relationship between family type and level of cultural complexity is curvilinear. Both the simplest and most complex societies have independent families. Extended families are most common in societies at intermediate levels of complexity.

Despite much theorizing and considerable theory testing, we still know very little about the origin and extension of the incest taboo. Genetic, psychological, and socio-cultural factors all seem important, but more research is needed.

We know beyond any reasonable doubt that a developmental sequence exists involving postmarital residence rules, rules of descent, and kinship terminology. We have learned also that the relative importance of male versus female subsistence contributions is not the key determinant of postmarital residence rules that many once thought it was. Instead, we have learned that type of warfare (internal or external) somehow influences postmarital residence rules. We need more research on the causes of multilocal, neolocal and avunculocal residence and unilineal descent.

We know that neither the incest-phobia nor the proximity hypothesis of kin avoidances withstands empirical testing. Ritualized kin relations is a complex topic. More work is needed.

While we have not learned a great deal about inheritance, the work of Goody and his associates at Cambridge has established a framework for future research. It seems reasonable to assume that inheritance practices are related to the type of subsistence economy and the nature of kin relations.

Expressive Culture

We do not yet know if Durkheim's contention—that the organization of the religious system of a society mirrors the social organization of the society—holds for the world in general. The evidence from two independent studies is contradictory. But we do know that child rearing practices are clearly related to beliefs about the nature of the supernatural. And we know that cultural complexity is related to the nature and complexity of religious practices, but not necessarily to the nature of religious beliefs. Of the four major evolutionary theories of religious development, only one has been tested holoculturally. We know that there is a general similarity among the people of the world in the emotions expressed during bereavement. Among factors that tend to shorten and ease bereavement are final funeral rites, change of residence by the survivor, and a taboo on the name of the deceased. There is much room for more holocultural research on religion.

We have not yet separated out the trustworthy theories of the origin and function of the postpartum sex taboo and menstrual taboo from the untrustworthy ones. The tests conducted so far are not of such quality to allow any theories to be classified as trustworthy. But we do know that the importance of the postpartum sex taboo as a cause of other cultural practices has been exaggerated.

And, we do know that societies are not entirely consistent nor inconsistent in their patterning of rules governing extramarital sex, premarital sex, rape, homosexuality, modesty, chastity, and kin avoidances. It seems, though, that the more complex a culture, the more restrictive will be its rules governing sexual behavior. Why this is so is not yet clear. Again, more research is needed.

We know also that games serve as expressive models of other cultural activities. Games of strategy are models of the kind of social interaction found among people in stratified societies. Games of chance are models of an uncertain social and physical world. We also know that games evolve in a clear developmental sequence, with games of physical skill appearing first, games of chance second, and games of strategy last.

Similarly, we suspect that art, music, and dance styles are also models of other cultural activities. While the findings of holocultural research suggest this deduction, the evidence is not yet conclusive. We do know that Lomax's notion that music style reflects level of cultural complexity has been largely discredited.

Socialization

We know that two important influences on parental behavior are the household structure and the nature of the subsistence economy. Alternative caretakers in the home generally ensure that infants will be indulged and children accepted. Children will more likely be rejected in mother-child households. The nature of the subsistence economy (food accumulation versus non-accumulation) helps determine whether children will be raised to be compliant and cooperative or independent and self-reliant. We do not yet know why the subsistence economy influences child rearing practices. Other possible influences on the way parents raise their children include birth order, level of cultural complexity, climate, and physiological factors.

We know from dozens of holocultural studies that certain child rearing practices and conditions are related to certain cultural practices and adult personality characteristics. Many of these studies follow a psychoanalytic model in which some psychodynamic mechanism such as anxiety or fixation is seen as mediating between the cause and effect. Actually, in these studies the psychodynamic mechanism is rarely measured, or, if measured, is done so with a questionable indirect measure. Thus, while we know that holo-cultural research supports a wide range of hypotheses derived from psychoanalytic personality theory, we wonder if these hypotheses are really tested.

We do not know why some societies have initiation rites while others do not. None of the five psychogenic or six sociogenic hypotheses tested so far has been convincingly supported. As a group, though, these theory tests suggest that initiation rites serve to smooth the transition from childhood to adulthood in societies where individual personality or sociocultural factors may interfere with that transition.

Social Problems, Deviance, and Social Control

We know that human aggression is at least as much the result of cultural patterning favoring aggression in certain societies as it is an innate drive. We know also that frustration does not invariably lead to aggression, although certain frustrations do seem to produce regularly the same aggressive responses. It seems that adult aggression may be related to childhood experiences, but we need more research to clarify the relationship.

We know that level of cultural complexity is a major determinant of the reasons a society goes to war and the strategy and tactics used in warfare. In small-scale societies and in non-industrialized civilizations it seems that preparedness for war only begets war. Preparedness for war seems to encourage rather than deter war. And, we know that the best assurance of stable peace is contact between political units. We also know that the presence of fraternal interest groups is associated with frequent feuding.

We know that thwarting disorientation situations in which the victim blames someone else for his or her loss of social ties is associated with suicide frequency.

Preliminary studies suggest links between theft and a feeling of being unloved, a high level of cultural complexity and social stratification. We do not know if a faulty father-son relationship makes it more likely that the son will be a criminal. The holocultural evidence is contradictory.

We do not know the cause of alcoholism; four major theories have been tested holoculturally. Each of these theories (anxiety-reduction, dependency-conflict, power motivation, and social disorganization) has been both questioned by some studies and supported by others.

We know that female status and power can be accurately measured from the ethnographic record if the focus is on specific behaviors rather than on gross assessments by the ethnographer. Using precise measures also controls any male bias problems with the data, although we do not yet have any means of measuring and controlling errors arising from differences in male and female perceptions of the world. We know that the relative importance of female subsistence contributions does not much affect female status and power. We also know that in matrilineal societies female autonomy is greatest when brothers and husbands share control over women. The nature of the division of labor by sex in small-scale societies is well established. But we do not know why there is such a division. Is it attributable to male/female differences in physical strength, or to female child care responsibilities, or to economy of effort? More holocultural theory testing is needed.

We have not learned much about aging and the treatment of the aged from holocultural research. But, it does seem that the aged have higher status and more power when they control vital information.

Holocultural studies have given us a short list of factors that may influence reproductive practices and the fertility and population growth rates in small-scale societies. Two findings we can trust are that a sizeable economic contribution by children is associated with population growth; and female subservience to men is unassociated with the population growth rate.

We know that social control in small-scale societies is often maintained through both coordinate and super-ordinate control mechanisms. We know that both do control violence. And, we know as well that witchcraft, sorcery, oaths, and ordeals are coordinate controls found often in small-scale societies.

REFERENCES

Aberle, David F.
  1961 Matrilineal Descent in Cross-Cultural Perspective. *In* Matrilineal
    Kinship. David Schneider and Kathleen Gough, eds. pp. 655-727.
    Berkeley: University of California Press.
Aberle, David F., Urie Bronfenbrenner, Eckhard H. Hess, Daniel R. Miller,
David M. Schneider and James N. Spuhler
  1963 The Incest Taboo and the Mating Patterns of Animals. American
    Anthropologist 65:253-265.
Abrahamson, Mark
  1969 Correlates of Political Complexity. American Sociological Review
    34:690-701.
Ackerman, Charles
  1968 Conjunctive Affiliation and Divorce. *In* A Modern Introduction to
    the Family. Norman W. Bell and Ezra F. Vogel, eds. pp. 469-478. New
    York: Free Press.
Adams, Richard N.
  1960 An Inquiry into the Nature of the Family. *In* Essays in the Science of
    Culture. Robert L. Carneiro and Gertrude E. Dole, eds. pp. 30-49. New
    York: Thomas Crowell.
Alland, Alexander, Jr. and Bonnie McCay
  1973 The Concept of Adaptation in Biological and Cultural Evoluation. *In*
    Handbook of Social and Cultural Anthropology. John J. Honigmann, ed.
    pp. 143-178. Chicago: Rand McNally.
Allen, Martin G.
  1967 Childhood Experience and Adult Personality—A Cross-Cultural
    Study Using the Concept of Ego Strength. Journal of Social Psychology
    71:53-68.
  1972 A Cross-Cultural Study of Aggression and Crime. Journal of Cross-
    Cultural Psychology 3:259-271.
Anderson, E. N., Jr.
  1972 Some Chinese Methods of Dealing with Crowding. Urban Anthro-
    pology 1:141-50.
Andrew, R. J.
  1971 Review of Ethology. Science 171:53-54.
Apple, Dorrian
  1956 The Social Structure of Grandparenthood. American Anthropologist
    58:656-663.
Ardener, Edwin W.
  1972 Belief and the Problem of Women. *In* The Interpretation of Ritual:

Essays in Honour of A. I. Richards. J. S. Fontaine, ed. pp. 135-158. London: Tavistock.

1975 Belief and the Problem of Women, and the "Problem" Revisited. *In* Perceiving Women. Shirley Ardener, ed. pp. 1-17, 19-27. New York: John Wiley.

Ardrey, Robert
1961 African Genesis. New York: Atheneum.
1966 The Territorial Imperative. New York: Atheneum.
1970 The Social Contract. New York: Atheneum.

Aronoff, Joel and William D. Crano
1975 A Re-examination of the Cross-Cultural Principles of Task Segregation and Sex Role Differentiation in the Family. American Sociological Review 40:12-20.

Ashby, W. R.
1964 An Introduction to Cybernetics. London: Chapman and Hall.

Avedon, Elliott M. and Brian Sutton-Smith
1971 The Study of Games. New York: John Wiley.

Ayres, Barbara
1967 Pregnancy Magic: A Study of Food Taboos and Sex Avoidances. *In* Cross-Cultural Approaches. Clellan S. Ford, ed. pp. 111-125. New Haven: HRAF Press.
1968 Effects of Infantile Stimulation on Musical Behavior. *In* Folk Song Style and Culture. Alan Lomax, ed. pp. 211-221. Washington, D. C.: American Association for the Advancement of Science.
1973 Effects of Infant-Carrying Practices on Rhythm in Music. Ethos 1:387-404.
1974 Bride Theft and Raiding for Wives in Cross-Cultural Perspective. Anthropological Quarterly 51:238-252.

Bacon, Margaret K.
1974 The Dependency-Conflict Hypothesis and the Frequency of Drunkenness. Quarterly Journal of Studies on Alcohol 35:863-876.

Bacon, Margaret K., Herbert Barry III and Irvin L. Child
1965 A Cross-Cultural Study of Drinking: II. Relations to Other Features of Culture. Quarterly Journal of Studies on Alcohol, Supplement 3:29-48.

Bacon, Margaret K., Irvin L. Child and Herbert Barry III
1963 A Cross-Cultural Study of the Correlates of Crime. Journal of Abnormal and Social Psychology 66:291-300.

Baks, C., J. C. Breman and A. T. J. Nooij
1966 Slavery as a System of Production in Tribal Society. Bijdragen tot de Taal-, Land- en Volkenkunde 122:90-109.

Banks, Arthur S. and Robert B. Textor
1963 A Cross-Polity Survey. Cambridge: M.I.T. Press.

Barber, B.
1941 Acculturation and Messianic Movements. American Sociological Review 6:663-669.

Barnes, J. A.
1971 Three Styles in the Study of Kinship. Berkeley: University of California Press.

Barnouw, Victor

1971   An Introduction to Anthropology: Ethnology. Homewood, Ill.: Dorsey Press.

Barrett, Gerald V. and Richard H. Franke
1970   Psychogenic Death: A Reappraisal. Science 167:304-306.

Barry, Herbert III
1957   Relationship between Child Training and the Pictorial Arts. Journal of Abnormal and Social Psychology 54:380-383.
1967   Ethnographic Atlas: Punched IBM Card Version. Pittsburgh: University of Pittsburgh.
1968   Sociocultural Aspects of Alcohol Addiction. In The Addictive States. A. Winkler, ed. pp. 455-471. Baltimore: Williams and Wilkens.
1969   Cross-Cultural Research with Matched Pairs of Societies. Journal of Social Psychology 79:25-33.

Barry, Herbert III and Leonora M. Paxon
1971   Infancy and Early Childhood: Cross-Cultural Codes 2. Ethnology 10:461-508.

Barry, Herbert III and John M. Roberts
1972   Infant Socialization and Games of Chance. Ethnology 11:296-308.

Barry, Herbert III, Margaret K. Bacon and Irvin L. Child
1957   A Cross-Cultural Survey of some Sex Differences in Socialization. Journal of Abnormal and Social Psychology 55:327-332.
1967   Definitions, Ratings, and Bibliographic Sources for Child Training Practices in 110 Cultures. In Cross-Cultural Approaches. Clellan S. Ford, ed. pp. 293-331. New Haven: HRAF Press.

Barry, Herbert III, Irvin L. Child and Margaret K. Bacon
1967   Relation of Child Training to Subsistence Economy. In Cross-Cultural Approaches. Clellan S. Ford, ed. pp. 146-258. New Haven: HRAF Press.

Barry, Herbert III, Lili Josephson, Edith Lauer and Catherine Marshall
1976   Traits Inculcated in Childhood: Cross-Cultural Codes 5. Ethnology 15:83-114.
1977   Agents and Techniques for Child Training: Cross-Cultural Codes 6. Ethnology 16:191-230.

Beardsley, Richard K., Preston Holder, Alex D. Krieger, Betty J. Meggers and John B. Rinaldo
1956   Functional and Evolutionary Implications of Community Patterning. Memoirs of the Society for American Archaeology, no. 11. American Antiquity 22, No. 2, Part II.

Becker, Ernest
1962   The Birth and Death of Meaning. New York: Free Press.

Becker, Howard S.
1963   Outsiders. New York: Free Press-Macmillan.

Befu, Harumi
1966   Political Complexity and Village Community: Test of an Hypothesis. Anthropological Quarterly 39:43-52.

Bellah, Robert
1964   Religious Evolution. American Sociological Review 29:358-374.

Bender, Donald R.
1967   A Refinement of the Concept of Household: Families, and

Domestic Functions. American Anthropologist 69:593-504.

Benedict, Ruth
1946   Patterns of Culture. New York: New American Library.

Bennett, Wendell C. and Robert M. Zingg
1935   The Tarahumara: An Indian Tribe of Northern Mexico. Chicago: University of Chicago Press.

Berleant-Schiller, Riva
1977   Comment. Current Anthropology 18:702.

Berlin, Brent and Paul Kay
1969   Basic Color Terms: Their Universality and Evolution. Berkeley and Los Angeles: University of California Press.

Berreman, Gerald D.
1978   Scale and Social Relations. Current Anthropology 19:225-237.

Berry, Brian J. C.
1967   Geography of Market Centers and Retail Distribution. Englewood Cliffs, N. J.: Prentice-Hall.

Berry, R., J. Boland, J. Laxson, D. Hayler, M. Sillman, R. Fein and P. Feldstein.
1974   The Economic Costs of Alcohol Abuse and Alcoholism—1971. Washington, D. C.: National Institute on Alcohol Abuse and Alcoholism.

Berting, J. and H. Philipsen
1960   Solidarity, Stratification and Sentiment: The Unilateral Cross-Cousin Marriage According to the Theories of Lévi-Strauss, Leach, and Homans and Schneider. Bijdragen tot de Taal-, Land- en Volkenkunde 116:55-80.

Beteille, André
1971   Caste, Class, and Power. Berkeley: University of California Press.

Bettelheim, Bruno
1954   Symbolic Wounds, Puberty Rites and the Envious Male. Glencoe, Ill.: Free Press.

Binford, Louis R.
1971   Mortuary Practices: Their Study and Their Potential. *In* Approaches to the Social Dimensions of Mortuary Practices. James A. Brown, ed. pp. 6-29. Washington, D.C.: Society for American Archaeology.

Blum, Richard H.
1969   A Cross-Cultural Study of Drugs. *In* Society and Drugs. Vol. I. Richard H. Blum and Associates, eds. pp. 135-186. San Francisco: Jossey-Bass.

Blumberg, Rae L. and Robert F. Winch
1972   Societal Complexity and Familial Complexity: Evidence for the Curvilinear Hypothesis. American Journal of Sociology 77:898-920.

Boas, Franz
1955   Primitive Art. New York: Dover.

Bohannan, Paul
1960   African Homicide and Suicide. Princeton: Princeton University Press.
1963   Social Anthropology. New York: Holt, Rinehart and Winston.
1968   An Alternative Residence Classification. *In* Marriage, Family, and Residence. Paul Bohannan and John Middleton, eds. pp. 317-323. Garden City, N. Y.: Natural History Press.

Bohannan, Paul and John Middleton, eds.

1968 Marriage, Family, and Residence. Garden City, N.Y.: Natural History Press.

Bornstein, Marc H.
1973 The Psychophysiological Component of Cultural Differences in Color Naming and Illusion Susceptibility. Behavior Science Notes 8:41-101
1975 The Influence of Visual Perception on Culture. American Anthropologist 77:774-798.

Botwinick, Jack
1973 Aging and Behavior. New York: Springer.

Bourguignon, Erika
1972 Dreams and Altered States of Consciousness in Anthropological Research. *In* Psychological Anthropology. New edition. Francis L. K. Hsu, ed. pp. 403-434. Cambridge: Schenkman.
1973 Religion, Altered States of Consciousness, and Social Change. Columbus: Ohio State University Press.

Bourguignon, Erika and Thomas L. Evascu
1977 Altered States of Consciousness within a General Evolutionary Perspective: A Holocultural Analysis. Behavior Science Research 12:197-216.

Bourguignon, Erika and Lenora Greenbaum
1973 Diversity and Homogeneity in World Societies. New Haven: HRAF Press.

Bowden, Edgar
1969a An Index of Sociocultural Development Applicable to Precivilized Societies. American Anthropologist 71:454-461.
1969b Indices of Sociocultural Development and Cultural Accumulation: An Exponential Cultural Growth Law and a "Cultural Surgency" Factor. American Anthropologist 71:1112-1115.
1972 Standardization of an Index of Sociocultural Development for Precivilized Societies. American Anthropologist 74:1122-1132.

Brant, Charles S.
1972 A Preliminary Study of Cross-Sexual Joking Relationships in Primitive Society. Behavior Science Notes 7:313-329.

Brenner, Charles
1957 An Elementary Textbook of Psychoanalysis. New York: Doubleday Anchor Books.

Broude, Gwen J.
1975 Norms of Premarital Behavior: A Cross-Cultural Study. Ethos 3:381-402.
1976 Cross-Cultural Patterning of Some Sexual Attitudes and Practices. Behavior Science Research 11:227-262.

Broude, Gwen J. and S. J. Greene
1976 Cross-Cultural Codes on Twenty Sexual Attitudes and Practices. Ethnology 15:409-429.

Brown, Judith K.
1963 A Cross-Cultural Study of Female Initiation Rites. American Anthropologist 65:837-853.
1969 Adolescent Initiation Rites among Preliterature People. *In* Studies in

Adolescence. Second edition. Robert E. Grinder, ed. pp. 59-68. New York: Macmillan.

1970 A Note on the Division of Labor by Sex. American Anthropologist 72:1073-1078.

Brown, Julia
1952 A Comparative Study of Deviations from Sexual Mores. American Sociological Review 17:135-146.

Buckley, Walter, ed.
1968 Modern Systems Research for the Behavioral Scientist: A Source Book. Chicago: Aldine.

Burnett, Jacquetta H. with Sally W. Gordon and Carol J. Gormley
1974 Anthropology and Education: An Annotated Bibliographic Guide. New Haven: HRAF Press for the Council on Anthropology and Education.

Burton, Roger V. and John W. M. Whiting
1963 The Absent Father and Cross-Sex Identity. *In* Studies in Adolescence. Robert E. Grinder, ed. pp. 107-117. New York: Macmillan.

Caillois, R.
1961 Man, Play and Games. New York: Free Press.

Calhoun, John B.
1962 Population Density and Social Pathology. Scientific American 296:139-148.

Campbell, Donald T. and Donald W. Fiske
1959 Convergent and Discriminant Validation by the Multitrait-Multimethod Matrix. Psychological Bulletin 56:81-105.

Carneiro, Robert L.
1968 Ascertaining, Testing, and Interpreting Sequences of Cultural Development. Southwestern Journal of Anthropology 24:354-474.

1970 Scale Analysis, Evolutionary Sequences, and the Rating of Cultures. *In* A Handbook of Method in Cultural Anthropology. Raoul Naroll and Ronald Cohen, eds. pp. 834-871. Garden City, N. Y.: Natural History Press. Reprinted 1973. New York: Columbia University Press.

1973a Classical Evolutionism. *In* Main Currents in Cultural Anthropology. Raoul Naroll and Frada Naroll, eds. pp. 57-122. New York: Appleton-Century-Crofts.

1973b The Four Faces of Evolution: Unilinear, Universal, Multilinear, and Differential. *In* Handbook of Social and Cultural Anthropology. John J. Honigmann, ed. pp. 89-110. Chicago: Rand McNally.

Carneiro, Robert L. and Stephen F. Tobias
1963 The Application of Scale Analysis to the Study of Cultural Evolution. Transactions of the New York Academy of Sciences, Ser. 2, 26:196-207.

Carr-Saunders, A. H.
1922 The Population Problem. Oxford: Oxford University Press.

Cavan, Ruth S.
1969 Juvenile Delinquency. Philadelphia: Lippincott.

Chagnon, Napoleon A.
1968 Yanomamo: The Fierce People. New York: Holt, Rinehart and Winston.

Chaney, Richard P.

1966a Typology and Patterning: Spiro's Sample Re-examined. American Anthropologist 68:1456-1470.

1966b A Reply to Spiro, or On the Misplaced Banderillas. American Anthropologist 68:1474-1476.

Chaney, Richard P. and R. Ruiz-Revilla
1969 Sampling Methods and Interpretation of Correlation: A Comparative Analysis of Seven Cross-Cultural Samples. American Anthropologist 71:597-633.

Chang, K. C.
1958 Study of the Neolithic Social Grouping: Examples from the New World. American Anthropologist 60:298-334.

1962 A Typology of Settlement and Community Patterns in Some Circumpolar Societies. Arctic Anthropology 1:28-41.

1968 Settlement Archaeology. Palo Alto: National Press.

1972 Settlement Patterns in Archaeology. Addison-Wesley Module in Anthropology, no. 24.

Child, Irvin L., Herbert Barry III and Margaret K. Bacon
1965 A Cross-Cultural Study of Drinking: III. Sex Differences. Quarterly Journal of Studies on Alcohol, Supplement 3:49-61.

Child, Irvin L., Thomas Storm and Joseph Veroff
1958 Achievement Themes in Folk Tales Related to Socialization Practices. *In* Motives in Fantasy, Action, and Society. John W. Atkinson, ed. pp. 479-492. Princeton: Van Nostrand.

Childe, V. Gordon
1941 War in Prehistoric Societies. Sociological Review 33:126-38.

Chilton, R. J.
1964 Continuity in Delinquency Area Research: A Comparison in Baltimore, Detroit, and Indianapolis. American Sociological Review 29:71-83.

Chorley, Richard J. and Peter Haggett, eds.
1967 Socio-Economic Models in Geography. London: Methuen.

Chu, Hsien-Jen and J. Selwyn Hollingsworth
1969 A Cross-Cultural Study of the Relationship between Family Types and Social Stratification. Journal of Marriage and the Family 31:322-327.

Clark, M. Margaret
1973 Contributions of Anthropology to the Study of the Aged. *In* Cultural Illness and Health. Laura Nader and Thomas W. Maretzki, eds. pp. 78-88. Washington, D. C.: American Anthropological Association.

Clarke, David L.
1968 Analytical Archaeology. London: Methuen.

Clarke, Edith
1957 My Mother Who Fathered Me: A Study of the Family in Three Selected Communities in Jamaica. London: Ruskin House.

Clough, G. C.
1965 Lemmings and Population Problems. American Scientist 53:199-212.

Cohen, Ronald, Alice Schlegel, Lawrence W. Felt and Earle Carlson
1968 The Tribe as a Sociopolitical Unit. *In* Essays in the Problem of Tribe. June Helm, ed. pp. 120-249. Seattle: University of Washington Press for the American Ethnological Society.

Cohen, Yehudi A.

1961 Food and Its Vicissitudes: A Cross-Cultural Study of Sharing and Non-Sharing. *In* Social Structure and Personality: A Casebook. Yehudi A. Cohen, ed. pp. 312-350. New York: Holt, Rinehart and Winston.

1964a The Transition from Childhood to Adolescence: Cross-Cultural Studies of Initiation Ceremonies, Legal Systems, and Incest Taboos. Chicago: Aldine.

1964b The Establishment of Identity in a Social Nexus: The Special Case of Initiation Ceremonies and Their Relation to Value and Legal Systems. American Anthropologist 66:529-552.

1969 Ends and Means in Political Control: State Organization and the Punishment of Adultery, Incest, and the Violation of Celibacy. American Anthropologist 71:658-687.

Colby, Kenneth M.
1963 Sex Differences in Dreams of Primitive Tribes. American Anthropologist 65:1116-1122.

Cole, G. D. H.
1932 Inheritance. *In* Encyclopedia of the Social Sciences. Edwin R. A. Seligman, ed. pp. 35-43. New York: Macmillan.

Colson, Elizabeth
1953 Social Control and Vengeance in Plateau Tonga Society. Africa 23:199-212.

Coppinger, Robert M. and Paul C. Rosenblatt
1968 Romantic Love and Subsistence Dependence of Spouses. Southwestern Journal of Anthropology 24:310-319.

Coult, Allan D.
1965 Terminological Correlates of Cross-Cousin Marriage. Bijdragen tot de Taal-, Land- en Volkenkunde 121:121-139.

Coult, Allan D. and Robert W. Habenstein
1965 Cross Tabulations of Murdock's World Ethnographic Sample. Columbia, Mo.: University of Missouri Press.

Cozby, Paul C. and Paul C. Rosenblatt
1971 Privacy, Love, and In-Law Avoidance. *In* American Psychological Association, 79th Annual Convention, Proceedings. pp. 277-278. Washington, D. C.: American Psychological Association.

D'Andrade, Roy G.
1966 Sex Differences and Cultural Institutions. *In* The Development of Sex Differences. Eleanor E. Maccoby, ed. pp. 174-204. Stanford: Stanford University Press.

Darwin, Charles
1859 The Origin of the Species. London: J. Murray.

Davidson, C. S.
1970 Nutrition, Geography, and Liver Diseases. American Journal of Clinical Nutrition 23:417-436.

Davie, Maurice R.
1929 The Evolution of War: A Study of Its Role in Early Societies. New Haven: Yale University Press.

Davis, Kingsley and Judith Blake
1956 Social Structure and Fertility: An Analytic Framework. Economic Development and Cultural Change 4:211-235.

Davis, William D.
1971 Societal Complexity and the Nature of Primitive Man's Conception of the Supernatural. Ph.D. Dissertation, University of North Carolina, Chapel Hill. Ann Arbor: University Microfilms, 72-10, 707.

Davis, William N.
1964 A Cross-Cultural Study of Drunkenness. B. A. Thesis, Harvard College, Cambridge, Massachusetts.

DeLeeuwe, Jules
1970 Society, System and Sexual Life. Bijdragen tot de Taal-, Land- en Volkenkunde 126:1-36.
1971 Replication in Cross-Cultural Research: Descent, Marriage System, and Mode of Production. Bijdragen tot de Taal-, Land- en Volkenkunde 127:82-145.

DeLint, Jan and Ronald Cohen
1960 On Factor Magic: A Discussion of Murdock's Theory of Social Evolution. Anthropologica 2:95-104.

Devereux, George
1955 A Study of Abortion in Primitive Societies. New York: Julian Press.

DeWaal Malefijt, Annemarie
1968 Religion and Culture: An Introduction to the Anthropology of Religion. New York: Macmillan.

Diebold, A. Richard
1966 The Reflection of Coresidence in Mareno Kinship Terminology. Ethnology 5:37-79.

Divale, William T.
1970 An Explanation for Primitive Warfare: Population Control and the Significance of Primitive Sex Ratios. New Scholar 2:172-193.
1971 Warfare in Primitive Societies: A Selected Bibliography. Los Angeles: California State College, Center for the Study of Armament and Disarmament.
1972 Systemic Population Control in the Middle and Upper Paleolithic: Inferences Based on Contemporary Hunter-Gatherers. World Archaeology 4:222-243.
1974a The Causes of Matrilocal Residence: A Cross-Ethnohistorical Survey. Ph.D. Dissertation, State University of New York at Buffalo. Ann Arbor: Xerox University Microfilms, 75-7742.
1974b Migration, External Warfare, and Matrilocal Residence. Behavior Science Research 9:75-133.
1976 Female Status and Cultural Evolution: A Study in Ethnographer Bias. Behavior Science Research 11:169-212.
1977 Living Floor Area and Marital Residence: A Replication. Behavior Science Research 12:109-116.

Divale, William T., Frosine Chamberis and Deborah Gangloff
1976 War, Peace and Marital Residence in Preindustrial Society. Journal of Conflict Resolution 20:57-78.

Divale, William T. and Marvin Harris
1976 Population, Warfare, and the Male Supremacist Complex. American Anthropologist 78:521-538.

Dixon, W. J., ed.

1964   BMD: Biomedical Computer Programs. Los Angeles: School of Medicine, University of California at Los Angeles.

Dole, Gertrude E.

1965   The Lineage Pattern of Kinship Nomenclature: Its Significance and Development. Southwestern Journal of Anthropology 21:36-61.

1972   Developmental Sequences of Kinship Patterns. *In* Kinship Studies in the Morgan Centennial Year. Priscilla Reining, ed. pp. 134-165. Washington, D. C.: Anthropological Society of Washington.

1973   Foundations of Contemporary Evolutionism. *In* Main Currents in Cultural Anthropology. Raoul Naroll and Frada Naroll, eds. pp. 247-280. New York: Appleton-Century-Crofts.

Dollard, John, L. Doob, N. E. Miller, O. H. Mowrer and R. R. Sears

1939   Frustration and Aggression. New Haven: Yale University Press. Reprinted 1969.

Douglas, Mary

1957   Animals in Lele Religious Thought. Africa 27:47-58.

1966   Purity and Danger. London: Routledge and Kegan Paul.

1968   Pollution. International Encyclopedia of the Social Sciences 12: 336-342.

Draper, Patricia

1973   Crowding among Hunter-Gatherers: The Kung Bushmen. Science 182:301-303.

1974   Comparative Studies in Socialization. *In* Annual Review of Anthropology. Volume 3. Bernard Siegel, ed. pp. 263-278. Palo Alto: Annual Reviews.

Driver, Harold E.

1956   An Integration of Functional, Evolutionary, and Historical Theory by Means of Correlations. Indiana University Publications in Anthropology and Linguistics, Memoir 12:1-26.

1961   Indians of North America. Chicago: University of Chicago Press.

1966   Geographical-Historical versus Psycho-Functional Explanations of Kin Avoidances. Current Anthropology 7:131-148.

1969   Girls' Puberty Rites and Matrilocal Residence. American Anthropologist 71:905-908.

1970a Statistical Studies of Continuous Geographical Distributions. *In* A Handbook of Method in Cultural Anthropology. Raoul Naroll and Ronald Cohen, eds. pp. 620-639. Garden City, N. Y.: Natural History Press. Reprinted 1973. New York: Columbia University Press.

1970b Innovations in Cross-Cultural Method from Ethnomusicology: A Review. Behavior Science Notes 5:117-124.

1973   Cross-Cultural Studies. *In* Handbook of Social and Cultural Anthropology. John J. Honigmann, ed. pp. 327-368. Chicago: Rand McNally.

Driver, Harold E. and William C. Massey

1957   Comparative Studies of North American Indians. Transactions of the American Philosophical Society 47:165-456.

Driver, Harold E. and Karl F. Schuessler

1957   Factor Analysis of Ethnographic Data. American Anthropologist 56:655-663.

1967   Correlational Analysis of Murdock's 1957 Ethnographic Sample.

American Anthropologist 69:332-352.

Dublin, L. I.
1963 Suicide. New York: Ronald.

Dumont, Louis
1966 Descent or Intermarriage? A Relational View of Australian Descent Systems. Southwestern Journal of Anthropology 22:231-250.
1968 Marriage Alliance. International Encyclopedia of the Social Sciences 10:19-23.

Durkheim, Emile
1898 La Prohibition de l'Inceste et Ses Origines. L'Anée Sociologique 1:1-70.
1915 The Elementary Forms of the Religious Life. New York: Free Press.
1951 Suicide. Glencoe, Ill.: Free Press.

Eckhardt, Kenneth W.
1971 Exchange Theory and Sexual Permissiveness. Behavior Science Notes 6:1-18.

Eckhardt, William
1975 Primitive Militarism. Journal of Peace Research 12:55-62.

Efron, Vera, Mark Keller and C. Gurioli
1974 Consumption of Alcohol and Alcoholism; 1974 edition. New Brunswick: Rutgers Center of Alcohol Studies.

Eggan, Fred
1950 Social Organization of the Western Pueblos. Chicago: University of Chicago Press.
1955a The Cheyenne and Arapaho. *In* Social Organization of North American Tribes. Fred Eggan, ed. pp. 33-95. Chicago: University of Chicago Press.
1955b Social Organization of North American Tribes. Chicago: University of Chicago Press.
1966 The American Indian. Chicago: Aldine.

Eibl-Eibesfeldt, I.
1970 Ethology. New York: Holt, Rinehart and Winston.

Eliade, Mircea
1958 Birth and Rebirth: The Religious Meaning of Initiation in Human Culture. William R. Trask, trans. New York: Harper.

Ember, Carol R.
1974 An Evaluation of Alternative Theories of Matrilocal versus Patrilocal Residence. Behavior Science Research 9:135-149.
1975 Residential Variation among Hunter-Gatherers. Behavior Science Research 10:199-227.
1981 A Cross-Cultural Perspective on Sex Differences. *In* Handbook of Cross-Cultural Human Development. Ruth H. Munroe, Robert L. Munroe and Beatrice B. Whiting, eds. pp. 531-580. New York: Garland.

Ember, Carol R. and Melvin Ember
1972 The Conditions Favoring Multilocal Residence. Southwestern Journal of Anthropology 28:382-400.
1973 Cultural Anthropology. New York: Appleton-Century-Crofts.

Ember, Carol R., Melvin Ember and Burton Pasternak
1974 On the Development of Unilineal Descent. Journal of Anthro-

pological Research 30:69-94.

Ember, Melvin

1961 A Preliminary Survey of Cross-Cultural Studies Relating to Health. Final Progress Report, Grant Number M-3090 (A), Division of Research Grants, National Institutes of Health. New Haven: Human Relations Area Files.

1962 Political Authority and the Structure of Kinship in Aboriginal Samoa. American Anthropologist 64:964-971.

1963 The Relationship between Economic and Political Development in Non-industrialized Societies. Ethnology 2:228-248.

1967 The Emergence of Neolocal Residence. New York Academy of Sciences, Transactions, Series II, 30:291-302.

1973 An Archaeological Indicator of Matrilocal versus Patrilocal Residence. American Antiquity 38:177-182.

1974a Conditions that May Favor Avunculocal Residence. Behavior Science Research 9:203-281.

1974b Warfare, Sex Ratio and Polygyny. Ethnology 13:197-106.

1975 On the Origins and Extension of the Incest Taboo. Behavior Science Research 10:249-281.

1978 Size of Color Lexicon: Interaction of Cultural and Biological Factors. American Anthropologist 80:362-367.

Ember, Melvin and Carol R. Ember

1971 The Conditions Favoring Matrilocal versus Patrilocal Residence. American Anthropologist 73:571-594.

1979 Male-Female Bonding: A Cross-Species Study of Mammals and Birds. Behavior Science Research 14:37-56.

Erickson, Edwin E.

1968 Self-Assertion, Sex Role, and Vocal Rasp. *In* Folk Song Style and Culture. Alan Lomax, ed. pp. 104-210. Washington, D. C.: American Association for the Advancement of Science.

1974 Galton's Worst: A Note on Ember's Reflection. *In* Studies in Cultural Diffusion: Galton's Problem. James M. Schaefer, ed. HRAFlex Book W6-002. New Haven: Human Relations Area Files.

1976 Tradition and Evolution in Song Style: A Reanalysis of Cantometric Data. Behavior Science Research 11:277-308.

1977 Cultural Evolution. American Behavioral Scientist 20:669-680.

Evans-Pritchard, E. E.

1965 The Position of Women in Primitive Societies and in Our Own. *In* The Position of Women in Primitive Societies and Other Essays in Social Anthropology. E. E. Evans-Pritchard, ed. pp. 37-58. New York: Free Press.

Evascu, Thomas L.

1975 A Holocultural Study of Societal Organization and Modes of Marriage: A General Evolutionary Model. HRAFlex Books. New Haven: Human Relations Area Files.

Eyde, David B. and Paul M. Postal

1961 Avunculocality and Incest: The Development of Unilateral Cross-Cousin Marriage and Crow-Omaha Kinship Systems. American Anthropologist 63:747-771.

Faris, Robert E. L.
  1948   Social Disorganization. New York: Ronald Press.
Fenichel, Otto
  1945   The Psychoanalytic Theory of Neuroses. New York: W. W. Norton.
Field, Peter B.
  1962   A New Cross-Cultural Study of Drunkenness. *In* Society, Culture
    and Drinking Patterns. David G. Pittman and Charles R. Snyder, eds.
    pp. 48-74. New York: Wiley.
Firth, Raymond
  1957   We, the Tikopia: Kinship in Primitive Polynesia. Boston: Beacon
    Press.
Fischer, Jack L.
  1961   Art Styles as Cultural Cognitive Maps. American Anthropologist
    63:79-93.
Fisher, Seymour and Roger P. Greenberg
  1977   The Scientific Credibility of Freud's Theories and Therapy. New
    York: Basic Books.
Ford, Clellan S.
  1945   A Comparative Study of Human Reproduction. Yale University
    Publications in Anthropology No. 32. New Haven: Yale University Press.
Ford, Clellan S. and Frank A. Beach
  1951   Patterns of Sexual Behavior. New York: Harper and Row.
Fortes, Meyer
  1949   Time and Social Structure: An Ashanti Case Study. *In* Social
    Structure: Studies Presented to A. R. Radcliffe-Brown. Meyer Fortes,
    ed. pp. 54-84. London: Oxford University Press.
  1950   Kinship and Marriage among the Ashanti. *In* African Systems of
    Kinship and Marriage. A. R. Radcliffe-Brown and Daryll Forde, eds.
    pp. 252-284. London: Oxford University Press.
Fortune, Reo
  1932   Incest. Encyclopedia of the Social Sciences 7:620-622.
Fox, Robin
  1967   Kinship and Marriage. Baltimore: Penguin Books.
Fraser, Douglas
  1968   Village Planning in the Primitive World. New York: George
    Braziller.
Frazer, Sir James George
  1959   The New Golden Bough. Theodore H. Gaster, ed. New York:
    Criterion Books. First Published 1890.
Freedman, Jonathan L.
  1972   Population Density, Juvenile Delinquency and Mental Illness in New
    York City. *In* Population Distribution and Policy. Sara M. Maize, ed.
    pp. 515-523. Washington, D. C.: Government Printing Office.
  1973   The Effects of Population Density on Humans. *In* Psychological
    Perspectives on Population. James T. Fawcett, ed. pp. 209-238. New
    York: Basic Books.
Freedman, Maurice
  1970   Lineage Organization in Southeastern China. London School of
    Economics, Monographs on Social Anthropology, no. 18. London:

Athlone Press.

Freeman, John D.
1955   Agriculture: A Report on the Shifting Cultivation of Hill Rice by the Iban of Sarawak. London: Her Majesty's Stationery Office.

Freeman, Linton C.
1957   An Empirical Test of Folk-Urbanism. Unpublished Ph.D. Dissertation, Northwestern University, Evanston, Illinois.

Freeman, Linton C. and Robert F. Winch
1957   Societal Complexity: An Empirical Test of Typology of Societies. American Journal of Sociology 62:461-466.

Freud, Sigmund
1918   Contributions to the Psychology of Love. The Taboo of Virginity. *In* The Collected Papers of Sigmund Freud. Vol. 4. pp. 217-235. London: Hogarth Press.
1924   Collected Papers. Vol. I. J. Rickman, trans. London: Hogarth Press.
1928   The Future of an Illusion. W. D. Robsonscott, trans. Edinburgh: Horace Liveright.
1936   The Problem of Anxiety. H. A. Bunker, trans. New York: Norton.
1938   A General Introduction to Psychoanalysis. J. Riviere, trans. New York: Garden City Publishing.
1950   Totem and Taboo. London: Routledge and Kegan Paul.
1953   The Interpretation of Dreams. J. Strachey, trans. *In* The Standard Edition of the Complete Psychological Works of Sigmund Freud. Vols. 4 and 5. London: Hogarth Press.
1955   Moses and Monotheism. New York: Vantage Books.
1956   Mourning and Melancholia. *In* Collected Papers of Sigmund Freud. Vol. 4. pp. 152-170. London: Hogarth.
1959   Beyond the Pleasure Principle. J. Strachey, trans. New York: Bantam Books.
1960   The Ego and the Id. J. Riviere, trans. New York: Norton.
1961   Civilization and Its Discontents. J. Strachey, trans. New York: Norton.

Fried, Morton
1967   The Evolution of Political Society. New York: Random House.

Friedl, Ernestine
1967   The Position of Women: Appearance and Reality. Anthropological Quarterly 39:97-108.
1975   Women and Men: An Anthropologist's View. New York: Holt, Rinehart and Winston.

Fuller, Richard C. and Richard R. Myers
1941   Some Aspects of a Theory of Social Problems. American Sociological Review 6:24-32.

Gardner, Robert
1964   Dead Birds. (16-mm. film, 83 min.). Cambridge: Peabody Museum, Harvard University.

Gearing, Frederick O. and B. Allan Tindall
1973   Anthropological Studies of the Education Process. *In* Annual Review of Anthropology. Bernard J. Siegel, ed. pp. 95-106. Palo Alto: Annual Reviews.

Geertz, Clifford
   1966   Religion as a Cultural System. *In* Anthropological Approaches to
   the Study of Religion. Michael Banton, ed. pp. 1-26. London: Tavistock.
Gerth, H. H. and C. Wright Mills, eds. and trans.
   1958   From Max Weber: Essays in Sociology. New York: Oxford University Press.
Gibbs, J. P. and W. Martin
   1964   Status Integration and Suicide. Eugene: University of Oregon Press.
Gilbert, William H., Jr.
   1955   Eastern Cherokee Social Organization. *In* Social Organization of
   North American Tribes. Fred Eggan, ed. pp. 283-338. Chicago: University of Chicago Press.
Gillis, A. R.
   1974   Population Density and Social Pathology: The Case of Building
   Type, Social Allowance, and Juvenile Delinquency. Social Forces
   3:306-314.
Gluckman, Max
   1956   Custom and Conflict in Africa. Glencoe: Free Press.
   1962   Les Rites de Passage. *In* Essays in the Ritual of Social Relations.
   Max Gluckman, ed. pp. 1-52. Manchester: Manchester University
   Press.
Glueck, Sheldon and Eleanor T. Glueck
   1950   Unraveling Juvenile Delinquency. New York: Commonwealth
   Fund.
Goffman, Erving
   1961   Encounters: Two Studies in the Sociology of Interaction. Indianapolis: Bobbs-Merrill.
   1967   Interaction Ritual: Essays on Face-to-Face Behavior. New York:
   Anchor Books.
Goodale, Jane
   1971   Tiwi Wives. Seattle: University of Washington Press.
Goodenough, Ward H.
   1955   A Problem in Malayo-Polynesian Social Organization. American
   Anthropologist 57:71-83.
   1969   Basic Economy and Community. Behavior Science Notes 4:291-298.
   1970   Description and Comparison in Cultural Anthropology. Chicago:
   Aldine.
Goody, Jack
   1959   The Mother's Brother and the Sister's Son in West Africa. Journal
   of the Royal Anthropological Institute of Great Britain and Ireland
   89:61-88.
   1969a   Comparative Studies in Kinship. Stanford: Stanford University
   Press.
   1969b   Inheritance, Property, and Marriage in Africa and Eurasia.
   Sociology 3:55-76.
   1970a   Cousin Terms. Southwestern Journal of Anthropology 26:125-142.
   1970b   Sideways or Downwards? Lateral and Vertical Succession,
   Inheritance and Descent in Africa and Eurasia. Man n.s. 5:627-638.
   1973   Bridewealth and Dowry in Africa and Eurasia. *In* Bridewealth and

Dowry. Jack Goody and S. J. Tambiah, eds. pp. 1-58. Cambridge: Cambridge University Press.

1976   Production and Reproduction: A Comparative Study of the Domestic Domain. Cambridge Studies in Social Anthropology Number 17. Cambridge: Cambridge University Press.

Goody, Jack and Joan Buckley
1974   Cross-sex Patterns of Kin Behavior: A Comment. Behavior Science Research 9:185-202.

Goody, Jack, Barrie Irving and Nicky Tahany
1970   Causal Inferences Concerning Inheritance and Property. Human Relations 24:295-314.

Gorer, Geoffrey
1935   Book One: Senegalese. *In* Africa Dances: A Book about West African Negroes. pp. 25-79. London: Farber and Farber.
1948   The American People. New York: W. W. Norton.

Gough, Kathleen E.
1959   The Nayars and the Definition of Marriage. Journal of the Royal Anthropological Institute of Great Britain and Ireland 89:23-34.
1961   Variations in Residence. *In* Matrilineal Kinship. David M. Schneider and Kathleen E. Gough, eds. Berkeley: University of California Press.

Gouldner, Alvin W. and Richard A. Peterson
1962   Notes on Technology and the Moral Order. Indianapolis: Bobbs-Merrill.

Granzberg, Gary
1973a   The Psychological Integration of Culture: A Cross-Cultural Study of Hopi Type Initiation Rites. Journal of Social Psychology 90:3-7.
1973b   Twin Infanticide: A Cross-Cultural Test of a Materialistic Explanation. Ethos 1:405-412.

Graves, Theodore D.
1967   Acculturation, Access, and Alcohol. American Anthropologist 69:306-321.

Greenwood, Davydd J. and William A. Stini
1977   Nature, Culture, and Human History: A Bio-Cultural Introduction to Anthropology. New York: Harper and Row.

Gudeman, Stephen
1977   Morgan in Africa. Reviews in Anthropology 4:575-580.

Gummerman, George J., ed.
1971   The Distribution of Prehistoric Population Aggregates. Proceedings of the Southwestern Anthropological Research Group. Anthropological Reports 1. Prescott, Ariz.: Prescott College Press.

Gunders, Shulamith and John W. M. Whiting
1964   The Effects of Periodic Separation from the Mother during Infancy upon Growth and Development. Paper presented at the seventh International Congress of Anthropological and Ethnological Sciences, Moscow.
1968   Mother-Infant Separation and Physical Growth. Ethnology 7:196-206.

Guthrie, George M.

1971 Unexpected Correlations and the Cross-Cultural Method. Journal of Cross-Cultural Psychology 2:315-323.

Haas, Michael
1967 Social Change and National Aggressiveness, 1900-1960. *In* Quantitative International Politics: Insights and Evidence. J. David Singer, ed. pp. 214-374. New York: Free Press.

Haeckel, Josef
1970 Source Criticism in Anthropology. T. A. Tatje and E. M. Shepers, trans. *In* A Handbook of Method in Cultural Anthropology. Raoul Naroll and Ronald Cohen, eds. pp. 147-164. Garden City, N.Y.: Natural History Press. Reprinted 1973. New York: Columbia University Press.

Haggett, Peter
1965 Locational Analysis in Human Geography. London: Edward Arnold.

Haggett, Peter and Richard J. Chorley, eds.
1971 Network Analysis in Geography. London: Edward Arnold.

Hall, A.D. and R.E. Fagen
1968 Definition of a System. *In* Modern Systems Research for the Behavioral Scientist: A Source Book. Walter Buckley, ed. pp. 81-92. Chicago: Aldine.

Hall, Calvin S.
1954 A Primer of Freudian Psychoanalysis. New York: Mentor Books.

Hall, Edward T.
1968 Proxemics. Current Anthropology 9:83-109.

Halpern, Joel M.
1958 A Serbian Village. New York: Columbia University Press.

Harner, Michael J.
1970 Population Pressure and the Social Evolution of Agriculturalists. Southwestern Journal of Anthropology 26:67-86.

Harrington, Charles
1968 Sexual Differentiation in Socialization and Some Male Genital Mutilations. American Anthropologist 70:951-956.

Harrington, Charles and John W. M. Whiting
1972 Socialization Process and Personality. *In* Psychological Anthropology. New edition. Francis L. K. Hsu, ed. pp. 469-508. Cambridge: Schenkman.

Harris, Marvin
1968 The Rise of Anthropological Theory. New York: Crowell.

Hays, David G., Enid Margolis, Raoul Naroll and Dale Revere Perkins
1972 Color Term Salience. American Anthropologist 74:1107-1121.

Heath, Dwight B.
1958 Sexual Divison of Labor and Cross-Cultural Research. Social Forces 37:77-79.

Hempel, Carl G.
1965 Aspects of Scientific Explanation and Other Essays in the Philosophy of Science. New York: Free Press.

Henry, Andrew F. and James F. Short
1954 Suicide and Homicide. Glencoe, Ill.: Free Press.

Henry, Jules
1972 Jules Henry on Education. New York: Vintage Books.

Herskovits, Melville J.
  1948 Man and His Works. New York: Knopf.
Herzog, John D.
  1962 Deliberate Instruction and Household Structure: A Cross-Cultural Study. Harvard Educational Review 32:301-342.
Hiatt, Betty
  1970 Woman the Gatherer. Australian Aboriginal Studies 32:2-9.
Hickman, John M.
  1962 Dimensions of a Complex Concept: A Method Exemplified. Human Organization 21:214-218.
Hines, Dwight and Colin Martindale
  1974 Possible Rhinencephalic Influences on Human Maternal Behavior: A Cross-Cultural Study. Paper presented at the second International Conference on Cross-Cultural Psychology, Kingston, Ontario.
Hirayama, T.
  1970 A Prospective Study on the Influence of Cigarette Smoking and Alcohol Drinking on the Death Rates for Total and Selected Causes of Death in Japan. Smoke Signals 16:1-6.
Hoben, Allan
  1973 Land Tenure among the Amhara of Ethiopia: The Dynamics of Cognatic Descent. Chicago: University of Chicago Press.
Hobhouse, L. T., G. C. Wheeler and M. Ginsburg
  1915 Material Culture and Social Institutions of the Simpler Peoples: An Essay in Correlation. London: Chapman and Hall.
Hochschild, Arlie R.
  1973 A Review of Sex Role Research. American Journal of Sociology 78:1011-1029.
Hoebel, E. Adamson
  1940 The Political Organization and Law—Ways of the Comanche Indians. American Anthropological Association, Memoir 54.
  1954 The Law of Primitive Man. Cambridge: Harvard University Press.
  1966 Anthropology: The Study of Man. Third edition. New York: McGraw-Hill
Homans, George C. and David M. Schneider
  1962 Marriage, Authority, and Final Causes: A Study of Unilateral Cross-Cousin Marriage. *In* Sentiments and Activities: Essays in Social Science. George C. Homans, ed. pp. 202-256. New York: Free Press.
Honigmann, John, ed.
  1973 Handbook of Social and Cultural Anthropology. Chicago: Rand McNally.
Horton, Donald
  1943 The Functions of Alcohol in Primitive Societies: A Cross-Cultural Study. Quarterly Journal of Studies on Alcohol 4:199-320.
Hudson, F. S.
  1970 A Geography of Settlements. London: MacDonald and Evans.
Huizinga, J.
  1955 Homo Ludens: A Study of the Play Element in Culture. Boston: Beacon Press.
Human Relations Area Files

1967 The HRAF Quality Control Sample Universe. Behavior Science Notes 2: 81-88.

Hunter, David E. and Phillip Whitten, eds.
1976 Encyclopedia of Anthropology. New York: Harper and Row.

Inkeles, Alex and Daniel J. Levinson
1954 National Character: The Study of Modal Personality and Socio-cultural Systems. *In* Handbook of Social Psychology. Vol. 2. Gardner Lindzey, ed. pp. 977-1020. Cambridge: Addison-Wesley.

Jackson, Gary B. and A. Kimball Romney
1973 Historical Inference from Cross-Cultural Data: The Case of Dowry. Ethos 1:517-520.

Jones, Emrys
1966 Human Geography. New York: Praeger.

Jorgensen, Joseph G.
1966 Addendum: Geographical Clustering and Functional Explanations of In-Law Avoidances: An Analysis of Comparative Method. Current Anthropology 7:161-169.

Justinger, Judith M.
1977 The Anthropological Study of Religion: Past and Future. American Behavioral Scientist 20:711-720.

Kaberry, Phyllis M.
1939 Aboriginal Woman, Sacred and Profane. London: Routledge.

Kaeppler, Adrienne L.
1978 Dance in Anthropological Perspective. *In* Annual Reviews of Anthropology. Vol. 7. Bernard J. Siegel, ed. pp. 31-40. Palo Alto: Annual Reviews.

Kalin, Rudolph, William N. Davis and David C. McClelland
1966 The Relationship between Use of Alcohol and Thematic Content of Folk Tales in Primitive Societies. *In* The General Inquirer. Phillip J. Stone, Dexter C. Dunphy, Marshall S. Smith and Daniel M. Ogilvie, eds. pp. 569-588. Cambridge: M.I.T. Press.

Kang, Gay E.
1976a Solidarity Theory: A Cross-Cultural Test of the Relationships among Exogamy, Cross-Allegiance, Peace, and Survival Value. Un-published Ph.D. Dissertation, State University of New York at Buffalo.
1976b Conflicting Loyalties Theory: A Cross-Cultural Test. Ethnology 15: 201-210.
1979 Exogamy and Peace Relations of Social Units: A Cross-Cultural Test. Ethnology 18:85-99.

Kaplan, Bert and Richard Lawless
1965 Culture and Visual Imagery: A Comparison of Rorschach Responses in Eleven Societies. *In* Context and Meaning in Cultural Anthropology. Melford E. Spiro, ed. pp. 295-311. New York: Free Press.

Kardiner, Abram
1939 The Individual and His Society. New York: Columbia University Press.

Keller, Mark and Vera Efron
1959 Selected Statistics on Alcoholic Beverages and Alcoholism: With a Bibiography of Sources. New Haven: Journal of Studies on Alcohol.

Keesing, Roger M.
   1973   Kin Groups and Social Structure. New York: Holt, Rinehart and
   Winston.
Kiev, Ari
   1960   Primitive Therapy: A Cross-Cultural Study of the Relationship
   between Child Training and Therapeutic Practices Related to Illness.
   Psychoanalytic Study of Society 1:185-217.
Kitahara, Michio
   1974   Living Quarter Arrangements in Polygyny and Circumcision and
   Segregation of Males at Puberty. Ethnology 13:401-413.
   1975   Significance of the Father for the Son's Masculine Identity. Behavior
   Science Research 10:1-17.
Klausner, Samuel Z.
   1964   Sacred and Profane Meanings of Blood and Alcohol. Journal of
   Social Psychology 64:27-43.
Kloos, Peter
   1963   Marital Residence and Local Endogamy: Environmental Knowledge
   or Leadership. American Anthropologist 65:854-862.
Kluckhohn, Clyde
   1939   Theoretical Bases for an Empirical Method of Studying the
   Acquisition of Culture by Individuals. Man 39:98-105.
   1941   Patterning as Exemplified in Navaho Culture. *In* Language, Culture
   and Personality: Essays in Memory of Edward Sapir. Leslie Spier,
   A. Irving Hallowell and Stanley S. Newman, eds. pp. 109-130. Menasha:
   Sapir Memorial Publication Fund.
Kluckhohn, Clyde and Dorothea Leighton
   1946   The Navaho. New York: Doubleday.
Köbben, A. J. F.
   1952   New Ways of Presenting an Old Idea: The Statistical Method
   in Social Anthropology. Journal of the Royal Anthropological Institute
   of Great Britain and Ireland 82:129-146.
   1967   Why Exceptions? The Logic of Cross-Cultural Analysis. Current
   Anthropology 8:3-19.
Köbben, A. J. F., L. Verrips and L. N. J. Brunt
   1974   Lévi-Strauss and Empirical Inquiry. Ethnology 13:215-223.
Krauss, Herbert H.
   1966   A Cross-Cultural Study of Suicide. Unpublished Ph.D. Dissertation,
   Northwestern University, Evanston, Illinois.
   1970   Social Development and Suicide. Journal of Cross-Cultural Psychology 1:159-167.
Krauss, Herbert H. and Beatrice J. Krauss
   1968   Cross-Cultural Study of the Thwarting Disorientation Theory of
   Suicide. Journal of Abnormal Psychology 73:353-357.
Krauss, Herbert H. and Abraham Tesser
   1971   Social Contexts of Suicide. Journal of Abnormal Psychology 78:222-
   228.
Kroeber, Alfred L.
   1909   Classificatory Systems of Relationship. Journal of the Royal Anthropological Institute of Great Britain and Ireland 39:77-84.

1948   Anthropology: Race, Language, Culture, Psychology, Prehistory. New York: Harcourt, Brace.
Krzywicki, Ludwig
1934   Primitive Society and Its Vital Statistics. London: Macmillan.
Kunstadter, Peter
1963   A Survey of the Consanguine or Matrifocal Family. American Anthropologist 65:56-66.
Lagacé, Robert O.
1977   (ed.) Sixty Cultures: A Guide to the HRAF Probability Sample Files (Part A). New Haven: Human Relations Area Files.
1979   The HRAF Probability Sample: Retrospect and Prospect. Behavior Science Research 14:211-229.
Lambert, William W., Leigh Minturn Triandis and Margery Wolf
1959   Some Correlates of Beliefs in the Malevolence and Benevolence of Supernatural Beings: A Cross-Societal Study. Journal of Abnormal and Social Psychology 58:162-169.
Lamphere, Louise
1974   Strategies, Cooperation and Conflict among Women in Domestic Groups. *In* Woman, Culture and Society. Michelle Zimbalist Rosaldo and Louise Lamphere, eds. pp. 97-112. Stanford: Stanford University Press.
Landauer, Thomas K.
n.d.   Effects of Infantile Vaccination on Growth. Unpublished manuscript.
Landauer, Thomas K. and John W. M. Whiting
1964   Infantile Stimulation and Adult Stature of Human Males. American Anthropologist 66:1007-1028.
Leach, Edmund R.
1951   The Structural Implications of Matrilateral Cross-Cousin Marriage. Journal of the Royal Anthropological Institute of Great Britain and Ireland 81:23-55.
1954   Political Systems of Highland Burma. Cambridge: Harvard University Press.
1961   Rethinking Anthropology. London School of Economics Monographs in Anthropology, 22. London: Athlone Press.
1964   Anthropological Aspects of Language: Animal Categories and Verbal Abuse. *In* New Directions in the Study of Language. E. Lenneberg, ed. pp. 23-63. Cambridge: M.I.T. Press.
1966   Review of Murdock, Culture and Society. American Anthropologist 68: 1517-1518.
1969   Kachin and Haka Chin: A Rejoinder to Lévi-Strauss. Man 4:277-285.
Leary, James R.
1961   Food Taboos and Level of Culture: A Cross-Cultural Study. Appendix A, Final Report, USPHS Grant No. A-3557.
Lee, Richard B. and Irven DeVore, eds.
1968   Man the Hunter. Chicago: Aldine.
Leis, Nancy B.
1974   Women in Groups: Ijau Women's Associations. *In* Woman, Culture

and Society. Michelle Zimbalist Rosaldo and Louise Lamphere, eds. pp. 223-242. Stanford: Stanford University Press.

Lenski, Gerhard and Jean Lenski
  1970 Human Societies: An Introduction to Macrosociology. New York: McGraw-Hill.

Lessa, William E. and Evon Vogt, eds.
  1972 Reader in Comparative Religion: An Anthropological Approach. New York: Harper and Row.

Lester, David
  1967a Suicide, Homicide, and the Effects of Socialization. Journal of Personality and Social Psychology 5:466-468.
  1967b The Relation between Discipline Experiences and the Expression of Aggression. American Anthropologist 69:732-737.
  1968 National Motives and Psychogenic Death Rates. Science 161:1260.
  1969 The Fear of the Dead in Nonliterate Societies. Journal of Social Psychology 77:283-284.
  1970 Adolescent Suicide and Premarital Sexual Behavior. Journal of Social Psychology 82:131-132.
  1971 The Incidence of Suicide and the Fear of the Dead in Non-Literate Societies. Journal of Cross-Cultural Psychology 2:207-208.
  1975 The Fear of Death in Primitive Societies. Behavior Science Research 10:229-232.

LeVine, Robert A.
  1960 The Role of the Family in Authority Systems: A Cross-Cultural Application of the Stimulus-Generalization Theory. Behavioral Science 5: 291-296.
  1962 Witchcraft and Co-Wife Proximity in Southwestern Kenya. Ethnology 1: 39-45.
  1973 Culture, Behavior and Personality. Chicago: Aldine.
  1978 Adulthood and Aging in Cross-Cultural Perspective. Items 31/32:1-5.

Levinson, David
  1977a What Have We Learned from Cross-Cultural Surveys? American Behavioral Scientist 20:757-791.
  1977b (ed.) A Guide to Social Theory: Worldwide Cross-Cultural Tests. New Haven: Human Relations Area Files.
  1979 Population Density in Cross-Cultural Perspective. American Ethnologist 6:742-751.

Levinson, David and Elizabeth G. Morgan
  n.d. Coded Data for the Probability Sample Files. Behavior Science Research (in press).

Levinson, David and Eleanor Swanson
  n.d. Female Power and Female Trade: A Preliminary Cross-Cultural Study. Unpublished Manuscript. New Haven.

Lévi-Strauss, Claude
  1956 The Family. In Man, Culture and Society. Harry L. Shapiro, ed. pp. 261-285. New York: Oxford University Press.
  1963 Structural Anthropology. New York: Basic Books.
  1968 The Family. In Studies in Social and Cultural Anthropology. John Middleton, ed. pp. 128-155. New York: Thomas Y. Crowell.

1969   The Elementary Structures of Kinship. James Harle Bell, John Richard von Sturmer and Rodney Needham, trans. Boston: Beacon Press.
Levy, Marion J.
1949   The Family Revolution in Modern China. Cambridge: Harvard University Press.
Levy, Marion J. and Lloyd A. Fallers
1959   The Family: Some Comparative Considerations. American Anthropologist 61:647-651.
Lévy-Bruhl, Lucien
1926   How Natives Think. Lilian A. Clare, trans. London: Allen and Unwin.
1931   Primitives and the Supernatural. Lilian A. Clare, trans. London: Allen and Unwin.
Lewis, Oscar
1956   Comparisons in Cultural Anthropology. In Current Anthropology: A Supplement to Anthropology Today. W. L. Thomas, ed. pp. 259-292. Chicago: University of Chicago Press.
Linton, Ralph
1936   The Study of Man. New York: D. Appleton-Century.
1943   Nativistic Movements. American Anthropologist 45:230-240.
Linton, Sally
1971   Woman the Gatherer: Male Bias in Anthropology. In Woman in Cross-Cultural Perspective: A Preliminary Sourcebook. Sue-Ellen Jacobs, ed. pp. 9-20. Urbana: University of Illinois, Department of Urban and Regional Planning.
Lippert, Julius
1931   The Evolution of Culture. New York: Macmillan.
Lofland, Lyn H.
1973   A World of Strangers. New York: Basic Books.
Lomax, Alan
1968a   Social Solidarity. In Folk Song Style and Culture. Alan Lomax, ed. pp. 170-203. Washington, D. C.: American Association for the Advancement of Science.
1968b   Song as a Measure of Culture. In Folk Song Style and Culture. Alan Lomax, ed. pp. 117-169. Washington, D. C.: American Association for the Advancement of Science.
Lomax, Alan and Conrad M. Arensberg
1977   A Worldwide Evolutionary Classification of the Cultures by Subsistence Systems. Current Anthropology 18:659-701.
Lomax, Alan, Irmgard Bartenieff and Forrestine Paulay
1968   Dance Style and Culture. In Folk Song Style and Culture. Alan Lomax, ed. pp. 222-247. Washington, D. C.: American Association for the Advancement of Science.
Lomax, Alan, with Norman Berkowitz
1972   The Evolutionary Taxonomy of Culture. Science 177:228-239.
Lorenz, Konrad
1966   On Aggression. New York: Harcourt, Brace and World.
Lorimer, Frank L., Meyer Fortes, K. A. Busia, Audrey I. Richards, Priscilla

Reining and Giorgio Mortara
  1954 Culture and Human Fertility. Paris: UNESCO.
Lounsbury, Floyd G.
  1962 Review of R. Needham, Structure and Sentiment. American Anthropologist 64:1302-1310.
Lowie, Robert H.
  1920 Primitive Society. New York: Liveright.
  1928 Relationship Terms. Encyclopedia Britannica. 14th ed. 19:84-90.
  1948 Social Organization. New York: Rinehart.
Luce, R. D. and Howard Raiffa
  1967 Games and Decisions: Introduction and Critical Survey. New York: John Wiley.
Mackay, D. M.
  1968 Towards an Information-Flow Model of Human Behavior. *In* Modern Systems Research for the Behavioral Scientist. Walter Buckley, ed. pp. 359-368. Chicago: Aldine.
Mair, Lucy
  1971 Marriage. New York: Pica Press.
Malinowski, Bronislaw
  1922 Argonauts of the Western Pacific. New York: E. P. Dutton.
  1927 Sex and Repression in Savage Society. London: Routledge and Kegan Paul.
  1941 War—Past, Present, and Future. *In* War as a Social Institution: The Historian's Perspective. J. Clarkson and T. Cochran, eds. pp. 20-30. New York: Columbia University Press.
  1954 Magic, Science and Religion and Other Essays. Garden City, N. Y.: Doubleday Anchor Books.
Maloney, Clarence, ed.
  1976 The Evil Eye. New York: Columbia University Press.
March, James A.
  1955 Group Autonomy and Internal Group Control. Social Forces 33:322-326.
Marett, R.
  1909 The Threshold of Religion. London: Methuen.
Marsden, H. M.
  1970 Crowding and Animal Behavior. Paper presented at the annual meeting of the American Psychological Association, Miami.
Marsh, Robert
  1967 Comparative Sociology. New York: Harcourt Brace.
Marshall, Donald S.
  1971 Sexual Behavior on Mangaia. *In* Human Sexual Behavior. Donald S. Marshall and Robert C. Suggs, eds. pp. 103-162. New York: Basic Books.
Martin, M. Marlene
  1978 Women in the HRAF Files: A Consideration of Ethnographic Bias. Behavior Science Research 13:303-314.
Masamura, Wilfred T.
  1977a Law and Violence: A Cross-Cultural Study. Journal of Anthropological Research 33:388-399.
  1977b Social Integration and Suicide: A Test of Durkheim's Theory.

Behavior Science Research 12:251-270.

Matza, David
    1969 Becoming Deviant. Englewood Cliffs, N. J.: Prentice-Hall.

Mauss, Marcel
    1967 The Gift: Forms and Functions in Archaic Societies. Ian Cunnison, trans. New York: Norton.

Maxwell, Robert J.
    1967 Onstage and Offstage Sex: Exploring an Hypothesis. Cornell Journal of Social Relations 1:75-84.

Maxwell, Robert J., Eleanor Krassen-Maxwell and Philip Silverman
    1978 The Cross-Cultural Study of Aging: A Manual for Coders. HRAFlex Books. New Haven: Human Relations Area Files.

Maxwell, Robert J. and Philip Silverman
    1970 Information and Esteem: Cultural Considerations in the Treatment of the Aged. Aging and Human Development 1:361-392.

McAllister, J. Gilbert
    1955 Kiowa-Apache Social Organization. In Social Organization of North American Tribes. Fred Eggan, ed. pp. 97-169. Chicago: University of Chicago Press.

McClelland, David C.
    1961 The Achieving Society. Princeton: D. Van Nostrand.

McClelland, David C., William N. Davis and Rudolf Kalin
    1966 A Cross-Cultural Study of Folk Tale Content and Drinking. Sociometry 29:308-333.

McClelland, David C., William N. Davis, Eric Wanner and Rudolf Kalin
    1972 A Cross-Cultural Study of Folk Tale Content and Drinking. In The Drinking Man. David C. McClelland, ed. pp. 48-72. New York: Free Press.

McCord, Arline and William McCord
    1977 Urban Social Conflict. St. Louis: C. V. Mosby.

McNett, Charles W., Jr.
    1970a A Cross-Cultural Method for Predicting Nonmaterial Traits in Archeology. Behavior Science Notes 5:195-212.
    1970b A Settlement Pattern Scale of Cultural Complexity. In A Handbook of Method in Cultural Anthropology. Raoul Naroll and Ronald Cohen, eds. pp. 872-886. Garden City, N. Y.: Natural History Press. Reprinted 1973. New York: Columbia University Press.
    1973 Factor Analysis of a Cross-Cultural Sample. Behavior Science Notes 8:233-257.

Mead, Margaret
    1928 Coming of Age in Samoa. New York: Morrow:
    1930 Growing Up in New Guinea. New York: Morrow.
    1953 National Character. In Anthropology Today. A. L. Kroeber, ed. pp. 642-667. Chicago: University of Chicago Press.
    1963 Socialization and Enculturation. Current Anthropology 4:184-188.

Mencher, Joan P.
    1965 The Nayars of South Malabar. In Comparative Family Systems. Meyer Nimkoff, ed. pp. 163-191. Boston: Houghton Mifflin.

Menninger, Karl

1938   Man against Himself. New York: Harcourt, Brace and World.
Merriam, Alan P.
1964   The Anthropology of Music. Evanston: Northwestern University Press.
Merton, Robert K.
1957   Social Theory and Social Structure. Glencoe, Ill.: Free Press.
Messenger, John C.
1971   Sex and Repression in an Irish Folk Community. *In* Human Sexual Behavior. Donald S. Marshall and Robert C. Suggs, eds. pp. 3-37. New York: Basic Books.
Michaelson, Evelyn and Walter Goldschmidt
1976   Family and Land Peasant Ritual. American Ethnologist 3:87-96.
Middleton, John, ed.
1968   Studies in Social and Cultural Anthropology. New York: Thomas Y. Crowell.
Minturn, Leigh
1965   A Cross-Linguistic Analysis of Freudian Symbols. Ethnology 4:336-342.
Minturn, Leigh and William Lambert
1964   The Antecedents of Child Training: A Cross-Cultural Test of Some Hypotheses. *In* Mothers of Six Cultures. Leigh Minturn and William Lambert, eds. pp. 164-175, 343-346. New York: John Wiley.
Minturn, Leigh, Martin Grosse and Santoah Haider
1969   Cultural Patterning of Sexual Beliefs and Behavior. Ethnology 8:301-318.
Montagu, M. F. Ashley, ed.
1968   Man and Aggression. New York: Oxford University Press.
Montgomery, Rita E.
1974   A Cross-Cultural Study of Menstruation, Menstrual Taboos and Related Social Variables. Ethos 2:137-170.
Moore, B., Jr.
1942   The Relation between Social Stratification and Social Control. Sociometry 5:230-250.
Morris, Desmond
1967   The Naked Ape. London: J. Cape.
1969   The Human Zoo. London J. Cape.
Morris, J. N.
1964   The Uses of Epidemiology. Baltimore: Williams and Wilkens.
Mukhopadhyay. Carol C.
1979   The Function of Romantic Love—A Reappraisal of the Coppinger and Rosenblatt Study. Behavior Science Research 14:57-64.
Munroe, Robert L. and Ruth H. Munroe
1969   A Cross-Cultural Study of Sex Gender and Social Structure. Ethnology 8:206-211.
1977   Cross-Cultural Human Development. Monterey: Brooks/Cole.
Munroe, Robert L., Ruth H. Munroe, and John W. M. Whiting
1973   The Couvade: A Psychological Analysis. Ethos 1:30-74.
Munroe, Robert L., John W. M. Whiting and David J. Hally
1969   Institutionalized Male Tranvestism and Sex Distinctions. American

Anthropologist 71:87-91.

Munroe, Ruth H., Robert L. Munroe and Beatrice B. Whiting, eds.
  1981   Handbook of Cross-Cultural Human Development. New York: Garland.

Murdock, George P.
  1937   Correlations of Matrilineal and Patrilineal Institutions. *In* Studies in the Science of Society. George P. Murdock, ed. pp. 445-470. New Haven: Yale University Press.
  1949   Social Structure. New York: Macmillan.
  1957   World Ethnographic Sample. American Anthropologist 59:664-687. Reprinted 1961. *In* Readings in Cross-Cultural Methodology. Frank W. Moore, ed. pp. 195-220. New Haven: HRAF Press.
  1964   Cultural Correlates of the Regulation of Premarital Sex Behavior. *In* Process and Pattern in Culture: Essays in Honor of Julian H. Steward. Robert A. Manners, ed. pp. 339-410. Chicago: Aldine.
  1967a Ethnographic Atlas. Pittsburgh: University of Pittsburgh Press.
  1967b Postpartum Sex Taboos. Paideuma 13:143-146.
  1968   Patterns of Sibling Terminology. Ethnology 7:1-24.
  1969   Correlations of Exploitative and Settlement Patterns. Bulletin of the National Museums of Canada 230:129-146.
  1971   Cross-Sex Patterns of Kin Behavior. Ethnology 10:359-368.
  1977   Major Emphases in My Comparative Research. Behavior Science Research 12:217-222.

Murdock, George P. and Catarina Provost
  1973a Factors in the Division of Labor by Sex: A Cross-Cultural Analysis. Ethnology 12:203-225.
  1973b Measurement of Cultural Complexity. Ethnology 12:379-392.

Murdock, George P. and Douglas White
  1969   Standard Cross-Cultural Sample. Ethnology 8:329-369.

Murdock, George P. and Suzanne F. Wilson
  1972   Settlement Patterns and Community Organization: Cross-Cultural Codes. Ethnology 11:254-295.

Murphy, Robert F.
  1957   Intergroup Hostility and Social Cohesion. American Anthropologist 59:1018-1036.

Nadel, Siegfried F.
  1955   Review of Gillin, For a Science of Social Man. American Anthropologist 57:345-347.

Nader, Laura, ed.
  1965   The Ethnography of Law. American Anthropologist 67. Part 2.

Nag, Moni
  1962   Factors Affecting Human Fertility in Nonindustrial Societies: A Cross-Cultural Study. New Haven: Yale University Publications in Anthropology.

Nammour, Valerie W.
  1974   Drums and Guns: A Cross-Cultural Study of the Nature of War. Unpublished Ph.D. Dissertation, University of Oregon, Eugene.

Naroll, Frada, Raoul Naroll and Forrest H. Howard
  1961   Position of Women in Childbirth: A Study in Data Quality Control.

American Journal of Obstetrics and Gynecology 82:943-954.

Naroll, Raoul

    1956   A Preliminary Index of Social Development. American Anthropologist 58: 687-715.

    1962a   Data Quality Control—A New Research Technique: Prolegomena to a Cross-Cultural Study of Culture Stress. New York: Free Press.

    1962b   Floor Area and Settlement Population. American Antiquity 27:587-589.

    1963   Thwarting Disorientation and Suicide. Institute for Cross-Cultural Studies. Mimeo.

    1967   The Proposed HRAF Probability Sample. Behavior Science Notes 2:70-80.

    1969   Cultural Determinants and the Concept of the Sick Society. *In* Changing Perspectives in Mental Illness. Stanley C. Plog and Robert B. Edgerton, eds. pp. 128-155. New York: Holt, Rinehart and Winston.

    1970a   The Culture-Bearing Unit in Cross-Cultural Surveys; Cross-Cultural Sampling; Data Quality Control in Cross-Cultural Surveys. *In* A Handbook of Method in Cultural Anthropology. Raoul Naroll and Cohen, eds. pp. 721-926, 889-926, 927-945. Garden City, N. Y.: Natural History Press. Reprinted 1973. New York: Columbia University Press.

    1970b   What Have We Learned from Cross-Cultural Surveys? American Anthropologist 72:1227-1288.

    1973a   Holocultural Theory Tests. *In* Main Currents in Cultural Anthropology. Raoul Naroll and Frada Naroll, eds. pp. 309-353. New York: Appleton-Century-Crofts.

    1973b   Reply to Discussion and Criticism of the Standard Ethnographic Sample. Current Anthropology 14:141-142.

    1976   Galton's Problem and HRAFLIB. Behavior Science Research 11:123-148.

Naroll, Raoul, Winston Alnot, Janice Caplan, Judith Friedman Hansen, Jeanne Maxant and Nancy Schmidt.

    1970   A Standard Ethnographic Sample: Preliminary Edition. Current Anthropology 11:234-248.

Naroll, Raoul, E. D. Benjamin, F. K. Fohl, R. D. Hildreth and J. M. Schaefer

    1971   Creativity: A Cross-Historical Pilot Survey. Journal of Cross-Cultural Psychology 2:181-188.

Naroll, Raoul, Vern Bullough and Frada Naroll

    1974   Military Deterrence in History: A Pilot Cross-Historical Survey. Albany: State University of New York Press.

Naroll, Raoul and Ronald Cohen, eds.

    1970   A Handbook of Method in Cultural Anthropology. Garden City, N. Y.: Natural History Press. Reprinted 1973. New York: Columbia University Press.

Naroll, Raoul and William T. Divale

    1976   Natural Selection in Cultural Evolution: Warfare versus Peaceful Diffusion. American Ethnologist 3:97-128.

Naroll, Raoul, Donald F. Griffiths, Gary L. Michik and Frada Naroll

    1977   HRAFLIB: HRAF Hologeistic Computer Program Library, Parts One and Two. New Haven: Human Relations Area Files.

Naroll, Raoul and Enid Margolis
1974 Maximum Settlement Size: A Compilation. Behavior Science Research 9:319-326.
Naroll, Raoul, Gary L. Michik and Frada Naroll
1974 Hologeistic Theory Testing. *In* Comparative Studies by Harold E. Driver and Essays in His Honor. Joseph G. Jorgensen, ed. pp. 121-148. New Haven: HRAF Press.
1976 Worldwide Theory Testing. New Haven: Human Relations Area Files.
1980 Holocultural Research Methods. *In* Handbook of Cross-Cultural Psychology. Vol. 2. Harry Triandis, ed. pp. 479-521. Boston: Allyn and Bacon.
Naroll, Raoul and Richard G. Sipes
1973 Standard Ethnographic Sample: Second Edition. Current Anthropology 14:111-140.
Naroll, Raoul and Rolf Wirsing
1976 Borrowing versus Migration as Selection Factors in Cultural Evolution. Journal of Conflict Resolution 20:187-212.
Naroll, Raoul and Harold Zucker
1974 Reply to More on the Standard Ethnographic Sample. Current Anthropology 15:316-317.
Needham, Rodney
1958 A Structural Analysis of Purum Society. American Anthropologist 60:75-101.
1962 Structure and Sentiment. Chicago: University of Chicago Press.
Nerlove, Sara
1974 Woman's Workload and Infant Feeding Practices: A Relationship with Demographic Implications. Ethnology 13:207-214.
Nerlove, Sara and A. Kimball Romney
1967 Sibling Terminology and Cross-Sex Behavior. American Anthropologist 69:179-187.
Nettl, Bruno
1956 Music in Primitive Culture. Cambridge: Harvard University Press.
Nie, Norman H., C. Hadlai Hull, Jean J. Jenkins, Karin Steinbrenner and Dale H. Bent
1975 SPSS: Statistical Package for the Social Sciences. Second edition. New York: McGraw Hill.
Nieboer, H. J.
1900 Slavery as an Industrial Ssytem. The Hague: Martinus Nijhoff.
Nimkoff, Meyer F.
1965 Types of Family: The Social System and the Family. *In* Comparative Family Systems. M.F. Nimkoff, ed. pp. 12-60. Boston: Houghton-Mifflin.
Nimkoff, Meyer F. and Russell Middleton
1960 Types of Family and Types of Economy. American Journal of Sociology 66:215-225.
Norbeck, Edward, Donald E. Walker and Mimi Cohen
1962 The Interpretation of Data: Puberty Rites. American Anthropologist 64:463-485.

Oliver, Pamela E.
   1972 Women and Men in Social Exchange: A Cross-Cultural Study.
      Unpublished M.A. Thesis, University of North Carolina, Chapel Hill.
Opler, Morris E.
   1945 Themes as Dynamic Forces in Culture. American Journal of
      Sociology 52:198-206.
Osmond, Marie W.
   1964 Toward Monogamy: A Cross-Cultural Study of the Correlates of
      Types of Marriage. Unpublished M.S. Thesis, Florida State University,
      Tallahassee.
   1969 A Cross-Cultural Analysis of Family Organization. Journal of
      Marriage and the Family 31:302-310.
Otterbein, Keith F.
   1965 Caribbean Family Organization: A Comparative Analysis. American
      Anthropologist 67:66-79.
   1968 Internal War: A Cross-Cultural Study. American Anthropologist
      277-289.
   1969 Basic Steps in Conducting a Cross-Cultural Survey. Behavior Science
      Notes 4:221-236.
   1970 The Evolution of War: A Cross-Cultural Study. New Haven: HRAF
      Press.
   1971 Comment on Correlates of Political Complexity. American Soci-
      ological Review 36:113-114.
   1972 Comparative Cultural Analysis: An Introduction to Anthropology.
      New York: Holt, Rinehart and Winston.
   1973 The Anthropology of War. In Handbook of Social and Cultural
      Anthropology. John J. Honigmann, ed. pp. 923-958. Chicago: Rand
      McNally.
   1976 Sampling and Samples in Cross-Cultural Studies. Behavior Science
      Research 11:107-121.
   1977 Warfare: A Hitherto Unrecognized Critical Variable. American
      Behavioral Scientist 20:693-710.
Otterbein, Keith F. and Charlotte Swanson Otterbein
   1965 An Eye for an Eye, a Tooth for a Tooth: A Cross-Cultural Study of
      Feuding. American Anthropologist 67:1470-1482.
Paige, Jeffry M.
   1974 Kinship and Polity in Stateless Societies. American Journal of Soci-
      ology 80:301-320.
Palmer, Stuart
   1965 Murder and Suicide in Forty Non-Literate Societies. Journal of
      Criminal Law, Criminology, and Police Science 56:320-324.
   1970 Aggression in Fifty-Eight Non-Literate Societies: An Exploratory
      Analysis. Annales Internationales de Criminologie 9:57-69.
Parsons, Jeffrey R.
   1972 Archaeological Settlement Patterns. In Annual Review of Anthro-
      pology. Bernard J. Siegel, ed. pp. 127-150. Palo Alto: Annual Reviews.
Parsons, Talcott
   1949 Essays in Sociological Theory, Pure and Appied. Glencoe, Ill.: Free
      Press.

Parsons, Talcott and Robert F. Bales
   1955 Working Papers in the Theory of Action. Glencoe: Free Press.
Passin, Herbert
   1943 The Place of Kinship in Taruhumara Social Organizatin. Acta
      Americana 1:360-495.
Pasternak, Burton
   1976 Introduction to Kinship and Social Organization. Englewood Cliffs,
      N. J.: Prentice-Hall.
Pearson, Lu Emily
   1957 Elizabethans at Home. Stanford: Stanford University Press.
Popper, Karl
   1968 The Logic of Scientific Discovery. New York: Harper and Row.
Pospisil, Leopold.
   1974 Anthropology of Law: A Comparative Theory. New Haven: HRAF
      Press.
Precourt, Walter
   1975 Initiation Ceremonies and Secret Societies as Educational Institu-
      tions. In Cross-Cultural Perspectives on Learning. Richard Brislin, Walter
      Lonner and S. Bochner, eds. pp. 231-250. Beverly Hills: Sage.
Prescott, James W.
   1975 Body Pleasure and the Origins of Violence. Bulletin of the Atomic
      Scientists 31:10-20.
Pressman, I. and A. Carol
   1969 Crime as a Diseconomy Scale. Paper presented at the meeting of the
      Operations Research Society of America, Denver.
Prince, A. M., L. Leblanc, K. Krohn, R. Masseyeff and M. E. Alpert
   1970 SH Antigen and Chronic Liver Disease. Lancet 2:717-718.
Prince Peter of Greece and Denmark
   1965 The Tibetan Family System. In Comparative Family Systems.
      Meyer F. Nimkoff, ed. pp. 192-208. Boston: Houghton Mifflin.
Prothro, E. Terry
   1960 Patterns of Permissiveness among Preliterate Peoples. Journal of
      Abnormal and Social Psychology 61:151-154.
Pryor, Fredric L.
   1977 The Origins of the Economy. New York: Academic Press.
Quigley, Carroll
   1961 The Evolution of Civilizations. New York: Macmillan.
Quinney, Richard
   1965 Suicide, Homicide, and Economic Development. Social Forces
      43:401-406.
Radcliffe-Brown, A. R.
   1935 Patrilineal and Matrilineal Succession. Iowa Law Review 10:286-303.
   1950 Introduction. In African Systems of Kinship and Marriage. A. R.
      Radcliffe-Brown and Daryll Forde, eds. pp. 1-85. International Affairs
      Institute. Oxford: Oxford University Press.
   1952 Structure and Function in Primitive Society. Glencoe, Ill.: Free Press.
   1964 The Andaman Islanders. New York: Free Press.
Raphael, Dana L.
   1969 The Lactation-Suckling Process within a Matrix of Supportive

Behavior. Ph.D. Dissertation, Columbia University, New York. Ann
Arbor: University Microfilms, 69-15, 580.
Rapoport, Amos
  1969   House Form and Culture. Englewood Cliffs, N. J.: Prentice-Hall.
Read, Margaret
  1960   Children of Their Fathers. New Haven: Yale University Press.
Reynolds, Barrie
  1968   The Material Culture of the Peoples of the Gwembe Valley. New
         York: Frederick A. Praeger.
Rivers, W. H. R.
  1906   The Todas. London: Macmillan.
  1924   Social Organization. London: Kegan Paul.
Robbins, Michael C.
  1966a House Types and Settlement Patterns. Minnesota Archaeologist
         28:2-26.
  1966b Material Culture and Cognition. American Anthropologist
         68:745-748.
Robbins, Michael C., Billie R. DeWalt and Pertti J. Pelto
  1972   Climate and Behavior: A Biocultural Study. Journal of Cross-Cul-
         tural Psychology 3:331-344.
Roberts, John M.
  1967   Oaths, Autonomic Ordeals, and Power. In Cross-Cultural
         Approaches. Clellan S. Ford, ed. pp. 169-195. New Haven: HRAF Press.
  1976   Belief in the Evil Eye in World Perspective. In The Evil Eye.
         Clarence Maloney, ed. pp. 223-278. New York: Columbia University
         Press.
Roberts, John M., Malcolm J. Arth and Robert R. Bush
  1959   Games in Culture. American Anthropologist 61:597-605.
Roberts, John M. and Herbert Barry III
  1976   Inculcated Traits and Game-Type Combinations: A Cross-Cultural
         View. In The Humanistic and Mental Health Aspects of Sports, Exercise,
         and Recreation. Timothy T. Craig, ed. pp. 5-11. Chicago: American
         Medical Association.
Roberts, John M. and Michael L. Forman
  1971   Riddles: Expressive Models of Interrogation. Ethnology 10:509-533.
Roberts, John M. and Thomas Gregor
  1971   Privacy: A Cultural View. Cornell University, Latin American
         Studies Program, Reprint Series 41:199-225.
Roberts, John M. and Brian Sutton-Smith
  1962   Child Training and Game Involvement. Ethnology 1:166-185.
  1966   Cross-Cultural Correlates of Games of Chance. Behavior Science
         Notes 1:131-144.
Roberts, John M., Brian Sutton-Smith and Adam Kendon
  1963   Strategy in Games and Folk Tales. Journal of Social Psychology
         61:185-199.
Rohner, Ronald P.
  1975   They Love Me, They Love Me Not: A Worldwide Study of the
         Effects of Parental Acceptance and Rejection. New Haven: HRAF Press.
  1977   Advantages of the Comparative Method in Anthropology. Behavior

Science Research 12:117-144.
Rohner, Ronald P., Herbert Barry III, William T. Divale, Edwin E. Erickson, Raoul Naroll, James M. Schaefer and Richard G. Sipes
1978 Guidelines for Holocultural Research. Current Anthropology 19: 128-129.
Rohner, Ronald P., Billie R. DeWalt and Robert C. Ness
1973 Ethnographer Bias in Cross-Cultural Research: An Empirical Study. Behavior Science Notes 8:275-313.
Rohner, Ronald P. and Caroline C. Nielsen
1978 Parental Acceptance and Rejection: A Review and Annotated Bibliography of Research and Theory. HRAFlex Books. New Haven: Human Relations Area Files.
Romney, A. Kimball
1965 Variations in Household Structure as Determinants of Sex-Typed Behavior. In Conference on Sex and Behavior. Frank A. Beach, ed. pp. 208-220. New York: Wiley.
Rosaldo, Michelle Zimbalist
1974 Woman, Culture, and Society: A Theoretical Overview. In Woman, Culture, and Society. Michelle Zimbalist Rosaldo and Louise Lamphere, eds. pp. 17-42. Stanford: Stanford University Press.
Rosaldo, Michelle Zimbalist and Louise Lamphere, eds.
1974 Woman, Culture, and Society. Stanford: Stanford University Press.
Rosenblatt, Paul C.
1966 A Cross-Cultural Study of Child Rearing and Romantic Love. Journal of Personality and Social Psychology 4:336-338.
1967 Marital Residence and the Functions of Romantic Love. Ethnology 6:471-480.
Rosenblatt, Paul C. and Paul C. Cozby
1972 Courtship Patterns Associated with Freedom of Choice of Spouse. Journal of Marriage and the Family 34:689-695.
Rosenblatt, Paul C. and Michael R. Cunningham
1976 Sex Differences in Cross-Cultural Perspective. In Exploring Sex Differences. Barbara Lloyd and John Archer, eds. pp. 71-94. London: Academic Press.
Rosenblatt, Paul C., Stephen S. Fugita and Kenneth V. McDowell
1969 Wealth Transfer and Restrictions on Sexual Relations during Betrothal. Ethnology 8:319-328.
Rosenblatt, Paul C. and Walter J. Hillabrant
1972 Divorce for Childlessness and the Regulation of Adultery. Journal of Sex Research 8:117-127.
Rosenblatt, Paul C. and Elizabeth L. Skoogberg
1974 Birth Order in Cross-Cultural Perspective. Development Psychology 10:49-54.
Rosenblatt, Paul C. and David Unangst
1974 Marriage Ceremonies. Journal of Comparative Family Studies 5:41-56.
Rosenblatt, Paul C., R. Patricia Walsh and Douglas A. Jackson
1976 Grief and Mourning in Cross-Cultural Perspective. New Haven: HRAF Press.

Ross, Marc Howard and Elizabeth Homer
    1976   Galton's Problem in Cross-National Research. World Politics 29:1-28.
Rothman, K. and A. Keller
    1972   The Effect of Joint Exposure to Alcohol and Tobacco on Risk of
    Cancer of the Mouth and Pharynx. Journal of Chronic Diseases
    25:711-716.
Russell, Elbert W.
    1972   Factors of Human Aggression: A Cross-Cultural Factor Analysis of
    Characteristics Related to Warfare and Crime. Behavior Science Notes
    7:275-312.
    1973   An Additional Warfare Element in Territorial Expansion. Behavior
    Science Notes 8:201-207.
Ryder, James W. and Margaret B. Blackman
    1970   The Avunculate: A Cross-Cultural Critique of Claude Lévi-Strauss.
    Behavior Science Notes 5:97-115.
Sahlins, Marshall D.
    1960   Evolution: Specific and General. *In* Evolution and Culture. Marshall
    D. Sahlins and Elman R. Service, eds. pp. 12-44. Ann Arbor: University of
    Michigan Press.
Sahlins, Marshall D.
    1965   On the Ideology and Composition of Descent Groups. Man
    65:104-107.
Sahlins, Marshall D. and Elman R., Service, eds.
    1960   Evolution and Culture. Ann Arbor: University of Michigan Press.
Sanday, Peggy R.
    1973   Toward a Theory of the Status of Women. American Anthropologist
    75:1682-1700.
    1974   Female Status in the Public Domain. *In* Woman, Culture, and
    Society. Michelle Zimbalist Rosaldo and Louise Lamphere, eds. pp.
    189-206. Stanford: Stanford University Press.
Saucier, Jean-François
    1972   Correlates of the Long Postpartum Taboo: A Cross-Cultural Study.
    Current Anthropology 13:238-249.
Sawyer, Jack and R. A. LeVine
    1966   Cultural Dimensions: A Factor Analysis of the World Ethnographic
    Sample. American Anthropologist 68:708-731.
Schaefer, James M.
    1969   A Comparion of Three Measures of Social Complexity. American
    Anthropologist 71:706-708.
    1973   A Hologeistic Study of Family Structure and Sentiment, Super-
    natural Beliefs, and Drunkenness. Ph.D. Dissertation, State University of
    New York at Buffalo. Ann Arbor: University Microfilms, 73-29, 131.
    1976   Drunkenness and Culture Stress: A Holocultural Test. *In*
    Cross-Cultural Approaches to the Study of Alcohol. Michael Everett,
    Jack O. Waddell, and Dwight B. Heath, eds. pp. 287-321. The Hague:
    Mouton.
Schaefer, James M. and David Levinson
    1977   The Growth of Hologeistic Studies: 1889-1975. Behavior Science
    Research 12:71-108.

Schapera, Isaac
1953 Some Comments on Comparative Method in Social Anthropology. American Anthropologist 55:353-361.
Scheffler, Harold W.
1964 The Genesis and Repression of Conflict: Choiseul Island. American Anthropologist 66:789-804.
1970 Review of Lévi-Strauss, The Elementary Structures of Kinship. American Anthropologist 72:251-268.
1973 Kinship, Descent, and Alliance. In Handbook of Social and Cultural Anthropology. John J. Honigmann, ed. pp. 747-794. Chicago: Rand McNally.
Scheffler, Harold W. and Floyd G. Lounsbury
1971 A Study in Structural Semantics: The Siriono Kinship System. Englewood Cliffs, N. J.: Prentice-Hall.
Schlegel, Alice
1972 Male Dominance and Female Autonomy: Domestic Authority in Matrilineal Societies. New Haven: HRAF Press.
Schmid, Calvin F.
1933 Suicide in Minneapolis, Minnesota, 1928-1932. American Journal of Sociology 39:30-49.
Schmid, Calvin F. and Maurice D. van Arsdol, Jr.
1955 Completed and Attempted Suicides: A Comparative Analysis. American Sociological Review 20:273-283.
Schmidt, W.
1931 The Origin and Growth of Religion: Facts and Theories. New York: Lincoln McVeagh.
Schmitt, R. C.
1957 Density, Delinquency, and Crime in Honolulu. Sociology and Social Research 41:274-276.
1966 Density, Health, and Social Disorganization. Journal of American Institute of Planners 32:38-40.
Scholte, Bob
1966 Epistemic Paradigms: Some Problems in Cross-Cultural Research on Social Anthropological History and Theory. American Anthropologist 68:1192-1201.
Schwartz, Richard D. and James C. Miller
1964 Legal Evolution and Societal Complexity. American Journal of Sociology 70:159-169.
Schwartzman, Helen B.
1976 The Anthropological Study of Children's Play. In Annual Review of Anthropology. Vol. 5. Bernard J. Siegel, ed. pp. 289-328. Palo Alto: Annual Reviews.
Seeley, J. R.
1962 The Ecology of Alcoholism: A Beginning. In Society, Culture, and Drinking Patterns. David Pittman and Charles Snyder, eds. pp. 330-344. New York: Wiley.
Segall, Marshall H., Donald Campbell and Melville J. Herskovits
1966 Influence of Culture on Visual Perception. Indianapolis: Bobbs-Merrill.

Seligman, Brenda Z.
1929 Incest and Descent. Journal of the Royal Anthropological Institute of Great Britain and Ireland 59:231-272.
Service, Elman R.
1966 The Hunters. Englewood Cliffs, N. J.: Prentice-Hall.
1971 Primitive Social Organization. New York: Random House.
Shapiro, Harry L., ed.
1956 Man, Culture, and Society. New York: Oxford University Press.
Sheils, H. Dean
1971 Monogamy and Independent Families. Behavior Science Notes 6:221-228.
1972 The Importance of Agriculture from the Perspective of Neoevolutionary Theory. Rural Sociology 37:167-188.
Sherratt, Andrew
1977 Comment on Lomax and Arensberg's, A Worldwide Evolutionary Classification of Cultures by Subsistence Systems. Current Anthropology 18:704.
Shirley, Robert W. and A. Kimball Romney
1962 Love Magic and Socialization Anxiety: A Cross-Cultural Study. American Anthropologist 64:1028-1031.
Shubik, Martin, ed.
1964 Game Theory and Related Approaches to Social Behavior. New York: John Wiley.
Silverman, Philip and Robert J. Maxwell
1978 How Do I Respect Thee? Let Me Count the Ways: Deference towards Elderly Men and Women. Behavior Science Research 13:91-108.
Simmel, Georg
1955 Conflict and the Web of Group Affiliations. Kurt H. Wolff and Reinhard Bendix, trans. New York: Free Press.
Simmons, Leo W.
1937 Statistical Correlations in the Science of Society. *In* Studies in the Science of Society. George P. Murdock, ed. pp. 495-517. New Haven: Yale University Press.
1945 The Role of the Aged in Primitive Society. New Haven: Yale University Press.
Sipes, Richard G.
1972 Rating Hologeistic Method. Behavior Science Notes 7:157-198.
1973 War, Sports, and Aggression: An Empirical Test of Two Rival Theories. American Anthropologist 75:64-86.
1974 A Hologeistic Investigation of the Effects of Three Sociocultural Variables on Population Growth Rate. Unpublished Ph.D. Dissertation, State University of New York at Buffalo.
1976 A Test for Coder Bias. Behavior Science Research 11:149-168.
Slater, Miriam K.
1959 Ecological Factors in the Origin of Incest. American Anthropologist 61:1042-1059.
Slater, Philip E. and Dori A. Slater
1965 Maternal Ambivalence and Narcissism: A Cross-Cultural Study. Merrill-Palmer Quarterly of Behavior and Development 11:241-259.

Smith, R. T.
1956 The Negro Family in British Guiana. London: Routledge and Kegan Paul.
Solien, Nancie L.
1959 The Consanguineal Family Household among the Black Carib of Central America. Unpublished Ph.D. Dissertation, University of Michigan, Ann Arbor.
Spencer, Herbert
1862 First Principles. London: William and Norgate.
1876-1896 Principles in Sociology. 3 vols. London: Williams and Norgate.
Spencer, Walter B. and James Gillin
1927 The Arunta: A Study of a Stone Age People. London: Macmillan.
Spengler, Oswald
1928 The Decline of the West. Francis Atkinson, trans. New York: Knopf.
Spiro, Melford E.
1961 Social Systems, Personality, and Functional Analysis. *In* Studying Personality Cross-Culturally. B. Kaplan, ed. pp. 93-128. Evanston, Ill.: Row, Peterson.
1965 A Typology of Social Structure and the Patterning of Social Institutions: A Cross-Cultural Study. American Anthropologist 67:1097-1119.
1966a A Reply to Chaney or It All Depends on Whose Ox Is Being Gored. American Anthropologist 68:1471-1474.
1966b Religion: Problems of Definition and Explanation. *In* Anthropological Approaches to the Study of Religion. Michael Banton, ed. pp. 85-126. London: Tavistock.
Spiro, Melford E. and Roy G. D'Andrade
1967 A Cross-Cultural Study of Some Supernatural Beliefs. *In* Cross-Cultural Approaches. Clellan S. Ford, ed. pp. 196-206. New Haven: HRAF Press.
Spooner, Brian
1976 Anthropology and the Evil Eye. *In* The Evil Eye. Clarence Maloney, ed. pp. 279-286. New York: Columbia University Press.
Steiner, Franz
1956 Taboo. London: Cohen and West.
Steinmetz, S. R.
1930 Classification des Types Sociaux et Catalogue des Peuples. Zur Ethnologie and Sociologie. Vol. II. Gesammalte Kleinere Schriften. Groningen: P. Noordhoff.
Stephens, William N.
1962 The Oedipus Complex: Cross-Cultural Evidence. New York: Free Press.
1963 The Family in Cross-Cultural Perspective. New York: Holt, Rinehart and Winston.
1967 A Cross-Cultural Study of Menstrual Taboos. *In* Cross-Cultural Approaches. Clellan S. Ford, ed. p. 67-94. New Haven: HRAF Press.
1972 A Cross-Cultural Study of Modesty. Behavior Science Notes 7:1-28.
Stephens, William N. and Roy D'Andrade
1962 Kin-Avoidance. *In* The Oedipus Complex: Cross-Cultural Evidence.

By William N. Stephens. pp. 124-150. New York: Free Press.
Steward, Julian H.
  1955   Theory of Culture Change: The Methodology of Multilinear Evolution. Urbana: University of Illinois Press.
Stewart, Frank H.
  1977   Fundamentals of Age-Group Systems. New York: Academic Press.
Stewart, Robert A. C. and Kenneth J. Jones
  1972   Cultural Dimensions: A Factor Analysis of Textor's A Cross-Cultural Summary. Behavior Science Notes 7:37-81.
Strauss, David J. and Martin Orans
  1975   Mighty Sifts: A Critical Appraisal of Solutions to Galton's Problem and a Partial Solution. Current Anthropology 16:573-594.
Sumner, William G.
  1911   War and Other Essays. New Haven: Yale University Press.
Sumner, William G. and Albert G. Keller
  1927   The Science of Society. New Haven: Yale University Press.
Swanson, Guy E.
  1960   The Birth of the Gods: The Origin of Primitive Religion. Ann Arbor: University of Michigan Press.
  1971   An Organizational Analysis Collectivities. American Sociological Review 36:607-624.
Sweetser, Dorrian A.
  1966a Avoidance, Social Affiliation, and the Incest Taboo. Ethnology 5:304-316.
  1966b On the Incompatibility of Duty and Affection: A Note on the Role of the Mother's Brother. American Anthropologist 68:1009-1013.
  1967   Path Consistency in Directed Graphs and Social Structure. American Journal of Sociology 73:287-293.
Tatje, Terrence A.
  n.d.   On Main Sequence Kinship Theory. Unpublished Manuscript. State University of New York at Buffalo.
Tatje, Terrence A. and Francis L. K. Hsu
  1969   Variations in Ancestor Worship Beliefs and Their Relations to Kinship. Southwestern Journal of Anthropology 25:153-172.
Tatje, Terrence A. and Raoul Naroll
  1970   Two Measures of Societal Complexity: An Empirical Cross-Cultural Comparison. In A Handbook of Method in Cultural Anthropology. Raoul Naroll and Ronald Cohen, eds. pp. 766-833. Garden City, N. Y.: Natural History Press. Reprinted 1973. Columbia University Press.
Taylor, Ian, Paul Walton and Jock Young
  1973   The New Criminology: For a Social Theory of Deviance. Boston: Routledge and Kegan Paul.
Taylor, Robert B.
  1973   Introduction to Cultural Anthropology. Boston: Allyn and Bacon.
Tax, Sol
  1955   The Social Organization of the Fox Indians. In Social Organization of North American Tribes. Fred Eggan, ed. pp. 241-282. Chicago: University of Chicago Press.
Tax, Sol and Leslie G. Freeman, eds.

1977   Horizons of Anthropology. Second ed. Chicago: Aldine.
Tefft, Stanton K. and Douglas Reinhardt
    1974   Warfare Regulation: A Cross-Cultural Test of Hypotheses among Tribal Peoples. Behavior Science Research 9:151-172.
Textor, Robert B.
    1967   A Cross-Cultural Summary. New Haven: HRAF Press.
Thoden van Velzen, H. U. E. and W. van Wetering
    1960   Residence, Power Groups and Intra-Societal Aggression. International Archives of Ethnography 49:169-200.
Tiger, Lionel
    1969   Men in Groups. New York: Random House.
Titiev, Mischa
    1943   The Influence of Common Residence on the Unilateral Classification of Kindred. American Anthropologist 45:511-530.
    1956   The Importance of Space in Primitive Kinship. American Anthropologist 58:854-865.
Tjim, J.
    1933   Die Stellung der Frau bei den Indianern der Vereinigten Staaten and Canadas. Zutphen: W. J. Thieme.
Toynbee, Arnold
    1957   A Study of History. Abridged in two volumes by D. Somerville. Oxford: University Press.
Triandis, Leigh Minturn and William W. Lambert
    1961   Sources of Frustration and Targets of Aggression: A Cross-Cultural Study. Journal of Abnormal and Social Psychology 62:640-648.
Trigger, Bruce G.
    1963   Settlement as an Aspect of Iroquoian Adaptation at the Time of Contact. American Anthropologist 65:86-101.
    1965   History and Settlement in Lower Nubia. New Haven: Yale University Publications in Anthropology, No. 69.
    1967   Settlement Archaeology—Its Goals and Promise. American Antiquity 32:149-160.
    1968   The Determinants of Settlement Patterns. In Settlement Archaeology. K. C. Chang, ed. pp. 53-78. Palo Alto: National Press Books.
Turner, Victor
    1969   The Ritual Process: Structure and Antistructure. Chicago: Aldine.
Turney-High, Harry H.
    1949   Primitive War: Its Practices and Concepts. Columbia: University of South Carolina Press.
Tutko, Thomas A.
    1979   Personality Change in the American Sport Scene. In Sports, Games, and Play: Social and Psychological Viewpoints. Jeffrey H. Goldstein, ed. pp. 101-114. Hillsdale, N. J.: Laurence Erlbaum.
Tylor, Edward B.
    1871   Primitive Cultures. London: J. Murray.
    1889   On a Method of Investigating the Development of Institutions: Applied to Laws of Marriage and Descent. Journal of the Royal Anthropological Institute of Great Britain and Ireland 18:245-272. Reprinted 1961. In Readings in Cross-Cultural Methodology. Frank W.

Moore, ed. pp. 1-25. New Haven: HRAF Press.
Ucko, Peter J., Ruth Tringham and G. W. Dimbleby, eds.
1972   Man, Settlement, and Urbanism. Cambridge: Schenkman.
Udy, Stanley H., Jr.
1959a   'Bureaucracy' and 'Rationality' in Weber's Organization Theory. American Sociological Review 24:791-795.
1959b   Organization of Work: A Comparative Analysis of Production among Nonindustrial Peoples. New Haven: HRAF Press.
1962   Administrative Rationality, Social Setting, and Organizational Development. American Journal of Sociology 68:299-305.
1970   Work in Traditional and Modern Society. Englewood Cliffs, N. J.: Prentice-Hall.
Underhill, Ruth M.
1946   Papago Indian Religion. New York: Columbia University Press.
Unwin, J. D.
1934   Sex and Culture. London: Oxford University Press.
van der Bij, T. S.
1929   On Tstaanen en Eerste Ontwikkeling van de Oorlog. Groningen: Wolters.
van Gennep, Arnold
1960   The Rites of Passage. Chicago: The University of Chicago Press.
Vickers, Geoffrey
1968   Is Adaptability Enough? *In* Modern Systems Research for the Behavioral Scientist. Walter Buckley, ed. pp. 460-473. Chicago: Aldine.
Vogt, Evon Z.
1956   An Appraisal of "Prehistoric Settlement Patterns in the New World." *In* Prehistoric Settlement Patterns in the New World. Gordon R. Willey, ed. p. 173-182. Viking Fund Publications in Anthropology No. 23. New York: Wenner-Gren Foundation for Anthropological Research.
Wallace, Anthony F. C.
1956   Revitalization Movements. American Anthropologist 58:264-281.
1966   Religion: An Anthropological View. New York: Random House.
Wallis, C. P. and R. Maliphant
1967   Delinquency Areas in the County of London: Ecological Factors. British Journal of Criminology 7:250-284.
Watson, Robert I., Jr.
1973   Investigation into Deindividuation Using a Cross-Cultural Survey Technique. Journal of Personality and Social Psychology 25:342-345.
Webb, Eugene J., Donald T. Campbell, Richard D. Schwartz and Lee Sechrest
1966   Unobstrusive Measures: Nonreactive Research in the Social Sciences. Chicago: Rand-McNally.
Weisner, Thomas S. and Ronald Gallimore
1977   My Brother's Keeper: Child and Sibling Caretaking. Current Anthropology 18:169-190.
Weiss, Charles
1966   Motives for Male Circumcision among Preliterate Peoples. The Journal of Sex Research 2:69-88.
Westermarck, Edward
1894   The History of Human Marriage. London: Macmillan.

1905   The Position of Women in Early Civilization. American Journal of Sociology 10:408-421.

White, Douglas R.
1967   Concomitant Variation in Kinship Structures. Unpublished Master's Thesis, University of Minnesota, Minneapolis.

White, Douglas R., Michael L. Burton and Lilyan A. Brudner
1977   Entailment Theory and Method: A Cross-Cultural Analysis of the Sexual Division of Labor. Behavior Science Research 12:1-24.

White, Leslie A.
1948   The Definition and Prohibition of Incest. American Anthropologist 50:416-435.
1949   The Science of Culture. New York: Grove Press.
1959   The Evolution of Culture: The Development of Civilization to the Fall of Rome. New York: McGraw-Hill.
1960   Foreword. In Evolution and Culture. By Marshall D. Sahlins and Elman R. Service. pp. v-xii. Ann Arbor: University of Michigan Press.

Whiting, Beatrice B.
1950   Paiute Sorcery. New York: Viking Fund.
1965   Sex Identity Conflict and Physical Violence: A Comparative Study. In The Ethnography of Law. American Anthropologist Special Publication 67, no. 6, part 2. Laura Nader, ed. pp. 123-140.

Whiting, John W. M.
1954   The Cross-Cultural Method. In Handbook of Social Psychology. Gardiner Lindzey, ed. pp. 523-531. Reading, Mass.: Addison-Wesley.
1960   Resource Mediation and Learning by Identification. In Personality Development in Children. Ira Iscoe and Harold Stevenson, eds. pp. 112-126. Austin: University of Texas Press.
1964   Effects of Climate on Certain Cultural Practices. In Explorations in Cultural Anthropology: Essays in Honor of George Peter Murdock. Ward H. Goodenough, ed. pp. 511-544. New York: McGraw-Hill.
1965   Menarcheal Age and Infant Stress in Humans. In Sex and Behavior. Frank A. Beach, ed. p. 221-233. New York: John Wiley.
1967   Sorcery, Sin and the Superego: A Cross-Cultural Study of Some Mechanisms of Social Control. In Cross-Cultural Approaches. Clellan S. Ford, ed, pp. 147-168. New Haven: HRAF Press.
1968a   Socialization. In International Encyclopedia of the Social Sciences. David L. Sills, ed. Vol. 14. pp. 545-551. New York: Macmillan.
1968b   Methods and Problems in Cross-Cultural Research. In Handbook of Social Psychology. Second edition. Gardner Lindzey and E. Aronson, eds. pp. 693-728. Reading, Mass.: Addison-Wesley.
1977   A Model for Psychocultural Research. In Culture and Infancy: Variations in Human Experience. P. Herbert Leiderman, Steven R. Tulkin and Anne Rosenfeld, eds. pp. 29-48. New York: Academic Press.

Whiting, John W. M. and Barbara Ayres
1968   Inferences from the Shape of Dwellings. In Settlement Archaeology. K. C. Chang, ed. pp. 117-133. Palo Alto: National Press Books.

Whiting, John W. M., Eleanor H. Chasdi, Helen Antonovsky and Barbara C. Ayres

1974   The Learning of Values. *In* Culture and Personality. Robert A. LeVine, ed. pp. 155-187. Chicago: Aldine.

Whiting, John W. M. and Irvin L. Child
1953   Child Training and Personality: A Cross-Cultural Study. New Haven: Yale University Press.

Whiting, John W. M., Richard Kluckhohn and Albert Anthony
1958   The Function of Male Initiation Ceremonies at Puberty. *In* Readings in Social Psychology. Third edition. Eleanor E. Maccoby, Theodore M. Newcomb and Eugene L. Hartley, eds. pp. 359-370. New York: Holt, Rinehart and Winston.

Whiting, John W. M., Thomas K. Landauer and T. M. Jones
1968   Infantile Immunization and Adult Stature. Child Development 39:59-67.

Whiting, John W. M. and Beatrice B. Whiting
1975   Aloofness and Intimacy of Husbands and Wives: A Cross-Cultural Study. Ethos 3:183-207.

Whitt, H. P., C. C. Gordon and J. R. Hofley
1972   Religion, Economic Development, and Lethal Aggression. American Sociological Review 37:193-201.

Whyte, Martin K.
1978a   Cross-Cultural Studies of Women and the Male Bias Problem. Behavior Science Research 13:65-80.
1978b   The Status of Women in Pre-Industrial Societies. Princeton: Princeton University Press.

Willey, Gordon R., ed.
1956   Prehistoric Settlement Patterns in the New World. Viking Fund Publications in Anthropology No. 23. New York: Wenner-Gren Foundation for Anthropological Research.

Williams, Thomas, R.
1972   Human Culture Transmitted: An Introduction to the Study of the Socialization Process. St. Louis: C. V. Mosby.

Wimberly, Howard
1973   Legal Evolution: One Further Step. American Journal of Sociology 79:78-83.

Winsborough, H. H.
1965   The Social Consequences of High Population Density. Law and Contemporary Problems 30:120-126.

Wirsing, Rolf
1973   Political Power and Information: A Cross-Cultural Study. American Anthropologist 75:153-170.

Witkowski, Stanley R.
1972   A Cross-Cultural Test of the Proximity Hypothesis. Behavior Science Notes 7:243-263.
1977   Kinship. American Behavioral Scientist 20:657-668.

Wolf, Eric R.
1977   The Study of Evolution. *In* Horizons of Anthropology. Second edition. Sol Tax and Leslie G. Freeman, eds. pp. 33-45. Chicago: Aldine.

Wolf, Margery
1972   Women and the Family in Rural Taiwan. Stanford: Stanford

University Press.

Wolfe, Alvin W.
1969 Social Structural Basis of Art. Current Anthropology 10:3-29.

Wright, George C.
1970 Projection and Displacement: A Cross-Cultural Study of Folk Tale Aggression. *In* Cross-Cultural Studies. D. R. Price-Williams, ed. pp. 348-360. Baltimore: Penguin.

Wright, Quincy
1942 A Study of War. Vol. I. Chicago: University of Chicago Press.

Wundt, Wilhelm
1916 The Elements of Folk Psychology. Edward L. Schaub, trans. London: Allen and Unwin.

Wynder, E. L. and I. J. Bross
1961 A Study of Etiological Factors in Cancer of the Esophagus. Cancer 14:389-413.

Wynder, E. L., I. J. Bross and R. M. Feldman
1957 A Study of Etiological Factors in Cancer of the Mouth. Cancer 10:1300-1323.

Young, Frank W.
1962 The Function of Male Initiation Ceremonies: A Cross-Cultural Test of an Alternative Hypothesis. American Journal of Sociology 67:379-396.
1965 Initiation Ceremonies: A Cross-Cultural Study of Status Dramatization. Indianapolis: Bobbs-Merrill.

Young, Frank W. and Albert Bacdayan
1967 Menstrual Taboos and Social Rigidity. *In* Cross-Cultural Approaches. Clellan S. Ford, ed. pp. 95-110. New Haven: HRAF Press.

Zelditch, Morris
1955 Role Differentiation in the Nuclear Family: A Comparative Study. *In* Family, Socialization and Interaction Process. Talcott Parsons and Robert F. Bales, eds. pp. 307-352. Glencoe, Ill.: Free Press.

Zelman, Elizabeth A. C.
1975 Women's Rights and Women's Rites: A Cross-Cultural Study of Womanpower and Reproductive Ritual. Ph.D. Dissertation, University of Michigan, Ann Arbor. Ann Arbor: University Microfilms,75-859.

Zern, David
1969 The Relevance of Family Cohesiveness as a Determinant of Premarital Sexual Behavior in a Cross-Cultural Sample. Journal of Social Psychology 78:3-9.
1970 The Influence of Certain Child Rearing Factors upon the Development of a Structured and Salient Sense of Time. Genetic Psychology Monographs 81: 197-254.
1972 The Relationship between Mother/Infant Contact and Later Differentiation of the Social Environment. Journal of Genetic Psychology 121:107-117.
1976 Further Evidence Supporting the Relationship between Mother/Infant Contact and Later Differentiation of the Social Environment. Journal of Genetic Psychology 129:169-170.

APPENDIX A
Methodological Procedures Used in Holocultural Research

This Appendix reports the documentation for the conclusions we have reached about the methodological rigor of the holocultural studies reviewed in the volume. The data presented here is taken from that listed in *A Guide to Social Theory: Worldwide Cross-Cultural Tests* (Levinson 1977b), and the unpublished *Supplement I* to the *Guide*.

Sixteen items of information about each holocultural study cited in the text are listed here. Full descriptions of these items, the coding procedures, and evidence for their accuracy and reliability can be found in Levinson (1977b).

The first column (Study) cites the holocultural study by the author's last name and the publication date. The references contain full bibliographic citations to the studies. The second column (Sample Size) lists the sample size. When a particular study uses samples of varying sizes, the range for all samples is given. The third column (Statistical Test) lists a code for the type of statistical test used:

D — data comparison, no formal test
C — correlation, regression
F — factor analysis
S — scaling
X^2 — chi square
A — analysis of variance
ST — significance test

The remaining thirteen columns contain information pertaining to specific methodological procedures. In all cases, a + sign indicates that yes, the procedure was followed in the study, a - sign indicates that no, the procedure was not followed, and a 0 indicates that the procedure was not applicable. By author, we mean the author of the cited holocultural study.

345

Data Collection

(CU)   *Coder Unawareness*—Does the author claim or imply that the coder(s) of the data for the hypothesis test was unaware of the hypothesis? If all of the data were taken directly from sources of coded data, this item is coded "not applicable."

(CT)   *Coder Training*—Does the author claim or imply that the coder(s) of the data for the hypothesis test was qualified or trained to perform the required tasks? If all of the data were taken directly from sources of coded data, this item is coded "not applicable."

(MV)   *Measure Validity*—Does the author provide evidence that the measures are valid indicators of the theoretical variables?

(P)   *Page Citations*—Does the author supply source and page citations to the ethnographic reports from which the data were taken? This item applies only to studies using either original ethnographic or historical reports or the HRAF Files as their data source.

(R)   *Coder Reliability*—Does the author report the results of intercoder reliability tests for data taken either from ethnographic reports, the HRAF Files, or historical reports?

Sampling

(U)   *Unit Definition*—Does the author define the sample units consistently? If not, is a reasonable rationale for not doing so discussed?

(S)   *Probability Sample*—Does the author claim that the sample was selected by means of probability sampling techniques?

(G)   *Formal Interdependence Test (Galton's Problem)*—Does the author use a formal test to check the independence of the sample units? When the hypothesis is a measure, this item is coded "not applicable."

Data Analysis

(M)   *Multivariate Analysis*—Does the author attempt to discredit plausible rival hypotheses through multivariate analysis, or through the direct testing of those rivals? When the hypothesis is a measure, this item is coded "not applicable."

(DC)   *Deviant Case Analysis*—Does the author attempt to explain
       at least one of the cases that does not conform to the pattern
       predicted by the hypothesis? When the hypothesis is not
       supported, this item is coded "not applicable."

(D)   *Systematic Error*—Does the author test to determine if the
       results of the hypothesis test may be influenced by sys-
       tematic errors in the data? Does the author test for the
       influence of any one of the following quality control mea-
       sures of the data collection process: (1) field worker length
       of stay in the field; (2) time focus; (3) native language
       familiarity; (4) systematic checks on informants' statements;
       (5) earlier publications cited; (6) any other data quality
       control measures specifically related to the variables of
       interest?

(GS)   *Group Significance*—When a large number of associations
       are computed from the same data, what are the chances that
       a certain number of those associations would be statistically
       significant by chance alone? We answer this question by
       reporting the results of group significance tests computed
       for *A Guide to Social Theory*, when authors report none of
       their own. We report the results of the group significance
       test as either above .10 or below .10.

Methodological Procedures Documented

Study	Sample Size	Statistical Test	CU	CT	MV	P	R	U	S	G	RV	M	DC	D	GS
Aberle (1961)	41-564	X²,C	0	0	+	0	0	+	-	-	+	-	-	-	+
Abrahamson (1969)	38	C	0	0	+	0	+	+	-	-	0	+	-	-	+
Ackerman (1968)	11-28	C	0	+	+	-	-	+	-	-	0	-	+	-	0
Allen (1967)	48-58	C	+	+	+	-	+	+	-	-	-	+	-	-	0
Allen (1972)	32-58	C	0	+	+	0	0	+	-	-	-	-	-	-	+
Apple (1956)	24-51	X²,ST	+	0	+	-	+	+	-	-	+	-	-	-	0
Aronoff & Crano (1975)	862	D	0	+	+	0	0	+	-	-	+	0	0	-	0
Ayres (1967)	25-36	ST,D	+	0	+	-	-	+	-	-	0	-	-	-	+
Ayres (1968)	47	D	0	+	+	-	+	+	-	-	+	+	+	-	0
Ayres (1973)	54	X²	+	0	+	-	+	+	+	+	+	+	-	-	0
Ayres (1974)	18-48	X²,ST	0	+	+	-	+	+	+	+	0	+	+	-	+
Bacon (1974)	38	C	+	+	+	-	+	+	-	-	0	-	-	-	+
Bacon, Barry & Child (1965)	39-84	C,D,ST	+	+	+	-	+	+	-	-	-	+	-	-	+
Bacon, Child & Barry (1963)	19-44	C	+	+	+	0	+	+	-	-	-	-	-	-	0
Baks, Breman & Nooji (1966)	57	D	0	+	+	0	-	+	-	-	-	+	+	-	0
Barry (1957)	28-30	C,D	-	0	+	0	0	+	-	-	-	-	-	-	+
Barry (1968)	13-52	D,C	0	0	+	0	0	+	-	-	0	-	-	-	0
Barry (1969)	24	C	0	0	+	0	0	+	-	+	-	-	-	-	+
Barry & Roberts (1972)	48-78	C	0	+	+	-	-	+	-	-	0	+	-	-	+
Barry, Child & Bacon (1967)	79-104	C,ST	+	+	+	-	-	+	-	-	-	-	-	-	+
Barry, Bacon & Child (1957)	35-64	C	0	+	+	-	-	+	+	-	+	+	-	-	+
Befu (1966)	30-366	C,D	-	+	+	-	-	+	-	-	0	-	-	-	0
Berlin & Kay (1969)	98	D	0	+	+	0	+	+	-	-	-	+	-	-	+
Berting & Philipsen (1960)	21-42	D,ST	0	+	+	0	-	+	-	-	0	-	+	-	0
Binford (1971)	40	D	0	+	+	+	-	+	-	-	0	-	-	-	+
Blum (1969)	Unknown	X²	0	0	+	-	+	+	-	-	-	-	-	+	+
Blumberg & Winch (1972)	45-933	C	0	+	+	0	0	+	-	-	-	-	-	-	0
Bornstein (1973)	13-126	D	-	+	+	-	-	+	-	-	+	+	-	-	0
Bourguignon (1972)	54	X²	+	+	+	-	-	+	-	-	-	+	+	-	0

Study	N	Code
Bourguignon & Evascu (1977)	488, 84	C
Bowden (1969a)	55	F,ST
Brant (1972)	38-55	C
Broude (1975)	30-55	X²,D,C
Broude (1976)	163	S,C
Brown, J.K. (1963)	75	X²
Brown, J. (1952)	50	C
Burton & Whiting (1963)	12-64	D
Carneiro (1968)	100	D
Carneiro (1970)	100	S
Chaney (1966a)	265-565	X²,D
Child, Barry & Bacon (1965)	53-89	ST,X²
Child, Storm & Veroff (1958)	9-44	C
Chu & Hollingsworth (1969)	531	X²
Cohen, Schlegel, Felt & Carlson (1968)	36	D
Cohen, (1961)	66	X²,D
Cohen (1964a,b)	65	X²
Cohen (1969)	53	D
Colby (1963)	75	X²
Coppinger & Rosenblatt (1968)	55	C
Coult (1965)	177-477	C
Cozby & Rosenblatt (1971)	20-41	D
Davis, W.N. (1964)	21-153	D,X²
Davis, W.P. (1971)	60	C
DeLeeuwe (1970)	39-300	ST
DeLeeuwe (1971)	200-300	D,ST
Divale (1972)	99	D
Divale (1974 a,b)	43-1179	C,F
Divale (1976)	16	C
Divale (1977)	57	C
Divale & Harris (1976)	561	ST
Divale, Chamberis & Gangloff (1976)	21-28	C

Methodological Procedures Documented, continued

Study	Sample Size	Statistical Test	Data Collection						Sampling			M	Data Analysis		
			CU	CT	MV	P	R	U	S	G	RV	M	DC	D	GS
Dole (1965)	61	D	-	+	+	-	-	+	-	-	-	-	+	-	0
Dole (1972)	33	S	-	+	+	-	+	+	-	0	0	0	-	-	0
Driver (1969)	75	C	0	0	+	0	0	+	-	-	-	-	+	-	+
Driver & Schuessler (1967)	565	F	0	0	+	0	0	+	-	-	+	+	-	-	+
Eckhardt, K.W. (1971)	144	C	0	+	+	-	-	+	-	-	-	+	-	-	-
Eckhardt, W. (1975)	43-87	C,X²	0	0	+	0	0	+	-	-	+	+	-	+	+
Ember, C. (1974)	13-42	ST,C	0	0	+	0	0	+	-	-	0	+	+	+	+
Ember, C. (1975)	21-50	ST,A	0	+	+	0	0	+	-	-	0	+	+	-	+
Ember, C & Ember M. (1979)	31-688	C,ST,X²	0	+	+	-	-	+	-	-	-	+	-	+	+
Ember, Ember & Pasternak (1974)	14-560	ST,C,A	-	+	+	-	+	-	-	-	-	-	+	-	+
Ember, M. (1961)	36	C,X²	0	0	+	0	+	+	-	-	0	+	+	-	+
Ember, M. (1963)	23-24	C,S	-	+	+	-	+	+	-	-	0	+	+	+	0
Ember, M. (1967)	17	C	-	+	+	-	+	+	+	-	0	+	-	-	0
Ember, M. (1973)	22	D	0	0	+	0	-	+	+	-	0	+	-	-	0
Ember, M. (1974a)	27-146	C	0	+	+	0	+	+	+	-	-	+	-	-	0
Ember, M. (1974b)	16-48	C,D	+	+	+	+	+	+	+	-	0	+	-	+	0
Ember, M. (1975)	49-744	X²,C	0	+	+	0	+	+	-	-	-	+	+	+	0
Ember, M. (1978)	31	ST	0	+	+	0	0	+	-	-	+	+	+	-	+
Ember, M. & Ember, C. (1971)	18-288	X²,C,ST	0	+	+	0	0	+	+	+	+	+	+	0	+
Ember, M. & Ember, C. (1979)	135	C	+	+	+	+	+	+	+	+	+	+	+	0	-
Erickson (1968)	31-76	C	0	0	+	-	-	+	+	+	+	+	+	-	+
Erickson (1976)	125	F	0	+	+	0	0	+	+	+	+	+	+	+	+
Evascu (1975)	74-98	C	0	0	+	0	0	+	+	+	+	-	-	-	+
Eyde & Postal (1961)	89-564	C	0	0	+	0	0	+	-	-	-	+	-	-	0
Field (1962)	14-55	D,C,X²	0	-	+	+	+	+	-	-	+	+	-	-	+
Fischer (1961)	30	ST	-	+	+	0	0	+	-	0	0	0	-	-	0
Freeman (1957)	52	S	-	+	+	-	+	+	-	0	-	0	-	+	+
Freeman & Winch (1957)	48	C	-	+	+	-	-	+	-	-	-	0	-	-	0

Reference	N	Code													
Goodenough (1969)	40-42	D	o	-	-	-	o	-	-	+	-	-	+	+	-
Goody (1970a)	863	D,C	o	-	-	-	+	-	-	+	o	o	+	o	o
Goody (1970b)	863	D,C	o	-	-	-	+	-	-	+	o	o	+	o	o
Goody (1973)	857	D	o	-	-	-	+	-	-	+	o	o	+	o	o
Goody & Buckley (1974)	133-179	X²,D	+	+	-	-	+	+	+	+	+	o	+	+	o
Goody, Irving & Tahany (1970)	60	C	o	-	+	+	-	-	-	+	o	o	+	+	o
Gouldner & Peterson (1962)	71	F,D,C	o	-	-	-	-	-	-	+	+	-	+	o	+
Granzberg (1973a)	70	X²	o	+	-	+	-	-	-	+	+	-	+	+	+
Granzberg (1973b)	32	X²	+	-	-	-	o	+	+	-	-	-	-	+	-
Gunders & Whiting (1968)	69	ST	o	-	+	-	o	-	-	+	-	o	+	o	-
Harner (1970)	797	X²	o	-	-	-	-	-	-	+	o	-	+	+	o
Harrington (1968)	101	A	o	-	-	-	+	-	-	+	o	o	+	+	-
Hays et al. (1972)	6-121	C	o	+	o	+	-	-	-	-	-	-	+	o	-
Heath (1958)	386-398	X²	+	+	-	-	-	-	-	+	o	o	+	+	+
Herzog (1962)	14-91	D,X²,ST	o	-	-	-	o	-	-	+	-	-	+	+	o
Hickman (1962)	70	F	o	-	-	-	+	o	-	+	-	-	+	+	o
Hines & Martindale (1974)	45	C	+	+	+	+	o	-	+	+	-	o	+	+	o
Hobhouse et al. (1915)	41-535	D	o	-	+	+	-	+	-	+	o	o	+	o	-
Homans & Schneider (1962)	33	ST	+	-	-	-	o	-	+	+	-	o	+	o	-
Horton (1943)	21-56	X²	+	-	+	-	+	-	-	+	o	+	+	+	o
Jackson & Romney (1973)	24	D	+	-	-	-	o	-	-	+	+	-	+	+	o
Jorgensen (1966)	89	C	+	-	+	+	+	-	-	+	-	o	+	o	o
Kalin et al. (1966)	46	C	+	-	-	-	+	-	-	+	o	o	+	o	o
Kang (1976a)	50	C	o	-	-	-	o	-	-	+	o	o	+	+	+
Kaplan (1965)	11	X²,D,C	o	-	+	+	+	-	-	+	o	-	+	o	o
Kiev (1960)	18-34	X²	o	-	-	+	-	+	-	+	-	o	+	+	o
Kitahara (1974)	33-78	X²	+	+	+	+	o	+	+	+	o	o	+	+	o
Kitahara (1975)	87-152	X²	+	+	-	+	o	+	+	+	o	o	+	+	+
Klausner (1964)	11-37	C	o	+	+	-	-	+	+	+	+	o	+	+	-
Kloos (1963)	20-24	D	o	+	-	-	-	-	-	+	-	-	+	+	o
Köbben et al. (1974)	16-507	D,X²	o	-	+	-	-	-	-	+	o	o	+	o	o
Krauss (1966)	35-58	C	+	+	+	-	-	+	+	+	o	o	+	+	+
Krauss (1970)	58	X²	o	+	-	-	-	+	+	-	-	-	+	-	o
Krauss & Krauss (1968)	58	X²,D,ST,C	o	+	-	-	-	+	+	+	+	-	+	+	+

Methodological Procedures Documented, continued

Study	Sample Size	Statistical Test	CU	CT	MV	P	R	U	S	G	RV	M	DC	D	GS
					Data Collection				Sampling			Data Analysis			
Krauss & Tesser (1971)	58	C	0	+	+	0	0	+	+	+	-	+	-	+	0
Lambert et al. (1959)	14-46	D	+	+	+	0	+	+	-	+	-	+	-	+	+
Landauer & Whiting (1964)	36	ST	+	+	+	-	+	+	-	-	+	+	-	+	+
Leary (1961)	100	D	0	0	+	-	-	+	-	-	-	-	-	-	0
Lester (1967a)	33	X²	0	+	+	0	0	+	-	-	0	0	0	-	0
Lester (1967b)	9-33	ST,D	-	0	+	-	-	+	-	-	0	0	0	-	0
Lester (1968)	17	C	0	0	+	-	-	+	-	-	0	-	-	-	0
Lester (1969)	25	ST	0	0	+	0	0	+	-	-	0	0	0	-	0
Lester (1970)	11	C	0	0	+	0	0	+	-	-	0	0	0	-	0
Lester (1971)	13-33	C	0	0	+	0	0	+	-	-	0	0	0	-	0
Lester (1975)	8-19	C	0	0	+	0	0	+	-	-	0	-	-	-	+
LeVine (1960)	518	X²	0	0	+	0	0	+	-	-	+	0	0	+	0
LeVine (1962)	61	D	-	+	+	+	+	+	-	+	-	-	-	-	0
Levinson (1979)	50	C	-	+	-	-	-	+	+	+	0	0	0	+	0
Levinson & Swanson (n.d.)	31	C	-	+	+	-	+	+	-	+	0	-	-	-	-
Lomax (1968a)	30-233	C,D	+	+	+	-	+	+	-	+	+	+	-	+	+
Lomax (1968b)	28-150	C	+	+	+	-	+	+	-	+	+	+	-	+	+
Lomax et al. (1968)	43	C	+	+	+	-	+	+	-	+	0	+	-	+	+
March (1955)	15	C,ST	-	+	+	-	-	+	-	-	0	-	-	-	0
Masamura (1977a)	47	C	-	+	+	-	+	+	-	+	0	+	-	+	0
Masamura (1977b)	35	C	-	+	+	-	-	+	-	+	0	-	-	-	0
Maxwell (1967)	54-93	X²,ST,D	0	0	+	-	0	+	-	+	0	-	-	-	0
Maxwell & Silverman (1970)	26	C	+	+	+	-	+	+	-	+	-	+	+	+	+
McClelland et al. (1972)	40-52	C	0	+	+	0	+	+	-	+	-	-	-	-	0
McNett (1970a)	37-48	C	0	+	+	0	0	+	-	+	0	+	-	+	+
McNett (1970b)	48	X²,C	0	+	+	-	-	+	-	+	0	-	-	+	+
McNett (1973)	48	F	0	0	+	0	0	+	+	+	0	+	+	+	0
Michaelson & Goldschmidt (1976)	46	X²	-	-	+	+	-	+	-	-	0	-	-	-	0

Reference	N	Code												
Minturn (1965)	10	X²	−	+		−	0			−	+	0	+	−
Minturn et al. (1969)	17–93	C,X²	+	+	−	+		+	+	−	+	−		+
Minturn & Lambert (1964)	38–62	D,C	+	+	−	+	+	+	+	−		+		0
Montgomery (1974)	19–41	X²	−	+	−	+	+	+	+	+	+		−	+
Moore (1942)	23–36	D	−	0	−	+	+	+	−	0	0	0	−	0
Mukhopadhyay (1979)	55	C	+	−	+	+	−	+	+	−	+			+
Munroe & Munroe (1969)	9	C	+	−	−	+	−	+	+		+	+	−	0
Munroe, Munroe and Whiting (1973)	74	X²	+			+	+	−	+		−	+		−
Munroe, Whiting and Halley (1969)	47	ST	−		−	+		−	+		−	+		0
Murdock (1949)	50–250	D,C	0	−	+	+	0	0	+	−		0		0
Murdock (1964)	180	D	0	−	+	+	0	0	+	−	−	0	−	0
Murdock (1967b)	166	D	0	−	+	+	0	0	+	−	−	0	−	0
Murdock (1968)	665–800	D,X²	0	−	+	+	0	0	+	+	−	0	−	0
Murdock (1969)	192–322	D	0	−	+	+	0	0	+	−	−	+	−	0
Murdock (1971)	83–120	D	0	+	+	+	0	0	+	+	−	−	−	0
Murdock & Provost (1973a)	141–185	D,X²,F	0	+	+	+	0	+	+	+	+	+	+	+
Murdock & Provost (1973b)	186	D	+	+	+	+	+	+	+	+	+	+	+	+
Murdock & Wilson (1972)	164–186	D	+	+	+	+	+	+	+	+	+	+	+	+
Nag (1962)	12–48	ST,D	−		+	+	+				−	+		0
Naroll (1956)	30	C	−	−	+	+	+	−	−	+	+	+		0
Naroll (1962b)	18	C	−	0	+	+	+	0	0	−	+	+	+	+
Naroll (1963)	58	C	−	0	+	+	+	0	+	+	+	+	+	0
Naroll (1969)	58	C	+	0	−	+		+	+	+	+	+	+	0
Naroll et al. (1971)	12–28	C	+	+	+	+	+	+	+		−	+	0	+
Naroll, Bullough and Naroll (1974)	20	C	−	−	+	+	+	−	−		−	+		0
Naroll & Wirsing (1976)	234	ST	−	+	+	+	+	+	0	+	+	+	+	0
Naroll & Divale (1976)	49	C	0	−	+	+	0	0	+	−	0	+	0	+
Nerlove (1974)	83	ST	+	+	+	+	+	+	+	−	−	+	+	0
Nerlove & Romney (1967)	41	X²	+	−	−	+	−	−	−			+		0
Nieboer (1900)	340	D	0	−		−	−	+	−		−	+	+	0
Nimkoff (1965)	160–560	X²	0	−	−	+	−	−	−			+		−

Methodological Procedures Documented, continued

Study	Sample Size	Statistical Test	CU	CT	MV	P	R	U	S	G	RV	M	DC	D	GS
				Data Collection					Sampling				Data Analysis		
Nimkoff & Middleton (1960)	302-549	X^2	0	+	+	0	0	+	-	-	-	+	+	-	+
Osmond (1964)	52-550	C,X^2	0	+	+	0	0	+	-	-	+	+	-	-	+
Osmond (1969)	410	C	-	+	+	0	0	+	-	-	-	+	-	-	+
Otterbein (1968)	36-47	C	+	+	+	0	0	+	+	+	0	+	-	-	+
Otterbein (1970)	15-46	C,D	-	0	+	-	+	+	+	-	0	+	+	+	+
Otterbein (1971)	42-47	C	-	+	+	-	-	+	+	-	0	-	-	-	+
Otterbein & Otterbein (1965)	50	C	-	+	+	0	0	+	+	-	0	+	-	-	+
Paige (1974)	21-52	C	0	0	+	0	0	+	-	-	-	-	-	-	0
Palmer (1965)	40	D	-	-	+	-	-	+	-	-	0	-	-	-	0
Palmer (1970)	58	D	-	+	+	-	-	+	-	-	-	-	-	+	+
Precourt (1975)	23-37	C	-	+	+	0	+	+	+	+	0	+	+	-	0
Prescott (1975)	49-63	D	+	0	+	0	0	+	-	-	-	+	-	+	+
Prothro (1960)	36	F	0	0	+	-	0	+	-	-	0	-	-	-	0
Pryor (1977)	60	C	-	+	+	-	+	+	+	+	-	+	-	-	+
Raphael (1969)	168	D	-	0	+	0	-	+	-	-	0	-	-	-	0
Robbins (1966a)	50	X^2	0	0	+	-	0	+	+	+	-	0	0	-	+
Robbins (1966b)	30	D	+	+	+	0	+	+	-	-	0	-	-	-	0
Robbins et al. (1972)	32-109	C,ST	0	+	+	-	-	+	-	-	0	0	-	-	+
Roberts (1967)	56-545	X^2,D	0	+	+	-	-	+	-	-	-	-	-	-	+
Roberts (1976)	128-186	C	0	+	+	0	0	+	-	0	-	+	-	-	+
Roberts & Barry (1976)	96	C	-	+	+	-	-	+	-	-	+	0	-	-	+
Roberts & Forman (1972)	49-146	X^2,C	0	+	+	-	-	+	-	-	-	-	-	-	+
Roberts & Gregor (1971)	41-42	C	0	0	+	0	0	+	-	-	0	-	-	-	+
Roberts & Sutton-Smith (1962)	43-53	ST,D	0	0	+	0	0	+	-	-	-	-	-	-	+
Roberts & Sutton-Smith (1966)	118	C	0	+	+	-	+	+	-	-	-	-	-	-	-
Roberts et al. (1963)	25-39	D,C	0	+	+	+	+	+	-	-	-	-	-	+	-
Roberts et al. (1959)	18-49	D	-	+	+	+	+	+	-	-	0	+	-	+	0
Rohner (1975)	11-101	C,D,X^2	-	+	+	+	+	+	+	+	+	+	+	+	+
Romney (1965)	35	D	0	0	+	0	0	+	-	-	0	-	-	-	0

Rosenblatt (1966)	16-18	C	0	+	+	-	+	+	-	-	0	-	-	-	+
Rosenblatt (1967)	75	A	+	+	+	-	-	+	-	-	-	-	+	-	0
Rosenblatt & Cozby (1972)	30-35	C	0	+	+	-	+	+	-	+	0	+	-	-	+
Rosenblatt et al. (1969)	27	D	0	+	+	0	0	+	-	-	0	-	0	-	0
Rosenblatt & Hillabrant (1972)	6-51	C,ST	+	+	+	-	+	+	-	+	+	-	+	-	0
Rosenblatt & Skoogberg (1974)	8-21	ST	+	+	+	-	+	+	-	+	0	+	-	-	+
Rosenblatt & Unangst (1974)	43-45	ST	0	+	+	0	0	+	+	-	+	-	-	-	0
Rosenblatt, Walsh & Jackson (1976)	10-58	ST,C	+	+	+	-	+	+	+	+	-	+	+	+	+
Rosenblatt et al. (1969)	27	D	0	+	+	0	0	+	-	-	0	-	0	-	0
Russell (1972)	400	F	0	0	+	0	0	+	-	-	+	+	-	-	0
Russell (1973)	40	C	0	0	+	0	0	+	+	-	0	-	-	-	0
Ryder & Blackman (1970)	27	D	0	+	+	-	-	+	-	-	0	0	0	-	0
Sanday (1973)	12-499	S,D	-	+	+	-	-	+	-	-	+	-	+	-	0
Sanday (1974)	12	C	+	+	+	-	-	+	-	-	0	-	+	+	0
Saucier (1972)	58-174	X^2	0	0	+	0	0	+	+	-	+	-	-	-	+
Schaefer (1973)	22-55	C	+	+	+	+	+	+	+	+	+	+	+	+	+
Schaefer (1976)	22-55	C	+	+	+	+	+	+	+	+	+	+	+	+	+
Schlegel (1972)	27-64	D,X^2,C	+	+	+	+	+	+	+	+	+	+	+	+	+
Schwartz & Miller (1964)	51	D,X^2,S	+	+	+	-	+	+	-	-	-	-	+	-	0
Sheils (1971)	483	C	0	0	+	0	0	+	-	-	-	-	-	-	0
Sheils (1972)	63	ST	-	-	+	-	-	+	+	-	-	+	+	-	0
Shirley & Romney (1962)	39	X^2	-	+	+	-	-	+	-	-	0	0	-	-	0
Silverman & Maxwell (1978)	32	C	-	+	+	0	-	+	-	+	0	+	-	-	-
Simmons (1945)	22-679	C	0	+	+	-	-	+	-	-	-	+	-	-	-
Sipes (1973)	20	C	-	+	+	+	+	+	-	+	0	-	+	+	0
Sipes (1974)	17	C	-	+	+	+	+	+	-	+	+	-	-	+	+
Slater & Slater (1965)	30-69	X^2	0	+	+	-	+	+	-	-	-	+	-	-	+
Spiro (1965)	60	X^2	0	0	+	0	0	+	-	-	-	+	-	-	0
Spiro & D'Andrade (1967)	11	C	0	+	+	-	+	+	-	-	0	-	-	-	+
Stephens (1962)	20-74	ST,X^2,C	-	+	+	-	+	+	-	+	-	+	-	-	+
Stephens (1963)	30-51	D	+	+	+	-	-	-	-	-	-	-	-	-	0
Stephens (1967)	55	C,D	0	+	+	-	+	+	-	-	-	-	-	-	+
Stephens (1972)	48	D	-	+	+	-	-	+	-	-	0	-	+	-	0

Methodological Procedures Documented, continued

Study	Sample Size	Statistical Test	Data Collection CU	CT	MV	P	R	U	Sampling S	G	RV	M	Data Analysis DC	D	GS
Stephens & D'Andrade (1962)	33-49	X²,C	0	+	+	–	+	+	–	–	0	+	–	–	+
Stewart & Jones (1972)	98	F	+	0	+	0	0	+	+	–	+	+	–	–	·
Swanson (1960)	19-50	X²,C	+	+	+	–	+	+	+	–	0	+	+	–	0
Swanson (1971)	29-39	X²	+	+	+	0	–	+	–	–	0	–	–	–	+
Sweetser (1966a)	110	ST,X²,C	0	+	+	–	+	+	–	–	–	+	–	–	·
Sweetser (1966b)	21-102	ST	–	0	+	–	–	+	–	–	–	+	–	–	0
Sweetser (1967)	29	ST	0	0	+	0	0	+	–	–	0	0	–	–	0
Tatje & Naroll (1970)	58	C	–	+	+	+	+	+	+	+	–	+	+	+	+
Tefft (1975)	29-44	C	–	+	+	–	–	+	+	–	0	–	+	–	+
Tefft & Reinhardt (1974)	44-49	C	–	+	+	–	–	+	+	–	0	–	–	–	·
Thoden van Velzen & van Wetering (1960)	50	X²	0	0	+	0	0	+	–	–	0	–	+	–	0
Triandis & Lambert (1961)	30-42	X²	+	+	+	–	+	+	–	–	0	+	–	–	·
Tylor (1961)	28-132	D	–	+	+	+	–	+	–	+	–	+	+	+	0
Udy (1959a)	54-150	C,ST	+	+	+	–	–	+	+	–	–	–	–	–	+
Udy (1959b)	150	C	–	+	+	+	–	+	–	–	–	+	+	–	+
Udy (1962)	33-34	C,X²,S	+	+	+	+	+	+	–	–	0	+	–	–	0
Udy (1970)	41-359	D	–	+	+	–	–	+	–	–	–	–	–	–	0
Unwin (1934)	80	D	+	+	+	+	+	+	–	–	+	+	–	–	0
Watson (1973)	23	X²	–	+	+	–	–	+	+	+	0	–	–	–	0
White et al. (1977)	186	S,C	+	+	+	0	–	+	–	+	+	+	+	–	·
Whiting, B. (1950)	20-50	C,ST	–	0	+	+	+	+	–	–	+	–	+	–	0
Whiting, J. (1964)	66-177	X²	+	+	+	–	+	+	–	–	+	–	–	–	0
Whiting, J. (1965)	24-47	X²,D,C	0	0	+	0	–	+	–	–	0	+	–	–	+
Whiting, J. (1967)	28-45	ST,C,D,X²	0	0	+	–	0	+	–	+	0	–	–	–	0
Whiting, J. & Ayres (1968)	30-121	D	0	0	+	0	+	+	+	–	–	+	–	–	0
Whiting et al. (1974)	18-30	ST	–	0	+	–	0	+	–	–	0	–	–	–	+
Whiting & Child (1953)	20-51	C,ST	+	+	+	–	+	+	–	–	+	+	+	–	0
Whiting et al. (1958)	56	X²,D	+	+	+	–	–	–	–	–	–	–	–	–	0

Reference	Test	N													
Whiting & Whiting (1975)	D,phi	39-159	+	−	−	−	+	−	−	+	+	○	+	○	○
Whyte (1978b)	C	93	+	+	+	+	+	+	−	+	+	+	+	+	+
Williams (1972)	D	128	○	+	+	○	−	−	−	+	−	+	+	+	−
Wimberly (1973)	C	48	○	+	+	○	○	○	−	+	+	−	+	+	○
Wirsing (1973)	C	25	+	+	−	+	○	+	+	+	+	−	+	+	−
Witkowski (1972)	C	60-87	○	−	○	○	−	−	−	+	○	−	+	○	○
Wright, G. (1970)	ST	33	+	−	−	−	○	−	−	+	+	○	+	+	−
Wright, Q. (1942)	D	448-590	○	−	−	−	+	−	−	+	−	−	+	+	○
Young (1962)	C	54	○	−	−	+	−	−	−	+	+	−	+	+	−
Young (1965)	D	44-54	○	+	+	−	−	−	−	+	+	−	+	+	+
Young & Bacdayan (1967)	D,C	46-58	+	−	−	+	−	−	−	+	+	−	+	+	−
Zelditch (1955)	D	19-37	○	−	+	−	○	−	−	+	−	+	+	+	−
Zelman (1975)	C	60	+	+	−	+	−	−	−	+	−	○	+	+	○
Zern (1969)	X²,C	37-41	○	−	+	−	○	−	−	+	+	−	+	+	○
Zern (1970)	C	42-47	+	−	−	+	+	−	−	+	+	−	+	+	○
Zern (1972)	X²,D	11-33	○	+	−	−	○	−	−	+	−	−	+	+	○
Zern (1976)	X²	66	○	−	+	−	−	−	−	+	−	−	+	+	○

Language Universals

Cecil H. Brown and Stanley R. Witkowski

Introduction

Language universals constitute an important focus of contemporary linguistics since their description may shed considerable light on the nature of the human language faculty. With the rise of transformational-generative grammar and related linguistic theories, it has been convincingly argued that the basic design principles of human language are innate. The study of language uniformities is one approach to fleshing out the cognitive framework innately shared by humankind upon which individual languages such as Chinese, English, Navaho, and so on, are all constructed.

Studies of language universals have focused on regularities in all three components of language: phonology, grammar, and the lexicon. Historically, however, phonological and grammatical uniformities have received the most attention. While examples of the latter will be reviewed here, this discussion examines in greatest detail universals in the lexicon which have been investigated chiefly by linguistic anthropologists during the past ten years. In this chapter we will also outline explanatory principles through which universals pertaining to all three components of language are linked.

Grammatical and Phonological Universals

A well-known grammatical regularity involves word order in the main clause of declarative transitive sentences. All languages have a normal or preferred word order for nominal subject (S), verb (V), and nominal object (O). In English, for example, it is SVO as in "Mary loves John" or "The dog chased the cat." Of the six logically possible word order types, the patterns SVO, VSO, and SOV are common cross-linguistically, while OVS and OSV never occur, and VOS is extremely rare. The three common orders all share the generalization that subject noun precedes object noun while verb placement is variable. Thus there is an overwhelming tendency for the subject noun to precede the object noun in all human languages (Greenberg 1963).

Other syntactic features are correlated with basic word order. Verb initial (VSO) languages, for instance, almost always employ prepositions, while verb final languages strongly tend to employ postpositions. Verb medial (SVO) languages are variable with respect to this feature. English, of course, has prepositions. When an inflected auxiliary is used in constructions with a main verb, VSO languages always place the auxiliary before the main verb, while SOV languages place it after the main verb. Again, SVO languages are variable, some placing the auxiliary before and some after the main verb. English places it before, as in "is going" and "is running."

The universals described above are *biconditional* in form (Greenberg 1963). Biconditional relationships exist when the occurrence of one language feature implies the occurrence of a second feature and vice versa. Excluding SVO languages which are variable, if a language has prepositions, then it will have VSO word order; if it has VSO word order, then it will have prepositions. Similarly, if a language has inflected auxiliaries before the main verb, it will have VSO word order and vice versa.

Languages also have *unconditional* or *implicational* relationships. These differ from biconditional relationships in that the presence of one language feature implies the presence of a second feature, *but not necessarily the other way around.* Ferguson (1963), for example, presents a series of implicational regularities involving nasal consonants. The occurrence of either a palatal nasal (ñ) or a velar nasal (ŋ) in a language's phonological inventory implies the presence of a bilabial nasal (m), but not the reverse (m can be present when ñ and ŋ are absent). Similarly, the presence of m implies an alveolar nasal (n), but not vice versa (n can be present when m is absent). There are, therefore, severe constraints on the composition of nasal consonant inventories of languages, since only four types of inventories out of many logically possible types occur: (1) no nasal consonants, (2) n alone, (3) n and m, and (4) n, m, ñ and/or ŋ. These regularities can be presented as a chain of implicational relationships: n < m < ñ or ŋ (where < reads "is implied by").

Implicational relationships are weaker than biconditional relationships since knowledge of the latter permits more accurate predictions concerning the co-occurrence of language features than knowledge of the former. Given a biconditional relationship, if we know that a certain feature is present, we can accurately predict that a second feature is present and vice versa. Given an implicational relationship such as that between n and m, if we know that m is present, we can predict that n is present, but we cannot accurately predict the occurrence of m from the occurrence of n. Even though implicational relationships are not as strong as biconditional ones, they are considerably more pervasive in cross-language research. They are also more pervasive in cross-cultural research, but the two types of relationships are not usually separated analytically (Kang 1972; Witkowski 1971, 1972, 1976).

The generalizations reviewed above for the grammatical and phonological spheres of language are only a very small sample of those described in the literature (see, for example, *Stanford University, Working Papers in Language Universals,* 1966-present). Beyond discovering language universals, an important challenge is formulation of theories that will explain regularities and predict additional ones. Recognition of *marking principles* is a significant step in this direction.

Marking

Marking principles are based on implicational relationships. In such relationships the implied feature is unmarked and the implying feature is marked. For example, the implicational chain for nasal consonants, n < m < ñ or ŋ, forms a marking sequence where ñ and ŋ are marked vis-à-vis m and n, and m is marked vis-à-vis n which is unmarked.

There are a set of features that tend to co-occur in typical marking relationships. These are as follows:

Unmarked Item	*Marked Item*
1. The implied in an implicational relationship	1. The implier in an implicational relationship
2. Greater frequency of use (in text or spoken language)	2. Lesser frequency of use
3. Appears in neutral environments	3. Does not appear in neutral environments
4. Less complex (phonologically or morphologically)	4. More complex
5. Earlier child acquisition	5. Later child acquisition

| 6. Greater frequency of occurrence across languages | 6. Lesser frequency of occurrence |
| 7. Survives if merger occurs | 7. Does not survive if merger occurs |

Marking frequently finds expression in adjectival oppositions such as deep/shallow and wide/narrow where one item will be unmarked and its counterpart marked (Greenberg 1966). An unmarked member of an adjectival pair tends to occur more frequently in ordinary language use than its marked opposite (see feature 2 above). This is especially noticeable in neutral linguistic environments (feature 3). In English, for example, queries concerned with depth are framed more often with the unmarked form "deep" rather than with the marked form "shallow." Thus we customarily ask "How deep is the river?" not "How shallow is the river?" when we do not have presuppositions about the depth of the river—when the context of inquiry is neutral. In addition, marked items tend to be phonologically more complex than unmarked items (feature 4). The marked form "shallow," for instance, is disyllabic while its unmarked counterpart "deep" is monosyllabic and, therefore, simpler.

Phonological complexity (feature 4) is sometimes realized through *overt marking* of the marked item. Overt marking in the lexicon involves use of the label for the unmarked item modified by an additional lexical element. This complex construction constitutes a label for the marked item. In Spanish, for example, "deep" is *profundo* and "shallow" is *poco profundo* (literally, "little deep").

Another marking characteristic pertains to child language acquisition (feature 5). Unmarked items tend to be acquired by children before corresponding marked ones. Thus, for example, English speaking children tend to acquire "deep" before "shallow."

An example of marking in the grammatical sphere is the universal marking of passive sentences in non-ergative languages (Greenberg 1966). Active sentences, such as the English "John hit Harry," are always unmarked, while their passive counterparts, such as "Harry was hit by John," are marked. Active sentences are more frequently used in ordinary language than passive ones. In addition, the processes of forming them are acquired by children before passive forming processes. Active sentences are also less complex than their passive counterparts. English active sentences, for instance, contain fewer morphemes than their passive realizations.

A classic case of marking involves the relationship between oral and nasal vowels. All languages have oral vowels, while some possess nasal vowels and some do not (French does, English does not). Oral vowels then are more frequent across languages than nasal vowels (feature 6), and thus are unmarked, while nasal vowels are marked. In addition, text counts of the intralanguage frequency of nasal versus oral vowels always are higher for the latter. Also, if a nasal vowel and its oral counterpart merge at some point in a language's history, it is always the oral vowel that survives (feature 7).

Zipf (1935, 1949) demonstrated some years ago that frequency of use of lexical items correlates with their phonological length. High frequency is associated with short length and, thus, with less complexity, and low frequency is associated with greater length and, thus, with more complexity. This association explains the co-occurrence of marking features 2, 4, and 5 (listed above). If lexical items increase in frequency of use, they tend to be shortened or replaced by shorter forms (*television* becomes *TV* or *telly* or *the tube*). Frequency of use and lesser complexity are also correlated in the grammatical sphere as in active and passive sentences. Phonologically, oral vowels are simpler than nasal vowels, which correlates with their greater frequency of occurrence both cross-linguistically and intra-linguistically. That children acquire high frequency, less complex unmarked language traits before their more complex and less frequently occurring marked counterparts is not surprising. Presumably the relative simplicity and common occurrence of unmarked items leads to their early learning.

Marking features 1, 6, and 7 are different ways of formulating the same underlying regularity. In the nasal consonant example, n and m can both be present in language or absent in language, but if only one is present, it is always n (the unmarked segment). Thus if these two merge, it is always n which is the survivor. Also, since many languages have n and lack m, while all languages that have m also have n, it follows that n will be more frequent cross-linguistically. Similarly, the existence of m implies the existence of n but not the other way around.

The two sets of marking features (1, 6, and 7) and (2, 4, and 5), are tied together by the positive correlation between high intralanguage frequency of use and greater cross-language frequency of occurrence. Thus within English text, n occurs more frequently than m. Similarly, n is more frequent than m cross-linguistically. It follows then that n is universally unmarked relative to m, while m is universally marked relative to n.

Universal marking relationships such as this and others discussed above are ubiquitous in language. Why these panhuman marking preferences exist is not yet fully understood.

Lexical Universals

This section discusses lexical universals from the domains of ethnobiology and color classification. Literature describing uniformities in the lexicon is now sizeable and it would be impossible to treat it all here. Those interested in surveys of this literature can refer to Witkowski and Brown (1978, n.d.).

Ethnobiology

All humans classify plants and animals into labeled categories of greater and lesser inclusiveness. For speakers of American English, for example, white oaks, pin oaks, and post oaks are kinds of oaks; oaks, walnuts, and maples are kinds of trees; and trees, vines, and grasses are kinds of plants. Each labeled biological category is associated with an "ethnobiological rank" (Berlin 1972, 1973, 1976; Berlin, Breedlove, and Raven 1973, 1974). For instance, in English the most inclusive class, *plant*, belongs to the "unique beginner" rank; *tree*, *vine*, and *grass* belong to the "life-form" rank; *oak*, *walnut*, and *maple* to the "generic" rank; and *white oak*, *pin oak*, and *post oak* to the "specific" rank. Finer distinctions are made at a lower or "varietal" rank (see Figure B.1).

Ethnobiological ranks are regularly associated with certain types of labels. For example, categories of the most inclusive ranks (generics, life-forms, and the unique beginner) are usually labeled by "primary lexemes," while classes of the least inclusive ranks (specifics and varietals) are usually labeled by "secondary lexemes." A primary lexeme is usually a linguistically simple label such as *oak*, *tree*, or *plant*. A secondary lexeme consists of a word for the category in which the class it labels is immediately included and a modifying element, such as *white oak* and *pin oak*.

While biological taxonomies may lack all categories of the unique beginner and life-form ranks (Brown 1977a; Berlin et al. 1973), classes of the generic and specific ranks are always present. Thus in biological classification, use of generic and specific categories

Figure B1. *Relationship of Ethnogiological Ranks*
(With Sample Botanical Classes from American English)

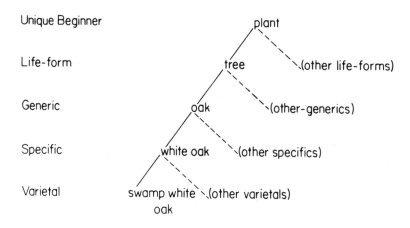

constitutes a cross-language universal. Within this universal core classificatory system generics are always more numerous than specifics. In addition, specific classes are always marked relative to unmarked generic categories in which they are immediately included. The marking relationship between generics and specifics in the universal core system is usually direct and overt. For example, *white oak* is a specific class immediately included in the generic category *oak*. The modifier *white* is a direct overt mark attached to the basic term *oak*.

Folk biological taxonomies are expanded beyond the universal core system with the addition of life-form classes. This addition follows an invariant "lexical encoding sequence" (Brown 1977a). Lexical encoding sequences are marking sequences which, like marking sequences in phonology and grammar, are based on implicational relationships.

Folk Botanical Life-Forms

Figure B.2 presents the lexical encoding sequence for folk botanical life-forms. The regularities in Figure B.2 are based on implicational relationships present in 105 languages (Brown 1977a). For

Figure B2. *Folk Botanical Life-Form Encoding Sequence*

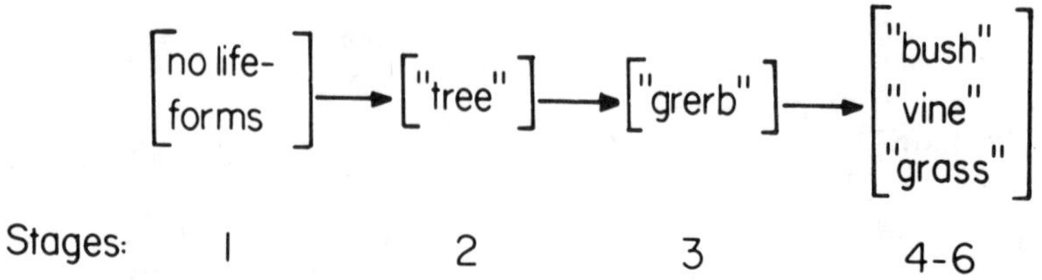

$$\begin{bmatrix} \text{no life-} \\ \text{forms} \end{bmatrix} \longrightarrow \begin{bmatrix} \text{"tree"} \end{bmatrix} \longrightarrow \begin{bmatrix} \text{"grerb"} \end{bmatrix} \longrightarrow \begin{bmatrix} \text{"bush"} \\ \text{"vine"} \\ \text{"grass"} \end{bmatrix}$$

Stages: 1   2   3   4-6

example, if a language has only one botanical life-form term, it always labels a large ligneous plant category that can be roughly glossed "tree." If a language has two botanical life-form terms, one is always "tree" and the other labels a small herbaceous plant category or "grerb." The occurrence of "grerb" implies the occurrence of "tree" but not necessarily the reverse. Thus in the growth of botanical life-form lexicons "tree" is always added before "grerb." The critical features associated with the five botanical life-forms of the encoding sequence are:

"tree"   large plant (relative to the plant inventory of a particular environment) whose parts are chiefly ligneous (woody)

"grerb"   small plant (relative to the plant inventory of a particular environment) whose parts are chiefly herbaceous (green, leafy, nonwoody). (The word *plant* is typically used by American English speakers as a label for this life-form. Since *plant* is also used as a unique beginner term referring to botanical organisms in general, it is not employed as a life-form gloss to avoid ambiguity of reference.)

"bush"   plant of intermediate size (relative to "tree" and "grerb")

"grass"   herbaceous plant with narrow, often bladelike or spear-shaped leaves

"vine"   plant exhibiting a creeping or twining or climbing stem habit

The lexical encoding sequence of Figure B.2 represents a series of stages in the growth of folk botanical life-form vocabularies. Stage 1 languages have no botanical life-forms. At Stage 2 "tree" is encoded. "Tree" in early stage languages is often considerably broader in actual plant membership than "tree" in later stage languages. It frequently includes bushes and shrubs, and sometimes even ligneous vines, in addition to trees. At Stage 3 a second life-form, "grerb," is lexically encoded which includes most plants not included in the "tree" life-form.

From Stage 4 to Stage 6 "bush," "vine," and "grass" are lexically encoded but in no significant order. These additional categories are composed of plants previously included in "grerb" and "tree." Thus, the lexical encoding of "bush," for example, involves pulling bushes and shrubs from the range of "grerb" or "tree," or from the ranges of both, as the case may be. Consequently, as life-forms are added from Stage 4 to Stage 6, the ranges of "grerb" and "tree" tend to shrink.

Explanatory Principles

Four general principles underlie regularities in botanical life-form growth and other encoding regularities to be described presently. These are (1) conjunctivity (including binary opposition), (2) criteria clustering, (3) dimension salience, and (4) marking (Witkowski and Brown 1978).

The encoding priority of "tree" and "grerb" exemplifies classification by means of binary opposition. This type of classification is particularly apparent in the adjectival component of vocabularies. The oppositional characteristics of dimensional concepts (height, width, depth) are usually encoded by two terms and only rarely are finer lexical distinctions carved out. This results in such familiar adjectival oppositions as wide/narrow, deep/shallow, hard/soft.

"Tree" and "grerb" encode the binary opposition "large plant"/ "small plant." In the Delaware language, for example, the "tree"/ "grerb" opposition is based on the size of human adults (Miller 1975). Delaware "tree" refers to any plant over human height and "grerb" to plants shorter than humans. The "large plant"/"small plant" contrast also occurs in child acquisition of American English botanical life-forms (Dougherty 1979).

Binary opposition is one way in which the principle of *conjunctivity* is realized in natural language categorization. The encoding of binary oppositions such as large/small, deep/shallow, and wide/narrow creates the dimensions size, depth, and width respectively. An alternative way of encoding a dimension would be to name its midsection with a term and its extremes with another; "medium size" could be labeled by one term and "extreme size, both large and small" by a second term. This labeling, however, never occurs in dimensional naming because it would violate conjunctive constraints. A category combining dimensional extremes would be disjunctive and such categories are rare in human naming systems. Binary opposition (dividing a dimension into two more or less equal parts) is the only way of partitioning a dimension by use of two terms which does not violate conjunctivity. The encoded opposition "tree"/"grerb" contrasts plants along a size dimension. Languages could categorize botanical objects through attention to size by assigning a name to all mid-sized plants and another to all very large and very small plants. Such a division of the botanical world, however, is not attested. To treat plants so would violate conjunctivity. A category combining very large plants and very small plants (minus mid-sized plants) would be disjunctive. The contrast "tree"/"grerb" or "large plant"/"small plant" represents the only way of categorizing plants in terms of size by use of two terms which does not violate conjunctivity. Consequently, oppositional classification of objects in terms of underlying dimensions is also due to conjunctivity constraints.

The "tree"/"grerb" distinction also involves *criteria clustering*. This clustering occurs when certain defining features of natural objects correlate so that the presence of any one feature is highly predictive of the presence of other features. Bruner, Goodnow, and Austin (1956:47) illustrate this principle by citing the example of "bird," an animal possessing feathers, wings, and a bill. A creature's possession of feathers is highly predictive of wings and a bill, so much so that we build up the expectation of all these features being present together. This expectation can lead to the lexical encoding of "bird." Through criteria clustering "natural breaks" occur in the physical world which tend to be followed in the classification of objects (Bruner, Goodnow, and Austin 1956:47; Hunn 1977:46).

Plants demonstrate continuous variation along two dimensions, size and ligneousness versus herbaceousness (woodiness versus nonwoodiness). These two dimensions tend to cluster: large plants are usually ligneous while small plants are usually herbaceous. This clustering provides a natural break for distinguishing plants by binary opposition and leads to the "tree"/"grerb" distinction.

The development of life-form categories through binary opposition always involves the dimension size (Brown 1979a; Witkowski and Brown 1978). The importance of size in biological classification illustrates the principle of *dimension salience*. Highly salient dimensions pertain to large and varied sets of objects. Dimensions of low salience apply to only a small number of different objects. Since all biological organisms vary by size, there is a strong tendency to incorporate this dimension into classificatory strategies. The encoding priority of "tree" relative to "grerb" (Figure B.2) involves the framework of *marking*. "Tree" is universally unmarked and "grerb" is universally marked (Brown 1977a: 334). "Tree" is unmarked since its occurrence is always implied by "grerb." In addition, a number of languages add a modifier to "tree" and use this overtly marked form for "grerb" (Brown 1977a:334-335, 1979b).

The unmarked status of "tree" vis-à-vis "grerb" is attributable to a *zero to infinity* principle. Greenberg (1975:90) cites several adjectival oppositions—"deep"/"shallow," "wide"/"narrow," "long"/ "short," and "large"/"small"—which enter into universal marking patterns. In all cases the marked item of the adjectival pair is associated with the "zero" point of the relevant dimension, while the unmarked item is associated with deviation from the zero point, the "infinite" end. For all dimensions with a clear physical interpretation and a zero point there is a tendency to treat the "infinite" pole preferentially, resulting in its unmarked status. This tendency also occurs in botanical life-form classification where "tree" or "large plant" universally emerges as unmarked vis-à-vis "grerb" or "small plant." The dimension involved is, of course, size.

As noted earlier, marking sequences can extend to three or more language features. The lexical encoding of "bush," for example, involves further attention to the size dimension underlying the "tree"/"grerb" or "large plant"/"small plant" opposition. "Bush" is intermediate in size. Only when the "tree"/"grerb" distinction is encoded and both poles labeled, will "bush" be encoded. Thus "tree," "grerb," and "bush" form a marking sequence in which "tree" is least marked and "bush" is most marked.

Basic Color Categories

Berlin and Kay (1969) assembled evidence from ninety-eight languages demonstrating implicational relationships among "basic color categories." Since then numerous field studies of native color vocabularies have been published (Berlin and Berlin 1975; Hage and Hawkes 1975; Heinrich 1972; Snow 1971). This new evidence supports Berlin and Kay's general conclusion that basic color terms are added to languages in an invariant order and has led only to minor changes in the lexical encoding sequence for color. Figure B.3

gives the Berlin and Kay color encoding sequence, including the latest revisions and amendments.

In Figure B.3 a term in quotation marks refers to the "focus" of a color category which is the most typical or representative member of that class in the judgment of informants. An expression in uppercase type designates a composite category. These are various combinations of black and white and of the hues red, yellow, green, and blue. Berlin and Kay (1969) have shown that the foci of all basic color categories fall into eleven small areas of color space.

Languages with two terms always encode the composite categories "macro-white" and "macro-black." Macro-white includes whites and most warm hues (reds, yellows, oranges, pinks, and purples) and macro-black includes blacks and most cool hues (blues and greens). The focus of macro-black is always "black," while the focus of macro-white is either "white" or "red." Two additional composite categories, "macro-red" and "grue," occur in the encoding sequence for color (Figure B.3). Macro-red includes most warm hues and is always focused in "red." Grue encompasses most cool hues and is focused in either "green" or "blue."

The encoding of macro-red at Stage II consists in separating warm hues from light hues and white, thus dividing the macro-white category into macro-red and white. Similarly, the encoding of grue involves the separation of most cool hues from very dark hues and black, thus dividing the macro-black category into grue and black. The lexical encoding of the remaining color classes involves subdividing ranges of macro-red and grue.

In Figure B.4 only focal hues are considered. Figure B.4 shows that red is always encoded first (Stage A), followed by yellow, green and/or blue, but in no particular order (Stage B). These in turn are followed by brown, pink, purple, and orange, again in no particular order (Stage C). This formulation is in accord with all existing color nomenclature data (Witkowski and Brown 1977).

Several authors (Bornstein 1975; Bornstein, Kessen, and Weiskopf 1976; Kay and McDaniel 1978; and von Wattenwyl and Zollinger 1979) have argued that the four hue classes, red, yellow, green, and blue, and the additional categories, black and white, are neurophysiologically "wired" or "programmed" in human beings. A useful summary of the ethological, neurophysiological, behavioral, and psychological evidence bearing upon the existence of wired color categories has been organized by Bornstein (1975). Figure B.4 shows that the four natural or wired hue categories are encoded first, while

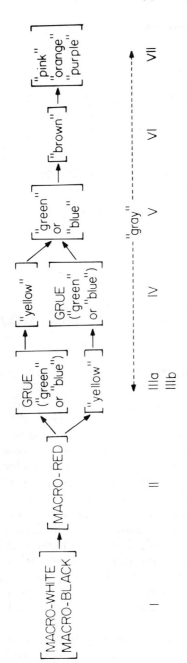

Figure B3. *Revised Berlin-Kay Color Encoding Sequence*

Taken from Witkowski and Brown (1977).

Figure B4. *Encoding Sequence for Hue*

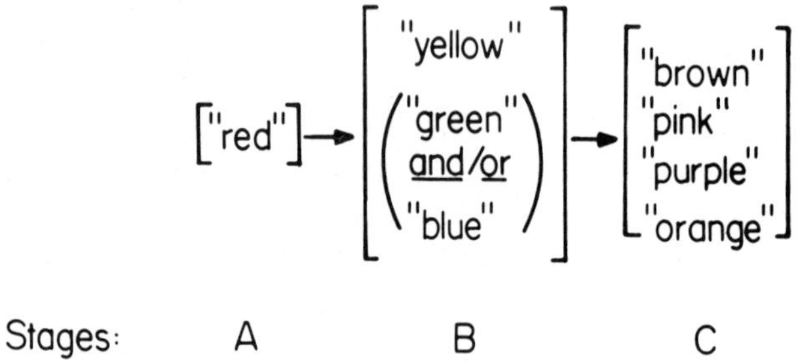

$$\left[\text{"red"}\right] \rightarrow \left[\begin{array}{c} \text{"yellow"} \\ \left(\begin{array}{c}\text{"green"} \\ \underline{\text{and}/\text{or}} \\ \text{"blue"}\end{array}\right) \end{array}\right] \rightarrow \left[\begin{array}{c}\text{"brown"} \\ \text{"pink"} \\ \text{"purple"} \\ \text{"orange"}\end{array}\right]$$

Stages: A   B   C

Taken from Witkowski and Brown (1977).

Color terms in quotation marks are focal. The "focus" of a color category is the most typical or representative member of that category in the judgment of informants.

the classes brown, pink, purple, and orange emerge only secondarily.

The color encoding sequence is also a marking sequence (see Figure B.4). Red is unmarked relative to yellow, green, and blue. Data gathered by Bornstein, Kessen, and Weiskopf (1976) show red to be especially salient. In addition to determining the existence of natural categories of hue, Bornstein and his collaborators also found evidence indicating that of the four wired hue classes, red is the most salient (1976:202). Finally, the color categories of Stage C (see Figure B.4) are marked vis-à-vis those of Stage B, the wired status of Stage B categories accounting for their unmarked condition relative to Stage C classes. D. G. Hays, Margolis, Naroll and Perkins (1972) have shown that intralanguage frequency of use also correlates with this marking sequence for color, and Durbin (1972:271) has shown a correlation between the sequence and the phonological length of color terms. Short terms tend to occur early in the sequence and long terms later.

Black, white, and gray relate to a separate brightness dimension. Together they form a marking sequence distinct from the hue sequence. Gray is marked relative to black and white. The brightness dimension is treated similarly to the size dimension underlying "tree," "grerb," and "bush"; namely, an opposition is encoded and only later is a middle segment distinguished.

It is interesting to note that the principle of criteria clustering has two realizations: (1) as discontinuities in nature, and (2) as discontinuities programmed into the neural circuitry of humans. "Natural breaks" in the physical world are associated with the emergence of categories such as "tree" and "grerb," while "neurophysiologically wired breaks" are associated with the emergence of the hue categories red, yellow, green, and blue and the brightness categories black and white.

Despite their wired status, the latter six categories are never the first color classes to be lexically encoded. Composite color categories always precede red, yellow, green, blue, black, and white in the development of color lexicons (Figure B.3).

Six combinations of the four primary hue classes are possible in composite categories: 1) red-yellow (macro-red); 2) yellow-green— a rare but attested category (Bornstein 1973); 3) green-blue (grue); 4) blue-yellow; 5) red-blue; and 6) red-green. Only the first three of these actually occur. The nonattested macro-colors provide evidence that a dimension based on wavelength order—red-yellow-green-blue—is important in human color categorization. Only conjunctive primary colors, those adjacent to each other in wavelength order, can be combined in composite classes. Nonadjacent combinations, 4-6, would be disjunctive, and, hence, do not occur. Conjunctivity considerations, then, provide important constraints limiting the variety of composite color classes.

Encoding macro-black and macro-white involves two pairs of binary oppositions. Oppositional characteristics of both brightness and hue are encoded. Macro-black (black-green-blue) and macro-white (white-red-yellow) oppose light and dark along a brightness dimension and warm and cool hues along a hue dimension, always associating dark colors with cool hues and light colors with warm hues (see Figure B.5). The encoding of macro-red (red-yellow) and grue (green-blue) involves separation of the brightness dimension from the hue dimension by segregating macro-red from white and grue from black (Witkowski and Brown 1977).

Wiring underlies the pairing of warm hues with white and cool hues with black in the categories macro-white and macro-black respectively. The cross-language focus of yellow is located in the

Figure B5. *Binary Distinctions Pertaining to the Encoding of Macro-Black and Macro White*

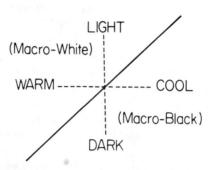

Adapted from Witkowski and Brown (1977).

light area of color space toward white, while the cross-language foci of the three other wired hue classes, red, blue, and green, are in the medium to dark brightness range (Berlin and Kay 1969; Witkowski and Brown 1977). Thus yellow is naturally associated with white, and red goes along with yellow in a macro-white class because of conjunctivity considerations. As a result, warm colors are universally associated with white in a macro-white category and cool colors with black in a macro-black category.

Processes yielding the opposition macro-white/macro-black are similar to those resulting in the contrast "tree"/"grerb" or "large plant"/"small plant." In both cases two dimensions are pertinent, hue and brightness for colors and size and woodiness for plants. Both contrasts partition two dimensions using only two terms. One is based on discontinuities in nature and the other on discontinuities in neurophysiological wiring.

Conjunctivity in Grammar and Phonology

In the preceding discussion we show that conjunctivity pertains to certain lexical regularities in the domains of ethnobotany and color classification. The principle of conjunctivity also extends to uni-.formities in other spheres of language.

Many languages, including English, distinguish singular from plural nouns. Others, such as Ancient Greek and many American Indian languages, make a further distinction between dual (two) and plural (three or more). In languages such as Chinese and Korean, on the other hand, grammatical number is entirely ignored. Cross-linguistically, singular, plural, and dual are implicationally related and form a marking sequence in which dual is marked relative to plural and singular, and plural is marked relative to singular—which is unmarked (Greenberg 1966).

A fourth type of system is possible, one which recognizes dual and combines singular and plural. Such a system would grammatically distinguish entities in twos (dual) from entities in numbers greater or lesser than two (combined singular and plural). Systems of this type, however, do not exist because they would violate conjunctivity constraints. The grammatical lumping of "one" and "three or more" would be disjunctive. Such a combination is disallowed for the same reason that a botanical class encompassing both very large and very small plants (minus mid-sized plants) is disallowed. Thus if a language is to make a two-way distinction in grammatical number, it must do so conjunctively.

Conjunctivity constraints also apply to phonological contrasts. No language, for instance, distinguishes partially nasalized vowels and opposes them to a combined category of fully oral and fully nasal vowels. The latter category, of course, would be disjunctive and, therefore, does not occur. Similarly, in languages such as Navaho, which distinguish two levels of lexical tone, tones are always high versus low, not mid versus a combined very high/very low category.

Sarci, a language closely related to Navaho, has innovated a third tone, a mid tone falling between the original high and low tones. This innovation is similar to the lexical encoding of "bush" (or mid-sized plant). Sarci mid tone and "bush" mediate linguistically recognized contrasts, high tone/low tone and "tree"/'grerb" respectively. Only after the poles of such oppositions are distinguished will mediating elements emerge. This process also explains the markedness of dual number vis-à-vis singular and plural. Dual is distinguished only after the conjunctive contrast singular/plural is recognized, dual (two) is an intermediate category between singular (one) and plural (three or more).

Binary contrasts are widespread in all areas of language because humans tend strongly to avoid disjunctive categories. Bruner, Goodnow, and Austin (1956) demonstrated that humans have more difficulty learning disjunctive concepts than conjunctive ones, a result which is consistent with the observations above. Distinguishing a mid category and opposing it to one combining opposing extremes is cognitively cumbersome, since it requires making two conceptual distinctions rather than one. In such a case, each extreme is separated from the mid category while in binary contrasts extremes are simply separated from each other. The cognitive usefulness of a category encompassing two extremes is also questionable. Such a category would be awkward and opaque in ordinary language use because the hearer would have to rely on context to determine which extreme is intended. For these reasons, binary opposition is the preferred way of making two-way distinctions in all components of language.

The Human Language Faculty

As mentioned earlier, language universals are an important focus in contemporary linguistics because their description can contribute greatly to the study of the human language faculty. In discussing the nature of this faculty a distinction is drawn between knowledge of an individual language such as Chinese, English, or Navaho—knowledge which is entirely learned—and knowledge of the design principles of language itself. Recently it has been argued that the underlying design pattern of human language is innate. Chomsky (1975:219) proposes that humans start life with innate knowledge of "the form and character of grammars and the principles by which grammars operate."

At issue is the degree of specificity of these design principles. Chomsky's discussion of syntactic universals stresses the detailed specificity of these uniformities. He rejects attempts to account for language universals by appealing to very general, non-specific design principles. Cognitive psychologists and others tend to appeal to information processing models of the human language faculty. They explain language learning by innate but very general mechanisms for processing primary linguistic data. We adopt a position combining detailed design and information processing, a rich cognition model. This model proposes that some aspects of language involve detailed design principles; however, the remainder and much the larger part of the human language faculty is attributed to innate information processing devices, most of which are very general.

The preceding discussion, especially of lexical uniformities, indicates that both detailed design and more general principles constitute aspects of the human language faculty. Basic naming principles that apply to botanical life-form encoding, to basic color category encoding, and to the encoding of adjectival oppositions, are not domain-specific—suggesting that the design principles underlying them are relatively general. The principles of conjunctivity (including binary opposition), criteria clustering, marking, and dimension salience are aspects of naming behavior which relate to cognitive faculties involving information processing rather than detailed design. On the other hand, color encoding is in part explained through reference to four natural categories of hue and two of brightness which are wired in detailed specificity into the neural circuitry of humans.

Lexical universals suggest that general design principles play a considerably more important role in shaping actual language than do specific design principles. The character of lexicons would be quite different without binary opposition and marking principles. On the other hand, language would be much the same if humans were not programmed for black, white, red, yellow, green, and blue. Lack of specific design for botanical categorization, for example, has not prevented lexical encoding of general plant classes. If detailed design principles for color did not exist, there is no reason to believe that languages would not encode basic color classes, although probably somewhat different ones.

Since some aspects of the human language faculty are based on detailed design, it is not inconceivable that further examples will emerge as investigation of language universals proceeds. It seems unlikely, however, that detailed specifications will figure prominently in explanations of language universals. In any case, neither the information processing model nor the detailed design model alone sufficiently captures the variety and complexity of the human language faculty. Rather, a rich cognition model, one allowing for both possibilities, appears warranted by present evidence.

Language Change

The kinds of universals described in this chapter have important implications for the study of language change. Understanding processes of language change, especially lexical change, provides principles for recovering language history and sheds light on the conceptual inventory of humans living thousands of years before the first appearance of written records.

The botanical life-form and color encoding sequences are both positively related to societal complexity (Brown 1977a; Naroll 1970; Ember 1978). Languages having few plant life-forms and basic color terms are usually spoken by peoples living in small-scale societies; they demonstrate little of the political integration, social stratification, and technological elaboration of speakers of languages possessing many of these items. The strong tendency for the number of terms in these encoding sequences to increase with increases in societal complexity implies that these sequences are basically additive in nature, since societal complexity has generally increased during the course of human history.

Because of their additive nature, the encoding sequences for plant life-forms and basic color classes provide constraints on the lexical reconstruction of earlier language states. Not all encoding sequences, however, are positively associated with societal complexity (Witkowski and Burris n.d.). In such cases, change does not involve the invariant accumulation of lexical items and as a consequence these sequences are less useful in recovering language history.

The tendency for the number of items in additive encoding sequences to increase with increases in societal complexity also implies that earlier language states had fewer of these items than present states. Since the last several millennia of human history have generally witnessed increases in societal complexity, it is unlikely that languages spoken thousands of years ago had more botanical life-forms and basic color terms than, or even the same number as, their respective contemporary daughter languages. Lexical reconstructions reported by Brown (1979b), Witkowski and Brown (n.d.), and Brown and Witkowski (n.d.) accord with this prediction.

Brown (1979b), for example, reconstructs folk botanical life-form terms for various proto-stages in Mayan language history. This reconstruction indicates that development of Mayan botanical life-form vocabularies from Proto-Mayan times to the present has involved precisely the kinds of lexical addition predicted by the botanical life-form encoding sequence (Figure B.2). Proto-Mayan, spoken about 4000 years ago, possessed only one botanical life-form term, "tree." After 3000 years of little change, Mayan botanical life-form lexicons began to increase in size. Today all Mayan languages have "tree" and "grerb" and many have life-forms beyond these.

Witkowski and Brown (n.d.) reconstruct basic color term inventories for Proto-Mayan, Proto-Polynesian, and Proto-Miwok (see Branstetter 1977; Callaghan 1979). A three term system, "black," "white," and "red," reconstructs for all three proto-languages. Most of the respective contemporary daughter languages have larger systems than this and none have smaller systems. In addition, color term growth in each language family from proto-language times to the present has conformed with the lexical encoding sequence for basic color categories (Figure B.3).

Since the lexical encoding sequences for botanical life-forms and basic color categories are basically additive in nature, it is possible to recover in a general way the lexical inventories of human groups of the distant past. For example, it is unlikely that languages of 10,000 or more years ago had general plant classes such as "tree" and "grerb." Thus they possessed botanical taxonomies with only generic and specific classes, the universal core system. In addition, it is unlikely that these languages had more than two color terms, macro-black and macro-white respectively.

Why were these lexical items less useful in societies of the past than today? The notion of societal complexity does not explain lexical growth in any particular domain. It merely designates a host of developments that tend to occur together. Different indices of societal complexity, for example, use different sets of variables, such as those developed by Freeman (1957), Marsh (1967), and Naroll (1956). All of these indices, however, correlate highly with each other (Schaefer 1969).

To explain lexical growth, more specific variables that are themselves related to overall societal complexity should be examined. Such a variable for the color encoding sequence might be increasing technological control over color in the form of dyeing, painting, and other color manipulation activities. This variable should be positively related to societal complexity. As color manipulating activities increase, an expanding basic color lexicon should prove increasingly useful.

The greater usefulness of general terms for plants in complex societies probably relates to the increasing separation of humans from direct reliance and dependence on the natural world as societies become more complex. The typical individual in a small-scale soceity can commonly name and identify 400 to 800 separate plant species (Berlin et al. 1974; Conklin 1954; T.E. Hays 1976), while the typical member of modern urban society might manage to name and identify only forty to eighty such species. Several observers have noted that folk systems of plant and animal nomenclature tend to lose terms from the bottom up; in other words, terms of the generic, specific, and varietal ranks are lost (see Figure B.1) as societies become more complex (Berlin 1972; Brown 1977a, 1979a; Dougherty 1978). As detailed terms disappear from folk systems, general terms, such as life-form names, become increasingly useful, so useful that they tend to increase in number. Addition of botanical life-form classes to languages, then, indexes an overall decrease of interest in and interaction with the plant world.

Developments in ethnobotanical classification and color categorization have proceeded in opposite directions. The basic color lexicon has increased and become more specific with increasing societal complexity. Total plant vocabulary, on the other hand, has decreased in modern societies. Only general, non-specific botanical terms such as life-form names show an increase. This increase is ironic, since it develops in response to decreasing concern and interaction with the plant world.

Burris (1979) describes an encoding sequence for geometric figure categories such as "circle" and "square"; this sequence is also positively associated with societal complexity. Burris found that a term for "circle" or "circular figure" is always added to lexicons before a term for "square" or "angular figure." Languages can have both or lack both, but if they have only one, it is always "circular figure." Thus "circle" is unmarked and "square" is marked, the latter implying the former.

To explain the positive association of this encoding sequence with societal complexity, Burris appeals to the carpentered world hypothesis of Segall, Campbell, and Herskovits (1966). This hypothesis was developed to explain differential cross-cultural susceptibility to certain visual illusions. These authors note that as societies increase in complexity, building and construction activity increases, and this activity introduces more and more sharp angles into the everyday environment. People in carpentered worlds are then more susceptible to certain angular illusions such as the Müller-Lyer effect. Burris (1979) argues that the negligible amount of carpentering in small-scale societies accounts for the relatively late addition to languages of angular geometric figure terms such as square and triangle. Ten thousand years ago languages probably lacked terms for angular figures and possibly terms for circular figures as well.

The lexicon is that part of language which most closely reflects human cultural concerns and relationships with the natural environment. As these concerns and relationships change, there are concomitant changes in associated areas of the lexicon, some involving lexical addition and some, lexical loss. Witkowski and Burris (n.d.) have considered the effects of such changes on the overall lexicons of languages. They report a high positive association between societal complexity and size of overall vocabulary. Large-scale complex societies have considerably larger overall lexicons than small-scale societies. However, when specialist terms (such as terminologies of academicians, bureaucrats, technicians) are excluded from consideration, this correlation falls off sharply. Thus the ordinary, nonspecialist vocabularies of people in any society, small-scale and large-scale alike, probably do not vary in size to any significant degree. What does vary from small societies to large complex ones, however, are the domain areas (such as plants, colors, geometric figures) lexically elaborated. Thus languages spoken in societies of widely varying complexity contain radically different constellations of terms.

Investigation of lexical regularities involving change amounts to a kind of human conceptual prehistory that has the potential of contributing much richness and detail to more conventional methods—such as archaeology and historical linguistics—of recovering the human past.

Summary

We have selectively illustrated universals pertaining to the phonological, syntactic, and lexical spheres of language. Uniformities within each of these components frequently fit into the same framework, usually implicational or unconditional in nature, and often have implications for language change. In addition, certain explanatory principles, including conjunctivity and binary opposition, marking relationships, criteria clustering, and dimension salience, are shown to have wide application in interpreting language regularities.

REFERENCES

Berlin, Brent
    1972 Speculations on the Growth of Ethnobotanical Nomenclature. Language in Society 1:51-86.
    1973 Folk Systematics in Relation to Biological Classification and Nomenclature. Annual Review of Ecology and Systematics 4:259-271.
    1976 The Concept of Rank in Ethnobiological Classification: Some Evidence from Aguaruna Folk Botany. American Ethnologist 3:381-399.

Berlin, Brent and Elois Ann Berlin
  1975 Aguaruna Color Categories. American Ethnologist 2:61-87.
Berlin, Brent, Dennis E. Breedlove and Peter H. Raven
  1973 General Principles of Classification and Nomenclature in Folk
    Biology. American Anthropologist 75:214-242.
  1974 Principles of Tzeltal Plant Classification: An Introduction to the
    Botanical Ethnography of a Mayan-Speaking People of Highland Chiapas.
    New York: Academic Press.
Berlin, Brent and Paul Kay
  1969 Basic Color Terms: Their Universality and Evolution. Berkeley:
    University of California Press.
Bornstein, Marc H.
  1973 The Psychophysiological Component of Cultural Difference in Color
    Naming and Illusion Susceptibility. Behavior Science Notes 8:41-101.
  1975 The Influence of Visual Perception on Culture. American Anthropol-
    ogist 77:774-798.
Bornstein, Marc H., William Kessen and Sally Weiskopf
  1976 The Categories of Hue in Infancy. Science 191:201-202.
Branstetter, Katherine B.
  1977 A Reconstruction of Proto-Polynesian Color Terminology. Anthro-
    pological Linguistics 19:1-25.
Brown, Cecil H.
  1977a Folk Botanical Life-Forms: Their Universality and Growth.
    American Anthropologist 79:317-342.
  1977b Lexical Universals and the Human Language Faculty. *In* George-
    town University Round Table on Languages and Linguistics. M. Saville-
    Troike, ed. pp. 75-91. Washington, D.C.: Georgetown University Press.
  1979a Folk Zoological Life-Forms: Their Universality and Growth.
    American Anthropologist 81:791-817.
  1979b Growth and Development of Folk Botanical Life-Forms in the
    Mayan Language Family. American Ethnologist 6:366-385.
Brown, Cecil H. and Stanley R. Witkowski
  n.d. Growth and Development of Folk Zoological Life-Forms in the
    Mayan Language Family. American Ethnologist (in press).
Bruner, Jerome S., J. J. Goodnow and G. A. Austin
  1956 A Study of Thinking. New York: Wiley.
Burris, Harold W., Jr.
  1979 Geometric Figure Terms: Their Universality and Growth. The
    Journal of Anthropology 1(2):18-41.
Callaghan, Catherine A.
  1979 Miwok Color Terms. International Journal of American Linguistics
    45:1-4.
Chomsky, Noam
  1975 Reflections on Language. New York: Pantheon.
Conklin, Harold C.
  1954 The Relation of Hanunoo Culture to the Plant World. Ph.D. Disser-
    tation, Yale University, New Haven, Conn.
Dougherty, Janet W. D.
  1978 Salience and Relativity in Classification. American Ethnologist

5:66-80.

1979   Learning Names for Plants and Plants for Names. Anthropological Linguistics 21:298-315.

Durbin, Marshall
1972   Basic Colors—Off Color? Semiotica 6:257-277.

Ember, Melvin
1978   Size of Color Lexicon: Interaction of Cultural and Biological Factors. American Anthropologist 80:364-367.

Ferguson, Charles A.
1963   Assumptions about Nasals. A Sample Study in Phonological Universals. *In* Universals of Language. Joseph H. Greenberg, ed. pp. 53-60. Cambridge, Mass.: M.I.T. Press.

Freeman, L. C.
1957   An Empirical Test of Folk-Urbanism. Ann Arbor: University Microfilms.

Greenberg, Joseph H.
1963   Some Universals of Grammar with Particular Reference to the Order of Meaningful Elements. *In* Universals of Language. Joseph H. Greenberg, ed. pp. 73-113. Cambridge, Mass.: M.I.T. Press.

1966   Language Universals with Special Reference to Feature Hierarchies. The Hague: Mouton.

1975   Research on Language Universals. Annual Review of Anthropology 4:75-94.

Hage, Per and Kristen Hawkes
1975   Binumarien Color Categories. Ethnology 14:287-300.

Hays, David G., Enid Margolis, Raoul Naroll and Dale Revere Perkins
1972   Color Term Salience. American Anthropologist 74:1107-1121.

Hays, Terence E.
1976   An Empirical Method for the Identification of Covert Categories in Ethnobiology. American Ethnologist 3:489-507.

Heinrich, Albert C.
1972   A Non-European System of Color Classification. Anthropological Linguistics 14:220-227.

Hunn, Eugene
1977   Tzeltal Folk Zoology: The Classification of Discontinuities in Nature. New York: Academic Press.

Kang, Tai S.
1972   Linking Form of Hypothesis to Type of Statistic: An Application of Goodman's Z. American Sociological Review 37:357-365.

Kay, Paul and Chad K. McDaniel
1978   The Linguistic Significance of the Meanings of Basic Color Terms. Language 54:610-646.

Marsh, Robert M.
1967   Comparative Sociology: A Codification of Cross-Societal Analysis. New York: Harcourt, Brace, and World.

Miller, Jay
1975   Delaware Alternative Classification. Anthropological Linguistics 17:434-444.

Naroll, Raoul
    1956   A Preliminary Index of Social Development. American Anthropologist 58:687-715.
    1970   What Have We Learned from Cross-Cultural Surveys? American Anthropologist 72:1227-1288.
Segall, Marshall H., Donald T. Campbell and Melville J. Herskovits
    1966   The Influence of Culture on Visual Perception. New York: Bobbs-Merrill.
Schaefer, James M.
    1969   A Comparison of Three Measures of Social Complexity. American Anthropologist 71:706-708.
Snow, D. L.
    1971   Samoan Color Terminology: A Note on the Universality and Evolutionary Ordering of Color Terms. Anthropological Linguistics 13:385-390.
von Wattenwyl, André and Heinrich Zollinger
    1979   Color-Term Salience and Neurophysiology. American Anthropologist 81:279-288.
Witkowski, Stanley R.
    1971   A Universalist Account of Kinship Semantics. Ph.D. Dissertation, University of Iowa, Iowa City.
    1972   Guttman Scaling of Semantic Distinctions. *In* Kinship Studies in the Morgan Centennial Year. Priscilla Reining, ed., pp. 167-188. Washington, D.C.: Anthropological Society of Washington.
    1976   Hypothesis Form and Diffusibility. Behavior Science Research 11: 103-106.
Witkowski, Stanley R. and Cecil H. Brown
    1977   An Explanation of Color Nomenclature Universals. American Anthropologist 79:50-57.
    1978   Lexical Universals. Annual Review of Anthropology 7:427-451.
    n.d.   Lexical Encoding Sequences and Language Change: Color Terminology Systems. American Anthropologist (in press).
Witkowski, Stanley R. and Cecil H. Brown, eds.
    n.d.   Lexical Universals. New Haven: HRAF Press (in press).
Witkowski, Stanley R. and Harold W. Burris, Jr.
    n.d.   Societal Complexity and Lexical Growth. Behavior Science Research (in press).
Zipf, G. K.
    1935   The Psycho-Biology of Language. Boston: Houghton Mifflin.
    1949   Human Behavior and the Principle of Least Effort. Cambridge, Mass.: Addison-Wesley.

Subject Index

Author Index

About the Authors

David Levinson (Ph.D., State University of New York at Buffalo) is an Associate in Research with the Human Relations Area Files in New Haven, Connecticut. His previous cross-cultural research on social problems, cultural evolution, and methodology led to publications in such journals as *Current Anthropology, American Ethnologist, Behavior Science Research, American Behavioral Scientist* and *Journal of Operational Psychiatry*. His fieldwork on skid rows in the United States led to publications in *Urban Anthropology* and the *International Journal of Social Psychiatry*.

Martin J. Malone (M.A., Southern Illinois University) is a Ph.D. candidate in sociology at Indiana University. He was formerly an Associate in Research with the Human Relations Area Files.

Cover design by Marylou Finch.